Alfred Edward Humphreys

The Epistles to Timothy and Titus

with introduction and notes

Alfred Edward Humphreys

The Epistles to Timothy and Titus
with introduction and notes

ISBN/EAN: 9783337728939

Printed in Europe, USA, Canada, Australia, Japan

Cover: Foto ©Lupo / pixelio.de

More available books at **www.hansebooks.com**

The Cambridge Bible for Schools and Colleges.

General Editor:—J. J. S. PEROWNE, D.D.
Bishop of Worcester.

THE EPISTLES TO

TIMOTHY AND TITUS

WITH INTRODUCTION AND NOTES

BY

THE REV. A. E. HUMPHREYS, M.A.,
RECTOR OF FAKENHAM, NORFOLK;
LATE FELLOW AND ASSISTANT TUTOR OF TRINITY COLLEGE, CAMBRIDGE.

STEREOTYPED EDITION.

Cambridge:
AT THE UNIVERSITY PRESS
1897

PREFACE

BY THE GENERAL EDITOR.

THE General Editor of *The Cambridge Bible for Schools* thinks it right to say that he does not hold himself responsible either for the interpretation of particular passages which the Editors of the several Books have adopted, or for any opinion on points of doctrine that they may have expressed. In the New Testament more especially questions arise of the deepest theological import, on which the ablest and most conscientious interpreters have differed and always will differ. His aim has been in all such cases to leave each Contributor to the unfettered exercise of his own judgment, only taking care that mere controversy should as far as possible be avoided. He has contented himself chiefly with a careful revision of the notes, with pointing out omissions, with suggesting occasionally a reconsideration of some question, or a fuller treatment of difficult passages, and the like.

Beyond this he has not attempted to interfere, feeling it better that each Commentary should have its own individual character, and being convinced that freshness and variety of treatment are more than a compensation for any lack of uniformity in the Series.

CONTENTS.

*** The Text adopted in this Edition is that of Dr Scrivener's *Cambridge Paragraph Bible*. A few variations from the ordinary Text, chiefly in the spelling of certain words, and in the use of italics, will be noticed. For the principles adopted by Dr Scrivener as regards the printing of the Text see his Introduction to the *Paragraph Bible*, published by the Cambridge University Press.

'Heresy is the school of Pride.'

Jacula Prudentum.

'I HAVE resolved to set down the Form and Character of a true Pastor, that I may have a Mark to aim at: which also I will set as high as I can, since he shoots higher that threatens the Moon, than he that aims at a Tree.'

G. HERBERT.

'BISHOPS and Priests, blessèd are ye, if deep
(As yours above all offices is high)
Deep in your hearts the sense of duty lie;
Charged as ye are by Christ to feed and keep
From wolves your portion of His chosen sheep:
Labouring as ever in your Master's sight,
Making your hardest task your best delight,
What perfect glory ye in Heaven shall reap!—
But in the solemn Office which ye sought
And undertook premonished, if unsound
Your practice prove, faithless though but in thought,
Bishops and Priests, think what a gulf profound
Awaits you then, if they were rightly taught
Who framed the Ordinance by your lives disowned!'

W. WORDSWORTH.

INTRODUCTION.

A. THE GENUINENESS AND DATE OF THE EPISTLES.

CHAPTER I.

External Evidence.

THERE was never any doubt in the Church, from the first century down to the present, but that St Paul was the author of these epistles. The rejection by Marcion, as has been well pointed out, increases the force of this testimony, as it shews that attention was expressly called to the subject. And Marcion's Canon of Scripture was fixed not by the evidence of authenticity, but by his own approval of the contents, of any book.

The attack made in the present century upon the genuineness of the epistles relies upon arguments drawn from their internal characteristics. In estimating the weight to be attached to these arguments it is of importance to be first sufficiently impressed by the strength of the external evidence. Instead therefore of dismissing this side of the question in a sentence, it is well to place in view the different groups of testimonies down to the acknowledged position given to the epistles by the Church in Canon and Council.

(*a*) The witness of the Apostolic Fathers.

Epistle of Barnabas, c. A.D. 75. 'Behold again it is Jesus, not a son of man, but the Son of God, and He was revealed in the flesh in a figure.' Compare 1 Tim. iii. 16.

Clement of Rome, c. A.D. 95. 'Lifting up pure and undefiled hands unto Him' (1 *ad Cor.* c. 29). Compare 1 Tim. ii. 8. 'King of the ages' (c. 61). Compare 1 Tim. i. 17.

Ignatius of Antioch, c. A.D. 112. 'Be not seduced by strange doctrines nor antiquated fables which are profitless' (*ad Magn.* c. VIII.). Compare Tit. i. 13, iii. 9. 'Please the Captain in whose army ye serve' (*ad Polyc.* c. VI.). Compare 2 Tim. ii. 4.

Polycarp of Smyrna, c. A.D. 112. 'But the love of money is the beginning of all troubles. Knowing therefore that we brought nothing into the world, neither can we carry anything out, let us arm ourselves with the armour of righteousness' (*ad Philipp.* c. 4). Compare 1 Tim. vi. 7, 10.

Epistle to Diognetus, c. A.D. 117 (Westcott), c. A.D. 150 (Lightfoot).—'One of the noblest and most impressive of early Christian apologies' (Lightfoot), not improbably addressed to Diognetus, the tutor of Marcus Aurelius. 'When the season came which God had ordained when henceforth He should manifest His goodness and power (O the exceeding great tenderness and love of God).' Compare Tit. iii. 4.

(*b*) The witness of the Greek Apologists.

Justin Martyr, c. A.D. 146, who, as a Christian philosopher in the public walk at Ephesus, held a discussion with the Jew Trypho proving from the Old Testament that Jesus was the Christ.

'The kindness of God and His love toward man' (*Dial. c. Tryph.* c. 47). Compare Tit. iii. 4.

Theophilus of Antioch, c. A.D. 168, its sixth bishop, who wrote to convince a learned heathen friend of the truth of Christianity.

'Further, respecting the being in subjection to rulers and authorities and praying for them, the divine utterance commands us that we lead a tranquil and quiet life' (*ad Autolyc.* III. 14). Compare Tit. iii. 1; 1 Tim. ii. 2.

(*c*) The witness of the Early Heretics.

Basilides, c. A.D. 110, a younger contemporary of Cerinthus, has perhaps in the phrase 'in his own times' a quotation from 1 Tim. ii. 6.

Marcion, c. A.D. 140, excluded the three epistles from his Canon, as witnessing against his Gnostic and Docetic views, and is therefore a witness to them.

Heracleon, c. A.D. 150, a familiar friend of Valentinus the Gnostic, claims the title of the first commentator on the New Testament; and the fragments of his commentary contain an allusion to 2 Tim. iii. 13.

Theodotus, c. A.D. 150, also a writer of the Valentinians, quotes 1 Timothy according to Epiphanius.

Tatian, c. A.D. 160, the head of the Encratites, combining the Valentinian doctrine of Æons with the asceticism of Marcion, affirmed according to Jerome that the Epistle to Titus was most certainly St Paul's.

(*d*) The witness of the Ancient Versions.

The *Peshitto-Syriac* Version, c. A.D. 130, of the 2nd century, completed shortly after the Apostolic age, and having special weight through the absence of all uncanonical books from this earliest version, contains all three epistles.

The *Old Latin* Version, c. A.D. 150, 'perhaps coeval with the introduction of Christianity into Africa'—in one shape or other the most important early witness to the text and interpretation of the whole Bible—also contains all three epistles.

Westcott (*Canon of New Testament*, p. 243) thus sums up the testimony of these most ancient Versions, "They give the testimony of Churches, not of individuals. They furnish a proof of the authority of the books which they contain, wide spread, continuous, reaching to the utmost verge of our historic records. Their real weight is even greater than this; for when history first speaks of them, it speaks as of that which was recognised as a heritage from an earlier period, which cannot have been long after the date of the Apostles."

(*e*) The witness of the Churches.

(1) *The Gallican Church.*

A.D. 177. The Epistle of the Churches of Vienne and Lyons to the brethren in Asia and Phrygia quotes 1 Tim.,

'Vehemently fell their rage upon...Attalus of Pergamos, a pillar, and ground of the whole district.' Compare 1 Tim. iii. 15.

Irenaeus, Bishop of Lyons, c. A.D. 180, begins his preface with quoting 1 Tim. i. 4, adding 'as the Apostle saith,' and quotes 1 Tim. i. 9, vi. 20; 2 Tim. iv. 9—11; Tit. iii. 10.

(2) *The Alexandrian Church.*

Clement of Alexandria, c. A.D. 180, Head of the Catechetical school at Alexandria A.D. 190—200, quotes 1 Tim. iv. 1, vi. 20; Tit. i. 12, referring to 'the blessed Paul,' 'the Apostle,' 'the noble Paul' as the author. He and Origen his successor undoubtedly include these epistles in their Canon of Scripture.

(3) *The African Church.*

Tertullian of Carthage, c. A.D. 200, quotes e.g. 1 Tim. vi. 20; 2 Tim. i. 14; Tit. iii. 10, 11, and speaking of Marcion says, 'I wonder since he received a letter written to an individual, the Epistle to Philemon, that he rejected two to Timothy and one to Titus written on the subject of Church order.'

The Canon of the African Church includes these epistles.

(4) *The Roman Church.*

Hippolytus, Bishop at Portus, c. A.D. 220, has, in his undoubted writings, quotations from these epistles, as from all the acknowledged books except Philemon and 1 John. In the list of his works is one entitled 'Verses about all the Scriptures.' Lightfoot regards these as metrical descriptions of the Old and New Testament, and the *Muratorian Fragment* as a part of one of these. It is in any case 'a summary of the opinion of the Western Church on the Canon,' and it includes 'one letter to Philemon, one to Titus, two to Timothy; letters of personal esteem and affection, but held in honour and regarded as Holy Scripture by the Catholic Church for their instruction in Church discipline.'

(*f*) The witness of the Historian.

The age of Diocletian brought persecution which raged with especial violence against the Scriptures. Among the results we find the testimony of the great *Eusebius the Historian*, c. A.D.

300, who describes the final steps in the history of the Canon, the forming of the books of the New Testament into distinct collections, 'a quaternion of Gospels,' 'fourteen Epistles of St Paul,' 'seven Catholic epistles.' In the Pauline group the Pastoral Epistles are included, and placed among the 'Acknowledged' Canonical writings.

(*g*) The witness of the Councils.

At this point it only remains to note that the Pastoral Epistles formed part of the contents of the three great MSS. of the Greek Bible, the Alexandrine (A), the Vatican (B, originally), the Sinaitic (ℵ), which belong to this period A.D. 300—450, the age of the great Councils; and that they form part of the Canon of the New Testament as authoritatively promulgated by the

Third Council of Carthage, A.D. 397. Included in the Scriptures of Athanasius, of Jerome, of Augustine, these Epistles kept their place unchallenged, while the Canon of the New Testament became 'no longer a problem but a tradition.'

CHAPTER II.

INTERNAL EVIDENCE.

I.

ST PAUL AND EARLY CHURCH ORDER.

THE Church has been, is, and always will be *one;* as its Founder, God in Christ, the "same yesterday, to-day, and for ever;" the central organism for the blessing of the world. That blessing was given in all the ages past, is given now, and will be ever given in many forms, by many agencies,—the working of natural laws, the rise and fall of nations, through all science and all history; but the central organism is spiritual, as any one would expect who recognises that "God is a Spirit," and man, the apex of creation, also spiritual; the action that is, of the supreme Creator and Governor upon the spirits of men through the evolution of spiritual forces. From Adam to Noah, from Noah to Abraham, from Abraham to Moses, from Moses to Malachi, from Malachi to John Baptist, from the Incarnation to the Resurrection, from the Resurrection to the descent of the Holy Spirit, from then till now, from now till the second Advent, these spiritual forces have been, are, and will be at work, gathering in strength and widening in sphere with the centuries.

> I doubt not thro' the ages one increasing purpose runs,
> And the thoughts of men are widened with the process of the suns.
>
> TENNYSON, *Locksley Hall.*

We are here concerned with the *Christian* Church in its beginnings, the relation of the Pastoral Epistles to that first century of the new life of the Church which commenced with the Pentecostal outpouring upon it of the Holy Spirit from its Incarnate Ascended Head.

We may conveniently note *four epochs* at about equal distances of one generation each, A.D. 33; 66; 99; 133. Round these four dates gathers most of the evidence that remains to us respecting the organisation and ministry of the Christian Church in its earliest days; and it is only by passing in review, chronologically, the literature of these dates, that we can see how appropriately in order of development the Church organisation of the Pastoral Epistles finds its place A.D. 66, 67, instead of one or two generations later.

FIRST EPOCH.

A.D. 33. We find *Apostles* chosen and appointed in readiness. The Gospels give great prominence to the choosing of the Twelve by our Lord, Matt. x. 1—5, Mk. iii. 14—19, Lk. vi. 12—16, Joh. vi. 67—71. "Our Lord chose them early in His public career. After their call as Apostles they appear to have been continuously with Him or in His service. The mother-church at Jerusalem grew up under their hands (Acts iii.—vii.); and their superior power and dignity were universally acknowledged by the rulers and the people (Acts v. 12 ff.)." Alford, *Dict. Bib.* p. 84. The ministerial office is not created by the Church but is ready for the Church. "Then they that gladly received his word were baptized, and the same day there were added unto them about three thousand souls. And they continued stedfastly in the Apostles' doctrine and in their fellowship, and in the breaking of bread, and in the prayers. And the Lord added to them daily such as were being saved" (Acts ii. 41).

SECOND EPOCH.

A.D. 35. The numbers increased very soon to five thousand, and with the roll daily increasing, some development of organisation was a necessity. The principle of the *Diaconate* was very soon established (Acts vi. 3) with popular selection but Apostolic ordination, A.D. 35; and during the 30 years that follow this date we find Deacons, Presbyters (called also Overseers or Bishops) and Apostles engaged in the direction of the Church. The *Presbyterate* appears as existing. Elders of Israel were attached to both city and synagogue, being admitted by the laying on of hands. It may be that the Apostles "found this Jewish organisation ready to hand, and when its members accepted the message of the Gospel, they continued their work, enlarging it by the peculiarities of the Christian scheme." Lefroy, *Christian Ministry*, p. 149. The earliest notice is of A.D. 45, when the relief for the poor brethren in Judæa was sent "to the elders" by the hand of Barnabas and Saul (Acts xi. 30). The Apostles, it is thought, having declared their resolve to have no more dealings with finance, and the deacons having only the task of administering, the presbyters as next in authority to the Apostles would receive the gift, which the deacons would then disburse. Again in A.D. 50 the 'Council' had an important *doctrinal* question before it, salvation without Jewish ceremonies. The presbyters were on the Council and are therefore seen to be entrusted with the ministry of the word; and were not, as Dr Hatch maintains, "like the Jewish elders, only officers of administration and discipline." Again in 1 Thessalonians, written almost certainly in A.D. 52, and therefore the earliest of the Christian writings we possess, St Paul exhorts "the church of the Thessalonians" "to know them that *labour among you*, and *are over you in the Lord*, and *admonish* you; and to esteem them exceeding highly in love for their work's sake," 1 Thess. v. 12, 13.

A.D. 57. Five years later in 1 Corinthians, written from Ephesus, St Paul lays stress on the "ministerial, evidential, and administrative" functions of the different and already numerous grades of ministers; and on all being the gift of the ascended Saviour; "God hath set some in the Church, first apostles, secondly prophets, thirdly teachers (*ministerial*), then miracles, then gifts of healings (*evidential*), helps, governments (*administrative*), divers kinds of tongues (*evidential*)," 1 Cor. xii. 28. And in the following year, A.D. 58, in addressing "the elders of the church" of Ephesus, whom he has sent for to Miletus, he says to them, "take heed unto yourselves and to all the flock in the which the Holy Ghost hath made you *bishops*, to *feed* the Church of God which he purchased with his own blood." And though Dr Hatch quotes the LXX. use (Acts xx. 28) of the Greek word for 'feed,' as shewing that 'rule' is meant, yet our Lord's use of the same word "feed, *tend*, feed," in giving the Apostolic Commission to St Peter is entirely against this; and the duties of the presbyter-bishops defined by this word certainly include the various offices of a shepherd, the leading, feeding, tending—'pasce mente, pasce ore, pasce opere, pasce animi oratione, verbi exhortatione, exempli exhibitione' (Bernard in Alford, quoted by Lefroy).

A.D. 61. Four years subsequently, the imprisonment at Cæsarea having taken place meanwhile, St Paul writes from Rome and salutes the "bishops" and "deacons" at Philippi, meaning evidently presbyters by "bishops." See Lightfoot, *Phil.* p. 94, "It is incredible that he should recognise only the first and third order and pass over the second, though the second was absolutely essential to the existence of a church and formed the staple of its ministry."

A.D. 62. A briefer list of functions of ministry, but similar to that which he sent to the Corinthians from Ephesus, St Paul sends now to the Ephesians themselves from Rome in A.D. 62. "He gave some to be apostles, and some prophets, and some evangelists (*itinerant*), and some pastors and teachers (*stationary*), for the perfecting of the saints unto the work of ministering, unto the building up of the body of Christ." In the Corinthian passage the point emphasised is the Divine harmony in variety of the different classes of functions. In this the stress is rather laid on the provision for all possible occasions and localities, and we can see the wide view of the Church Catholic which has alike her "itinerant or missionary clergy and stationary or localized clergy." This stationary and local duty, of being pastors and teachers, would be that especially of the presbyters (Lightfoot, *Phil.* exc. p. 192).

A.D. 63. And in the Epistle of St James another spiritual function is very definitely assigned to the presbyters, "Is any among you sick? Let him call for the elders of the church and let them pray over him, anointing him with oil in the name of the Lord," Jas. v. 14.

A.D. 65. In the Epistle to the Hebrews the writer, probably in Syria, "in the critical interval between A.D. 64, the government of Gessius Florus, and A.D. 67, the commencement of the Jewish war," speaks generally of a ministry of spiritual guidance and instruction, and of a sacred succession in it; "obey them that *have rule* over you and submit to them, for they watch in behalf of your *souls*," c. xiii. 17, and earlier, "remember them that *had the rule* over you, which *spake unto you the word of God*," xiii. 7.

And St Peter, writing most probably from Rome after St Paul's release and departure, and after Nero's persecution (A.D. 64), urges the "presbyters" belonging to the different Christian communities in Asia Minor to "do the work of bishops" with disinterested zeal. "The *elders* therefore among you I exhort, who am a fellow elder,...*tend* the flock of God which is among you, *exercising the oversight* not of constraint but willingly," 1 Pet. v. 1, 2.

We are thus brought on to the close of the *second epoch or generation*, and to the assumed date of the Pastoral Epistles. (See above, p. 14.)

A.D. 66. In 1 Timothy and Titus we find not so much "a distinct *advance in organisation* from the condition of the

Church exhibited in St Paul's other Epistles" (Wace, *Speaker's Comm.*, p. 764) as a more detailed exposition of the duties and functions belonging to the *apostolate*, the *presbyterate* and the *diaconate*, all of which offices we have seen already recognised. Such advance as there seems to be lies in the silence observed as to the other offices named in other passages; and, so far, preparation is divinely made for their gradual extinction. But in the generation which followed the Pastoral Epistles, as we shall see from the *Teaching of the Twelve Apostles*, they were still vigorous.

The apostolate is the main theme of both 1 Tim. and Titus. We assume the charge given alike to Timothy and Titus to be that of Vicar-apostolic, St Paul's representative (whether temporary or permanent), 1 Tim. i. 3; Tit. i. 5.

The *scope* of 1 Tim. is the maintenance of the deposit of the Catholic faith, "that he may charge some that they teach no strange doctrine,"—the purpose of the commandment being "love out of a pure heart and of a good conscience and of faith unfeigned," 1 Tim. i. 4—11; vi. 20, 21.

Its *sphere* is the oversight of public life and worship—prayer for all "that we may lead a quiet and peaceful life," 1 Tim. ii. 2.

Its *method* is the supply of sufficient and sufficiently qualified ministers of two grades, *bishops*, whose training and work are described in 1 Tim. iii. 1—7, and who are called "presbyters" in a further description, v. 17—19, and *deacons*, who are described in 1 Tim. iii. 8—13.

Its *efficiency* rests on Timothy's own example in conduct, study, use of spiritual gifts, bearing towards the old and the young, the poor and the rich, the widow and the slave, 1 Tim. iii. 14—vi. 21.

Similarly, we may place the instructions to Titus under the same heads, though they are briefer, and arranged independently.

The *scope* of the apostolate; the maintenance of the truth on which the life depends, and its "good works," Tit. i. 1—4, 10—16.

Its *sphere;* the oversight of public life and religion, ii. 11—14, iii. 1—8.

Its *method;* the supply of ministers—one grade only being named, that of "presbyters," here also called "bishops" i. 5—9.

Its *efficiency;* dependent on his own high example in doctrine, good works, and bearing towards the elder and younger, the heretical and orthodox, ii. 1—10, iii. 8—11.

A.D. 67. The personal outweighs the official in the fervent utterances of the Apostle's last words in 2 Timothy: we trace something of the same *scope* in i. 12—14, "guard the good deposit"; something of the same *sphere* in i. 1, 2, "life in Christ," with its double seal of holy devotion and devoted holiness, "the Lord knoweth them that are His," and "depart from unrighteousness"; something of the same *method* in ii. 2, 14, "commit thou the sound words to faithful men," "put them in remembrance"; but we see the dying father most solicitous for the personal conduct of his "beloved child," that he may "fulfil his ministry" and bear aloft the apostolic standard falling from his own hand, i. 3—11, ii. 1, 3—13, 15—26, iii. 10—17, iv. 1—10. The *efficiency* of the apostolate is more anxiously than ever made to rest on Timothy's own character and bearing, "Stir up the gift of God which is in thee," "Suffer hardship with me," "Give diligence to present thyself approved unto God," "Be instant in season, out of season," "For I am already being offered."

A.D. 69. Such evidence as is afforded by the Apocalypse of St John belongs most probably to the two or three years following St Paul's death. (See summary of arguments for this date, *Cambridge Companion to Bible*, p. 84.) The Epistles addressed to the Seven Churches of Asia are sent to the "angel" of each Church. If we allow for the Oriental and Hebraic symbolism of the form in which this portion, like the other portions of the Apocalypse, is cast, it will seem in keeping with the main theme of the Pastoral Epistles that the stress of responsibility should be laid on one presiding minister. Let us assume that, historically, the basis of this symbolic vision is a headship of some sort exercised in each Church for the time being by an itinerant or stationary apostolic delegate; that in the spirit of the Pastoral Epistles some similar provision (of which they give specimens) had been and was being generally made, wherever Churches were sufficiently settled; then in this delegated apostolate we get sufficient idea of the conception present to the inspired seer; and we seem to see divine confirmation of the plan, still only forming historically, for the one apostolic headship in each district. The "seven churches" indicate the vision of the Church in its covenanted completeness; the "seven stars in Christ's right hand" signify the complete apostolic authority, immediately and constantly derived from Him (Trench, *Seven Churches in Asia*, pp. 52, 53).

"The seven stars" are also "the seven angels," according to the wealth of Oriental imagery, "by a heavenly title transferred in O.T. already to men, Eccles. v. 6, Hag. i. 13, Mal. ii. 7; iii. 1, designating not the *personality* but the *office* of those heavenly beings by whom it is properly borne" (Trench, p. 56.)

Bishop Lightfoot's objection, that the time did not allow of change in organisation sufficient to establish a "bishop" proper, does not lie against the above explanation; and we might well urge that to the same extent the time does not allow of the change for the worse, apparently depicted in the condition of the Asiatic Churches. The truth seems to be that there *is no great change* of organisation *or* of life. It is another Apostle who is reviewing both, and is expressing himself with the vividness of a son of thunder, with the imagery of an oriental, and under the afflatus of prophetic symbolism.

Bp Lightfoot's other objection, that "the Angel is made responsible for the Church to a degree wholly unsuited to any human officer," seems also met by the thought of the O. T. identification of prophet with people.

To his own view that the stars, as opposed to the earthly fires of the candlesticks, are the heavenly representatives of the Churches, "the star shining steadily by its own inherent light," Dr Lee (*Speaker's Commentary*, vol. IV. p. 512) reasonably objects that, "were this so, each 'star' or 'angel' must surely be faultless; and yet the angels of the Churches of Smyrna and Philadelphia, alone of the seven, are spoken of without reproof."

After the gradually increasing light thus thrown on the organisation and ministry of the Church up to our second epoch, the close of the first generation, it is tantalising to find ourselves at present in darkness as to the years between A.D. 70 and 90 with regard to direct contemporary evidence. For though both Bp Lightfoot and Dr Salmon agree in dating the *Epistle of Barnabas* (probably a namesake of the Apostle) in the reign of Vespasian, 75 A.D., yet it contains no reference to the Church's ministry—"prophets" in § 1 being Old Testament prophets, and "teacher" being used generally and not technically.

Our next series of writings can be dated approximately A.D. 95. The *Third Epistle of St John*, which competes with his Gospel for the very latest place in the Canon of the New Testament, appears to indicate the same preeminence of one ecclesiastical officer in the rejection of St John's letter of communion and the missionary brethren the bearers of it by Diotrephes, "I wrote unto the church, but Diotrephes, who affects primacy over them receiveth us not," v. 9. We note further in both this and the Second Epistle St John gives himself the title of "The Presbyter" (2 John 1, 3 John 1), as St Peter had called himself "Fellow presbyter," 1 Pet. v. 1.

We now pass outside the N. T. Canon; and, at the same date, find in the *First Epistle of Clement*, written from Rome to Corinth, evidence of the same apostolic superintendence, and the same two grades of ministers, bishops or presbyters, and deacons.

He says of the Apostles, "they appointed the bishops and afterwards *they provided a continuance* that if these should fall asleep other approved men should succeed them." He speaks of "those bishops who were appointed by the apostles or afterward *by other men of repute*, with the consent of the whole Church," and continues, "it will be no light sin for us if we thrust out those who have offered the gifts of the *bishop's* office unblamably and holily. Blessed are those *presbyters* who have gone before, seeing that their departure was fruitful and ripe;

for they have no fear lest anyone should remove them from their appointed place" (c. xliv). In the italicised words we see traces first of the apostolic delegacy of the Pastoral Epistles and of the "angels" of the Revelation, and then of the identity of bishops and presbyters.

Of about the same date, according to the best critics, is the *Teaching of the Apostles*, "a Church manual of primitive Christianity," the text of which was recovered by Abp Bryennius in 1875 and published in 1883. The points bearing on the present topic are well summed up by Bp Lightfoot, *Apostolic Fathers*, p. 215. "The itinerant prophetic order has not yet been displaced by the permanent localised ministry, but exists side by side with it as in the lifetime of S. Paul, Eph. iv. 11, 1 Cor. xii. 28. Secondly, episcopacy has apparently not yet become universal. The word 'bishop' is still used as synonymous with 'presbyter,' and the writer therefore couples 'bishops' with deacons (§ 15), as S. Paul does, 1 Tim. iii. 1—8, Phil. i. 1, under similar circumstances."

Similarly Dr Salmon (*Int. N. T.*, pp. 613, 614), "In that part which treats of Church teachers, the foremost place is given to Apostles and Prophets. But the word 'Apostle' has not the limited meaning to which modern usage restricts it. The 'Apostles' are wandering missionaries or envoys of the Churches. Directions are given as to the respect to be paid to an Apostle, and the entertainment to be afforded him by a Church through which he might pass, but it is assumed that he does not contemplate making a permanent stay... The chief place in the instruction of the local Church is assigned to the 'prophets,' whose utterances were to be received with the respect due to their divine inspiration, and who were entitled to receive from their congregations such dues as the Jews had been wont to render to the high-priests. The possibility is contemplated that in the Church there might be no prophet. In that case the first-fruits are to be given to the poor. Mention is also made of teachers, by which I understand persons who gave public instruction in the Church, but who did not speak 'in the spirit' as the prophets did... The first mention is only of apostles and prophets; then directions are given for Sunday Eucharistic celebration, and then is added 'elect, *therefore*, to yourselves bishops and deacons.' These, we are told, are to be honoured with the prophets and teachers, as fulfilling like ministration. The inference then suggests itself that at the time this document was written the Eucharist was only consecrated by the president of the Church assembly, who held a permanent office, and who probably might also be a preacher; but that in the mind of the writer the inspired givers of public instruction held the higher place."

The passages referred to in these extracts will be found in the following selection from the Book, cc. xi.—xv. "But concerning the apostles and prophets, so do ye according to the ordinance of the Gospel. Let every apostle when he cometh to you be received as the Lord; but he shall not abide more than a single day, or, if there be need, a second likewise; but if he abide three days he is a false prophet.... And any prophet speaking in the Spirit ye shall not try nor discern; for every sin shall be forgiven, but this sin shall not be forgiven.... Every true prophet desiring to settle among you is worthy of his food. In like manner a true teacher is also worthy, like the workman of his food. Every firstfruit, then...thou shalt take and give as the firstfruit to the prophets, for they are your chief priests. But if ye have not a prophet, give them to the poor.... And on the Lord's own day gather yourselves together and break bread and give thanks, first confessing your transgressions, that your sacrifice may be pure... Appoint for yourselves, therefore, bishops and deacons worthy of the Lord, men who are meek, and not lovers of money, and true and approved; for unto you they also perform the service of the prophets and teachers. Therefore despise them not; for they are your honourable men along with the prophets and teachers."

It should be added that the false teachers, prophets and apostles, against whom so many warnings are directed by St Paul and St Peter in the former generation, and by St John in the present, are painfully in evidence in this Book. "If the apostle ask money, he is a false prophet.... From his ways the false prophet and the prophet shall be recognised.... If he has no craft, according to your wisdom provide how he shall live as a Christian among you, but not in idleness. If he will not do this, he is trafficking upon Christ. Beware of such men."

A.D. 99. This generation seems to be closed with the "*Shepherd" of Hermas*, if, according to the most recent view of Zahn and Salmon and others, a Hermas not otherwise known is assumed as the author, living about A.D. 90—100, and so acquainted with Clement, to whom a copy of his book is directed to be sent. The internal evidence, Bp Lightfoot (*Apost. Fathers*, p. 294) agrees, will suggest this date, especially the notices of the Christian ministry and of the condition of the Church generally. The prophetical office is particularly prominent. It would seem indeed as if Hermas himself were a prophet, and, as Dr Salmon suggests, "felt some jealousy of the superior dignity of the presbyters. Thus in one vision (3, 1) the Church who appears to him in the form of a lady bids him sit down. 'Nay,' he modestly answers, 'let the presbyters be seated first.' 'Sit down, as I bid you,' the lady replies" (*Int. N. T.* 593). The true and false prophet are strongly distinguished—"the one that hath the Spirit which is from above is gentle and tranquil and humble-minded, and abstaineth from all wickedness and vain desire of this present world"—the other, who "seemeth to have a spirit exalteth himself, and desireth to have a chief place, and straightway he is impudent and shameless and talkative and conversant in many luxuries and in many other deceits, and receiveth money for his prophesying, and if he receiveth not, he prophesieth not" (*Mand.* xi.).

The following passages suggest a ministry similar to that already depicted in this age. "The stones that are squared and white and that fit together in their joints, these are the apostles and bishops and teachers and deacons, who walked after the holiness of God and exercised their office of bishop and teacher and deacon in purity and sanctity for the elect of God" (*Vis.* III. 5). "'But the stones, Sir,' said I, 'that came from the deep, and were fitted into the building, who are they?' 'The first,' saith he, 'even the ten that were placed in the foundations are the first generation; the twenty-five are the second generation of righteous men; the thirty-five are God's prophets and His ministers; the forty are apostles and teachers of the preaching of the Son of God'" (*S.* 9. XV.). Again he writes of "apostles and teachers who preached unto the whole world" (*S.* 9. XXV.), of "deacons that exercised their office ill and plundered the livelihood of widows and orphans" (*S.* 9, XXVI.), and of "bishops, hospitable persons, who at all times without ceasing sheltered the needy and the widows in their ministration, and conducted themselves in purity at all times" (*S.* 9, XXVII.).

FOURTH EPOCH.

A.D. 117. The striking feature of the evidence from the Christian writings, arranged thus chronologically according to the most recent authority of sober criticisms, is the narrowing of the period during which the definite settled establishment of the local episcopate, and the definite disappearance of the prophetical office and apparently other itinerant ministries, must be held to have taken place; a period of fifteen or twenty-five years at most. For we come now to the evidence of the *Epistles of Ignatius*, A.D. 117—30, which have been examined of late years with great care. The following summary by Dr Plummer (*Pastoral Epistles*, p. 113) gives the conclusions that may be safely drawn. "The investigations of Lightfoot, Zahn, and Harnack, have placed the genuineness of the short Greek form of the Epistles of Ignatius beyond reasonable dispute. Their exact date cannot as yet be determined. The evidence is strong that Ignatius was martyred in the reign of Trajan; and if that is accepted, the letters cannot be later than A.D. 117. But even if this evidence be rejected as not conclusive, and the letters be dated ten or twelve years later, their testimony will be of the utmost importance. They prove that long before A.D. 150 episcopacy was the recognised form of government throughout the Churches of Asia Minor and Syria; and as Ignatius speaks of 'the bishops that are settled in *the farthest parts* of the earth,' they prove that according to his belief episcopacy was the recognised form everywhere (*Ephes.* iii.). This evidence is not a little strengthened by the fact that as all sound critics on both sides are now agreed, the Epistles of Ignatius were evidently not written in order to magnify the episcopal office or to preach up the episcopal system. The writer's main object is to deprecate schism, and all that might tend to schism. And in his opinion the best way to avoid schism is to keep closely united to the bishop. Thus the magnifying of the episcopal office comes about incidentally; because Ignatius takes for granted that everywhere there is a bishop in each church who is the duly appointed ruler of it, loyalty to whom will be a security against all schismatical tendencies......The office of prophets appears to have been extinct when Ignatius wrote; by prophets he always means the prophets of the Old Testament."

Of the seven epistles, six contain the clearest and most definite statements as to bishop, presbyters, and deacons; all six are evidently his fervent dying charges to love and unity through these. That to the Romans seems so full of an equally fervent dying charge to the Church there not to hinder his martyrdom, that no room is left for any other topic. It must suffice to give one passage from each epistle.

"That ye may obey the bishop and the presbytery without distraction of mind, breaking one bread which is the medicine of immortality." (*To the Ephesians*, c. 20.)

"Be ye zealous to do all things in godly concord, the bishop presiding after the likeness of God, and the presbyters after the likeness of the Council of the Apostles, with the deacons also who are most dear unto me since they have been entrusted with the diaconate of Jesus Christ." (*To the Magnesians*, c. 6.)

"Apart from the deacons, the bishop, and the presbyters, there is not even the name of a church......he that is without the sanctuary is not clean, that is, he that doeth aught without the bishop and presbytery and deacons." (*To the Trallians*, c. 3, 7.)

"I spake with a loud voice, with God's own voice, Give ye heed to the bishop and the presbytery and deacons ... Do nothing without the bishop...cherish union, shun divisions." (*To the Philadelphians*, c. 7.)

"Shun divisions as the beginning of evils. Do ye all follow your bishop as Jesus Christ followed the Father, and the presbytery as the Apostles, and to the deacons pay respect as to God's commandment. Let no man do aught of things pertaining to the Church apart from the bishop. Let that be held a valid eucharist which is under the bishop, or one to whom he shall have committed it." (*To the Smyrnæans*, c. 8.)

"Give ye heed to the bishop that God also may give heed to you. I am devoted to those who are subject to the bishop, the presbyters, the deacons. May it be granted me to have my portion with them in the presence of God. Toil together one with another, struggle together, run together." (*To St Polycarp*, c. 6.)

What Ignatius was as Bishop to Antioch, Polycarp was to Smyrna at this time; and *Polycarp's Letter to the Philippians* gives similar witness: "Polycarp and the presbyters that are with him unto the Church of God which sojourneth at Philippi... submitting yourselves to the presbyters and deacons as to God and Christ," cc. 1, 5.

This letter is especially interesting from its evident reminiscences of the Pastoral Epistles, as e.g., "But *the love of money is the beginning of all troubles*.... In like manner deacons should be blameless in the presence of his righteousness as deacons of God and of Christ and not of men; not calumniators, not double-tongued, not lovers of money, temperate in all things, compassionate, diligent, walking according to the truth of the Lord, who became a *minister* (*deacon*) *of all*...and the presbyters also must be compassionate...abstaining from all anger, respect of persons, unrighteous judgment being far from all love of money" (cc. 4, 5, 6.) We may add testimony of the Church of Smyrna in its letter to the Church at Philomelium relating the bishop's martyrdom. "In the number of these elect was this man, the glorious martyr Polycarp, who was found an apostolic and prophetic teacher in our own time, a bishop of the holy Church which is in Smyrna."

A.D. 133. This epoch closes with the name of Papias, the devout if somewhat credulous Bishop of Hierapolis at this same time, who, like Polycarp, was reputed a disciple of St John. Of the fragments preserved as his, none bear on the question of the ministry; but the passages from later authors which enshrine his sayings bear witness to his striking personality as bishop of Hierapolis; and the matter of the sayings, relating mainly to the care with which he treasured the deposit of the faith of the Gospel, shews us one whose aim was to fulfil the dying charge of St Paul to Timothy, "Guard that which is committed unto thee," "Hold the pattern of sound words."

To these great names, the best specimens possible of what the *episcopate* could be and should be as the now established successor of the apostolate, we may add a final evidence of the now settled ministry of the *presbyterate*, surviving all the itinerant offices and recognised as the proper body of preachers. It occurs in the document which is known as *The Second Letter of Clement*, but which is rather as Bishop Lightfoot judges "the earliest Christian homily extant," by an unknown author of about A.D. 130. The writing is, as he adds, interesting for its high moral tone and unswerving faith. It is a bright example of the aim of the Church's historic ministry to reach St Paul's Pastoral standard, "Preach the word; be instant in season, out of season."

"Let us therefore repent with our whole heart, lest any of us perish by the way. For if we have received commands, that we should make this also our business, to tear men away from idols and to instruct them, how much more is it wrong that a soul which knoweth God already should perish. Therefore let us assist one another, that we may also lead the weak upward as touching that which is good, to the end that we may all be saved: and let us convert and admonish one another. And let us not think to give heed and believe now only, while we are admonished by the presbyters; but likewise when we have departed home, let us remember the commandments of the Lord, and not suffer ourselves to be dragged off the other way by our worldly lusts; but coming hither more frequently, let us strive to go forward in the commands of the Lord, that we all having the same mind may be gathered together unto life" (c. 17).

NOTE. The translations given above are taken from Lightfoot and Harmer's *Apostolic Fathers*.

CHAPTER III.

INTERNAL EVIDENCE.

II.

ST PAUL'S LATEST STYLE AND CHARACTERISTICS.

I. There are peculiarities of language and of thought in the Pastoral Epistles compared with St Paul's earlier letters.

II. These peculiarities are nothing more than marks of natural growth and development.

III. Along with the differences there are abundant samenesses both in style and intrinsic character with what we recognise as essentially Pauline.

I. It is quite true that there are special peculiarities in vocabulary and syntax and also in modes of thought and teaching in the Pastoral Epistles, when we compare them with the earlier groups of St Paul's letters.

These peculiarities are well classified by Bp Lightfoot, *Biblical Essays*, p. 401, and adduced as a proof first that they belong to the same period with one another, and secondly that they cannot have been contemporaneous with the other epistles of St Paul. The following summary is taken mainly from his classification. Following Conybeare he designates the First and Second Epistles to Timothy and the Epistle to Titus by the letters *a*, *b*, *c* respectively, the number of occurrences, where more than one, being placed immediately above each letter.

1. *The Vocabulary.*

(*a*) A new set of terms to describe moral and religious states:

"profane" a^3b, not used elsewhere by St Paul (but Heb. xii. 16).

"godliness" a^8bc, the adverb bc, the verb a, 13 times in all, and not once elsewhere in St Paul's epistles.

"pure" $a^2b^2c^2$, in four out of the six cases used of the conscience; only once elsewhere in St Paul's epistles.

"good" or "beautiful" $a^{16}b^3c^5$, 24 times in the Pastoral Epistles and only 16 times elsewhere in St Paul.

"gravity" a^2c, "grave" a^2c. "Grave" occurs Phil. iv. 8 and nowhere else in N.T.

(*b*) A new set of terms relating to doctrine, many of them bringing out the contrast between true and false doctrine:

"teaching" $a^8b^3c^4$, used most frequently objectively as "doctrine"; four times only elsewhere in St Paul of "the art of teaching."

"questionings" a^2bc, not elsewhere in St Paul.

"strifes of words" ab, not elsewhere in N.T.

"the deposit of the faith" ab^2, not elsewhere in N.T.

"sound," "healthy," of doctrine, $a^2b^2c^5$, not elsewhere in St Paul, or in this sense in N.T. Also the opposite

"to be unhealthy" a, nowhere else in N.T.

(*c*) Certain formulæ and maxims:

"to witness before" ab^2, the verb only once elsewhere in St Paul.

"Grace, mercy and peace" ab, the earlier "grace and peace" c; see significance of this, notes, pp. 2, 74, 128.

"It is a faithful saying" a^3bc; peculiar to this group.

(*d*) Modes of speaking of God the Father and Christ:

"the blessed God" a^2, not elsewhere in St Paul.

"Saviour God" a^3c^3, not elsewhere in St Paul.

"appearing" in the sense of "presence" ab^3c, only "the appearing of his presence," 2 Thes. ii. 8.

(*e*) Other expressions peculiar to this group of Pauline epistles:

"to deny" ab^2c^2.

"diabolus, false accuser" *abc*.

"to decline" (1 Tim. iv. 7) a^2bc.

"despot" for "master," elsewhere in St Paul *Kyrios*.

2. *The Syntax.*

(*a*) It is stiffer and more jointed than in the earlier epistles; the clauses are marshalled together, with a tendency to parallelism.

e.g. 1 Tim. ii. 1, 2, iv. 12, 13, 15, vi. 9, 11, 12, 13, 15, 18.
2 Tim. ii. 11, 12, iii. 10—13, iv. 2, 4, 5, 7.
Tit. i. 7, 8, 9, ii. 7, 12, iii. 1—3.

(*b*) There is more sententiousness, abruptness and positiveness of form. Imperative clauses are frequent.

e.g. 1 Tim. v. 7, 8, 22—25.
2 Tim. iii. 1, 5, 12, 16.
Tit. i. 12—14, iii. 8—11.

3. *The Tone of thought.*

(*a*) There is an increased tendency to the directly moral side of duty. "Faith" and "grace" occupy a smaller, less prominent, space. Stress is laid upon good works; 1 Tim. ii. 10, v. 10, 25, vi. 18; 2 Tim. ii. 21; Tit. i. 16, iii. 7, 14. In describing the Christian state, the principles of "godliness" and "soberness" stand forward; with long lists of virtues and the minutiæ of practical life.

(*b*) At the same time the Apostle dwells more than formerly on orthodoxy of belief. There is more of the doctrine of Christianity as a creed and less as a life. The teaching generally is more definite and positive, with more of detail and less of principle.

4. *The Subject-matter of teaching.*

The main topic of ecclesiastical organisation is new, though there are some references to it in the epistle nearest in point of date, the Ephesians.

II. It is equally true that these peculiarities are nothing more than marks of growth and development such as would be naturally expected at a date like A.D. 66 and 67; in the same way as other marks of growth and development distinguish the epistles of the first Roman captivity (Philippians, Philemon, Colossians, Ephesians, A.D. 61, 62), from the four principal epistles (1 Corinthians, Galatians, 2 Corinthians, Romans, A.D. 56, 57); and as these are again similarly distinguished from the earliest epistles (1 and 2 Thessalonians, A.D. 51, 52). It is natural to expect that each of these successive quinquennial periods of time should shew changes of thought and corresponding changes of style according as the experiences and surroundings of the Apostle and all his Churches changed for better or worse. No modern bishop or parish priest could help testifying to such fluctuation and development of feeling, and life, and action, and speech, in connexion with pastoral works extending over a period of 20 years and over a variety of districts.

How the main subject-matter of the teaching in the successive groups of epistles changes, while the underlying Gospel foundation truth remains the same, is admirably worked out by Bp Lightfoot in *Biblical Essays*, p. 227, sq. By the word development, in this connexion, he points out, is meant, not that St Paul added to his doctrines, but that he altered the lights in which he placed them, making one point more prominent at one time than another. The whole doctrine is there from the first implicitly involved in the fundamental conception of the person of Christ, but the particular aspects are brought into special prominence by the varying requirements of the Church at large or the altered conditions of the Apostle's own life.

(1) The doctrine of the Second Advent is the subject of the earliest group, because the Resurrection, with Judgment on Sin and Reward for faithful service, was the central point in the teaching of the Twelve after Pentecost, and the necessary groundwork for the call to Repentance with which the ministry of St Paul in each new sphere commenced.

(2) The natural sequel to the teaching of Judgment to come and of the need of Repentance is found in the second group of epistles, where God's remedy for sin is fully told. Christ is the Redeemer as well as the Judge. Justification, Atonement, Sacrifice—the chief teaching on these all-important topics is found here. The legalism of the Jewish Convert and the license of the Greek were now St Paul's greatest difficulties; he meets both by the Cross of Christ; "Christ died for us," and "we must die with Christ." This is the busiest, stormiest time of St Paul's ministry, and the style and teaching reflect all his "bustling strained activity."

(3) The calm of two periods of imprisonment, at Cæsarea and Rome, followed; and in those quiet days of rest and thought St Paul's contemplation of the highest mysteries of the faith found expression in the teaching of the third group of epistles. From Christ upon the Cross he looks up and teaches his converts at Philippi, Colossæ, Ephesus, as they grow in grace, to look up to Christ upon the Throne. Christ is the King as well as the Redeemer; the Eternal Word, God manifest in the flesh, through Whom and in Whom each separate soul, and the whole Church, is sanctified and "raised to sit in heavenly places," and united to the Eternal Father. There is no angelic intermediary; "our citizenship is in heaven," "ye are complete in Him," the "One Lord."

(4) Returned from captivity, how naturally would St Paul seek to use the short interval of life and work which was all he could expect, so as to consolidate the Church in its inner doctrine and its outer organisation, before the withdrawal of the first teachers and founders. "Schisms and heresies were starting into life within the fold, and meanwhile the apostolate was dying out. Therefore a double necessity was laid upon 'Paul the aged' to meet this danger by strengthening and developing the Church's system of government. If we look at the Pastoral Epistles we find no new doctrine inculcated. The two notes which are struck again and again are (1) 'Hold fast the tradition, the deposit of the faith,' and (2) 'Preserve order in the Church.' In short this group of Epistles constitutes

St Paul's last will and testament in which he gives his final instructions for the maintenance and continuity of the faith."

Such being the character of the successive groups of the epistles, we can readily see how the tone of thought and the language employed will vary of necessity with the subject-matter of the period. The characteristic of the Pastoral Epistles, the inculcation of the steady-going quiet virtue that will last, the Sober Godliness that is chiefly known by its unobtrusive good works, is thus found to be the mark of genuineness, as the natural and necessary sequel to the earlier stages (1) of Repentance under the conviction of sin and judgment to come, (2) of the glad acceptance of a finished Atonement, and (3) of the realised joy of heavenly union and Sanctification in a living and loving Lord. The use of rhythmic phrase, and creed formula, and liturgic versicle, is what would be expected when the aim of the writing is to urge the keeping in the old paths. During 30 years of Christian life and worship the Church must have come to adopt some set forms of brief teaching and common prayer and praise. Again, it is a matter of present experience, how as years advance, men more and more express their faith and hope and joy in the old creeds and prayers and hymns of their early days. Why should not Paul the aged have been such an one also? The character of the syntax, so far as it is new and peculiar, seems to be sufficiently accounted for by the hortatory and dogmatic nature of the contents; while the vocabulary is not stranger than St Paul's habit, and the new subject and period, would lead us to expect.

For as Weiss points out (*Manual of Introduction to N. T.* p. 216), to make the four principal epistles the categorical standard of St Paul's lexical phraseology, in so far as it was not directly influenced by his doctrine, and to measure all that claims to be of Pauline origin by them, is a manifest blunder. Each one of the epistles shews a fulness of *hapax legomena*, many different expressions for the same thing, and manifold points of contact with other New Testament writers; for the linguistic treasure from which they all drew was essentially the same. Hence, according to Weiss's mode of reckoning phrases, it may be calculated that the first group of two epistles (seven chapters) contain 15 phrases not common to St Paul's other epistles; the second group of four epistles (51 chapters) contain 118 such phrases; the third group of four epistles (15 chapters) contain 48 such phrases; the fourth or Pastoral group (13 chapters) contain 51 such phrases. Or to take another comparison, noted by Bp Westcott (*Hebrews*, p. xlv.), Dr Thayer reckons the same number of peculiar words, 168, in the Pastoral Epistles and in the Epistle to the Hebrews, but the latter is longer in about the proportion of 21 to 15.

Finally, it is a pertinent question to ask as Schaff does (*History of the Church*, Eng. Trans. p. 806), why a forger should have chosen so many new words when he might have confined himself much more closely to the vocabulary of the other epistles of St Paul?

III. It is, further, equally true that along with these peculiarities there are abundant samenesses, indications of identity in style and tone of thought and teaching with what we recognise as essentially Pauline.

(*a*) If we take by way of example the Second Epistle to Timothy, we are struck, as Dean Howson points out (*Hulsean Lectures*, p. 144) by the exordium, where St Paul thanks God for the unfeigned faith which is in Timothy and assures him of his unceasing remembrance of him in his prayers (2 Tim. i. 3). Almost all St Paul's letters (except that to Titus and that to the Galatians, which is full of reproof,) begin with thanksgiving, and most of them add the assurance of continued prayer for his converts. That this characteristic of thanksgiving with prayer is not an epistolary trick but a devotional principle may be seen on a review of St Paul's life as given in the Acts. Again in verse 4, "remembering thy tears," we have an example of "the tenderness of friendship, the grief of separation, the cherished remembrance of the last parting," which marked St Paul's intercourse with his associates, that sympathy and affectionateness which both in the Acts and the Epistles displays itself again and again towards Churches and towards individuals, cf. Acts xx. 18, 19, 31, 37; Phil. ii. 27, 28; 1 Tim. v. 23; 2 Tim. iv. 20. Turning now to the end of the Epistle we may single out the passage emphasized by Dr Gwynne (*Speaker's Commentary*, *Intr. to Philippians*, p. 588), viz. iv. 6—8. "With Timothy at his side in the days of his first imprisonment he has written from Rome to the Philippians of his desire to 'depart,' his 'fight,' his willingness to be 'poured out' (i. 23; *ib.* 30; ii. 17); of himself as one 'pressing on' in a 'race' for a 'prize' (iii. 14). To Timothy, after the lapse of years, he writes as his second and final imprisonment in Rome draws towards its close, reminding him (as it seems) of that early anticipation of the end now imminent, and reverts to the same words—infrequent and exclusively Pauline—words; 'I am now being *poured out* and the time of my *departure* is at hand. I have fought the good *fight*, I have finished the *race*...there is laid up for me the *crown* of righteousness.'" Lastly, the closing verses of the Epistle furnish perhaps the most conspicuous example of St Paul's frequent but not invariable habit of personal salutation, with which we are familiar, for instance, at the close of the *Romans* and *Colossians*; and this in such a natural way both with old names and new names as to be entirely beyond the powers of a forger.

(*b*) More generally, throughout the Pastoral Epistles, we may find the same revelation conveyed to the Church by St Paul as is contained in his other writings. One of the most recent sketches of this Pauline revelation is given by Rev. R. F. Horton, *Revelation and the Bible*, p. 292 sq. And we will place under each of the characteristic heads, as given by him, references to these Epistles of our own selection, illustrating these topics and methods. This will be the more valuable, as the sketch of Pauline characteristics is given by Mr Horton in a different connexion, and he himself doubts whether the Pastoral Epistles should not "be relegated to the pseudepigraphical class of literature."

(1) *A Christ-filled personality—Christ an indwelling person.*
1 Tim. i. 11—17, especially 15, 16.
"Faithful is the saying and worthy of all acceptation, that

Jesus came into the world to save sinners, of whom I am chief: howbeit for this cause I obtained mercy, that in me as chief might Jesus Christ shew forth all his longsuffering, for an example of them which should hereafter believe on him unto eternal life."

2 Tim. i. 12.

"I know him whom I have believed, and I am persuaded that he is able to guard that which he hath committed unto me against that day."

2 Tim. iv. 17.

"The Lord stood by me and strengthened me, that through me the message might be fully proclaimed."

The Ep. to Titus has nothing of this thought. But neither have the Thessalonian epistles, while the Philippian Epistle is full of it.

(2) *A tentative theology*, containing a *doctrine of redemption.*

1 Tim. ii. 3—6.

"God our Saviour who willeth that all men should be saved, and come to the knowledge of the truth. For there is one God, one mediator also between God and man, himself man, Christ Jesus, who gave himself a ransom for all—the testimony to be borne in its own times."

Cf. 1 Tim. iii. 16. "Without controversy," &c.

Tit. iii. 4—7.

"But when the kindness of God our Saviour and his love toward man appeared, not by works done in righteousness which we did ourselves, but according to his mercy he saved us, through the washing of regeneration and renewing of the Holy Ghost, which he poured out upon us richly through Jesus Christ our Saviour; that being justified by his grace, we might be made heirs according to the hope of eternal life."

Cf. Tit. ii. 11—14. "The doctrine of God our Saviour," &c.

2 Tim. i. 9, 10.

"God, who saved us, and called us with a holy calling, not according to our works but according to his own purpose and grace, which was given us in Christ Jesus before times eternal, but hath now been manifested by the appearing of our Saviour Christ Jesus, who abolished death, and brought life and incorruption to light through the Gospel."

Cf. 2 Tim. ii. 8, 11—13. "Remember Jesus Christ," &c.

(3) *The constitution, methods, conduct of the early Churches.* Every one admits this to be the especial theme of the Pastoral Epistles; and it will suffice to give the following references, which embrace of course a large portion of the whole.

1 Tim. ii. 1, 2, 8, 9—12, iii. 1—7, 8—13; Tit. i. 5—9, 10—14, ii. 1—10, iii. 1, 2, 8—11, 13, 14; 2 Tim. i. 15—18, ii. 2, 14—18, iii. 6—9, iv. 9—15.

(4) *Ethical precepts*, lofty and based on the principle "work *from* life, not *for* life;" but *personal counsels* of right conduct not final or infallible or universal.

2 Tim. ii. 22.

"Flee youthful lusts, and follow after righteousness, faith, love, peace with them that call on the Lord out of a pure heart... The Lord's servant must not strive, but be gentle towards all."

Tit. ii. 11.

"The grace of God—bringing salvation, instructing us *to the intent that* denying ungodliness we should *live soberly, righteously and godly*—that he might redeem us—to be a people *zealous of good works.*"

Tit. iii. 8.

"Faithful is the saying, and concerning these things I will that thou affirm confidently to the end that they which have believed God may be careful to maintain good works."

1 Tim. ii. 12.

"I permit not a woman to teach."

1 Tim. v. 23.

"Be no longer a drinker of water."

(5) *A strong human personality.*

1 Tim. i. 20.

"Hymenæus and Alexander whom I delivered unto Satan that they be taught not to blaspheme."

Tit. i. 12.

"One of themselves, a prophet of their own, said, Cretians are always liars, evil beasts, idle gluttons. This testimony is true. Wherefore rebuke them sharply."

2 Tim. iii. 10, 11.

"But thou didst follow my teaching, conduct, purpose, faith, longsuffering, love, patience, persecution, sufferings, what things befel me at Antioch, at Iconium, at Lystra."

2 Tim. iv. 6—8.

"I am already being offered, and the time of my departure is come. I have fought the good fight, I have finished the course, I have kept the faith."

2 Tim. iv. 14—18.

"Alexander the coppersmith did me much evil, the Lord will render to him according to his works," &c.

(6) *Inexactness* as to (1) use of O.T., (2) expectation of the Second Advent.

1 Tim. v. 18.

"For the Scripture saith, Thou shalt not muzzle the ox when he treadeth out the corn."

2 Tim. iii. 8.

"And like as Jannes and Jambres withstood Moses, so do these also withstand the truth."

2 Tim. i. 12.

"Able to guard that which he has committed unto me against that day."

2 Tim. iii. 1.

"Know this that in the last days grievous times shall come."

Our conclusion may be summed up in the words of Schaff and Farrar, as representing (in spite of Dr Hatch's depreciation) the true weight of Biblical criticism in Germany and England under such names as Guericke, Thiersch, Huther, Wiesinger, Otto, Wieseler, Van Oosterzee, Lange, Herzog, von Hofmann, Beck, Alford, Wordsworth, Gloag, Fairbairn, Ellicott, Wace, Plumptre, Kölling, Plummer, Lightfoot. "Finally the peculiarities of style are counterbalanced by stronger resemblances and unmistakable evidences of Pauline authorship. 'There are flashes of the deepest feeling, outbursts of the most intense expression. There is rhythmic movement and excellent majesty in the doxologies, and the ideal of a Christian pastor drawn not only with an unfaltering hand, but with a beauty, fulness and simplicity which a thousand years of subsequent experience have enabled no one to equal, much less to surpass.'"

CHAPTER IV.

INTERNAL EVIDENCE.

III.

THE LAST JOURNEYS OF ST PAUL.

WAS St Paul released from the captivity described in Acts xxviii.? Did he travel after the end of that period?

The following reasons may be given for saying "yes" to each of these questions. See Dr Plummer, *Pastoral Epistles*, p. 14.

(1) "To assert that St Paul was released at the end of two years is to maintain a mere hypothesis: yet to assert that he was *not* released is equally to maintain a mere hypothesis."

(2) The writer of the *Pastoral Epistles* certainly believed that the Apostle did a good deal after the close of the Acts. No place can be found for all that is told or inferred within the limits of time fixed by the Acts.

(3) Clement of Rome (Cor. v.) speaks of St Paul "having reached the furthest bound of the West." In Clement's mouth at Rome this could hardly mean anything but Spain. If St Paul visited Spain as he intended (Rom. xv. 24, 28), it was after the period of the Acts.

(4) The Muratorian Fragment (c. 220 or 170 A.D.) names "the departure of Paul from the city to Spain."

(5) Eusebius, *H. E.* II. xxii. 2, says that at the end of the two years of imprisonment, according to tradition, St Paul went forth again upon the ministry of preaching; and in a second visit to the city ended his life by martyrdom under Nero, and that during this imprisonment he wrote the Second Epistle to Timothy.

(6) The objection that, if so, these last years would not have been unrecorded, is not valid. They *are* partly recorded in the *Pastoral Epistles.* Much of the rest of St Paul's life is unrecorded (2 Cor. xi.). So it is also with the other Apostles. The Holy Spirit designed no full biographies, but select lessons from select lives. *Ab uno disce omnes.*

If we seek to piece together such scattered notices of the years between A.D. 63 and A.D. 67 or 68 as may give a probable account of this last portion of the Apostle's life we are met by many possible combinations. It seems best therefore to present only one arrangement, not as more certain than others, but as fairly consistent and simple and sufficient. The "passages illustrated" which are set against the "order of events" themselves form the clue to the choice of routes.

PROBABLE FIRST JOURNEY EASTWARD.

Date A.D.	*Order of Events*	*Passages Illustrated*
63 *summer*	After the trial and release, St Paul, we may suppose, leaves Rome by the great Egnatian way, passes by Brundisium and *Dyrrachium* into Epirus and Macedonia, and visits *Philippi* according to his hope expressed from Rome; thence by the route through Troas direct to *Colossæ*, where again he had promised a visit; and so by Pergamos, Sardis and Hierapolis Laodicea	I trust in the Lord that I myself also shall come shortly. Phil. ii. 24. Withal prepare me also a lodging, for I hope that through your prayers I shall be granted unto you. Philem. 22.
63 *autumn*	to make a longer stay at *Ephesus*. In his farewell to its elders at Miletus, Acts xx. 29, he had led them to expect that to be his last visit; but as in the projected joint visit to Rome and Spain (Rom. xv. 28) and elsewhere 'circumstances	Grievous wolves shall enter in. Acts xx. 29.

Date	*Order of Events*	*Passages Illustrated*
	alter cases'; and his unexpected deliverance would lead him to revisit a place that had given him such foreboding anxiety as Ephesus did. The whole of 1 Tim. gives us the impression of a lengthened stay, during which the opposition of Hymenæus and Alexander and the services of Onesiphorus would alike find their natural place.	Hymenæus and Alexander I delivered unto Satan. 1 Tim. i. 20. In how many things Onesiphorus ministered at Ephesus thou knowest very well. 2 Tim. i. 18.
A.D. **64** *autumn* to **65** *spring*	After this year's stay he goes to *Crete* with Titus, where we may suppose he spends the winter at least. If a year's work at Ephesus with his 'son in the faith' is the natural basis on which the fact of the two letters to Timothy stands up subsequently, a winter's work with his other son in Crete gives the ground for the Epistle to Titus. During this year safely spent by the Apostle in the pastoral work at Ephesus and Crete the great fire broke out at Rome (19th July, 64).	The Emperor Nero "enjoyed the dreadful sight from a turret of his palace, singing and dancing the mime of the 'Burning of Troy' during the progress of the national catastrophe...and the tyrant succeeded in diverting the odium of the fire from himself to the innocent Christians, and gave them up to the refined and barbarous punishments of that which is called the first Christian persecution." Merivale, *St Paul at Rome*, pp. 145, 148.

PROBABLE SECOND JOURNEY WESTWARD.

Date	*Order of Events*	*Passages Illustrated*
A.D. **65** *spring*	Free now to think of a still 'larger hope' long entertained, St Paul sets sail from Crete, when the winter is past, trusting himself once again to a 'ship of Alexandria' bound for *Puteoli* and so by Rome (where his stay would be of the briefest) for *Carthago nova* and *Gades* in furthest Spain.	I will go on by you unto Spain. Rom. xv. 28. Having taught righteousness unto the whole world and having reached the furthest bound of the west. Clem. Rom. *Cor.* v. The departure of Paul from Rome for Spain. *Muratorian Fragment.*
65 *summer*	Thence by *Tarraco* to *Massilia* and Gaul (*Galatia*) generally including *Lugdunum*.	Crescens to Galatia. 2 Tim. iv. 10.
65 *autumn*	From Massilia back to Rome.	

Probable Third Journey Eastward and Westward.

Date A.D.	*Order of Events*	*Passages Illustrated*
66 *spring*	From Rome we may believe St Paul to have gone by one of the first ships after navigation was open to *Crete;*	For this cause left I thee in Crete. Tit. i. 5.
summer	from Crete he goes by *Miletus* again to *Ephesus;* journeys again to Colossæ and back;	This thou knowest that all that are in Asia turned away from me, of whom are Phygelus and Hermogenes. 2 Tim. i. 15. Alexander the coppersmith did me much harm. 2 Tim. iv. 14.
autumn	leaves Timothy at Ephesus, and by *Miletus*, where he leaves Trophimus, goes to *Troas*, where he leaves his cloke and books.	I exhorted thee to tarry at Ephesus on my going into Macedonia. 1 Tim. i. 3. Trophimus I left at Miletus sick. 2 Tim. iv. 20. The cloke that I left at Troas with Carpus bring when thou comest and the books. 2 Tim. iv. 13.
	Very possibly here at Carpus' house he writes the First Epistle to Timothy.	
	At this time he is intending, after his circular tour through Macedonia and Achaia, to return to Ephesus. He passes through *Philippi* to *Corinth.*	These things write I unto thee hoping to come unto thee shortly. 1 Tim. iii. 14.
	Here (or on the way here) he writes the Epistle to Titus.	
	He has intercourse with Zenas and Apollos, who, on leaving for Crete, are commended to Titus.	Set forward Zenas the lawyer and Apollos on their journey diligently. Tit. iii. 13.
	He changes his plans (whether through Nero being in the East or not) and determines to winter at *Nicopolis.*	There I have determined to winter. Tit. iii. 12.
	Crescens, Demas, Luke, Tychicus and Artemas are with him; and Erastus, who stays behind when the others go on to *Nicopolis.*	When I shall send Artemas unto thee or Tychicus, give diligence to come unto me to Nicopolis. Tit. iii. 12. Erastus abode at Corinth. 2 Tim. iv. 20.
	Here, under the pressure of danger beforehand, Demas forsakes the Fellowship.	Demas forsook me. 2 Tim. iv. 10.
	Artemas is sent to take Titus' place at Crete. After the arrival of Titus the plots against St Paul seem to have burst. They may have been hatched in Corinth, that dangerous centre of evil life and intercourse. He seems to have a presentiment that the end is near. He will not selfishly keep	

Date	*Order of Events*	*Passages Illustrated*
	his comrades to share his fate. The word of God must not be bound. Titus must go to Dalmatia, one open door into the "wild north," Crescens to Gaul, another open door into the "wild west." Only Luke his 'beloved physician' and Tychicus his 'beloved brother and faithful minister' insist on staying to tend him. So, for the last time, once more a prisoner, by Apollonia and Brundisium along the Egnatian way St Paul reaches *Rome*.	Titus to Dalmatia. 2 Tim. iv. 10. Crescens to Galatia. 2 Tim. iv. 10. Only Luke is with me. 2 Tim. iv. 10. Tychicus. 2 Tim. iv. 12.
A.D. **66** *winter*	He is closely confined now in one of the common criminal dungeons, so that Onesiphorus has difficulty in finding him.	I suffer hardships unto bonds as a malefactor. 2 Tim. ii. 9. When he was in Rome, he sought me diligently and found me. 2 Tim. i. 17.
67 *spring*	After his 'first defence,' all unbefriended, he writes the SECOND EPISTLE TO TIMOTHY, and sends it by Tychicus, begging Timothy to come to him before the navigation closes and bring Mark with him, that he may not go through another winter so forlorn.	At my first defence no one took my part. 2 Tim. iv. 16. Tychicus have I sent to Ephesus. 2 Tim. iv. 12. Do thy diligence to come before winter. 2 Tim. iv. 21. Take Mark and bring him with thee. 2 Tim. iv. 11.
67 June 29	But the Lord had other plans, and the executioner's sword set him free "before winter," even at midsummer, for his last brief journey to Paradise.	"Both alike (St Peter and St Paul) preached together as far as Italy and suffered martyrdom at the same time." Dionysius, Bp of Corinth A.D. 170, in Euseb. ii. 25. "The holy blessed apostles Peter and Paul were perfected on the 29th day of the month of June." *Acta Petri et Pauli*, § 88; cf. also Chrysost. *Opera*, v. 994.

CHAPTER V.

Internal Evidence.

IV.

St Paul and Early Gnosticism.

The heresy referred to by St Paul in the Pastoral Epistles, if fairly viewed, is seen to be the same as that of the Colossian Epistle—the earliest Judaic form of Gnosticism. Such differences as appear are sufficiently accounted for by the personal character of the letters and by the assumed lapse of some four or five years.

For the full statement of the arguments on which this conclusion rests, the reader is referred to Bp Lightfoot, *Introduction to Colossians*, p. 73 sq., and *Biblical Essays*, p. 411 sq.

The following summary gives in the main his view of the question. It is necessary (1) first to enquire what is the origin and meaning of Gnosticism. It is then (2) shewn that Essene Judaism was Gnostic; and (3) that the heresy of the Colossian Epistle was Judaic Gnosticism or Essene Judaism; and (4) the heresy of the Pastoral Epistles the same, advanced by one stage and more defined. And it is shewn (5) lastly that this heresy is very closely akin to the earliest Ophite Gnosticism, and leads naturally to the Cerinthian development of A.D. 90; and is therefore in its right place if dated A.D. 66, 67.

1. *What is the origin and meaning of Gnosticism?* Gnosticism, a system of religious beliefs and practices, which claimed to be possessed of *Gnosis*, a superior wisdom or *knowledge*, originated in the theosophic speculations of the East about the time of the Christian era, and appears to have formed an alliance with Judaism even before there was any contact with Christianity.

It has three characteristic features.

(1) It makes a distinction between the vulgar many who must be content with faith, blind faith, and the select few who

have knowledge. It introduces a separate intellectual *caste*, with a mysterious initiation, and an exclusive *aristocratic* spirit.

(2) Its field of speculation is natural and moral science; how to explain the work of creation, and how to account for the existence of evil; how to reconcile the creation of the world and the existence of evil with the conception of God as the absolute Being.

Since evil exists, and God could not create evil, so the argument ran, there must be some opposing principle independent of God and limiting His energy; and this was conceived to be the world of matter. Whether as a dead passive resistance, or a turbulent active power, evil thus resides in the material sensible world; and the result is a *dualism*, God perfectly good, matter the abode of evil. How then could God act upon matter, the Good communicate with the Evil? Only by some self-limitation, some evolution, some effluence of Deity. Thus the Divine Being germinates, as it were; and we obtain a series of successive *emanations*, the Divine element in each becoming feebler, until at length contact with matter is possible and creation ensues. These are the æons, spirits, or angels, of Gnosticism, more or less concrete and personal in different systems.

(3) Its rules of life and practice were moulded by these views; that a man might avoid this principle of evil and keep his higher nature unsoiled by matter. One rule was that of *rigid asceticism*, by which the material part of man should be subdued and mortified. The other was that of *unrestrained license*, the treating of matter as something alien, towards which there were no duties or obligations, and which could be used or left unused at will; so that the highest perfection consisted in the most complete contempt of mundane things.

2. *Essene Judaism was Gnostic and was in Asia Minor.* To the rigorous observance of the Mosaic law the Essene Jew added a rigid asceticism in respect to marriage, to drinks as well as meats, to oil for anointing, which went beyond Pharisaic obedience to external law and introduced the principle of

abstinence from externals as evil in themselves. Among his speculative tenets were a tendency to sun-worship, a denial of the resurrection of the body, a prohibition of sacrifices, an esoteric doctrine of angels, speculations on God and Creation, the belief in magical charms and certain "sacred books." He was an "exclusive," holding it a grievous offence to communicate his "mysteries" to the uninitiated and guarding the precious deposit by solemn oaths, by a long period of noviciate, and by a distinction of several orders in the community. Thus the three distinctive characteristics of Gnosticism reappear in the Essenes; and Essenism might be rightly designated as Gnostic Judaism. That Essene Judaism, at least in essential affinity of type, was to be found in Asia Minor may be inferred from the probabilities of the case; the union of Judaism and Oriental mysticism would produce the same results among the settlers in Asia Minor as in the Essene colonies by the Dead Sea; and Phrygia and Asia would be congenial soil, where the cosmological speculation of Thales, the mystic theosophy of Heraclitus, the fanatical worship of the Phrygian Cybele and the Ephesian Artemis, all had their home. The history of St Paul's visit to Ephesus (Acts xix. 13), with the incidents of the strolling Jews' exorcisms and the burning of their magical books by the Jewish converts, seems to indicate this connexion; since Josephus ascribes the practice of exorcism and of charms to the Essenes.

3. *The Colossian heresy was Judaic and Gnostic.* Its Judaism all will allow, from the references to circumcision, to the distinction of meats and drinks, to the observance of sabbaths and new moons (ii. 11, 16, 17, 21). It has also the three notes above marked of Gnosticism. (1) An *intellectual oligarchy* in religion is combated. St Paul contends for the universality of the Gospel, claiming to "warn *every* man and teach *every* man in *every kind of* wisdom, that he may present *every* man perfect in Christ Jesus" (i. 28). He takes up the language of his opponents, "wisdom," "intelligence," "knowledge," "perfect knowledge" (i. 9, ii. 2, 3, &c.), and translates it into a higher sphere. He dwells on the one universal comprehensive

mystery, the knowledge of God in Christ; which contains "all the treasures of wisdom and knowledge hidden" in it (i. 26, 27, ii. 2, iv. 3). (2) *The speculative tenets*, the cosmogony and theology, of Gnosticism are attacked. Against the doctrine of successive evolutions from the Divine nature, angelic mediators forming the successive links, St Paul sets the doctrine of the one Eternal Son, the Word incarnate (i. 15—20, ii. 9—15). Both in the natural and spiritual creation His initiative is absolute, His control is universal, His action is complete. He is the visible image of the invisible God. In Him resides the totality of the Divine powers and attributes, the *pleroma* or *plenitude*, according to the Gnostic term for this totality. Hence he is absolute Lord of all created things, whatever there may be, of "thrones, dominations, princedoms, virtues, powers." Angelolatry is therefore condemned as a denial of His perfect mediation. He is the centre of life, the mainspring of all energy; all therefore must be "in the Lord," and "unto the Lord" (ii. 18, iii. 18, 20, 23). (3) The *rigid asceticism*, which was one of the two practical results to which Gnostic doctrine led, appears in the Epistle as Essene rather than Pharisaic, Gnostic rather than Jewish (ii. 16, 21). These severities of discipline were intended "to check indulgence of the flesh," ignoring the cravings of the body and denying its wants. "Touch not, taste not, handle not." St Paul's treatment of this error does not, as in the case of the Galatian Judaism, point the contrast of law and grace; he deals with the *moral* aspects of these ascetic practices, as valueless for their purpose (ii. 23). He offers instead the elevation of the inner life in Christ, the transference of the affections into a higher sphere where the temptations of the flesh are powerless (iii. 1—5, 10).

The Colossian heresy is thus seen to be Gnostic as well as Judaic; and to have the very same characteristics as Essene Judaism. The two are in fact one and the same heresy, which according to the aspect in which it is viewed may be called either Judaic Gnosticism or Essene Judaism.

4. *The heresy of the Pastoral Epistles is the same, advanced one stage further and more defined.* Infancy has be-

come early childhood. But we have no full exposition, as in *Colossians*, where St Paul is confronting false opinion itself. Here he is writing to a friend and instructing him to deal practically with the question. Reference and allusion are sufficient. We have only a single word here and there, a descriptive epithet or attribute. But in the light of the Colossian Epistle these notes become clear. The heresy in both cases has its root on the same ground, in Asia Minor, the fittest meeting point of Oriental mysticism, of Greek thought, of Judaism and of Christianity.

(1) There is the same *esoteric spirit*, the exclusive intellectualism of Gnosticism; but there is an advance. "Knowledge" has now become the watchword of the sect, a title vaunted as peculiarly their own: "the knowledge falsely so called" (1 Tim. vi. 20). The contrast of the "different doctrine" is more marked, as the speculations of knowledge crowd out the "dispensation of God which is in faith" (1 Tim. i. 4). The Gospel is emphatically declared to be universal; "God our Saviour, who willeth that all men should be saved and come to the full knowledge of the truth" (1 Tim. ii. 4). And the true knowledge *is* faith; "God who is the Saviour of all men, specially of them that believe" (1 Tim. iv. 10). From this intellectualism were now arising very obtrusively and offensively the "vain talking" (1 Tim. i. 6), the "questionings and disputes of words" (1 Tim. vi. 4), the "profane babblings" (2 Tim. ii. 16), the "foolish and ignorant questionings" (2 Tim. ii. 23) which St Paul so frequently and so severely rebukes.

(2) In the *speculative theories*, the doctrine of emanations, there is the same leading thought, taken further. The somewhat vague and shadowy "worship of angels" (Col. ii. 18), as emanations of intermediary superior essences, appears now in the more definite shape of "genealogies" (Tit. iii. 9), "endless genealogies" (1 Tim. i. 4); a phrase clearly referring to the successive generations of the æons from the *pleroma*. The same speculations embodied in the concrete form of stories by the Gnostic teachers are labelled as "fables" or "myths" as well as "tiresome pedigrees"; "profane and old wives'

fables" (1 Tim. iv. 7); "Jewish fables" (Tit. i. 14); "turning aside unto fables" (2 Tim. iv. 4). The truth of the One only Mediator in opposition to these false mediators is emphasised, "one mediator between God and man, himself man, Christ Jesus" (1 Tim. ii. 5); the Word incarnate, the one "mystery of godliness," "He who was manifested in the flesh, justified in the spirit, revealed to all His creatures, angels and men, as Lord, and enthroned as King in glory" (1 Tim. iii. 16). The truth of the One God in opposition to the dualism of the Gnostic is enforced, "there is one God" (1 Tim. ii. 5), "to the King Eternal, the only God, be honour" (1 Tim. i. 17).

These speculations on the unseen and marvellous found expression in magical rites, the common refuge of oriental superstition. Hence St Paul calls these heretics "wizards," "enchanters" (2 Tim. iii. 13), misled by "doctrines of devils" (1 Tim. iv. 1).

(3) The resulting Gnostic rule of *rigid asceticism* still prevails in "commandments of men" (Tit. i. 14). The denial of the resurrection of the body (2 Tim. ii. 18) finds its motive here in the desire to be rid of the material, the home and abode of evil. The "abstaining from meats" (1 Tim. iv. 3) is based indeed on the Mosaic law, but doubtless went beyond the Mosaic distinction between meats clean and unclean. The "forbidding to marry," a very general Gnostic tenet, was independent of and contrary to the spirit of Judaism. The result of such a perverted asceticism, abstinence from things lawful, was the prevalence of other vices, avarice, selfishness, deceit; "supposing that godliness is a way of gain" (1 Tim. vi. 5).

But there are signs of a new departure; traces of the other Gnostic rule of *unbridled license* coming to be adopted; an indulgence in profligate habits and a pandering to the vices of others; "by their works they deny God, being abominable—to them that are defiled and unbelieving nothing is pure" (Tit. i. 16, 15), "silly women laden with sins led away by divers lusts" (2 Tim. iii. 6). These are the first beginnings of that wild profligacy in later Gnosticism which is a constant theme of reproach with writers of the Church.

5. *This heresy finally is very closely akin to the earliest Ophite Gnosticism, and leads naturally to the Cerinthian development of* A.D. 90; *and is therefore in its right place if dated* A.D. 66 *and* 67.

The Ophites were among the earliest Gnostic sects. The heathen element is still predominant in their teaching. Great prominence is given to Phrygian mysteries and rites; and their proper home would appear to have been Phrygia. Their name *Naassene*, derived from the Hebrew word for serpent (Ophite being from the Greek *ophis* a serpent), shews that there was also an admixture of Judaic elements. They professed to derive their Gnosis from James the Lord's brother. Hippolytus, Bishop at Portus, the harbour of Rome, A.D. 220, whose "Refutations of Heresies" was discovered about A.D. 1850, is our chief authority respecting the sect, and he places them first in the series of heresies, before Simon Magus and before Cerinthus. He implies that they were the first to call themselves Gnostics; names among their magical rites and mysteries those of Osiris, Samothrace, Eleusis and Cybele, later additions very probably to the mystical Judaic interpretations of the Old Testament; speaks of their teaching by myths, forbidding marriage, maintaining that the resurrection was spiritual, making genealogies a definite part of their system; and so forth. How largely the heresy of the epistles partook of this Ophite character is seen from the passages quoted above.

Cerinthus lived and taught in Proconsular Asia about A.D. 90 and was a contemporary of St John. According to Neander he "is best entitled to be considered as the intermediate link between the Judaizing and the Gnostic sects." Judaism was still prominent in his teaching: but already the Gnostic element was aggressive (1) in his cosmogony, (2) in his Christology.

(1) The world he asserted was not made by the highest God but by an angel or power, far removed from and ignorant of this Supreme Being. Thus his theory was linked on to the angelology of later Judaism founded on the angelic appear-

ances of the Old Testament. The Colossian epistle seems to represent the first stage of Gnostic teaching about this angelic demiurge as having an imperfect appreciation of the Supreme God (whence arose the imperfections of the natural world) but still a fit object of worship as mediator between God and man. The second stage was that of Cerinthus, representing the angel demiurge as ignorant of the good God. The third that of later Gnostics attributing to him direct antagonism.

(2) Again, as a Judaizer Cerinthus held that Jesus was only the son of Joseph and Mary born in the natural way. As a Gnostic he maintained that the Christ first descended in the form of a dove on the carpenter's son at his baptism ; that He revealed to him the unknown Father and worked miracles through him, and that at length He took His flight and left him, to return "to His own *pleroma*," so that Jesus alone suffered and rose.

The existence of vague and undeveloped germs of this latter doctrine appears in the emphasis with which, both in the Colossian and Pastoral Epistles, the eternal being and absolute sovereignty, and also the historic passion, resurrection, and ascension of Christ are asserted. In addition to the passages above quoted, compare "the whole *pleroma* abides permanently in Christ" (Col. i. 19, ii. 9) ; "ye received the doctrine of the Christ, even Jesus the Lord" (Col. ii. 6); "reconciled through the blood of Christ's cross," "in the body of His flesh through death" (Col. i. 20, 22) ; "given us in Christ Jesus before times eternal" (2 Tim. i. 9); "remember Jesus Christ risen from the dead, &c." (2 Tim. ii. 8) ; "the glory of our great God and Saviour Jesus Christ" (Tit. ii. 13).

The former doctrine, in its still undefined, undeveloped form, is met by the emphasis laid on the being and character of the one God throughout the Pastoral Epistles. "In the sight of God who quickeneth all things...who is the blessed and only Potentate, who only hath immortality" (1 Tim. vi. 13, 15). Cf. i. 17, "the only God," ii. 3, "God our Saviour—one God," iii. 15, iv. 10, "the living God." Cf. also the significant phrase three times repeated, "God our Saviour," Tit. i. 3, ii. 10, iii. 4, in each case followed by "Jesus Christ our Saviour," as though expressly to assert firstly the living love and power of the one Sovereign Father, and secondly the unity of Father and Son.

Thus we pass from St Paul to St John, who frames of this teaching a whole Epistle and Gospel, to meet the now fully spread and fully working poison of the Cerinthian Gnosticism. "I and the Father are one" (Joh. x. 30). "This is the antichrist, even he that denieth the Father and the Son" (1 Joh. ii. 22).

CHAPTER VI.

SUMMARY AND CONCLUSIONS.

THE *external evidence* in favour of St Paul's authorship of the Epistles is, as we have seen in Chap. I., very strong. They have been almost universally accepted as Pauline. They are used by the Apostolic Fathers, the Greek Apologists, the Early Heretics; have the witness of the Ancient Versions and the Ancient Churches; and are acknowledged alike by Historian, Canon, and Council. Down to the nineteenth century no one doubted their authenticity, even if any rejected them from dislike of their contents.

The *internal evidence* entitles us to assert strongly that the difficulties alleged by some modern critics in the way of this belief have no just foundation. One of the most widely-spread summaries of this (chiefly) foreign criticism is that of the late Dr Hatch, *Encyclopædia Britannica*, ed. IX. vol. XVIII. 381.

Baur, Holtzmann, and others raise four main objections.

1. The first point alleged is that

The ecclesiastical organisation implied is too advanced, the teaching about it too definite for St Paul.

This objection arises from an exaggerated view of both the advance and the definiteness.

A fairer judgment is to be obtained from a review of all the literary evidence that remains to us at successive epochs, A.D. 33; 66; 99; 133; as given in Chap. II.

From this, studied as a whole, we see that the duties of presidency and headship, with the power of delegation, are, in the period before A.D. 66, assumed throughout to be those of the first Apostles themselves; while in the periods which follow there is very definite and frequent reference to the delegated presidencies of 'apostles' or 'angels' or 'prophets'; until, with Ignatius, the name of 'bishop' appears singly to denote this office. It is further seen that subordinate offices and ministries appear from the first—'presbyters' (also called 'bishops' during the first century) and 'deacons' *along with others.* But throughout the period there is frequent and definite reference to these two offices as standing on a more settled footing than others.

It is, we conclude, quite natural that, with regard to the *apostolate*, St Paul, as in some sense the chief secretary of the Apostolic College, should be found laying down principles of guidance for successors when "the time of their departure was at hand."

It is quite natural that these instructions should embrace the method of dealing with the two more settled ministries of the *presbyterate* and *diaconate*, and should *not* deal with other offices.

The oral Gospel of the apostolic ministry is giving place to the written Gospel. As in the case of the selections made by the Evangelists, so now leading principles rather than exhaustive rules, specimens of method rather than complete codes, are what we should expect; and this is what we find.

The great Pauline principle for the apostolate is *character*; the great Pauline method is a *fit succession of "fellow-workers unto the kingdom."*

2. A second objection urged is that

The style and philological peculiarities of the epistles are foreign to St Paul.

We have indeed had reason to allow, in Chap. III., that there are peculiarities of both language and tone of thought in the Pastoral Epistles compared with St Paul's earlier letters. But we have shewn that these peculiarities are nothing more than marks of natural growth and development. And, further, along with the differences there are abundant samenesses both in style and intrinsic character with what we recognise as essentially Pauline.

3. A third objection brought is

The difficulty of reconciling the historical references with what is known from other sources of the life of St Paul.

We admit that the epistles cannot be placed at any period in the life of the Apostle up to the close of the two years named in Acts xxviii. 30: and we maintain that they were written subsequently. For the reasons and according to the account given in Chap. IV. we conclude that St Paul was released from captivity, made further missionary journeys, during which the First Epistle to Timothy and the Epistle to Titus were written, and was then re-imprisoned at Rome, from whence the Second Epistle to Timothy was written. It has been well urged that "until the epistles are proved forgeries, they are themselves competent witnesses as to the facts of the Apostle's history; and consistent even if differing theories respecting the position of the events named have been framed without difficulty. That these do differ is no argument for their impossibility; only that not enough data are to hand to fix between three or four possible combinations." Dr Riddle, *Encyclopædia Americana*, 1889, pp. 146, 7. The same writer forcibly adds:—"The historical difficulties themselves favour the genuineness. A forger [or, we may add, a pseudepigraphist of the century] skilful enough to deceive the church for 1800 years would have fitted his allusions to the Acts; and would not have invented 'the cloak' and other minor incidents."

4. A fourth objection is founded upon

The allusions to a too-developed Heresy, and too elaborate a debasement of Christianity.

In reply it may be shewn, as in Chap. V., that "the early and rapid growth of error is indicated in the undoubted Pauline Epistles." In particular we see that Essene Judaism was Gnostic, and that this was the heresy of the Colossian Epistle in its early stage, and of the Pastoral Epistles in the next stage; being next of kin to the earliest Ophite Gnosticism and leading naturally to the Cerinthian development of A.D. 90.

It is therefore in its right place if dated A.D. 66, 67. "Nor can there be found any particular age or error in the church after the apostolic period to which the language of these epistles would apply with such force as to suggest a forgery to meet that error in that age."

The conclusion, which we may draw with confidence, from both the external and internal evidence, is that all three Epistles are the genuine work of St Paul and belong to the last years of his life A.D. 66, 67. "The three stand or fall together. Every attempt to prove one of them Pauline and the others forgeries has failed from its inherent inconsistency." They *stand.* Dr Hatch is entirely in error in stating that "the majority of modern critics question or deny their authenticity." On the contrary, no considerable portion of Biblical scholars do so; and with the great majority of modern critics, some of whose names are given p. 39, we unhesitatingly maintain the complete authenticity of St Paul's crowning work.

B. THE FRIENDS ADDRESSED IN THE EPISTLES.

CHAPTER VII.

LIFE OF TIMOTHY.

A.D. 30. The birthplace of Timothy was most probably Lystra. We infer this from Acts xvi. 1, where we read that St Paul on his second missionary journey "came also to Derbe and Lystra (by road from Antioch in Syria), and behold a certain disciple was there named Timothy, the son of a Jewess which believed, but his father was a Greek. The same was well reported of by the brethren that were at Lystra and Iconium." The passage actually proves only that his home at the time was Lystra and that he had been sufficiently long there and at Iconium to be well known to the Christian Church. St Paul was well acquainted not only with his mother Eunice but with his grandmother Lois, who were distinguished among the Jewish converts; "when I call to remembrance the unfeigned faith that is in thee, which dwelt first in thy grandmother Lois, and thy mother Eunice." Lewin seems to refer this to their "devotional turn of mind" before conversion, and thinks that from the mention of the grandmother "an intimacy had subsisted between the two families from the earliest times." But if this intimacy existed, the nearness of Tarsus to Lystra would be likely to have brought them together during St Paul's stay at Tarsus after his conversion between A.D. 37 and 45, and so have led to their conversion before St Paul's first recorded missionary visit to Lystra, A.D. 45. If this was so, Timothy as a young boy enjoyed the results of this in early Christian training; we cannot be sure how early. But we can be sure that the trials of the first missionary journey made a deep impression upon him. Thou hast fully known...my persecutions, afflictions, which came unto me *at Antioch, at Iconium, at Lystra* (2 Tim. iii. 11). We cannot go so far as to infer with Lewin from this "that he had evidently been a convert at the date of Paul's first visit to Antioch in Pisidia, and in the place of Mark, who had withdrawn his services at Perga, had followed Paul successively to Iconium and Lystra." It may have been, as Bp Ellicott suggests, that these sufferings drew the lad on to throw in his lot with the cause championed by so brave and noble a leader. Such sufferings in one town of the district after another would be "household words" in Eunice's home, and young Timothy may well have dated his baptism and "laying on of hands" in Confirmation from that time (A.D. 45), if they had not taken place earlier. The phrases of St Paul's letters to him certainly imply this connexion between them then, if not earlier; "my true child in faith" (1 Tim. i. 2), "my beloved child" (2 Tim. i. 1); since at the second missionary visit he appears as a "disciple," "well reported of," not only in Lystra itself but in the district. In what way he had thus become known in his own town and at Iconium we can only conjecture; perhaps by some commencement of that work he did so successfully afterwards, that of being the messenger of the Churches.

A.D. 51. We take up his life now (Acts xvi. 1), with St Paul at Lystra upon his second missionary journey. He is, we may believe, a young man now of 21 years, devout, enthusiastic, sympathetic, trustworthy, just the youthful colleague after St Paul's own heart. As a Jew on his mother's side and a Greek on his father's he would feel for and with both portions of the communities to be visited. But to the Jews he would cause a difficulty from not having been circumcised, since the Jewish law required the rite in the case of mixed marriages where the mother was a Jewess. St Paul's precept and practice with regard to compliance with the law of Moses was to become all things to all men if by any means he might gain some: but where the liberty of the Gentile converts to be free from the law was at stake, there to "give way by subjection, no not for an hour." Accordingly, while he refused to circumcise Titus who was a Greek (Gal. ii. 3), he now "took and circumcised Timothy because of the Jews that were in those parts; for all knew that his father was a Greek" (Acts xvi. 3). The next step was to ordain and set him apart as an evangelist, an office apparently general and itinerant, suited to a "messenger of the churches" who was to be a vicar apostolic. "Do the work of an *evangelist*, fulfil thy ministry" (2 Tim. iv. 5). This was done by St Paul as *Apostle*, "the gift of God that is in thee by the putting on of my hands" (1 Tim. i. 18), but with, also, "the laying on of the hands of the *presbytery*" (2 Tim. i. 6). The ordination included "prophecy," that is, utterances or "charges," from "*prophets*," "the gift that is in thee which was given thee by prophecy" (2 Tim. i. 6). And we see in this scene a practical example of St Paul's words written to the Ephesians ten years later; "He gave some to be *apostles;* and some, *prophets;* and some, *evangelists;* and some, *pastors* and teachers" (Eph. iv. 11). Thus equipped the young evangelist went forth with Paul and Silas on the journey to "confirm the churches" already visited, and on their way through the cities to deliver the decrees of the Council at Jerusalem respecting the ceremonial observances of the Mosaic Law. Their course took them doubtless first to Iconium and Antioch, and we can be sure that these were among the Churches that now began to make great progress with the removal of this barrier to Gentile admission. What other "cities and churches" are included in the description given Acts xvi. 4, 5 we can only conjecture. Prof. Ramsay in his *Church in the Roman Empire*, p. 75 sqq., has shewn good reason for doubting the interpretation generally given in maps of St Paul's journeys to the account in verse 6, "they went through the region of Phrygia and Galatia, having been forbidden of the Holy Ghost to speak the word in Asia." One main road from Antioch went turning slightly south along the valley of the Lycus by Colossæ, Laodicea and Hierapolis to Ephesus. But in the Ep. to Colossians (i. 5) St Paul speaks of their having learned the Gospel not from himself but from Epaphras. Besides, Colossæ, Laodicea, and Hierapolis were all in the Asia of N. T., i.e. in Lydian Asia. The general account therefore given is that St Paul from Antioch "bent his steps northward," "making for Galatia which lay to the north," and so he would reach Pessinus, Ancyra and Tavium. Lewin has this view in his 4th edition, I. p. 172, though Prof. Ramsay misrepresents him as still taking St Paul to Colossæ. He gives however in his map the Roman provinces of Asia and Galatia as filling the whole space of the country west of Derbe, except for Bithynia on the northern, and Pamphylia on the southern coast of Phrygia; and we have only to add '*Phrygia Galatica*' as a further title of South-west Galatia, the district between Antioch and Iconium, to get the true corrected geography of Prof. Ramsay; whose interpretation is then to take Acts xvi. 6 as a recapitulation of *vv.* 4, 5; "at Antioch, St Paul was forbidden to preach in Asia;" then, "it seems to have occurred to St Paul to go on to the country immediately beyond, viz. West Bithynia; and the road by Dorylaion to Nikaia and Nikomedeia was a great route. But when they came opposite to Mysia, at Nakoleia, the 'Spirit of Jesus' suffered them not, they were compelled to turn westward and keeping along the southern frontier of Mysia they reached Troas."

Here St Luke joins them (Acts xvi. 10, "*we* sought to go forth"), partly it may be from anxiety for St Paul's health (cf. "Luke the beloved physician," Col. iv. 14). The vision calling them into Europe explains the refusal of the Spirit to allow the delay in Asia; and they cross to Philippi. Timothy shares in the first triumphs there of the Cross, escaping the imprisonment that fell to his chiefs; and apparently leaving Luke behind (since the 3rd person is resumed instead of the 1st in Acts xvi. 40), the party travel along the great Egnatian road to Thessalonica (Acts xvii. 1); where after three weeks' vain efforts for the conversion of the Jews they obtain signal success among the pagan population ("ye turned to God from idols," 1 Thess. i. 9). Here St Paul was "at one and the same time the Christian advocate and the industrious artisan"; "neither did we eat any man's bread for nought, but wrought with labour and travail night and day that we might not be chargeable to any of you" (2 Thess. iii. 8). The stress laid here upon this working would seem to require us to suppose that Silas and Timothy too would have their share in the earning of the daily bread. At the same time the Philippian converts sent support, "ye Philippians know that in Thessalonica also ye sent *once and again* unto my necessities" (Phil. iv. 15). The later work of Timothy shews how his "first love" went out in devoted labour both for Philippi and Thessalonica. After some months (see note Alf. *Prolegg.* 1 *Thess.* § 2) the Jewish enmity instigated the mob to an attack upon the Apostles at the house of Jason. Paul, Silas and Timothy were sent away by night by the brethren to Berœa (Acts xvii. 10, 14). There Timothy's zeal and knowledge in the Old Testament Scriptures (2 Tim. iii. 15) would help to kindle the "noble" desire of the Berœan Jews, who "received the word with all readiness of mind, examining the scriptures daily, whether these things were so" (Acts xvii. 11). From Berœa St Paul was hastily sent away *to go to the sea.* Timothy who had well won his spurs receives orders from St Paul at Athens to go from Berœa to Thessalonica and bring St Paul (A.D. 52, spring) the latest tidings of his flock (1 Thess. iii. 1—6); and Silas is instructed, we may assume, as he is not mentioned in 1 Thess. iii. 1—6, to stay on at Berœa; though at first St Paul had wished them to follow him to Athens at once. After completing his errand to Thessalonica in the satisfactory way described, 1 Thess. iii. 2, Timothy would rejoin Silas at Berœa, and both, bringing supplies "from Macedonia," rejoined St Paul, who by this time had reached Corinth, and, again in need, had been busily pursuing his trade as tentmaker in partnership with Aquila and Priscilla (Acts xviii. 2, 3, 5; 1 Thess. iii. 7; 2 Cor. xi. 8, 9). During the year (autumn) both Epistles to the Thessalonians are despatched, both bearing the names of Silas and Timothy after St Paul's. It is interesting to note this connexion of Timothy with the epistolary work of St Paul at the very commencement of the series of letters which, continued at intervals through the next fifteen years, closes with the touching outpour of personal affection and anxiety in a second letter to Timothy himself just before his end.

The joint labours of the three missionaries resulted at Corinth as elsewhere in violent opposition from the Jews, and they hired a meeting-room from Justus close to the synagogue. For 18 months they were undisturbed, and disciples multiplied, among whom we probably know of some ten names, Justus, Crispus, Stephanas, Fortunatus, Achaicus, Erastus, Caius, Chloe, Quartus, Tertius. The delightful work of baptizing these converts fell to Timothy and Silas, we suppose, since the Apostle debarred himself from taking part (1 Cor. i. 14). But we are expressly told of *their preaching* also, and of its significant directness: "The Son of God, Jesus Christ, who was preached among you by us, even by me and Silvanus and Timothy," 2 Cor. i. 19. In this great centre of Greek life not only would the full preaching power of all be put forth, but St Paul exercised also the apostolic gift of miracles. as we learn from 2 Cor. xii. 12, "truly the signs of an Apostle were wrought among you in all patience, by signs and wonders and mighty works." In June, A.D. 53, Gallio came to Corinth as governor of Achaia, an able and amiable Roman, before whom St Paul was in vain indicted. It may well have been that the Nazarite vow, often taken for 30 days by pious Jews in time of difficulty, was taken by St Paul in connexion with this deliverance. And if so "the many days" that St Paul "stayed on" (Acts xviii. 18) would be about a month, and the "cutting off the hair" at the expiration of the vow took place at Cenchreæ, the port of Corinth, just before starting for Ephesus. This Jewish observance is interesting, as we note the same liberty of practice in things indifferent claimed by St Paul for himself that was shewn in Timothy's circumcision. We have no knowledge whether Timothy accompanied St Paul on his journey by Ephesus to Jerusalem for the Feast of Tabernacles, and so on to Antioch (A.D. 53, Sept. 16). But there seems no reason against it; and we may think of him making his first acquaintance with the great "city of God" under St Paul's inspiring guidance; Silas may probably have remained there, but Timothy would go on with St Paul to Antioch.

A.D. 54. After a winter's stay there, the third missionary journey was commenced by going "through the region of Galatia and Phrygia in order," and Timothy would revisit with St Paul the old home on their way. Following one of Prof. Ramsay's interpretations of Acts xviii. 23 we suppose "the Galatian country" to refer to the Lycaono-Galatic country of Lystra and Derbe, and "Phrygia" to the Phrygo-Galatic district of Iconium and Antioch. "Phrygia" can hardly refer to "Phrygia Magna," which Paul would traverse after leaving the Galatic territory, since he had not been previously along the western road, and would have no disciples to "establish." It would indeed "confirm" those loving, devout disciples Eunice and Lois to hear of the great things God had wrought already by their young evangelist. The visit to Galatia shewed however the baneful influence of the Judaisers, and the fickle converts were ready with resentment instead of their first impulsive love, because the Apostle "told them the truth" respecting "their false teachers" and "the law" (Gal. iv. 16).

Reaching Ephesus, not by the valley of the Lycus but by the shorter hill road by the plain of Metropolis and the Cayster valley, they make a long stay of three years, during which great success attends their labours. "The word of God prevailed and grew mightily" (Acts xix. 20). But there were many difficulties and persecutions in the midst of the public and house-to-house ministration, as touchingly described by St Paul in his address to the elders of Ephesus, A.D. 58 (Acts xx. 18—21). And still stronger language is used in 1 Cor. iv. 9, xv. 32, an epistle written towards the close of the sojourn at Ephesus in the spring of A.D. 57. St Paul had previously, in preparation for revisiting the Churches of Macedonia and Achaia, sent Timothy forward with Erastus (Acts xix. 22), especially perhaps to get ready the contribution for the poor saints at Jerusalem (1 Cor. xvi. 1, 2). The immoralities and schisms among the Corinthians, of which news reached Ephesus after Timothy had left, determine St Paul to send a letter on at once to reach them sooner than his envoy would; and Timothy is accordingly "commended to their regard in terms which imply a fear of insult from the anti-Pauline party, and they are bidden to send him forth in peace that he might return to Paul" (1 Cor. iv. 17, xvi. 10). Later in the year Timothy rejoins the Apostle in Macedonia, very likely at Philippi, as his name appears with St Paul's in the salutation of the 2nd letter to Corinth (2 Cor. i. 1). It would seem most natural to place the Epistle to the Galatians during this interval of Timothy's absence One who had been so closely linked with St Paul in the two visits to Galatia and belonged to the neighbourhood would surely not be merged in the general phrase "all the brethren which are with me" (Gal. i. 2). According to Bp Lightfoot (Int. *Gal.*, 2nd ed. p. 58) the special truths common to the Galatian and Roman Epistles must have appeared in any letter written between them; but on p. 44 he well depicts the strong similarity in *tone and feeling* that does exist between 2 Corinthians and Galatians; and he would admit a *general identity of doctrine*, since he would assign to all the four letters of the second group the subject "Christ the Redeemer," or "Christ on the Cross." The special application of the subject varied with the special errors of the two Churches. A parallel case is that of Ignatius, who writes "Farewell" to seven Churches, but makes his special topic in six of the letters the need of unity under the bishop, but in the seventh, to the Romans, the appeal that nothing may be done to hinder his martyrdom.

Timothy now for the third time visits Corinth—a second time with St Paul—about November, probably of A.D. 57, when the Apostle had "gone through those parts," i.e. Macedonia, "and given them much exhortation" (Acts xx. 2). There they "abode three months," and there would be abundant work in the complete arrangement of the troubles and disorders and the reestablishment of filial love and piety. If in the midst of the Galatian trouble the 2nd Corinthians could be written, so now in the very heart of Corinthian cares and duties the Galatian topic is taken up and enlarged into a very manual and Gospel of the Faith in the shape of the Epistle to the Romans. Timothy is again joined in the salutations, the first of those who send greetings, "Timothy my fellow worker saluteth you" (Rom. xvi. 21), and shared doubtless to the full that interest in the capital of the world which led St Paul so ardently to cherish the desire, "I must also see Rome." But at present the path lay otherwise, and, by Passover time, March 27, A.D. 58, they were at Philippi, *en route* for Jerusalem, and were joined by St Luke, whose journal fixes the details of the voyage very minutely. The company at first included "Sopater of Berœa; Aristarchus and Secundus of the Thessalonians; Gaius of Derbe, and Timotheus; and of Asia, Trophimus and Tychicus" (Acts xx. 4). How far they all travelled with St Paul we cannot tell; we only know from the first person being used in the narrative that St Luke was one who remained, and from Acts xxi. 29 that Trophimus was another. We can hardly bring ourselves to believe that Timothy was left behind, and, as Plumptre points out (*Dict. Bib.* p. 1506), "the language of St Paul's address to the elders of Ephesus (Acts xx. 17—35) renders it unlikely that he was then left there with authority." We can the rather suppose that he would accompany St Paul to Jerusalem.

A.D. 59—61. Thus he would be at hand to supply all possible succour and service throughout the two years' imprisonment at Cæsarea. He may, for example, have visited Philippi more than once as St Paul's representative. As he is not named in Acts xxvii. we may perhaps conclude that he did not accompany the Apostle to Rome, but his company and comfort must have been welcomed before long, since three out of the four epistles of the third group bear witness to his active, trusty cooperation.

A.D. 62. If with Bp Lightfoot we assign the Philippian epistle to the earlier part of this imprisonment we may think of Timothy arriving at Rome in the spring of A.D. 62; and after a brief stay with his old chief, preparing to pay another visit to Philippi, "having been chosen for this purpose as one whose solicitude for the Philippians had become a second nature" (Phil. ii. 20). It is calculated that the journey would not take longer than a month, and Timothy would have returned long before the penning of the Epistles to Colossians and Philemon was taken in hand, A.D. 63, spring. Timothy is joined in the salutation in both of these, but not in that to the Ephesians written at the same time. The reason may be the encyclical or "essay" character of the "Ephesians" intended for all the Churches of Asia, as it also contains no salutations to any individuals. The subject-matter both of Colossians and Ephesians was one in which Timothy must have taken much interest. Not only were the earliest elements of Gnosticism largely "Ophite" and Phrygian, and therefore derived from the neighbourhood of his own home, but he must himself have already in his work at Ephesus met the germs of the Gnostic heresy and as a young man have felt his need of guidance and teaching, how to teach against it "the truth as it is in Jesus," "the life in Christ," which the Apostle here lays down.

A.D. 63, 64. On St Paul's release in the summer of A.D. 63 Timothy would, we may believe, accompany him in his first journey eastward, described p. 41.

A.D. 65, 66. Staying at Ephesus, when St Paul went on to Crete and Spain, he may have suffered accusation or imprisonment either there or in the course of journeys appointed him by St Paul to Corinth and elsewhere during his absence. Nero was in Greece at the time, and though the storm of persecutions away from Rome was not yet general, some zealous official might easily have thought to please the emperor by seizing Timothy. But from the passage in Hebrews xiii. 23, "Know ye that our brother Timothy has been discharged," the trouble seems to have been short-lived and he was free to join St Paul again in his third journey eastward, or to be joined by him at Ephesus. See Int. p. 43.

A.D. 66. There, at any rate in the autumn of A.D. 66, we find him left in charge (1 Tim. i. 3), and there most probably he stayed, receiving first in the autumn the "First Epistle to Timothy" and again in the spring the "Second Epistle," and busy with all the "care of the churches" which the contents of these letters disclose.

A.D. 67. Before he could start to join his aged "father" after the receipt of the letter, we may believe the end came to St Paul, June, A.D. 67, and he was left alone to play the man. With Plumptre (*Dict. Bib.* III. 1507), we may suppose that "the special charge committed to him in the Pastoral Epistles might not unnaturally give fixity to a life which had previously been wandering," and he would become the resident apostolic or prophetic head of the single Church of Ephesus rather than the superintendent of many Churches, having very probably been first used by God to establish earlier than elsewhere in the Churches of Asia this rule of a settled head, whether "prophet" or "apostle" or "presbyter" or "bishop," which was gradually to become universal. If this were so we shall recognise, under the oriental symbolic picture-language of St John, in the "angel of Ephesus," Timothy "the evangelist," "the brother," "the beloved son" of St Paul; and in the Revelation, written A.D. 69, we catch the last inspired view of him in the "Epistle to the Church of Ephesus." If we allow for the oriental character of the visions, and the vividness of style of the son of thunder in his character as "prophet," reproducing Old Testament vehemence of language, we may assent to Plumptre's identification; "both the praise and blame are such as harmonise with the impressions as to the character of Timotheus derived from the Acts and the Epistles. The refusal to acknowledge the self-styled apostles, the abhorrence of the deeds of the Nicolaitans, the unwearied labour, all this belongs to the 'man of God' of the Pastoral Epistles. And the fault is no less characteristic. The strong language of St Paul's entreaty would lead us to expect that the temptation of such a man would be to fall away from the glow of his 'first love,' the zeal of his first faith. The promise of the Lord of the Churches is in substance the same as that implied in the language of the Apostle" (2 Tim. ii. 4—6). We have this view confirmed by Eusebius, *H. E.* III. 14, who represents Timothy as continuing to act as Bishop of Ephesus.

He is further said (Niceph. *H. E.* III. 11) to have died a martyr's death under Domitian or Nerva, the day associated with his martyrdom being Jan. 24. "During the great annual feast of the Catagogii of Artemis, which consisted of processions bearing idols, with women lewdly dancing before them and ending in bloodshed, Timothy moved by righteous zeal rushed into the portico of the temple and exhorted the frenzied revellers to decency; but this so enraged them that they fell upon him with sticks and stones and killed him." (See Baring-Gould's *Lives of the Saints*, I. 360.)

CHAPTER VIII.

LIFE OF TITUS.

A.D. 29 or 30. THERE seems good reason for assuming some such date as A.D. 30 for the birth year of Titus. (1) In A.D. 66, to which year we assign the Epistle to Titus, he was evidently still a young man. The language used is very similar to that used in the case of Timothy, and the age may be taken as nearly the same, "Let no man despise thee (ii. 15). The younger men likewise exhort to be soberminded, in all things shewing thyself an ensample of good works" (ii. 6, 7); compared with "Let no man despise thy youth; but be thou an ensample to them that believe, in word, in manner of life, in love, in faith, in purity," 1 Tim. iv. 12. And again (2) in A.D. 50, the date generally assigned to the Council at Jerusalem, he was old enough to be selected as a member of the deputation from the Church at Antioch, which accompanied Paul and Barnabas to obtain a judgment respecting Jewish ceremonial. This we learn from Gal. ii. 1, "I went up again to Jerusalem with Barnabas, taking Titus also with me," Titus being therefore included under the phrase "certain other of them" in the account given Acts xv. 2, "the brethren appointed that Paul and Barnabas and certain other of them should go up to Jerusalem unto the apostles and elders about this question." (For the full arguments identifying these visits as one and the same, see Bp Lightfoot, *Galatians*, ed. 2, pp. 122 sqq.) Titus could hardly have been thus appointed under the age of 20 years or so. If we now look for notices of his life still earlier than A.D. 50 we find only one, but that very significant; in Tit. i. 4 St Paul addresses him as "Titus my true child after a common faith." He owed therefore his conversion to St Paul; and when we couple the *time* that must be supposed, such a reasonable time before A.D. 50 as to make it suitable for him to be a "select" representative, together with the *place* in which he first appears, Antioch in Syria, and with his *nationality*, "being a Greek," we are led to that remarkable year, A.D. 43—44, which witnessed St Paul's first great year of ministry, when Barnabas found a new and notable work being done at Antioch by the men of Cyprus and Cyrene "preaching the Lord Jesus to the *Greeks*" (as the right reading in Acts xi. 20). So great indeed was the movement that Barnabas "went forth to Tarsus to seek for Saul;" and "even for a whole year they were gathered together with the church and taught much people, and the disciples were called Christians first in Antioch." We can readily imagine the stir and movement of such a time; and in its way it would be very similar to the mission season at Lystra, a year later, when Timothy, a lad of fifteen, felt the fervent love and power of the Apostle.

A.D. 44. We may well think then of the lad Titus, at the same age of 14 or 15, when all the man begins to stir within the boy, catching fire from the same flame of heavenly zeal at Antioch in that great year, A.D. 44, when so many of his elders of the same Greek race "believed and turned to the Lord." Lewin graphically describes the scenes with which the heralds of Christianity found themselves surrounded at Antioch, "destined soon to be the metropolis of Gentile Christendom." "The market-place was teeming with swarthy Syrians and quick-witted Greeks, and with the children of Abraham, ever distinguished by their marked physiognomy. Here and there were observed troops of legionary soldiers, the conquerors of the world. The languages that greeted the ear were as diverse as the costumes that met the eye. Syriac and Hebrew, Greek and Latin, were heard in succession. Greek however predominated and formed the ordinary vehicle of communication between such discordant materials....The very place in which they prosecuted their ministry at Antioch has been recorded by John of Antioch, commonly called Malala, or the Orator, who lived at the close of the sixth century. In general, tradition is of little value; but in this instance a native of Antioch who quotes Domminus, an antiquary of a much earlier age, is entitled to some respect. According to Malala, Paul and Barnabas preached in Singon Street, near the Pantheon, in the south-western part of the city called Epiphania. No spot could have been fixed upon more suitable for their purpose, as it was in one of the most populous districts, and in the immediate neighbourhood of the Forum." *Life of St Paul*, I. 96. If our conclusion is right, we can realise more than has been generally done, of Titus's earlier years; and we see how his brisk, businesslike character would form itself, and how the very surroundings of his earliest Christian life in "faith that cometh by hearing," in baptism and laying on of hands and Christian service in Singon Street, Epiphania, would prepare him for the part he had to play afterwards in busy-stirring Corinth, and the care he was to bestow on his Churches in Crete that they should exhibit a life of practical godliness and "good works."

A.D. 50. We now take up his life at the time when he is deputed to attend Paul and Barnabas to Jerusalem, when the great question of Jewish ceremonial was to be settled. Titus as the representative, firm but modest, of his race was to be there to plead in person for the "liberty in Christ Jesus" which already St Paul had asserted by refusing to have him circumcised. Or at least he was there, a silent witness, to whom St Paul might point, of the Holy Spirit's blessing without the old Jewish rite, a bright God-fearing "true son after a common faith." We cannot doubt that, under God, young Titus played no unfit part in obtaining the judgment given "not to trouble them which from among the Gentiles turn to God" (Acts xv. 19).

A.D. 51—53. We hear nothing of Titus during the Second Missionary Journey of St Paul, which followed, and during which Timothy is taken up at Lystra. And from the express mention of Silas alone as leaving Antioch with the Apostle we may perhaps conclude that the work of Titus lay at home at Antioch for the present. This is the more likely when we note that St Luke, who joined the party at Troas, seems to have been unacquainted with Titus; at least there is no mention of him at all in the Acts. For though the true reading in Acts xviii. 7 gives Titus Justus as the name of the man in whose house St Paul preached at Corinth after leaving the synagogue, yet the description added that he was a proselyte, "one that worshipped God," points to some entirely different person. At the close of this ever-memorable campaign, in which the Holy War had been carried for the first time into Europe, St Paul returns from Jerusalem to Antioch (Acts xviii. 22).

A.D. 54. We may perhaps conclude that on the Third Missionary Journey St Paul took with him from Antioch both Timothy and Titus. It would certainly seem from the reference to Titus in Gal. ii. that he was known to the Galatian Church; and this occasion of St Paul's visit there when "he went through the region of Galatia and Phrygia in order, stablishing all the disciples" (Acts xviii. 23), would seem the most likely time for such an acquaintance to be formed. This supposition will bring Titus naturally to Ephesus with St Paul, and give him a share in the great work of those three years. So we find him on the spot, a ready and trusty messenger, when St Paul, on receipt of the bad news from Corinth respecting the schisms and its immoralities, is looking round for one to whom he may entrust the letter written at once to that Church—the "First Epistle to the Corinthians." Timothy had been commissioned previously to pay them a visit of enquiry and encouragement; now St Paul is glad to have so strong and firm and discreet a character as Titus in whose hands to place the unwelcome task of rebuke. For the full proof of this assumption that Titus was the bearer of 1 Cor., see Bp Lightfoot, *Journal of Classical and Sacred Philology*, II. pp. 201, 202, recently reprinted in *Biblical Essays*, p. 273 sq.; and cf. 2 Cor. xii. 18, "I exhorted Titus, and I sent the brother with him." Yet the Apostle is very anxious about the result, especially when Titus fails to meet him on his journey to Macedonia, as appointed at Troas (2 Cor. ii. 12). Further on in his journey, perhaps at Philippi or Thessalonica, Titus meets St Paul with the good news of his success; and in the references to this in 2 Corinthians we are shewn both the close tie of affection subsisting between St Paul and Titus and the zeal, the sympathy, and the strong feeling of Titus himself. "God comforted us by the coming of Titus; and not by his coming only, but also by the comfort wherewith he was comforted in you, while he told us your longing, your mourning, your zeal for me," "his spirit hath been refreshed by you all," "his inward affection is more abundantly toward you, whilst he remembereth the obedience of you all, how with fear and trembling ye received him," 2 Cor. vii. 6, 7, 13, 15. It had required no little judgment and tact to induce the vain and fitful Corinthians to take in good part the strong though necessary rebukes of the Apostle. It was proof of equally good business instincts and qualifications that the other Corinthian matter in which St Paul was much interested was also placed in the hands of Titus and carried through satisfactorily, the collection for the poor saints at Jerusalem. The practical godliness of such action as proving something deeper than the external froth of mere spiritual excitements, the practical proof of union between Jew and Gentile, afforded both at Corinth in the face of schisms, and at Jerusalem in the face of slanders against St Paul, all this may account for the stress laid by the Apostle on what might otherwise seem a mere detail or an unworthy serving of tables. And it is an undesigned coincidence, indeed, but an additional internal evidence of the genuineness of the Epistle to Titus, that we find a similar stress laid upon the carefulness of believers "to maintain good works," a precept exemplified later by the provision Titus is himself to make for Zenas and Apollos, and the addition of the charge that "our people also learn to maintain good works for necessary uses, that they be not unfruitful" (Tit. iii. 8, 13, 14). While Titus is with St Paul then at this time, he is, in his heart and mind, the living example of the union of two apparently opposite principles. On the one hand St Paul is writing to the Galatians and vehemently contending that "works" are nothing, "faith" is everything, "having begun in the Spirit they are fools to be now perfected in the flesh" (Gal. iii. 3); and we can imagine him turning to Titus and telling him that he will remind them of his case, just to the point, where he had absolutely refused to have him circumcised (Gal. ii. 3). And on the other hand, almost in the same week, when Timothy's arrival turns his mind full again on Corinth, he is writing his second letter to the Corinthians and equally vigorously contending that "faith" works by "love," that their faith and repentance must be shewn by their works; and we can almost see him turn to Titus and exhort him "that as he had made a beginning before, so he would also complete in them this grace also and the fellowship in the ministering to the saints" (2 Cor. viii. 7, 4). So Titus is sent back again from Macedonia to Corinth, with two trusty companions, Tychicus and Trophimus, in charge of the second Corinthian letter, and with the earnestly pressed commission for the completion of the alms. We gather that the work is a delicate and difficult one, not only from the character, otherwise learnt, of Titus himself, to whom it is committed, but from the care of St Paul in commending him lest he should say either too much or too little—too much, and so make him out a "mechanical delegate"—too little, and so leave him "an unauthorised volunteer." "Thanks be to God, which putteth the same earnest care for you into the heart of Titus. For indeed he accepted our exhortation; but being himself very earnest he went forth unto you of his own accord" (2 Cor. viii. 16, 17). St Paul follows slowly to Corinth.

A.D. 58. At Corinth he finds the work well done; he can sit down and write to the Romans the quiet reasoned essay of a mind calm and at leisure, gathering up all the tossing, vehement arguments of Galatian and Corinthian letters into a flawless manual of evangelical truth. And at the close he alludes with evident satisfaction to the successful issue of the effort for ministering unto the saints, as the completion of work which will enable him to fulfil his great wish of reaching Rome and Spain (Rom. xv. 28). With this last glimpse of the great aid given by Titus to his chief, in this the very crisis of St Paul's doctrinal energy, we lose sight of him for eight long years. He is not mentioned by St Paul in the salutations to the Roman Church, nor by St Luke in his list of the companions who were with St Paul on the journey from Corinth to Asia, and so to Cæsarea and Jerusalem; and we can only conclude that he may have been sent, or sent for, to his old home, Antioch, which perhaps St Paul was glad should be thus kept in touch still with the spread of the Gospel, in case he could no longer "report himself" there as of old.

A.D. 64, 65. When the Roman imprisonment came to an end, as we conclude, in A.D. 63, and St Paul was set free for active work, the notices scattered through the Epistles alone guide us as to the probable movements of the Apostle and his assistants. A sketch of one connected method of piecing these together consistently is given pp. 41—44. In accord with that we may here suppose Titus, either from Antioch or from such other centre of work as may have been appointed for him, joining St Paul at Ephesus, and going with him to Crete, to spend the winter (autumn, A.D. 64, to spring, A.D. 65). They would land at Heracleum (now Megalo Kastron), the port of Gnossus, the capital of Crete on its northern coast; and would, after their stay there, cross the island to Gortyna, a little inland from "Fair Havens," on the southern coast; and so go "throughout the cities" with the good news of the gospel (Tit. i. 5). From the character of the Cretans as immoral, and turbulent, and uncivilised, given in the Epistle, we see reason enough for the selection of the companion and helper whose decided discreet character would find ample scope and exercise. The original preaching of the Gospel may have come from those Cretans who were amongst the recipients of the gift of tongues on the day of Pentecost (Acts ii. 11). But the lack of organisation and the low standard of morality shown in the Epistle make it clear that St Paul in going there would not be "building on another man's foundation." And the impulse to visit the island may have been given by the brief view of it obtained in the stormy voyage of Acts xxvii.

A.D. 66. It would seem more natural and consistent with the tone of the Epistle to suppose, as the sketch does, that a second visit was paid by St Paul—which indeed he seems to have made a rule of his missionary work—and that after this second visit (A.D. 66, spring) the letter was written reviewing the progress made and consolidating the directions given verbally to Titus on leaving. This would bring us to the autumn of A.D. 66, after an interval spent at Ephesus. On the circular tour then planned he reaches Corinth, and from that place writes the Epistle to Titus (autumn), commending Zenas and Apollos to him, and telling him of his plan newly formed to winter at Nicopolis, and of his wish to see him there as soon as Artemas and Tychicus can take his place for a while. The Epistle emphasises work which no doubt Titus had been already doing well and manfully, in the selection of fit presbyters, the determined check to Judaising teachers, the inculcation of a high standard of Christian life and work, the reconciling the Christian slaves to their position and duty, the control of unruly movements, whether social, political, or theological.

Though St Paul sent for Titus to Nicopolis, and apparently, when plots thickened, and plans altered, sent him on a mission to Dalmatia, his last errand for his faithful squire, yet we may conclude from the letter that while it is in one sense a charge to the Church at large through Titus, it also assumes that Titus will make some definite stay in Crete to carry forward the work appointed. With this the specific and constant tradition of the island is in accord, making him indeed to be permanent bishop there, and assigning the modern capital Candia as his burial-place (see Cave's *Apostolici*, p. 42, quoted by Dr Howson, *Dict. Bib.* s.v.).

The following summary of the traditions preserved by Zenas and Peter, *De Natalibus*, gives an interesting, though as is evident, entirely untrustworthy account of the early life, conversion, and death of Titus (see Baring-Gould's *Lives of the Saints*, I. p. 55). It is interesting as an instance of the growth of literary myth from the one seed-word, Crete.

Titus it is said was born of Gentile parents, being descended from the ancient royal family of Crete. St Paul, after his first imprisonment, returning from Rome into the East, made some stay in the island of Crete, the governor of which, Rustitius, was married to the sister of Titus. Titus, living in the island of Crete, was learned in Greek literature, having been studious in youth. But the dreams of the poets and philosophers did not satisfy the inward craving of his soul after truth. One day when twenty years old he heard a voice say to him, "Titus, depart hence and save thy soul, for the learning of the Greeks will not profit thee unto salvation." Wondering in himself what this could mean he was bidden by the same voice to take up a Hebrew volume that he had long disregarded and open it. And the book was the prophet Isaiah, and the place of the Scriptures that his eye rested on was this, "Keep silence before me, O islands, and let the people renew their strength," and what follows, Is. xli. And he applied to himself the words, "thou whom I have taken from the ends of the earth, and called thee from the chief men thereof, and said unto thee, Thou art my servant; I have chosen thee, and not cast thee away." These were words very different from those of the poets of Greece, and gave an idea of God quite other from that formed by Homer, in whose writings he had found delight; so Titus left his Greek studies and his native island, and sought Jerusalem, the chief city of that people of whom the prophet spake such great things. And when he was there, he saw Jesus, and heard Him teach. Perhaps he was one of those Greeks whom St Andrew brought to Christ. He believed, and was of the number of the first disciples. He remained at Jerusalem after the Ascension, and the descent of the Holy Ghost. After he joined St Paul he accompanied him in most of his journeys. St Paul consecrated him to be Bishop of Crete and left him there. When death approached he saw angels coming from heaven in a glorious train to fetch his soul, and his face was lit up with joy at their approach and shone with supernatural splendour. He committed his people to God in long and earnest prayer, and then yielded up his spirit in peace to Christ his Saviour.

The body of Titus was kept with great veneration in the cathedral of Gortyna; but that city having been ruined by the Saracens, in A.D. 823, the metropolitan see was transferred to Candia, 17 miles from the ancient Gortyna; there the head of Titus was preserved till it was carried off by the Venetians, and it is now among the sacred treasures of St Mark's at Venice.

C. THE THEME AND CONTENTS OF THE EPISTLES.

CHAPTER IX.

Analysis of the Epistles.

The Apostolate; its scope, its sphere, its method, its efficiency; this has been shewn to be the main theme of the Pastoral Epistles. See above, Int. p. 18.

It is not unfolded in any set and formal way, because the Epistles are letters, first and foremost, to old friends and pupils. See Life of Timothy, p. 57, and Life of Titus, p. 68. But they are at the same time more than this, being guided by the Holy Spirit to form the transition from the oral gospels of the apostleship, and to be the Church's inspired abiding Manual of the Pastoral Care. See Int., pp. 14—19, 33.

In the same way, the treatment of heresy and error is not by formal refutation of the false doctrine, but by practical hints and instructions to friends, who were to induct sound fresh teachers into office. See above, Int., pp. 18, 19.

It only remains to give an analysis of the contents, as one point leads to another in the mind of "Paul the aged," anxious above all things that the young knights, who have worthily won their spurs with him, may "after the time of his departure" play the man in the "good fight of faith."

I TIMOTHY.

CH. i. Apostolic faithfulness.

1, 2. The greeting, with a specially touching addition of the word "mercy."

3—11. Timothy is exhorted to faithful ministry by a reminder of the glad tidings of the true Gospel.

12—20. He is further encouraged by a reminder of St Paul's own calling and commission and of the fall of some false teachers.

CH. ii. Apostolic regulation of Public Worship.

1—7. Directions are given for Common Prayer and Intercession because of the universality of the Gospel;

8—15. and for the parts to be taken in Public Worship by men and by women respectively.

CH. iii. Apostolic selection of the Assistant Ministry.

1—7. A sketch is drawn of the duties and characters of Bishops or Presbyters;

8—13. and of the duties and characters of Deacons, both men and women.

14—16. The importance of these directions is based on the character of the Church and its Head, the Incarnate Redeemer.

CH. iv. Apostolic government in regard to Doctrine.

1—6. The central truth is to be guarded, which false teachers violate by their false asceticism, the dogma of the Incarnate Redeemer.

6—16. Timothy's own strong hold of right doctrine and of right discipline is dwelt upon as essential for right government.

CH. v. Apostolic government in regard to Discipline.

1, 2. Advice is given as to Timothy's demeanour generally towards his flock;

3—16. as to his duties in regard to Widows;

17—25. his duties in regard to Presbyters;

vi. **1, 2.** and his duties in regard to Slaves.

CH. vi. Last words on Apostolic Doctrine and Duty.

3—10. A further warning is given against false teachers, and their covetousness;

11—16. and a further exhortation to a true life, in view of the LORD's appearing.

17—19. A last direction follows on the duties of the rich;

20, 21. and a last appeal, on the keeping of the Deposit of the Catholic Faith.

Parting salutation.

II TIMOTHY.

CH. i. Apostolic gifts and responsibilities.

1, 2. The greeting, with the same tender touch of 'mercy.'

3—7. The affectionate 'Father in God' grounds a warm appeal to Timothy on his inheritance of personal faith and ministerial gifts.

8—12. He makes the appeal itself—to be a brave champion both of the saving Work of Christ and of the suffering Witness of St Paul.

13, 14. The double ground of appeal is shewn to be also the double line of responsive action.

15—18. The appeal is enforced by a contrast of cases, a sad warning and a bright example.

CH. ii. Apostolic zeal and purity.

1—7. The anxious 'Overseer' resumes his appeal for personal and ministerial zeal, illustrating it by Parables from life—the soldier, the athlete and the farmer.

8—13. He gives a yet higher illustration from God's own plan of salvation—the Cross before the Crown.

14—26. He defines the especial sphere both of the personal and of the ministerial zeal to be (1) pure doctrine, (2) a pure life.

CH. iii. Apostolic life and doctrine.

1—5. The prophetic 'Teacher' further urges his appeal to Timothy for pure life, in view of the worse days and lives to come;

6—9. for pure doctrine, in view of the worse doctrines to come;

10—17. for pure life and doctrine, in view of both St Paul's own past and the evil future.

CH. iv. Apostolic succession and fellowship.

1—8. The old 'Evangelist' puts forward the last appeal, the same warning, the old example, to inspire Timothy to take up his work and fulfil the same ministry.

9—18. He tells of the scattering of friends, with entreaty for Timothy's presence, but with full assurance of the LORD's present help.

19—22. He says the last words of salutation, entreaty, benediction.

TITUS.

CH. i. The Apostolate; its scope and method.

1—4. The greeting; specially emphasizing the base and scope of the Apostolic office.

5—9. The commission of Titus is dwelt upon, in regard to the selection of duly qualified Bishops or Presbyters.

10—16. The scope of his office is shewn, in the repression through this method of the rival unruly teachers with a view to the life of practical godliness.

CH. ii. The Apostolate; its efficiency and its sphere.

1—10. The efficient discharge of his office is shewn to require from Titus the maintenance of a high standard of holy living, in his own person and in his control of others.

11—15. His sphere of duty is to claim all life—public, social and private—for God and religion.

CH. iii. The Apostolate; its ministry of goodwill and good works.

1—7. The duty is dwelt upon of promoting a life of goodwill and peace from the sense of God's love and through the Spirit's power.

8—14. When all is said and done, the practical holiness of good works is to abide.

15. Last words of salutation.

THE FIRST EPISTLE OF PAUL THE APOSTLE

TO

TIMOTHY.

PAUL, an apostle of Jesus Christ by the commandment 1
of God our Saviour, and Lord Jesus Christ, *which is*

TITLE.

The title given in A.V. agrees with that adopted by the Elzevir editions of 1624, 1633. But the best MSS. give only **First Epistle to Timothy**, as also for the 'Subscription.'

CH. I. APOSTOLIC FAITHFULNESS.

1, 2. GREETING.

1. *an apostle of Jesus Christ*] Read rather with the MSS. **an apostle of Christ Jesus**, and again with a similar transposition and omitting 'Lord,' **Christ Jesus our hope**; as in v. 21; 2 Tim. iv. 1; Tit. i. 4. Altogether, according to the best MSS., the change should be made nine times in these epp. The name 'Christ Jesus' is most frequently on the Apostle's lips in old age, occurring 22 times, while 'Jesus Christ' is used but seven times, 'our Lord Jesus Christ' but twice, see vi. 3. See further, Moule's *Colossians*, I. 1.

by the commandment of] Better, **by authority from**; this phrase (1) recalls to English ears official titles and announcements; and (2) suits each of the seven passages in St Paul's epistles where it occurs, suggesting the *commission* delegated from the supreme power of God: it gives as here, so in Titus i. 3, the warrant for St Paul's laying down the rules of Church order, and the warrant therefore for Timothy and Titus doing the same under their delegated commission. It is a clear gain to use the same word in these passages and in Tit. ii. 15, 'exhort, reprove, with all *authority*.'

God our Saviour] A new phrase in St Paul's language, three times used in this epistle and three times in ep. to Titus; cf. Jude, *v.* 25: the corresponding phrase *Christ our Saviour* four times in these epistles (previously in Eph. v. 23 and Phil. iii. 20, the word 'Saviour' is used not as a title but in a statement, as predicate not attribute—an evidently earlier stage), five times in the Second Epistle of St Peter.

2 our hope; unto Timothy, *my* own son in the faith: Grace,
mercy, *and* peace, from God our Father and Jesus Christ
our Lord.
3 As I besought thee to abide *still* at Ephesus, when I

Fairbairn suggests with reason that this title is given to *God* here rather than to Christ 'as a kind of counteractive to the false teaching'; this personal designation of God, as originating and carrying into effect the work of salvation, would indicate the true preservative against all arbitrariness in speculation and undue licence in practice.

Jesus Christ...our hope] Again a token of the later apostolic age. Christ, who is at first in His own words 'the Light,' 'the Way,' 'the Truth,' 'the Life,' is (with still further appropriation of the abstract) in the epistles of the first captivity 'our peace,' Eph. ii. 14, 'the hope of glory,' Col. i. 27, and now towards the days of the second captivity simply 'our hope.' This personification of the abstract has still further developed with the lapse of centuries, so that a modern writer can say,

O everlasting Health,
From which all healing springs,
Our Bliss, our Treasure, and our Wealth,
To Thee our spirit clings.

2. my *own son in the faith*] Better, **my true child in faith** with R.V.; **child**, because the word is used, as the Greek *teknon* is, (1) of specially tender affectionateness, (2) of the spiritual relationship of a disciple to a teacher; **true**, that is, shewing a real and marked resemblance in character to your 'father in God'; **in faith**, or as we should say, **spiritually**; apparently by this time a recognised adverbial or adjectival phrase, as in Tit. iii. 15, 'salute them that love us in faith,' or, as we should say, 'our *Christian* friends.' The same argument from the growth of this abstract applies here; the earlier and more concrete 'in the Lord' (1 Cor. iv. 17), and 'in the Gospel' (1 Thess. iii. 2) gives place to 'in faith,' or as in Tit. i. 4 'in communion of faith.'

Compare 2 Joh. 1, 'whom I love *in truth*,' St John's corresponding word for spiritual Christianity, and the combination in ch. ii. 7.

Grace, mercy, and *peace*] 'Mercy' here and in 2 Tim. i. 2; while in Tit. i. 4 according to the best MSS. it is 'grace and peace,' as in the salutations of St Paul's other epistles. 'Why,' asks Fairbairn, 'is "mercy" specially needed for St Paul's dear child of faith? The nearer he was in character to St Paul the more would *he* too feel himself "the chief of sinners," and so appreciate a prayer so truly faithful and sympathising; a lesson,' he adds, 'for all future ministers of the Gospel which it well becomes them to ponder.' St John's private letter to the 'Elect lady' has the same salutation.

God our Father] Read **God the Father**, as in 2 Tim. i. 2 and Tit. i. 4; 'our Father' was the usual form in the earlier epistles.

3—11. TIMOTHY IS EXHORTED TO FAITHFUL MINISTRY. HE IS REMINDED FIRST OF THE CHARACTER OF THE TRUE GOSPEL.

3. *As I besought thee*...so do] Rather **as I exhorted thee**...**so do I**

went into Macedonia, that thou mightest charge some that
they teach no other doctrine, neither give heed to fables and 4
endless genealogies, which minister questions, rather than
godly edifying which is in faith : *so do*. Now the end of the 5

now, i.e. **exhort thee.** The R.V. varies between 'beseech' and 'exhort' for *parakalein*, e.g. reading in Philem. 9, 'for love's sake I rather beseech.'

to abide still] Or **to tarry**; the force of the preposition in the verb is expressed by 'still'; the aorist is usual after verbs of hoping, &c.

when I went into Macedonia] The present participle is emphatic—**when I was going.** This journey into Macedonia cannot be fitted in anywhere during the period covered by the Acts. See Ellicott here, and Paley, *Hor. Paul.* ch. xi. Cf. Introduction, p. 43.

that thou mightest charge some] Rather **certain persons** slightingly, and indicating that he could name them if he would; the word for 'charge,' cf. v. 5, is in St Paul's mind in writing, and occurs seven times in this epistle.

no other doctrine] Better, **not to be teachers of a different doctrine,** as in Gal. i. 6, 'a different gospel,' i.e. different in kind; the word appears in our 'heterodoxy,' difference *for the worse* from the established view of things.

4. *fables and endless genealogies*] Ellicott following Chrysostom and the early Greek commentators regards the false teaching as arising from Jewish, perhaps Cabbalistic sources, and only an affluent afterwards of the later and more definite Gnosticism—Rabbinical fables and fabrications in history and doctrine, and vague rambling genealogies—in the proper sense, but very possibly combined with wild speculative allegories. See Introduction, pp. 45 sqq.; Appendix, B.

which minister questions] Rather with R.V. **the which minister questionings**—'the which' implying the force of the pronoun 'which are of such a kind as to'; and 'questionings' suggesting better the process and state of questioning which the form of the noun conveys. The compound noun which is the right reading implies painful, elaborate questionings, so the verb 1 Pet. i. 10 'searched diligently.'

godly edifying] Read with the best MSS. (and the Received Text which the A.V. has not followed here) **a dispensation of God**—the divine *economy* or scheme of salvation to be apprehended *by faith*. They whom Timothy was thus to correct had or might have learnt exactly what St Paul meant by this dispensing of grace on God's part from the eloquent passage in his own letter to them, Eph. iii.; 'the dispensation of that grace of God,' ver. 2; 'to make all men see what is the dispensation of the mystery,' ver. 9.

in faith] That is, as Theod. Mops. puts it, we lay hold of the plan of salvation by 'a historic faith'—'getting our proof of its truth from the facts themselves of the life of God incarnate.'

5. *Now the end of the commandment*] Better, **But the end of the charge,** 'but' rather than 'now' because it is not so much the com-

commandment is charity out of a pure heart, and *of* a good
6 conscience, and *of* faith unfeigned: from which some having
7 swerved have turned aside unto vain jangling; desiring to
be teachers of the law; understanding neither what they

mencement of a new paragraph as a positive statement of the true aim of the ministry to counteract the statement just made of false aims, so completing the paragraph. 'The charge,' the verb or noun occurs seven times in this epistle, and as thus constantly present to St Paul might almost give a second title to the epistle of 'The Chief Pastor's *Charge*,' iv. 11, v. 7, vi. 13—17. Here one of the best comments is in the Bishop's words at the Ordination of Priests in the English Prayer Book, 'Be thou a faithful dispenser of the word of God,' 'Take thou authority to preach the word of God.'

charity] **love**, a life of active love and union; the opposite of the 'strifes' which result from 'questionings,' 2 Tim. ii. 23. It is important to keep the English word 'love' as the equivalent of the Greek word *agapè* throughout the New Testament, as the Revisers have very properly done. It is a characteristic word, and only confusion is introduced in the mind of English readers by sometimes rendering it 'charity.'

a pure heart] thoroughly bent on turning from sin and youthful lusts, honestly growing in righteousness, 2 Tim. ii. 22.

of *a good conscience, and* of *faith unfeigned*] 'Conscience' is one of St Paul's most characteristic words; out of 32 places where it occurs in N.T. 23 are of his using either in speech or writing, six of these belonging to the Pastoral Epistles. See Appendix, D. Literally the word means 'knowing *with*' and Bp Westcott draws out this idea in his definition, "It presents man as his own judge. Man does not stand alone. He has direct knowledge of a law—a law of God—which claims his obedience, and he has direct knowledge also of his own conduct. He cannot then but compare them and give sentence. His 'conscience' as the power directing this process is regarded apart from himself (Rom. ix. 1; ii. 15)." See his Additional Note, Heb. ix. 9.

6. *from which*] Plural **from which things,** that is the love and its threefold helpers, in the grace, the life, and the creed.

having swerved] Lit. 'having missed the mark,' another of the words peculiar to these epistles, occurring only ch. vi. 21 and 2 Tim. ii. 18.

vain jangling] **empty talking**; the word occurs in the adjective form once again, in the still stronger warning against the same class of teachers in Tit. i. 10, where they are said to be mostly 'of the Circumcision,' and to give heed to 'Jewish fables.' The law of which they are **setting themselves up to be teachers** is of course the law of Moses, but corrupted by allegorical interpretations and philosophisings which whittled away the keen edge of its moral precepts and blunted all sense of the paramount necessity of holy living.

7. *understanding*] More exactly, **though they understand**; the negative particle used shews that the clause is subordinate to, not parallel

say, nor whereof they affirm. But we know that the law 8
is good, if a man use it lawfully; knowing this, that the 9
law is not made for a righteous *man*, but for the lawless
and disobedient, for the ungodly and for sinners, for unholy

with 'setting themselves up,' or 'desiring,' and expresses *their* thoughts. 'We choose to teach, without understanding.' Winer, § 55. 5 B, p. 607.

neither what they say, nor whereof] They neither understand the statements they make nor even what the questions are about which they make such confident assertions. **Confidently affirm** gives the force of the preposition in the compound verb; it occurs in Tit. iii. 8; but not elsewhere in N. T. The middle voice expresses the *secondary* kind of making firm, by speech, instead of act, as commonly in Class. Gr. Compare to *draw* up a narrative, Lk. i. 1; 'I *laid* before them the Gospel,' Gal. ii. 2; Winer, Pt. III. § 38, 2—6, p. 317.

8. *But we know*] **Yet we are all aware,** a correction or concession. St Paul uses 'we know' in a similar way, Rom. vii. 14, 'I grant that the law is spiritual'; 1 Cor. viii. 3, 'We are quite aware (with irony) that we all have knowledge.'

if a man use it lawfully] The regular Greek idiom corresponding with our passive, **if it be handled as law should be,** that is, by the teacher of the law. Ellicott gives the sense of the passage clearly, 'The false teachers on the contrary, assuming that it *was* designed for the righteous man, urged their interpretations of it as necessary appendices to the Gospel.'

For the play on the word 'law' compare 2 Tim. iii. 4, iv. 7, and better 1 Tim. i. 3, 5, 'charge,' 'charges.'

9. *knowing this*] The A.V. putting a full stop after 'lawfully' gives an entirely wrong turn here; the R.V. puts a comma and inserts 'as' in order to shew the connexion of 'knowing' with 'a man'; we may continue the above rendering rather more idiomatically, **if it be handled as law should be and with the knowledge that.**

the law is not made] There is no article, and we may with the R.V. translate, **law is not made**; not thereby drawing a marked distinction between 'law' here and 'the law' of Moses above, but following St Paul's instinct of language, and by the omission drawing attention to the play on words or the antithesis intended, in a crisper and more proverbial way. This explanation will satisfy all the cases of omission of article before 'law' quoted by Winer from Gal. ii. 21, iii. 11, 18, 21, iv. 5. Cf. Winer, § 19, Moulton n.; Lightfoot's *Gal.* II. 19. Here 'law' and 'the lawless' stand in sharper contrast without the article.

for a righteous man] By 'righteous' we may well understand one 'who has his measure of fruit in holiness' (Ellicott, quoting Hooker), in contrast to those who not only ignore the law as any check on their life, **lawless**, but are positively *disobedient* or **unruly**, delighting in open defiance of it; being **ungodly**, with no fear of God or sense of His presence before their mind; and **sinners**, marked as such by definite acts of sin (Lk. xviii. 13), (2 Pet. i. 6); (for the two words together compare Jude 15).

unholy] They are further breakers of the first and second command-

and profane, for murderers of fathers and murderers of
10 mothers, for manslayers, for whoremongers, for them that
defile themselves with mankind, for menstealers, for liars,
for perjured *persons*, and if *there be* any other *thing that* is
11 contrary to sound doctrine; according to the glorious gospel

ments; the word describes the disregard of *duty to God*, and only occurs here and 2 Tim. iii. 2; but the corresponding word for the performing of this duty occurs in 1 Tim. ii. 8, 'lifting up *holy* hands in worship.'

profane] breakers of the third and fourth commandments; the N. T. use of the word describes disregard of God's day, Matt. xii. 5; of God's house, Acts xxiv. 6; of God's law and truth, 1 Tim. iv. 7, vi. 20; 2 Tim. ii. 16; of God's name and birthright blessing, Heb. xii. 16.

murderers of fathers and murderers of mothers] breakers of the fifth commandment, cf. Exod. xxi. 15. In this and in the following words St Paul evidently singles out the *worst* breaches of the law, his argument being 'the law was meant to convict the vilest—you apply it to the holiest.' Hence, we must keep the stronger meaning 'parricide,' though the Greek word by its proper derivation means 'father-beater.' When it came to have the meaning 'parricide,' a different derivation was also assigned to it and the spelling a little altered accordingly. For similar corruptions in English to fit a supposed derivation compare 'reindeer,' 'causeway,' 'camel leopard.'

manslayers] breakers of the sixth commandment.

10. *whoremongers, for them that defile themselves with mankind*] breakers of the seventh commandment.

menstealers] breakers of the eighth commandment, the grossest theft; punishable with death, Exod. xxi. 16, by the Mosaic code, as also among the Greeks.

perjured persons] breakers of the ninth commandment. Cf. Lev. xix. 12.

and if there be *any other* thing that *is contrary to sound doctrine*] breakers of the tenth commandment as an inclusive summary embracing all sides and all aspects of each part of the duty to one's neighbour, 'not to covet nor desire other men's goods, but to learn and labour truly to get mine own living and to do my duty.' The mode of expression and the use of the particle are quite St Paul's; cf. Rom. xiii. 9, 'and if there be any other commandment,' Phil. iv. 8, 'if there be any virtue and any praise.'

sound doctrine] With R.V. render **the sound doctrine.** The word for 'doctrine' occurs 15 times in these epistles, against seven times in the rest of the N. T.; a mark that the original simple concrete word 'teaching' is gradually becoming the settled abstract term 'doctrine.' But it is still too soon for the idea of this general abstraction which is conveyed to our mind by the phrase 'sound doctrine.' The insertion of the article (according to the Greek) gives us just an English equivalent of the middle stage which the phrase has reached.

The nearest to the use of the Past. Epp. is Eph. iv. 14, where we ought to read 'every wind of the doctrine,' the article referring to all the work of apostles, prophets, evangelists and teachers just spoken of.

of the blessed God, which was committed to my trust.
And I thank Christ Jesus our Lord, who hath enabled me, 12
for that he counted me faithful, putting *me* into the ministry;

sound] 'healthful,' an epithet occurring with 'doctrine' or 'words' six times in these epistles and nowhere else; in contrast to a different form of error from any previously described, 'the sickly (ch. vi. 4) and morbid (2 Tim. ii. 17) teaching of Jewish gnosis,' Ellicott.

11. *according to the glorious gospel*] Rather with R.V. **according to the gospel of the glory.** How far back does St Paul look in 'according to the gospel'? Surely through the whole passage since the last *winding up* at the end of *v.* 3; just as the next passage winds up similarly at *v.* 17. (The marking of the paragraphs in the R.V. throughout will be worth careful notice.) The charge to insist on sound teaching—the end of the charge, a life of love unselfish out of faith unfeigned, instead of a laboured law of mystic perfectionism—the sound teaching of those who (as he had written them word, Eph. iv. 11) were given them by Christ for the purpose—all this was 'according to the gospel of the glory of God': for *the* chief and surpassing glory of God was seen not in the law but in the person, the life of Jesus Christ.

the blessed God] The epithet seems added from the rush of personal feeling as the sense of the present love and mercy of Christ (never long absent) comes to him strongly in penning the words. It occurs again in vi. 15 in a similar passage.

12—17. FAITHFUL MINISTRY. TIMOTHY IS FURTHER REMINDED OF ST PAUL'S OWN CALLING AND COMMISSION.

12. This strong feeling quite accounts for the abruptness with which once again (after many other utterances of his own religious experiences) he claims 'all the mercy' and acknowledges 'all the sin,' and offers 'all the service.' We must omit 'and,' reading with R.V. **I thank him that enabled me, even Christ Jesus our Lord.**

The whole paragraph which follows is the drawing out of all that came into his mind as he wrote *the Gospel—entrusted—to me.* The *ego* at the end of the verse, so emphatic, is ample connexion, especially when the first word of the new sentence is 'Thanks':—'To me—even to me; Jesus Christ be praised; He gave me pardon, He gave me work, He gave me strength.'

At the same time this statement of his own case is well fitted to carry on the two thoughts that have been in his mind, (1) the encouragement of Timothy to faithful ministry, (2) the saving and cheering power of the true doctrine compared with the condemning, despairing character of the law.

who hath enabled me] The aorist tense has the balance of authority here, and refers to the strength given, with and at the time of the commission. **I thank him that enabled me,** rather than 'hath enabled me.'

faithful] i.e. after the time of preparation that followed his Conversion, the years of retirement in Arabia and at Tarsus, A.D. 36—44, he was judged to be 'trusty,' 'trustworthy'; Barnabas 'brought him to

13 who was before a blasphemer, and a persecutor, and in-
jurious: but I obtained mercy, because I did *it* ignorantly
14 in unbelief. And the grace of our Lord was exceeding
abundant with faith and love which is in Christ Jesus.
15 *This is* a faithful saying, and worthy of all acceptation, that

Antioch' to be a 'prophet and teacher,' Acts xi. 26, xiii. 1, and then the Holy Spirit of Jesus said, 'Separate me Saul and Barnabas for the work whereunto I have called them,' Acts xiii. 2.

putting me *into the ministry*] Better **appointing me for service.** The present participle in English gives the exact force of the aorist here. 'He shewed that He counted me faithful by giving me work.'

As to *diakonia*, 'ministering,' 'service,' 'ministration,' 'ministry,' are used by R.V. in different places; the other passage where 'service' is used being Heb. i. 14, 'ministering spirits sent forth *to do service* for the sake of them that shall inherit salvation.' We may at any rate say that the noun could not have had, if we go by N. T. usage, so soon the formal meaning '*the ministry*,' whatever definiteness the word *diakonos*, 'minister, deacon,' may have now obtained; see note, iii. 1; Int. pp. 15, 16, 18; App. C.

13. *who was before a blasphemer*] A translation of the acc. masc. of the article taken with the participle. But the neuter of the article has the best support, and is taken with the adverb, giving it a slightly stronger force 'during the former days'; while the participle has the concessive sense, **though I was beforetime.**

a blasphemer, and a persecutor, and injurious] R.V. retains 'injurious' in spite of its having become a much weaker word since the 17th century, and so we have an anticlimax, whereas the Greek gives us a climax, the last word referring to deeds of outrage and contumely. Cf. Trench, *N. T. Syn.* § 29. In 1 Thess. ii. 2 and three other places, we have the verb translated 'shamefully entreated.' Tindale, Coverdale and Cranmer give 'tyraunt.' Translate, with Ellicott, **a doer of outrage.**

but I obtained mercy] **howbeit,** or 'but still,' gives a stronger force than simply 'but.' 'He had not like the worse part of the blaspheming and persecuting Pharisees sinned against his better convictions, Mk. iii. 28—30; he had not deliberately set at nought the counsel of God, and defied Heaven to its face.' Fairbairn.

14. *the grace of our Lord was exceeding abundant*] 'Overflowed its wonted channels,' and a stream of faith and love in me, having Jesus Christ for its source and life, flowed *side by side with* this full flood of grace and mercy. The removal of the comma (A.V. of 1611) after 'abundant' leaves the force of the 'with' ambiguous, as though the grace *abounded with* faith. See St Matt. xxvii. 34, 'wine mingled *with* gall,' 1 Tim. vi. 6, 'godliness *with* contentment,' for this full force of the preposition.

15. This is *a faithful saying*] More exactly, **Faithful is the saying,** 'gravissima praefandi formula,' says Bengel; the first of five occurrences in these epistles, where only it is found, iii. 1, iv. 9; 2 Tim. ii. 11; Tit. iii. 8. With it we may compare Rev. xxi. 5, and our Lord's

Christ Jesus came into the world to save sinners; of whom
I am chief. Howbeit for this cause I obtained mercy, that 16
in me first Jesus Christ might shew forth all longsuffering,
for a pattern to them which should hereafter believe on him

'Verily, verily I say unto you.' The special weight of each maxim or practical instruction thus introduced is examined in Appendix, E. See also Introduction, ch. III. ii. 1 c, p. 30.

faithful] That is, trustworthy and claiming implicit credit; more than merely 'true,' which is the rendering in the P. Bk. Communion Service, 'This is a true saying and worthy of all men to be received;' *worthy of all acceptation*, of every kind and degree, as there is no article with 'all'; to be received with every mark of regard and welcome, of confidence and affection.

What is the truth thus heralded? 'Christ Jesus as God in heaven; Christ Jesus come to this earth to save sinners; Christ Jesus come to save *me* the chief of sinners.' It is this personal dealing of the Saviour with the single soul, the personal laying hold by the separate soul of the Saviour's love and pardon, which is so specially precious to St Paul and gives new lustre to the jewel, the simple creed.

of whom I am chief] *am*, shewing his abiding sense of his sinfulness, and this at the close of his life, when he could say 'I have fought the good fight, I have kept the faith, &c.'

'And they who fain would serve Thee best
Are conscious most of wrong within.'

Cf. 1 Cor. xv. 9. So in Acts xxii. 4, 19, xxvi. 9, he takes every opportunity of referring with express self-condemnation to his past life.

16. *Howbeit*] A characteristic re-assertion with a new antithesis, 'Yes, I am indeed chief of sinners, but still I received mercy on this account, that I might also be chief exemplar of Jesus Christ's all-patience.'

Translate with R.V. **that in me as chief** (i.e. **of sinners) might Jesus Christ shew forth all his longsuffering.**

in me] 'in my case,' as in Gal. i. 16, 'it pleased God to reveal His Son *in me*,' 'to shew the Saviour's power in my conversion,' Gal. i. 24, 'they glorified God in me.'

all longsuffering] The longer form of the Greek word 'all' should be read, though only once used otherwise by St Paul, Eph. vi. 13; the position of the article coming before the 'all' is very unusual in N. T. and suggests the translation proposed by Dr Vaughan, 'His all-patience,' cf. Gal. v. 14, 'The whole law.' Winer, § 17. 10.

might shew forth] The right translation in our idiom of the subjunctive, which Hellenistic Greek uses for the optative when it would naturally follow the past tense, 'received mercy,' cf. *v.* 20; the verb 'shew forth' is middle, as always in N. T.; its force 'shew forth as His attribute.'

for a pattern to] R.V. **for an ensample of them which should hereafter believe.** According to the use of the word in the only place where it occurs besides, 2 Tim. i. 13, 'the pattern of sound words,' the phrase ought to be a simpler one 'for a pattern of believers,' and the

17 to life everlasting. Now unto the King eternal, immortal,
invisible, the only wise God, *be* honour and glory for ever
18 and ever. Amen. This charge I commit unto thee, son

longer form is substituted at the moment of writing. And it is not quite as Bengel puts it with emphasis on 'belief,' 'si credis ut Paulus salvabere ut Paulus,' but 'etiamsi peccaveris ut Paulus, ut Paulo poena tibi differetur, locum habebis poenitentiae ut Paulus.'

to life everlasting] We may shew better how this word is taken up, and with a turn of meaning suggests the form of the ascription, by rendering **unto life eternal: and to the King of the eternity...be honour and glory unto all eternity.**

'"Life eternal" is the divine life, the life that *is*'; 'not an endless duration of being in time, but being of which time is not a measure.' Westcott on 1 Joh. i. 2; v. 20.

In St John's use, the *present* living 'in Christ,' spiritual religion, is meant almost entirely to be emphasised, e.g. Joh. iii. 15, v. 24; 1 Joh. i. 2, v. 13.

In St Paul's use this is certainly so too in *one* passage, 1 Tim. vi. 12, where Timothy is now by a distinct effort and act (aorist imperative) to 'lay hold' of 'the eternal life'; that is, 'the special Messianic gift brought by Christ,' described (according to the true reading) in 1 Tim. vi. 19 as 'the life which is life indeed,' and in Eph. iv. 18 as 'the life of God.' So perhaps here, though probably more often St Paul's use of the phrase looks to the development of this life still *future*, e.g. Rom. ii. 7, vi. 22, 'and the end life eternal.' The phrase 'King of the eternity,' lit. 'King of the ages,' covers both uses: God is King and Giver of Life in all the cycles and stages of development through which the world and all in it pass.

This connexion of the phrases makes it probable that this allusive title of God 'King of the eternal' is left thus, strong and complete, and that the following epithets belong to the new title, making a climax **the incorruptible, invisible, only God** (not as A.V. and R.V.). The epithet 'wise' has not sufficient MS. authority here or in Jude 25.

17. *honour and glory*] This combination by itself is only found here. St Paul uses 'glory' with the article generally.

Such an ascription is with St Paul a most characteristic close of passages which are the evident outburst of strong warm feeling excited by some particular train of thought.

18—20. Faithful Ministry. Timothy is further reminded of the fall of some false Teachers.

18. *This charge*] From note on *v.* 5 we shall see no difficulty in the reference of the words here. St Paul has put 'the charge' of which he is full in two different ways in 3—11 and 12—17; he puts it now in another in 18—20. The pronoun 'this' should refer according to its proper usage to something already set forth rather than to something new; and so we may paraphrase, 'This is my charge to teach the old simple truths, with a heart and life that retain still the old penitent

Timothy, according to the prophecies which went before
on thee, that thou by them mightest war a good warfare;
holding faith, and a good conscience; which some having 19
put away, concerning faith have made shipwrack: of whom 20
is Hymeneus and Alexander; whom I have delivered unto
Satan, that they may learn not to blaspheme.

gratitude and devotion; I trust to you this life and work, as a precious jewel; so precious that to guard and keep it you must be never off duty, always Christ's faithful soldier and servant.'

son Timothy] As in verse 2, **my child Timothy.**

the prophecies which went before on thee] "The allusion is to prophecies uttered, as is supposed, at or before his ordination, given then for the purpose of encouraging the Church to make, and Timothy to accept the appointment, in view perhaps of his extreme youth, and possibly also slender frame: prophecies of the arduous nature of the work and of Divine aid in it." Fairbairn. They were utterances at Lystra by Silas (cf. Acts xv. 32) and others of the 'prophets' of the N.T., spoken under the influence of the Holy Spirit, as in St Paul's own case at Antioch, Acts xiii. 2; 'forth-tellings' of the Divine Will, to which St Paul refers partly as warranting him in his appointment of so young a man to so important a charge, partly as encouraging Timothy himself to brave effort. Cf. iv. 14; and Introduction, pp. 16, 58. The marginal rendering of R.V. 'which led the way to thee,' i.e. "the premonitions of the Holy Spirit which pointed to thee" modifies, as Bp Ellicott, unnecessarily the simple meaning both of noun and verb.

a good warfare] Rather render the whole clause **that in them thou mayest war the good warfare**; in them as his heavenly armour—to ward off scorn from without and doubt from within.

Compare the well-known hymn, translating St Paul's previous call to arms in his letter to the same parts, Eph. vi.

Stand then *in His great might*
With all His strength endued,
And take to arm you for the fight
The panoply of God.

19. *faith, and a good conscience*] Together as in ver. 5.

which some having put away] Probably both faith and good conscience, the relative agreeing in number only with the latter. Render rather **having thrust away**—a wilful casting away of rudder and compass.

concerning faith have made shipwrack] Accurately rendering aorist and article **made shipwreck concerning the faith.** 'The faith' here is quite independent of 'faith' above, and means rather what we mean by "the Catholic faith," the creed; so in iii. 9 'holding the mystery of the faith,' iv. 1 'some shall fall away from the faith,' vi. 10 'have been led away from the faith.'

20. *Hymeneus and Alexander*] The name Hymenæus occurs again in 2 Tim. ii. 17, and being uncommon and used in both places of an heretical person in the same locality may fairly be taken as referring to

2 I exhort therefore that, first of all, supplications, prayers,

the same person; the heresy condemned is practically the same; 'the profane babblings' there representing the 'vain talking' of verse 6 here, which is plainly echoed in verse 19—the test of orthodoxy being 'faith and a good conscience.'

The name Alexander also occurs again in 2 Tim. iv. 14; but being common, and having a distinguishing addition there 'the coppersmith,' and referring rather to a personal enemy of St Paul than to a heretic, may more probably refer to a different person, possibly the Alexander of Acts xix. 33. Fairbairn adds reasonably 'in the 2nd Epistle Philetus not Alexander is associated with Hymenæus, and Alexander is mentioned alone and apparently as a worker of evil, not at Ephesus but in Rome, though it is possible enough he may have belonged to the region of Asia.'

whom I have delivered unto Satan, that they may learn] The exact force of the tense is **whom I delivered**; of the mood, **that they might be disciplined.** In the N. T. the later usage holds of the subjunctive following the past tense instead of the optative and our idiom requires 'might.' A definite *time* and *act* of 'delivering' is thus seen to be referred to, explained by some ancient and modern commentators as being excommunication; e.g. Theod. Mops., Latin Version, "ecclesiae alienationem 'traditionem Satanae' vocans"; by others as the judicial infliction of bodily sickness or calamity, such as the blindness inflicted upon Elymas by St Paul, Acts xiii. 11; by Ellicott and Fairbairn, as both combined. "The term" says Wordsworth (on 1 Cor. v. 5, where the phrase is the same) "appears to have had its origin from consideration of the fact that physical evil is due to the agency of the Evil Spirit; cf. Job ii. 6; Lk. xiii. 16: Matt. viii. 30—32 (add 2 Cor. xii. 7 'a messenger of Satan'). But St Paul states the aim and end of the sentence of excommunication against the incestuous Corinthian to be that by the punishment of the flesh, and consequent mortification of the fleshly lusts and appetites, 'his *spirit* may be saved in the day of the Lord'; so in the case of Hymenæus and Alexander; and generally his spiritual weapons are given him for edification and not for destruction. Cf. 2 Cor. x. 8."

may learn] **might be disciplined**; the verb, meaning properly 'to train,' 'educate,' as in Acts vii. 22, is generally used of 'training by chastisement,' 'correcting'; cf. 1 Cor. xi. 32, 'when we are judged we are *chastened* of the Lord,' where the reference is to the sickness and death sent as chastisement for the desecration of the Lord's Table. Compare the old English use of 'teach' in Judges viii. 16, 'he took the thorns of the wilderness and briars, and with them he *taught* the men of Succoth.' Cf. the striking use in Lk. xxiii. 16, 'I will therefore *chastise* him and let him go.'

Ch. II. Apostolic Regulation of Public Worship.

1—7. Directions for Common Prayer and Intercession for all, since the Gospel is for all.

1. *I exhort therefore that, first of all*] Rather, **I exhort therefore**

intercessions, *and* giving of thanks, be made for all men;

first of all; as my first special injunction after my general charge and commission, ch. i. *vv.* 3—5, 18, 19; the verb itself partly suggests the taking up of the subject in new form.

that...supplications...be made] The position of the Greek verb suggests its being middle voice rather than passive. So R.V. margin and Alford following Chrysostom: 'I exhort to make supplications.' The present tense implies the habitual making; and the absence of a subject leaves it unemphatic. In a modern rendering it might run exactly "I recommend therefore first of all the practice of common supplication and prayer, of common intercession and thanksgiving, in behalf of all men." The middle is found in 17 places at least in N. T., in two of these governing the same word 'supplications,' Luke v. 33; Phil. i. 4. So Chrysostom in his comment here uses as the natural phrase 'for all the world... we make our supplication.' The only place where the passive occurs is in the perfect participle, Heb. xii. 27, 'as of things that have been made.'

supplications, prayers, intercessions] In the first word there is, from its derivation, the idea of a felt 'want' and petition for its supply; cf. esp. Phil. i. 4; Luke i. 13; 2 Tim. i. 3. Notice how in English, in the prayer of St Chrysostom, 'our common supplications' is explained by "requests" and by "desires and petitions."

In the second, the idea of vow and 'worship towards' God, cf. Matt. xxi. 13, '*my house* shall be called the house *of prayer*,' Acts ii. 42, 'they continued stedfastly...in the breaking of bread and the prayers.'

In the third, the idea of a personal interview and solicitation, such as Abraham's for Sodom: either (1) against, or (2) for some one: for (1) cf. Acts xxv. 24, 'made suit to me, crying that he ought not to live,' Rom. xi. 2, 'he pleadeth with God against Israel': for (2) Rom. viii. 26, 'The Spirit (and ver. 34 Christ Jesus) maketh intercession for us,' Heb. vii. 25 'He ever liveth to make intercession for us.' See note also on chap. iv. 5.

The plural of each as being a collection of concrete examples is the earlier way of representing the abstract noun; and it also helps to give the force, implied by the whole context, of *common, public*, prayer. Augustine says that the four words refer to the liturgical form of administration of Holy Communion: we may certainly say the converse that our 'Divine Liturgy' is modelled on this authorised rule, taking e.g. the modern 'Prayer for the Church Militant' with its express embodiment of this passage, or the ancient Gloria in Excelsis—(1) "In earth peace, goodwill towards men: (2) we bless thee, we worship Thee, O Lord, (3) Thou that takest away the sins of the world, have mercy upon us; (4) we give thanks to Thee, God the Father Almighty": or taking the service as a whole, we get (1) the *supplication* for mercy and grace in the Kyrie after each Commandment, in the collects for the Queen and that for the day and the Church Militant, (2) the *prayer of worship* in the prayers of humble access and consecration, (3) the intercession in the Lord's Prayer and following prayers, (4) the thanksgiving of the Gloria in Excelsis summarising all before.

2 for kings, and *for* all that are in authority; that we may
lead a quiet and peaceable life in all godliness and honesty.
3 For this *is* good and acceptable in the sight of God our
4 Saviour; who will have all men to be saved, and to come

2. *in authority*] R.V. **in high place.** The noun occurs only 1 Cor. ii. 1, 'I came not *with excellency* of speech,' but the participle in Rom. xiii. 1, 'the *higher* powers.'

Though there is no special reference to Roman emperors, yet as Wordsworth well says, under the circumstances of its writing, this exhortation is 'an evidence of the courage and divine commission of St Paul.' It is also a practical reply to the charge, so commonly brought at the time and after, of civil disaffection.

in all godliness and honesty] 'Godliness,' a constant devout realization of God's presence and greatness. The word occurs ten times in these epistles, and in 2 Pet. i. 3, 6, 7; its opposite in 1 Tim. i. 9. It is another characteristic word of the Pastoral Epistles. 'Honesty' appears to have the same sense as in the Marriage Service, 'that they may live together in godly love and honesty,' that is, purity and fidelity to the marriage vow, and therefore well to represent the Greek word which only occurs here and iii. 4, and Tit. ii. 7. The idea is that of *propriety of conduct*, the outward counterpart of *godliness*. The adjective which occurs 1 Tim. iii. 8, 11; Tit. ii. 2 and Phil. iv. 8 is in the last place rendered by A.V. 'honest,' by R.V. 'honourable.' Joseph in his thought and in his conduct exemplified both; "How can I do this great wickedness and sin against God?" Conybeare's rendering **gravity** has been adopted by the commentators and R.V. The Prayer for the Church Militant expressly echoes this verse, 'that under her we may be godly and quietly governed.'

quiet and peaceable] Rather, **peaceable and quiet**; 'outward peace and inward tranquillity' Olshausen and Ellicott, who translate 'quiet and tranquil': but the distinction is doubtful, and R.V. gives 'tranquil and quiet.'

life] 'Manner of life' according to the usual distinction between *bios* and *zoë*. See Trench, *N. T. Syn.* § 27.

3. *For this* is *good and acceptable*] We should omit *For*; for the apparent abruptness compare Phil. iv. 5, 'The Lord is at hand,' 2 Tim. iv. 18 (right reading), 'The Lord will deliver me.' The connexion by 'this' or 'these' occurs in every chapter of this epistle; cf. i. 18; iii. 14; iv. 11, 15; v. 7; vi. 2. It is especially characteristic of St John. Cf. Joh. i. 30; vi. 50, 58; 1 Joh. ii. 22; iv. 6; v. 6, 20.

good and acceptable] Are taken best together with 'in the sight of.' Cf. a similar coupling and similar added clause in iv. 4.

God our Saviour] Rather, **our Saviour God**, or 'our saving God.' The first of four places where this order is observed, Tit. i. 3, ii. 10, iii. 4; here there is an obvious emphasis, as the thought of the next verse comes into view.

4. *who will have*] The exact rendering is that of R.V. **who willeth that all men should be saved**—not the stronger word *bouletai*, 'desireth,' with a definite purpose. Chrysostom's comment is "if He

unto the knowledge of the truth. For *there is* one God, 5

willed to save all, do thou will it also; and if thou willest, pray for it": and Theod. Mops. in the Latin translation "evidens est quoniam omnes vult salvari, quia et omnes tuetur, quia est omnium Dominus." Thus the Greek fathers accepted St Paul's words in their *prima facie* sense. The Latin fathers seek to guard their application; and St Augustine actually says "by 'all' understand 'all the predestined,' because men of all sorts are among them." The phrase is not "willeth to save all," which would have been very near to *universalism*; but there is implied "the human acceptance of offered salvation on which even God's predestination is contingent" Alford.

be saved, and to come unto the knowledge of the truth] Notice the order of the words; salvation is according to the N. T. usage, *past*, *present* and *future*.

Past, 2 Tim. i. 9, 'God who saved us and called us.'
Tit. iii. 5, 'he saved us through the laver of regeneration.'
Present, Rom. xiii. 11, 'work out your own salvation.'
Acts ii. 42, 'The Lord added...those that were being saved.'
Future, 1 Pet. i. 5, 'guarded unto a salvation ready to be revealed in the last time.'
2 Tim. iv. 18, 'will save me unto his heavenly kingdom.'

And here we are evidently to understand by the two clauses first *a rescue* from ignorance and sin, from life in untruth, and then an advance from this first knowledge of one's true self as a sinner to the complete and perfect knowledge of the truth. So far then as the word 'salvation' and 'saved' are used to describe an experience of the first of these two stages, *and are understood to be so limited*, the language is Apostolic; and that indeed is a more incorrect usage which refers the word only to final safety, without guarding it as in our collect by a defining epithet "towards the attainment of *everlasting* salvation," and without remembering the express statement of the Prayer-Book Catechism that by Baptism we have been now "called to a state of salvation."

At the same time, so far as any teachers or evangelists regard all as finished and completed *at conversion*, they ignore and contradict the latter clause here; God willeth that *all* should come to *the full knowledge* of the truth, and not stay ever resting on a past acceptance of the message of forgiveness. The word for **full knowledge**, *epignosis*, is repeated four times in these Epistles, 2 Tim. ii. 25, iii. 7; Tit. i. 1, and is contrasted with the knowledge, falsely so called, of the heretical teachers, cf. vi. 20; Tit. i. 16.

The simple verb is rendered by Westcott, Joh. iii. 10, to 'perceive by the knowledge of progress, recognition.' See also on Joh. ii. 24.

The force of the distinction between the simple and compound word is well seen in 1 Cor. xiii. 12, "Now I am getting to know in part; but then I shall fully know, even as God knew me fully."

5. *For* there is *one God*] Usually taken as a proof of God's willing all men to be saved, as in the quotation from Theodore, ver. 4. But the parallel passage is ch. iii. 15, 16, where the test word 'the truth' leads at once to the recital of an apparently well-known elementary

and one mediator between God and men, *the* man Christ
6 Jesus; who gave himself a ransom for all, to be testified in
7 due time. Whereunto I am ordained a preacher, and an

creed. And so here, verses 5 and 6 give us a creed, a brief exposition of 'the truth'; and verse 7 is seen to have a much plainer connexion and stronger force—this creed, this Gospel, is what you have received with my *imprimatur* as apostle of the Gentiles, and is 'the truth,' whatever the teachers of false knowledge may say. See App. A III.

and one mediator...the *man*] Accurate rendering requires **one mediator also...(himself) man.** The word 'mediator' has now come to be applied without explanations to Christ; a token of the later use, even of creed formulary. The places in Hebrews viii. 6, ix. 15, xii. 24, where Christ is thus spoken of in contrast to Moses would lead on to this usage. 'Man,' not of the angelic race, whose aid some would wish to use for mediation, Col. ii. 18. Cf. Heb. ii. 16.

"The other equally essential condition that he should be God is not here insisted on, for the tendency of Gnosticism was to *Docetism*."

6. *a ransom*] The word is a compound naturally formed, as time passed, to represent Christ's own teaching, *antilutron* thus recalling the *lutron anti* of Matt. xx. 28; Mark x. 45. On this last verse Maclear distinguishes, from Trench's *Syn.*, p. 276, the three great circles of images in Scripture used to represent the purport of Christ's death:

(*a*) sin offering or propitiation, 1 John ii. 2, iv. 10.

(*b*) atonement, i.e. at-one-ment, reconciliation with an offended friend, Rom. v. 11; xi. 15; 2 Cor. v. 18, 19.

(*c*) ransom, or the price paid for the redemption of a captive from slavery, Rom. iii. 24; Eph. i. 7.

This third image, which is St Paul's latest love, occurs again, Tit. ii. 14, 'that he might redeem us from all iniquity,' and is chosen by St Peter, 1 Pet. i. 18, and the writer to the Hebrews, Heb. ix. 12.

Our Article II. like this creed, and unlike the Apostles', Nicene and Athanasian Creeds, adds a statement of the purport of Christ's death to its statement of the fact; but takes the first and second of these images to express it; "who truly suffered, was crucified, dead and buried, *to reconcile* His Father to us, and *to be a sacrifice* not only for original guilt but also for all actual sins of men." Cf. Art. XV.: 'He came to be the Lamb without spot, who by sacrifice of Himself once made should take away the sins of the world.'

to be testified in due time] R.V. **the testimony to be borne in its proper seasons**; the neuter substantive having its proper sense, 'that which was to be testified of.' The word may well have come into this creed from the familiarity of the Jewish Christians with its use (as Wordsworth suggests) in the Pentateuch, where it occurs 30 times in connexion with the Holy of Holies, the Tables of the law, the Tabernacle and the Ark. Cf. Acts vii. 44, 'Our fathers had the tabernacle of *the testimony* in the wilderness.' 'The redemption made by the Blood of Christ was the True Testimony which was reserved for its full revelation in its own appointed season,' Eph. i. 10, 'a dispensation of the fulness of the seasons to sum up all things in Christ.'

apostle, (I speak the truth in Christ, *and* lie not;) a teacher
of the Gentiles in faith and verity. I will therefore that 8
men pray every where, lifting up holy hands, without wrath

The reading is not doubtful, though from the apparent abruptness (sufficiently accounted for if part of a brief creed) the scribes in the MSS. seem to have stumbled at the clause, each giving some variety for smoothness. See note on verse 5 for the connexion; which makes the force and relevance of the familiar phrases strong and clear.

7. *Whereunto*] For the ministry of which, the True Testimony.

I am ordained] There is in the Greek an emphasis on 'I,' **Whereunto I—remember—was appointed.** St Paul is always filled with his special mission to proclaim the universality of the Gospel, and appropriately recals his commission as **teacher of the Gentiles.** Cf. Gal. ii. 9.

I speak the truth in Christ] Here the words 'in Christ' have no sufficient authority, and have been introduced from Rom. ix. 1.

in faith and verity] Better, **in faith and truth**; see note on i. 1; a teacher, not in politics or art, but in religion, its morals and doctrine; its spiritual *life*, that the soul may go out to God in faith that worketh by love and a good conscience; and its spiritual *knowledge*, that the historic facts revealed may be fully grasped, and the haze of false doctrine be dispelled.

8—15. COMMON PRAYER. THE PART TO BE TAKEN IN PUBLIC WORSHIP BY MEN AND BY WOMEN.

8. *I will therefore that men pray every where*] (1) the position of 'pray' shews the resumption of this subject as the main thought of the sentence, (2) the word used for 'men' and the article prefixed shew the contrast to women in verse 9, (3) we have *boulomai* not *thelô*: we may render therefore more accurately **I desire then that prayer be made by the men in every place**; 'in every place' where public prayer is made; for the limitation of 'every' by the surrounding circumstances of the passage, cf. Phil. iii. 8.

lifting up holy hands] For the exact force of 'holy' cf. note on 'unholy,' i. 9. With outstretched arms and uplifted palms was the Oriental and Roman attitude; cf. 'duplices tendens ad sidera palmas,' Virg. *Aen.* I. 93. 'The folding together of the hands in prayer has been shewn to be of Indo-Germanic origin.' Ellicott.

without wrath and doubting] It is a very even question of authority whether we should read the singular or plural, 'doubting' or 'doubtings.'

It is also a very even question of usage whether we understand 'inward disputings,' that is, 'doubtings' or 'outward disputations'; the former is the commoner meaning in N.T., cf. Luke xxiv. 38: but the latter is clearly found, Phil. ii. 14, and the verb, Mk. viii. 16, &c. Perhaps, as a preparation for prayer, to have faith, as well as charity, enjoined, gives the greater point: compare the preparation required for our Chief Act of Prayer 'To examine themselves, whether they...have a

9 and doubting. In like manner also, that women adorn
themselves in modest apparel, with shamefastness and
sobriety; not with broided hair, or gold, or pearls, or costly
10 array; but (which becometh women professing godliness)

lively faith in God's mercy...and be in charity with all men.' Prayer-Book Catechism, *s. fin.*

9. *In like manner also, that women adorn themselves*] The point of likeness consists in the fitting attitude of men and of women towards Public Worship and Common Prayer; for men, to lead in prayer with suitable posture and prepared spirit; for women, to attend in quiet dress and quiet behaviour, 'unadorned' but still 'adorned the most' with the halo of their church work. Cf. Tit. ii. 3.

modest apparel] Or, **seemly guise**, if we take the word (which occurs only here) to refer like the Latin *habitus* not solely to dress but also to demeanour. The simple noun occurs often, e.g. Luke xv. 22, 'bring out the best robe.' The compound verb is used by the 'town clerk of Ephesus,' Acts xix. 36, 'ye ought *to be composed*.'

with shamefastness and sobriety] The word 'shamefacedness' is a vulgar printer's corruption of the word used by the translators of the A.V. 'shamefastness,' now restored to the A.V. in the copies printed side by side with the R.V. The original word *aidôs* implies a reference to *external standards*; a feeling of what is due to another (God or man) irrespective of consequences (in contrast to *aischunê*, the same feeling through fear of harm); the other word *sôphrosunê*, characteristic of these epistles, implies restraint upon oneself from an *innate sense* of what is right. The English words of the A.V. may carry the same distinction. Compare Xen. *Cyrop.* VIII. i. 31, 'the shamefast shun what is openly disgraceful, the sober-minded what is disgraceful in secret also.' Cf. ch. iii. 2. Trench, *N. T. Syn.*, is not quite right.

broided hair] Lit. 'plaitings'; 'gold' seems to have the best support of MSS. here, though 'gold coins' is the best supported word in the parallel passage, 1 Pet. iii. 3, 'plaiting the hair and wearing a necklace of coins.'

costly array] The R.V. **raiment**; the word in its form suggests what we convey by the modern term 'wardrobe.'

10. *which becometh women professing godliness*] Best as A.V. and R.V. forming a parenthesis to justify the boldness of the dress recommended immediately after.

godliness] The noun occurs only here, the adjective only in Joh. ix. 31, 'a worshipper of God.' It seems to be distinguished from its kindred word above, verse 2, thus: *theosebeia* looks to the worship being that of *God* in contrast to *idols*, and embodies the phrase in use for converts from heathen polytheism to Judaism throughout the Acts, xiii. 43, 50, xvi. 14, xvii. 4, 17, xviii. 7, 'one that worshipped,' and in full 'one that worshipped God.' While *eusebeia*, above and in nine other places in these epistles, by its prefix goes deeper than the change of outward worship—heart reverence and devotion, 'the *best* worship': as the years went on a natural advance urged on the Christian converts in whom the seed was 'to grow

with good works. Let the woman learn in silence with 11
all subjection. But I suffer not a woman to teach, nor to 12
usurp authority over the man, but to be in silence. For 13
Adam was first formed, then Eve. And Adam was not 14
deceived, but the woman being deceived was in the trans-
gression. Notwithstanding she shall be saved in child- 15

secretly.'. In this place then, where it is a question of *public* worship and the right surroundings, the word chosen here is the exactly appropriate one; 'You profess the worship of *God* by your coming to the public prayers: your best dress is to be known and esteemed for your zeal in acts of love and service for Him in His church.'

with good works] R.V. **through**; the change of preposition suggests a change in the character of the phrase, that St Paul is now speaking metaphorically.

11. *Let the woman learn in silence*] The reference is still to the public assemblies. The exact rendering in our idiom of the article is, with R.V., **Let a woman learn**, in silence, **in quiet**, as in verse 2. Cf. 1 Cor. xiv. 34, 35.

12. The direction is made more emphatic by the position of the verb 'to teach' (according to the better supported reading) at the beginning of the clause: **But teaching I permit not to a woman.**

to usurp authority] The verb does not go so far as this in later Greek, only to the extent of the R.V. **to have dominion over**. From *authentikos* 'from first authority' we get our 'authentic' in its proper meaning (Trench's *Select Glossary*, p. 15; Cic. *ad Att.* x. 9) of 'coming from the pen of the writer to whom a work is attributed.' 'The Turkish "effendi" (lord) is from the same word.' Wordsworth.

13. 'The Apostle appeals to the original order and course of things. By inverting this relative position and calling—the helpmate assuming the place of the head or guide, and the head facilely yielding to her governance—was the happy constitution of Paradise overthrown.' Fairbairn.

14. *the woman being deceived was in the transgression*] The compound verb should be read as in 2 Cor. xi. 3, 'as the serpent beguiled Eve'; 'Adam was not beguiled,' a general negative, limited by the compound verb following, 'you may say he was not beguiled in comparison with the complete direct beguiling of Eve'; **the woman being beguiled is found in transgression.**

'Was' does not represent properly the perfect, lit. 'is become,' used, according to Greek idiom, because the past event is viewed as having a present influence, and continuing in its effects.

Here it helps the transition from the particular case of Eve in the past to the general case of women now. This is also aided by the further change to the future in 'shall be saved.'

15. *in childbearing*] R.V. gives the exact force of the Greek **through the childbearing**, and leaves unsettled which particular interpretation is correct (1) the A.V. 'in childbearing,' the preposition ren-

bearing, if they continue in faith and charity and holiness with sobriety.

3 *This is* a true saying, If a man desire the office of a

dering merely the circumstances, cf. Rom. iv. 11 'in uncircumcision';

or (2) the margin of R.V. 'through her childbearing': 'her childbearing which is her curse may be her highest blessing, as with man's doom, labour; her domestic life and duties, the sphere of woman's mission, St Paul lays great stress on good works, the performance of the common duties of life, in opposition to the irregularities of the times; and yet adds the necessary previous condition "if they abide in faith"'; so Conybeare;

or (3) 'through the Childbearing—the Incarnation of Christ,' an early interpretation quoted by Theophylact, and also given in the Ancient Catena recently recovered and published by Dr Cramer, and supported by Hammond, Ellicott and Wordsworth, on the grounds (*a*) that the parallel passage in 1 Cor. xi. 8—12 closes with a reference to the Incarnation, (*b*) that in speaking of the transgression and sentence it was in itself natural and appropriate to speak of the sustaining prophecy, (*c*) that 'saved' and 'through' both gain in fulness of force.

On the whole (2) seems most probable, this 'childbearing' being singled out from among the 'good works' of ver. 10. Compare ch. v. 13, 14, where the younger widows are urged not to be 'idle' (lit. 'workless') or 'busybodies' (lit. 'prying into the work of others') but to 'marry, *bear children*, rule the household'; and note that the verb there and the noun here for childbearing occur nowhere else in N.T. This thought of 'work'—woman's proper work—lasts on then to the end of the chapter, and gives the natural transition to other work, the 'good work' of a bishop in chap. iii.

if they continue] i.e. women, from 'the woman' of ver. 14; the aorist tense implies 'continue stedfastly.'

faith and charity and holiness] Rather as R.V. **love and sanctification**, the form of the latter word implying a process of repeated acts: so 'doubting' above, the harbouring of doubt upon doubt. The fundamental idea of the Greek noun is 'separation and, so to speak, consecration and devotion to the service of the Deity'; Trench, *N. T. Syn.*, p. 316. Cf. 2 Tim. i. 9, 'called us with a holy calling.' 'But the thought lies very near that what is set apart from the world and to God should separate itself from the world's defilements and should share in God's purity.' Hence the appropriateness of its being linked here with 'sobriety' so as to recal the feminine modesty and purity of ver. 9. Cf. Westcott, Heb. x. 10 'the initial consecration and the progressive hallowing.'

CH. III. APOSTOLIC SELECTION OF THE ASSISTANT MINISTRY.

1—7. THE DUTIES AND CHARACTERS OF BISHOPS OR PRESBYTERS.

Following the directions concerning the general arrangements for public worship come instructions as to the character and qualifications of the appointed ministers, the presbyterate, and the diaconate (male

bishop, he desireth a good work. A bishop then must be 2

and female). These are introduced by a well-known saying among them, declared to be 'faithful' or 'trustworthy.' See Appendix, E.

1. This is *a true saying*] Better, **It is a faithful saying**; R.V., as in i. 15, literally 'Faithful is the saying'; most probably to be referred, as there and in the other three passages, to the following sentence. So A.V. and R.V., though the margin of R.V. mentions that 'Some connect the words...with the preceding paragraph'; and Westcott and Hort in their text by the mode of printing so connect it. The early Greek Fathers are divided; Chrysostom, e.g. is for reference to the preceding, Theod. Mops. to the following, quoting our Lord's 'Verily, verily.' The various reading of D *anthrôpinos* (some Latin Versions have *humanus*) 'this is a *human* saying,' read also in i. 15, cannot very well be explained as by Ellicott, an equivalent of *benignus*, for how could *benignus* at all fairly represent *pistos*, faithful, trusty? Nor can it have arisen from the spread of the *nolo episcopari* feeling, causing this place to give offence, so that 'human,' 'carnal' was substituted; for when substituted it turns the context upside down, and the explanation could not hold in i. 15. We may look for the explanation rather in the use by St Paul of the phrase *kata anthrôpon*, *anthrôpinos*, Rom. vi. 19; Gal. iii. 15; 1 Cor. xv. 32, where the original idea is 'according to the way of ordinary human speaking.' So here 'the saying has won its way to acceptance in the common speech,' has become *proverbial*, representing the wisdom of many and the wit of one.

desire] R.V. **seeketh**, the word being stronger than that in the next clause and meaning literally 'stretcheth out to take'; it is used (in N. T.) only in vi. 10, 'love of money, which some reaching after,' and Heb. xi. 6 'a rewarder of them that seek after him.'

the office of a bishop] The episcopate, lit. 'overseership,' which Alford would retain as the translation, to avoid the later limitations suggested by 'the office of a bishop.' Fairbairn on the other hand urges 'pastorate.' But 'pastor' originally meant only 'bishop' in its English ecclesiastical use. It is clear that the originals of our *episcopate*, *diaconate* and *apostolate* were at first interchangeable as general terms; Acts i. 17, 'this diaconate,' 20 'his episcopate,' 25 'this diaconate and apostolate,' all used of the office from which Judas fell: *diaconate* expresses the service done for Christ, and *apostolate* the mission from Him; *episcopate* the oversight and care of those among whom the service is done and to whom the mission is.

For the first trace of separation of the term 'diaconate' to a distinct class cf. Acts vi. 1 and 2, contrasted with ver. 4; though the word is still used of St Paul's apostleship, 1 Tim. i. 12, and of Timothy's office, 2 Tim. iv. 5. A separate 'bishop' or 'overseer' and a separate 'deacon' or 'minister' come first in Phil. i. 1, 'all the saints with the *bishops* and *deacons*': then in Acts xx. 17, compared with ver. 28, 'the *presbyters* of Ephesus at Miletus'...'the Holy Ghost hath made you *bishops*,' we get a new name synonymous with bishop—'presbyter'; and later 2 Joh. i. 1 this new name 'presbyter' is used of the apostle St John and 1 Pet. v. 1 by St Peter of himself.

blameless, the husband of one wife, vigilant, sober, of good

We infer then that in N. T. times 'bishop' and 'presbyter' were both used of certain senior ministers and of the apostles, and that there were junior ministers called 'deacons'; but the word 'deacon' could still be used generally. The conclusion of Bp Wordsworth is that the reference of *episcopate* here, while mainly to be made to the office of *presbyter*, does not exclude the office to which Timothy was appointed in the room of the apostle, to which the term was afterwards restricted, and from which comes our word 'bishop.' See Introduction, pp. 13—28, 53, 54; Appendix, C.

he desireth a good work] With all commentators from Chrysostom we must lay stress on *good work;* 'non dignitates sed opus eo quod pro communi est utilitate constitutum.' Theod. Mops.

2. *A bishop*] R.V. **The bishop**, as St Mark iv. 3, 'the sower': so George Herbert, '*The* country Parson': 'A bishop' is however quite idiomatic too.

blameless] R.V. **without reproach**; twice again, ch. v. 7 and vi. 14, nowhere else in N. T.; 'giving no handle' is exact, though rather colloquial, implying in Greek and in R.V. the absence of definite acts or habits to give occasion for reproach. See note on *v.* 7.

the husband of one wife] A regulation apparently very simple, but one that has much exercised both ancient and modern commentators. We may pass by the view (1) 'husband of *a* wife,' i.e. 'a married man,' as ungrammatical; because the definite numeral has not lost its force '*one*' in N.T.; in all the 36 or 37 passages where it might be thought to approach the sense of the indefinite article there is something in the context which draws attention to the singleness, the individuality of the person or thing named in a way which is lost by simply rendering 'an' or 'a.' This is virtually the view of the Greek Church, which requires all priests to be married, but forbids a second marriage, and requires the priest who has lost his wife to cease from exercising his functions.

We may pass by also view (2), that of the Mormons, though at least grammatical, 'husband of one wife if not more.'

The weight of authority is divided between (3) 'not a digamist' and (4) 'not a bigamist.'

Alford, Wordsworth and Ellicott adopt (3) and understand a second marriage after the loss of the first wife, however happening, to be forbidden, *digamia;* relying on (*a*) the very early interpretation by many Greek and Latin Fathers, the action by many bishops and the enactment of some councils, (*b*) the supposed propriety of greater strictness for officers of the Church.

But as to (*a*), the more general interpretation by the prevailing 'voice of the Church' in the first and second centuries was for (4), and St Paul has express statements on this point, Rom. vii. 2; 1 Cor. vii. 39, countenancing second marriages; as to (*b*), St Paul's usage is *not* to make *laws* of a 'higher life' for ministers than for people, but to expect the same laws kept in a way to serve for ensample to the flock. We adopt (4) therefore—which is the *prima facie* meaning, and was the view of the Antiochene fathers (though Chrysostom seems to have

behaviour, given to hospitality, apt to teach; not given to 3

changed his mind when he came to annotate Tit. i. 6), and was acted upon by some of the Eastern bishops. Many converts to Christianity would have more than one wife. They are nowhere commanded to put away all but one; but it was not seemly that a man in such a position should be a Christian minister, who ought in all respects to be an ensample to the flock. See further on Tit. i. 6. The parallel passage in ch. v. 10 need cause no difficulty: then as now many a woman would change her partner and with or without a so-called re-marriage feel no scruple so long as she was faithful to the new partner. The elementary principle of Christian relationship needed then to be taught in Christian Asia, and needs teaching now in many still half-heathen circles of Christian England.

vigilant, sober] Rather **sober, pure**; the first word, from which *nephalism* comes, occurs only here and in verse 11 of the 'women deacons,' and in Tit. ii. 2 of 'the aged men,' and is rendered by R.V. 'temperate'; while the verb with which it is connected, occurring 1 Thess. v. 6 and 8, 2 Tim. iv. 5, and 1 Pet. i. 13, iv. 7, is rendered 'be sober.' The second word here and usually in the Pastoral Epistles, where it and its connexions occur nine times, is rendered by R.V. 'soberminded': in the passage however where both the verbs occur, 1 Pet.. iv. 7, we have 'be of *sound* (not sober) mind and be sober unto prayer.'

'Sober,' not indulging the desire of 'winebibbings, revellings, carousings'; 'pure,' not indulging in the thought of 'lasciviousness and lusts.' See 1 Pet. iv. 3 compared with 7. Cf. also 1 Thess. v. 6, and Tit. ii. 2.

of good behaviour] R.V. with Conybeare and Lewin **orderly**; the same word describes the 'modest' dress of the women above ii. 9, and occurs nowhere else in N. T. The root-idea of the word is the 'beauty of order,' such as made it an appropriate word to describe the *world*, '*kosmos*,' created out of bare blank *chaos*. Our word 'decent' had originally a somewhat similar force; see Prayer-Book rubrics in Communion Service, directing the alms to be received in a *decent*, i.e. fair and fitting bason, and the priest so to place the bread and wine that he may with the more readiness and *decency*, i.e. fair and holy order, break the bread.

Here the word expresses the character of the presbyter in his outward behaviour, 'modest' but not 'shy,' 'genial' but not 'noisy'—that of a Christian gentleman.

given to hospitality] The adjective occurs (excepting in the parallel account of the presbyter, Tit. i. 8) only in 1 Pet. iv. 9, the same passage from which we have just drawn two other of the characteristic words of the Pastoral Epistles. The subst. occurs however Rom. xii. 13 and Heb. xiii. 2. 'Brethren in their travels could not resort to the houses of the heathen, and would be subject to insult in the public deversoria.' Alford.

apt to teach] The only specially *ministerial* qualification, enlarged in Tit. i. 9, 'able both to exhort in the sound doctrine, and to convict the gainsayers.'

3. *not given to wine*] Margin R.V. expresses exactly the usage of

wine, no striker, not greedy of filthy lucre; but patient, not
4 a brawler, not covetous; one that ruleth well his own house,
5 having *his* children in subjection with all gravity; (for if a

the word, 'not quarrelsome over wine,' like the term so painfully familiar in our police-courts, 'drunk and disorderly': again peculiar to these Epp., here and Tit. i. 7. For the simpler word with St Paul, cf. 1 Cor. v. 11, 'a drunkard,' Eph. v. 18, 'be not drunken with wine.'

no striker] The necessity for specifying this and the preceding qualification, so elementary as they seem to us, shews a state of society in which the plainest, most obvious meaning for 'husband of one wife' is the one most likely to have been meant, as argued above.

not greedy of filthy lucre] Omit as not having MS. support and having come in from the parallel passage Tit. i. 7, and from ver. 8.

patient, not a brawler] R.V. rightly '**gentle, not contentious,**' 'patient' being too *weak* an attitude of the mind, and 'brawler' going *beyond* the mental attitude; whereas both words express 'an *active* attitude of the *mind*' in contrast to the *acts* of quarrelling and striking; '**gentle,**' i.e. 'anxious to shew considerateness and forbearance' according to the now well-known meaning of Phil. iv. 5, 'forbearance,' margin R.V. 'gentleness,' (cf. 1 Pet. ii. 18), 'offering to give up one's just rights': **not contentious,** not aggressive, averse to disputing, nearly as Conybeare renders 'peaceable'; only here and Tit. iii. 2.

not covetous] Rather, with R.V. **no lover of money**; the word only occurs here and in Heb. xiii. 5, and represents the 'avaricious' rather than the 'covetous,' which is *pleonektês*, a frequent word with St Paul in his other epistles; cf. 1 Cor. v. 10, 'with the covetous and extortioners.' See Trench, *N. T. Syn.* § 24. The qualification Interprets in a practical concrete form for daily life the Master's word, 'He that loveth his life loseth it, and he that hateth his life in this world shall keep it unto life eternal.'

4. *that ruleth well his own house*] In distinction to 'God's household' the Church, verses 5 and 15.

his *children*] Rather, from the emphatic position of 'children,' and the absence of the article, the sense is 'with a household of his own rightly under his rule, with children held in subjection.'

with all gravity] There should be, that is, all propriety of conduct on his part, according to the line 'maxima debetur pueris reverentia'; so Titus in order to commend his exhortations to the young men to be pure is himself 'to set an example of propriety,' Tit. ii. 7. There should be the same propriety on the children's part, according to the similar passage in Tit. i. 6, that they be 'not accused of riot.'

Compare St Paul's eloquent appeal to the Philippians to 'think thoughts true and *seemly*, righteous and pure,' thoughts of truth, *morality*, righteousness and purity, Phil. iv. 8.

5. *for if a man know not*] **but,** the force of the adversative conjunction being, 'You may think me needlessly particular in requiring this, but a straw will shew how the wind blows, a bad parent will make a bad pastor.' The negative is to be taken closely with the verb 'is

man know not how to rule his own house, how shall he
take care of the church of God?) Not a novice, lest being 6
lifted up with pride he fall into the condemnation of the
devil. Moreover he must have a good report of them 7
which are without; lest he fall into reproach and the snare

ignorant.' There is a preference, especially in later Greek, for the stronger negative where there is an antithesis or where there is special emphasis by the negativing of a single word. Cf. Winer, § 55, 2; James ii. 11; 1 Tim. v. 8; 2 Tim. ii. 14.

Both the words 'rule' and 'take care' have an obvious bearing on St Paul's conception of the ministry as being especially for government. So too what follows.

6. "Do not set a new convert to rule in high place lest 'pride come' again 'before a fall' as in Satan's case: and again, let your ruler be one at whom the world can throw no stone; or its reproaches will do harm and may drive him back into his old sins."

Not a novice] Lit. 'a neophyte,' a new convert. The objection raised against the authenticity of the Epistle from this verse cannot be sustained when the later date is granted, since we get a period of twelve years from A.D. 54, the commencement of St Paul's three years' work at Ephesus, to A.D. 66, the most probable date for this Epistle. See Introduction, ch. vi. *fin.*

lifted up with pride] Rather, **puffed up**. See note on vi. 4.

the condemnation of the devil] The same condemnation as that under which the devil came for pride; objective genitive. Compare '...what time his pride Had cast him out of heaven, with all his host Of rebel angels.' Milton, *Par. Lost*, I. 36.

7. *them which are without*] Outside the circle of believers, the Christian Church: the same phrase is used by St Paul, 1 Thess. iv. 12, 'walk honestly toward them that are without': cf. 1 Cor. v. 12, 13.

the snare of the devil] Probably we should take this as a separate phrase apart from 'reproach,' considering the use in 2 Tim. ii. 26, 'recover themselves out of the snare of the devil.' The genitive here must be subjective, 'the snare laid by the devil.' So Huther, 'It is a figurative name for the lying in wait of the devil, who is represented as a hunter.' See Appendix, K.

The devil entraps a man, that is, into 'proud despair' by the temptation arising out of the 'reproach' for the past thrown in his teeth; 'You can never be of use or in repute; these old sins will dog and clog you; you may as well return to your "wallowing in the mire"'; cf. 2 Sam. xii. 14, 'By this deed thou hast given great occasion to the enemies of the Lord to blaspheme.' We know the terrible struggle David's life was to him afterwards, through the weakening of his authority, in consequence of the old, well-known fall; how for example he was drawn again into deeds of violence and injustice by the sons of Zeruiah, who, as he bitterly complained, were 'too hard' for him.

8 of the devil. Likewise *must* the deacons *be* grave, not
doubletongued, not given to much wine, not greedy of
9 filthy lucre; holding the mystery of the faith in a pure

8—13. The duties and characters of Deacons, both Men and Women.

8. *the deacons*] There is no article; for 'deacons' in the accusative we must supply from verse 2 the remainder of the construction 'it is right that *deacons* be.' This elliptical abruptness is among the characteristics of the style of these Epistles. See Introduction, p. 31. The title 'deacons' is only used in this special sense here and Phil. i. 1. But the title 'deaconess' is given to Phœbe, Rom. xvi. 1. In other passages such as Rom. xiii. 4; 1 Tim. iv. 6; 1 Pet. iv. 10 the word still retains the general sense explained on iii. 1. Both in Phil. i. 1 and Rom. xvi. 1 we may trace a fitness in the mention from the office of *almoner*, the original function assigned to the deacons, Acts vi. 1. In writing to the Philippians St Paul, as Bp Lightfoot points out, mentions the officers, since the *contributions* were probably sent to him in their name as well as of the Church generally. In commending Phœbe to the Roman Church he speaks of her as 'a succourer of many and of mine own self.' Though the duties were now enlarged, St Paul still lays stress here on fitness for their first charge; they of all men must be 'not greedy of filthy lucre.' He had not mentioned this in speaking of the presbyters; though in Tit. i. 7 he does.

grave] Considering the emphasis laid on purity of life and bearing in the case of the presbyters 'pure,' 'orderly,' we see in this epithet the corresponding qualification of 'seemly morals and propriety,' cf. ii. 2.

not doubletongued] Or, better, **not talebearers**. The word is used here only in N.T. Xen. *de Equestri*, VIII. 2, uses the noun of repeating gossip. Polycarp has this very rare word, *ad Phil.* c. v., of the deacons. Bp Ellicott attributes the interpretation of Theodoret 'saying one thing to one and another to another' to Theodore; who has however a singular explanation of his own, 'non *bilingues*'; 'si enim deferunt illa quae mandantur a presbyteris sive viris sive mulieribus ad quos et mittuntur, iustum est eos sincero arbitrio sicut convenit implere quae sibi mandantur quae per eos mandantes audiunt.'

not given to much wine] The word for 'given' is used five times by St Paul in these Epistles, and nowhere else by him except in Acts xx. 28 to the elders of Ephesus, 'take heed to yourselves.' Lit. 'giving heed.'

9. *the mystery of the faith*] Apparently repeated again verse 16 as 'the mystery of godliness.' The word 'mystery' is significant. Coming from the Greek, 'to close the mouth,' and so 'to initiate,' it was originally used of the secret rites of Eleusis in Attica, into which each year the youth of Athens were initiated at the annual celebrations. Thence by the process so loved by St Paul of consecrating old words to higher use it becomes the pregnant expression of the truth, 'latet in vetere novum testamentum, vetus in novo patet.' It is a truth once hidden but now revealed, a truth which may be apprehended though not comprehended. So the Atonement is a mystery, 1 Cor. ii. 1, 2, 7, the

conscience. And let these also first be proved; then let 10
them use the office of a deacon, being *found* blameless.
Even so *must their* wives *be* grave, not slanderers, sober, 11
faithful in all *things*. Let the deacons be the husbands of 12
one wife, ruling *their* children and their own houses well.
For they that have used the office of a deacon well purchase 13

Catholicity of the Church is a mystery, Eph. iii. 3, 4, 9; the Incarnation is a mystery, 1 Tim. iii. 16. In St Paul's final thought of revelation in this chapter the 'secret now told' embraces the whole of God's saving love, in one or other of its aspects, here as the 'creed of creeds,' in verse 16 as the 'work of works,' here the life of Christ, there 'the life in Christ.' We are familiar with a somewhat similar use of 'mystery' in the 'mystery plays'; and compare the word 'mystery' in the Prayer-Book Communion Office as the equivalent of 'Sacrament,'—the union of the outward and visible sign and the inward and spiritual grace, the living spirit through the lifeless matter—'the dignity of that holy mystery'; 'He hath instituted and ordained holy mysteries'; 'have duly received these holy mysteries.' See further, Appendix, G.

10. *And let these also*] These, as well as the presbyters, for whom verse 7 defines a very searching test. Bp Ellicott's note, rightly explaining that the first conjunction is 'Also,' 'Moreover,' and the second 'and' in this phrase, shews that the stress must be on 'these,' the force of the first conjunction being necessarily limited to it. Yet Alford quotes the note while saying 'there is no connexion by means of the conjunctions with the former requirements concerning presbyters.' The test or proof here too is the judgment of the general community. Cf. 2 Tim. iii. 12 for the same conjunctions.

11. *Even so* must their *wives* be *grave*] The R.V. translates literally **Women in like manner must be grave**, i.e. women deacons, favouring the general view of the earliest commentators, as Chrysostom and Theod. Mops., 'mulieres quae diaconis officium implere statuuntur,' and the latest, as Bps Wordsworth and Ellicott. Fairbairn gives well the reasons; 'the mode of expression "likewise" apparently marking a transition to another class (as at *v.* 8, ii. 9; Tit. ii. 3, 6); also the absence of the article or the pronoun to connect the women with the men spoken of before; the mention only of qualifications for deacon work, while nothing is said of those more directly bearing on domestic duties.'

slanderers] The word is only used in these Epistles, here and Tit. ii. 3 of women; in 2 Tim. iii. 3 of men. It corresponds to the 'double-tongued' above. Theod. Mops. Lat. gives 'accusatrices,' and this shews well the identity of the word with that for the great 'accuser,' the devil (*diabolus*).

faithful in all things] That is, in all the duties of a deaconess.

12. *ruling* their *children*] The sentence gives compendiously the same requirements as to domestic relationships for deacons as for presbyters; the briefer form of the latter clause favours the interpreting 'all gravity' above of the children rather than the father.

13. *purchase to themselves a good degree*] The word for 'degree'

to themselves a good degree, and great boldness in the faith
which is in Christ Jesus.
14 These *things* write I unto thee, hoping to come unto
15 thee shortly: but if I tarry long, that thou mayest know

occurs only here in N.T., having been used in LXX. for a 'step' or 'threshold,' e.g. 1 Sam. v. 5, 'the threshold of Dagon in Ashdod.' It may be compared with vi. 19, 'a good foundation,' and may, from the drift of that phrase, be interpreted so as to combine something of all the three most general explanations, (*a*) a better degree or post, promotion to the priesthood; (*b*) esteem and regard from the Church for good service; (*c*) honour and promotion from God in the final day of reckoning. In vi. 19 the right use of wealth by the wealthy is the best *basis* for the whole of the life 'which is life indeed' to be gradually built up on, in the days yet to come on earth, and the unending day after: no spiritual life can be *sound* that is not built in and upon the faithful doing of our duty in that state of life to which it may please God to call us. An illustration of the metaphor may be taken from the building of Smeaton's Eddystone Lighthouse and all lighthouses of the kind since. 'All the lower courses of stone were joggled and *morticed into the rock*, hewn for that purpose into a series of *six steplike courses*. The lower portion of the building was solid throughout, and from its peculiar dovetailing practically *but one stone with the rock upon which it was raised*.' So we may translate here with R.V. **they that have served well as deacons gain to themselves a good standing**, and interpret 'good standing' not to mean a higher post but good solid work done by them as deacons, leading (*a*) to 'boldness of speech in the faith,' the acceptable performance of functions such as St Stephen and St Philip, though deacons, were privileged to perform. We then gain a force for 'to themselves' in accordance with (*b*), adopting Theodore's comment 'though second in rank to presbyters, they will themselves have an esteem second to none,' and (we may add) real 'freedom in speaking' too, from the consciousness of their people's sympathy and support. Finally the life now is part only of the whole life; and 'life is the use of the gifts of God according to the will of God'; hence good deacon's work now is the basis (*c*) for a joyous expectation of the Master's smile of approval, 'ye have done it unto Me,' a joyous acceptance of His seal of approval, 'Be thou ruler over many things.' See Appendix, K.

the faith which is in Christ Jesus] Here, like 'the faith of the Gospel' in Phil. i. 27; Gal. iii. 23 (see Bp Lightfoot), *objective;* the doctrine and scheme of 'Christianity.' Compare James ii. 1, 'the faith of our Lord Jesus Christ'; Jude 3, 'the faith once for all delivered unto the saints.'

14—16. THE IMPORTANCE OF THESE DIRECTIONS BASED ON THE CHARACTER OF THE CHURCH AND ITS HEAD.

14. *to come unto thee shortly*] The comparative adverb if retained will have the force given by Fairbairn 'more speedily than I at one

how *thou* oughtest to behave thyself in the house of God, which is the church of the living God, the pillar and ground

time thought or than would seem to call for more detailed communications,' cf. 2 Tim. i. 18, 'very well,' lit. 'better than I need say.' Westcott and Hort however with Lachmann follow MSS. ACD in reading the substantive and preposition 'with speed.' As to the supposed inconsistency of this intention with Acts xx. 25, 38, St Paul certainly there bids the Elders of Ephesus farewell, saying that they will 'see his face no more.' But circumstances alter cases. The Spirit did not give him definite knowledge of what would befall him in every place; and it is sufficient to say that at the time he was expecting bonds and possible martyrdom and was impressed with the belief, a mistaken one, that he would not return.

15. *how* thou *oughtest to behave thyself*] There is little in the Greek words and little in the context to decide us in translating either thus with A.V. and margin of R.V. or **how men ought to behave themselves,** with R.V. For (1), *Timothy himself* is in St Paul's mind throughout; the directions are given for his guidance in seeing to a properly qualified ministry; for (2), *presbyters and deacons* have just had their proper equipment and behaviour fully detailed. Perhaps the latter is to be preferred from the long phrase (for so brief a style) 'that thou mayest know how (one) ought to walk' instead of 'in order that thou mayest walk'; and from the brevity of the style solving by omission the difficulty of finding a phrase which should include bishops, deacons, and women deacons.

behave thyself] The verb is used by St Paul twice besides, 2 Cor. i. 12, 'we have (had our conversation) behaved ourselves in the world'; Eph. ii. 3, 'we also (had our conversation) lived in the lusts of the flesh'; and the cognate substantive in the next chapter, iv. 12, 'manner of life,' and twice besides, Gal. i. 13, 'my (conversation) manner of life in time past'; Eph. iv. 22, 'put off concerning the former (conversation) manner of life the old man.' It was represented exactly by the Latin *conversari* (conversatio), whence our A.V. 'conversation' in its old sense.

the house of God] In O.T. the Temple; cf. Mk. xi. 17, 'My house shall be called a house of prayer,' quoted from Isai. lvi. 7; and then spiritually God's household and temple the chosen people, cf. Heb. iii. 6, 'Moses was faithful in all God's house as a servant, Christ as a son over God's house,' quoted from Numb. xii. 7. St Paul had elaborated the metaphor in his letter to Ephesus, ii. 22; and so in the later Epistles it is natural and appropriate as a title of Christ's Church; Heb. x. 21, 'having a great high priest over the house of God'; 1 Pet. iv. 17, 'the time is come for judgment to begin at the house of God.' See Appendix, K.

which is the church of the living God] The lengthened form of the relative is used to give the characteristic attribute 'which is, to describe it aright, the Church.' 'The Church,' *ecclesia*, is used (1) simply for 'a gathering,' 'a calling together,' i.e. the regular law-court, Acts

16 of the truth. And without controversy great is the mystery

xix. 39; (2) for 'the congregation' of the children of Israel, in LXX. constantly; (3) from this, by our Lord twice for His own constituted community, Matt. xvi. 18, xviii. 17; (4) hence, 23 times in the Acts, the first history of that community, 62 times in the Epistles of St Paul its widest organiser, and 23 times in the Epistles and Apocalypse of St John, its venerable champion and prophet; sometimes of the Church at large, as here, 'holy and Catholic,' sometimes of one or other of its constituent parts, e.g. in Asia, Galatia, Judæa, Macedonia. See Bp Browne on Art. XIX., who quotes the following among other definitions of the earliest Fathers: 'Tertullian speaks of the Church as composed of all the Churches founded by Apostles or offsprings of Apostolic Churches, and living in the unity of the same faith and discipline. The Church according to Clement of Alexandria is the assembly of the elect, the congregation of Christian worshippers; the devout Christians being as it were the spiritual life of the body of Christ, the unworthy members being like the carnal part. Origen says, "the Church is the body of Christ, animated by the Son of God, the members being all who believe in Him." The visibility of the Church he expresses by saying that "we should give no heed to those who say, There is Christ, but show Him not in the Church, which is full of brightness from the East to the West and is the pillar and ground of the truth."'

the living God] At Lystra, where 'the gods' were thought to have come down in the likeness of men, St Paul besought them to 'turn from these vanities unto *the living God* which made heaven and earth and the sea'; so now at Ephesus, where the Jewish and oriental speculations of physical and moral sciences, 'the endless genealogies of emanations and æons,' were clouding the simple truth 'as it is in Jesus,' St Paul insists on all his teachers being 'good churchmen,' holding and teaching the faith in '*one living God*' manifested in Christ Jesus.

the pillar and ground of the truth] It will be felt unworthy of the rising greatness of the passage to refer this to Timothy or to the teachers; it is *the Church* penetrated through with this faith which, as the single central column in the chapter-house at Salisbury, supports and sustains and combines all the orb of truth, God's progressive revelation of Himself in Nature, Art, Conscience. 'Christ is the centre of mankind, and mankind is the centre of the world. If that be so, we have a central point round which all knowledge groups itself. The physical and the moral sciences have each their part in the building up of the great human temple in which God dwells; and the highest education is that which gives man a complete conception of the world thus viewed as centred in humanity and in Christ, its head.' Fremantle, *The Gospel of the Secular Life*, p. 98.

There is no difficulty in a certain shifting of the metaphor, any more than in the above passage, itself a modern undesigned expansion of the phrase. The Church is, first, the house of God, and the Son

of godliness: God was manifest in the flesh, justified in the

of the living God its centre; and then this house is itself a centre, the central pillar of a larger house, the world, God's home.

16. *without controversy*] We may render, **And confessedly mighty is that holy truth revealed**, the very grain and fibre of a reverent Christian life, which counts all as 'holy ground,' for Christ is 'all in all.'

God was manifest in the flesh] The controversy is well known which has so long prevailed as to the original reading; whether the passage should begin 'God' or 'who': the Greek abbreviated form of writing 'God' being very like the Greek for 'who,' $\overline{\Theta C}$ and OC. Since the minute inspection of the Alexandrine MS. by Bps Lightfoot, Ellicott, and others, there has been general belief in the reading being 'who,' as is also the reading of ℵ, and all the Versions older than the 7th century, of Origen, Epiphanius, Jerome, Theodore, and Cyril. The neuter relative is indeed found in one uncial MS. (D^1) in the It. and Vulg. and in all the Latin Fathers except Jerome, a correction apparently to make it agree with the neuter word *mustêrion*. The support of MSS., Versions and Fathers is comparatively weak for 'God': while 'it is a most significant fact that in the Arian controversy, no one of the Catholic champions except Gregory of Nyssa produces this passage, though it would have been their strong weapon.' Dean Burgon indeed sums up strongly against a relative masc. or neut., but it seems incredible that ΘC should have been altered into OC because of the difficulty of the reading. Moreover it is difficult to understand how it could be said that *God* was justified in spirit or seen of angels or received up in glory. We take the reading 'who' unhesitatingly, and refer it to 'an omitted though easily recognised antecedent, viz. Christ.' The Person is implied in the Mystery. In Col. i. 27, He is expressly called 'this mystery among the Gentiles.' In order to bring out the personal reference contained in the word 'mystery' as followed by the masculine relative, we must render in English with R.V. **the mystery of godliness; He who**. The abruptness and the rhythmical parallelism of the passage have been very probably accounted for by supposing it to be part of one of the earliest of the Christian creeds or hymns; as in Eph. v. 14, 'Wherefore *he* saith "Awake thou that sleepest"' where the words cannot be referred to any known passages of Holy Scripture. Westcott and Hort in their new critical edition of the Greek Testament have arranged the lines in both places according to this explanation; here in two divisions, the first two clauses in each pointing to *earthly*, the third to *heavenly* relation:—

'He Who was manifested in the flesh,
Was justified in His spirit,
Was shewn to the angels,
Was proclaimed among the nations,
Was believed on in the world,
Was taken up in glory.'

Spirit, seen of angels, preached unto the Gentiles, believed
on in the world, received up into glory.

4 Now the Spirit speaketh expressly, that in the latter times

The clauses have been however divided by Fairbairn and others into *pairs;* the first pair describing Christ's human nature—*in flesh* manifested as true man, *in spirit* judged or approved as sinless man 'fulfilling all righteousness'; the second pair recording the revelation of Himself by sight to the angels, by preaching to the Gentiles—the highest and the lowest of His subjects; the third pair closing with the acceptance of Himself by faith below, by ascension into glory above. We may shew something perhaps of the rhythmical effect thus for modern ears:

'Who in *flesh* was manifested,
Pure in *spirit* was attested;
By angels' vision witnessèd,
Among the nations heralded;
By faith accepted here,
Received in glory there!'

'Manifested in the flesh' is the first part of the statement of the Incarnation; 'an historical appearance of One Who had previously existed but had been kept from the knowledge of the world'; the flesh, the material part of Christ's human nature being the sphere of His manifestation. 'Justified in the spirit' is the second part; His spirit, the highest portion of the immaterial part of His human nature, is the sphere of His justification; the challenge which He made to the Jews, 'Which of you convicteth Me of sin' was one which He could make to *His own conscience.* He was *justified* when it spake and clear when it judged (Rom. iii. 4; Ps. li. 4). See Dr Plummer, *Pastoral Epistles*, pp. 135 sqq.

On the perfection of Christ's human nature, body, soul and spirit, see Appendix, A.

Ch. IV. Apostolic Government in regard to Doctrine.

1—5. False Teachers mar the Truth of the Incarnate Redeemer.

1. *Now the Spirit speaketh*] The connexion is this. The teachers and ministers of the Church must hold her central doctrine. It stands strong and firm—a rock pillar; 'Christ the Son of the living God,' (1) incarnate, (2) redeemer of the world. But there will be, notwithstanding, false teachers, evil heresies, subverting this great mystery of Godliness. See Bp Wordsworth's note. 'For example, *forbidding to marry* is heresy, since by His incarnation the Son of God has married our Nature, has espoused to Himself a Church and so has sanctified marriage. Eph. v. 23—32. *Commanding to abstain from meats* is heresy, since if (as is implied in the command) the flesh was created by the *evil principle*, and was therefore unclean, God could not have taken human flesh and united it for ever to the Godhead: and it is heresy too, since Christ, the second

some shall depart from the faith, giving heed to seducing spirits, and doctrines of devils; speaking lies in hypocrisy, 2

Adam, recovered for us the free use of all the creatures of God and recovered for them their original benediction.'

'The Spirit,' as very frequently, put alone for 'the Holy Spirit'; *where* 'the Spirit saith expressly' and distinctly that these heresies will arise, is not clear. The words of our Lord (Matt. xxiv. 11), of the prophets in various Christian Churches, of St Paul (2 Thess. ii. 3) are referred to. But it may be best to take the passage here as itself the new and more explicit utterance by the Spirit in St Paul of what is coming; in a manner similar to St Paul's statement at Miletus of what would befall himself and the Church at Ephesus, 'the Holy Ghost testifieth unto me in every city, saying that bonds and afflictions abide me...I know that... from among your ownselves shall men arise speaking perverse things.' Acts xx. 23, 29.

expressly] The Greek word is postclassical and occurs here only in N.T. As applied to the operation of the Spirit it is very remarkable as implying more than illumination or influence—direct communication understood to be such by the recipient.

in the latter times] Perhaps as R.V. **in later times**, as distinguishing this phrase from 'the last days,' 2 Tim. iii. 1. So Huther, 'The former points simply to the future, the latter to the last time of the future.' But the distinction must not be too much pressed: the 'later times' predicted here are surely the 'last hour' spoken of by St John (1 Joh. ii. 18) some 25 years later, if, as Bp Westcott says of the date of that letter, 'this may be fixed with reasonable likelihood in the last decade of the first century.' He adds on ii. 18, 'the last days are found in each of the seasons of fierce trial which precede the several comings of Christ. The phrase marks a period of critical change.'

shall depart from the faith] R.V. **fall away**, as the parent of a word afterwards used still more definitely, 'apostate.' 'The faith' objectively as above.

seducing spirits] Here opposed to 'the Spirit,' as in 1 Joh. iv. 6, giving the history of what is here prophecy, we have the cognate substantive: the adjective 'deceiving' or 'deceiver' occurs Matt. xxvii. 63, 'that deceiver said,' and 2 Cor. vi. 8, but is used in 2 Joh. 7, evidently with reference to the same heresy as here. The substantive has been rendered by A.V. sometimes 'deceit,' sometimes 'error;' by R. V. always 'error.' These deceiving spirits, as Bp Ellicott says, are the spiritual emissaries of Satan which work in their hearts; cf. Eph. vi. 12. See 1 Joh. iv. 3, where the proof of a spirit being 'not of God' is the failure to confess the Incarnation. 'The many false spirits represent one personal power of falsehood, the prince of the world (John xii. 31), the devil, whose "children" the wicked are (1 Joh. iii. 10). The many false prophets stand in a relation towards the Spirit like that which the "many Antichrists" occupy towards Christ. *Through them evil spiritual powers find expression.*' Westcott.

doctrines of devils] The last sentence seems an exact paraphrase of this clause, the instructions given by the evil spirits to the false teachers

3 having their conscience seared with a hot iron; forbidding
to marry, *and commanding* to abstain from meats, which
God hath created to be received with thanksgiving of them
4 which believe and know the truth. For every creature of

used by them as 'their organs through whom to speak.' 'Devils' or 'demons' is clearly thus a subjective genitive. The word 'demon' in general classical usage signified intermediate beings, the messengers of the Gods to men. The notion of *evil* demons was due to the later influences of the East, and in LXX. the word is generally used of the heathen idols, Ps. xcv. 3; cf. 1 Cor. x. 19, 20; but Josephus employs it always of evil spirits, *Bell. Jud.* vii. 6, § 3. Cf. Acts xix. 12, 13, James ii. 19. From the N.T. we gather certainly that the demons are agents of Satan in his work of evil, probably that they must be the same as 'the angels of the devil,' Matt. xxv. 41; Rev. xii. 7, 9, 'the principalities and powers' against whom we 'wrestle.' See Bp Barry, *Dict. Bib.*

2. *speaking lies in hypocrisy*] Rather, as R.V. **through the hypocrisy of men that speak lies**, that is, the 'false prophets,' 'many of whom,' we read, by the time of the writing of 1 Joh. iv. 1, 'are gone out into the world' as the scene of their activity; cf. Westcott's note there. 'The words point, as it appears, to the great outbreak of the Gentile pseudo-Christianity which is vaguely spoken of as Gnosticism, the endeavour to separate the ideas of the Faith from the facts of the historic Redemption.'

having their conscience seared] Lit. **branded as to their own conscience**, grown callous in their own case as flesh would with the branding of hot iron: the word is found nowhere else in N.T. Individually conscious of their *own* responsibility, they were like branded slaves who *knew* their guilt.

3. *forbidding to marry*] See on verse 1 and Introduction, pp. 46, 48, 50, 51. From the verb 'forbidding' must be supplied by the rule called *zeugma* (Winer, § 661 e), the positive 'bidding' with the infinitive 'to abstain from meats.' 'Meats' is to be understood in its older sense 'food for eating,' though abstinence from *animal food* was the distinctive rule of the developed Gnostic systems, such as that of the Encratites or Purists under Tatian.

to be received with thanksgiving of them which believe and know] The comma of A.V. (Parallel N.T.) after 'believe' (though inserted to prevent its being understood to mean 'believe the truth') has been omitted by R.V., apparently because there is only one article for the two clauses, and therefore they describe the same people under slightly different aspects: while the insertion might seem to make a higher class *among* those that believe, viz. those that know the truth fully, and to give the privilege of thus partaking to it only.

The word for 'know' is most exactly **have come to full knowledge of**, and implies that full experience of God's will and ways which is open to all who have become 'adherents of the faith,' 'faithful.' Cf. note on iii. 4.

4. *every creature of God is good*] Creation in all its parts is meant,

God *is* good, and nothing to be refused, if it be received
with thanksgiving: for it is sanctified by the word of God 5

everything made by God; for this use of the word 'creature' from Lat. *creatura* compare the Communion Office in the Prayer-Book, 'receiving these Thy creatures of bread and wine.' All God's workmanship 'is good, and was so pronounced by God Himself at the moment of creation.' Fairbairn.

'We read in Gen. viii. 21, "I will not again curse the ground any more for man's sake;" and the Psalms always speak of this earth and of all created things as if there was no curse at all on them; saying that "all things serve God, and continue as they were at the beginning;" and that "He has given them a law which cannot be broken;" and in the face of those words let who will talk of the earth being cursed, I will not; and you shall not if I can help it.' Kingsley, *Good News of God*, p. 35.

'Oh the yearning when one sees a beautiful thing to make someone else see it too! Surely it is of Heaven!...Every creature of God is good if it be sanctified with prayer and thanksgiving! This to me is the master truth of Christianity! I cannot make people see it, but it seems to me that it was to redeem man and the earth that Christ was made man and used the earth.' Kingsley, *Letters*, Abr. ed., I. p. 72.

nothing to be refused] The form of the Greek favours the making this a separate sentence as R.V., **nothing is to be rejected**.

5. *for it is sanctified by the word of God and prayer*] Rather, **through**. The 'word of God' is most commonly in N.T. 'the gospel' generally, Acts iv. 31, 1 Cor. xiv. 36, Col. i. 25, 1 Thess. ii. 2, 8, 9, 13, Rev. xx. 4; sometimes more pointedly 'the word which *God speaks* through His messengers or immediately in the heart of each man, Heb. iv. 12, 1 Pet. i. 23, Tit. i. 3; sometimes still more specifically, the very Son of God Himself, the Word incarnate, Joh. i. 1, 1 Joh. i. 1, Rev. xix. 13. But it is also the record of God's will and truth as declared by the Old Testament lawgivers and prophets, Mk. vii. 13, Rom. ix. 6. And so with Huther, Ellicott, Conybeare, Lightfoot and Alford, we understand it here of O.T. declarations of God's creating and sustaining goodness incorporated in the 'invocation.' We take it to imply that the thanksgiving was commonly made in some Scriptural words, such as those quoted from a primitive grace before meat (*Apostolical Constitutions*, VII. 49), which begins 'Blessed art thou, O Lord, Who nurturest me from my youth up, Who givest food to all flesh.' Compare the Latin Version of Ps. cxlv. 15:

Oculi omnium in Te sperant, Domine,
Et Tu das escam illis in tempore.

The word for 'prayer' here is the same as that rendered 'intercessions' in ii. 1, where the meaning is discussed. Here perhaps it is chosen as more directly expressing the recognition of God's particular providence; each recipient of 'daily bread,' after reciting the very words of God speaking to him and giving him every good gift, is to speak in his turn face to face with God and pray with thankful heart for blessings to others, '*Our* Father, give *us* our daily bread.' The *whole* life of a Christian

6 and prayer. If thou put the brethren in remembrance of
these *things*, thou shalt be a good minister of Jesus Christ,
nourished up in the words of faith and of good doctrine,

(and therefore everything of which he partakes) is sanctified through the word of God and prayer.

The bearing of this passage on the social and religious question of total abstinence from alcoholic drink is seen in the following note of Fairbairn; all the better because he is evidently not thinking specially of that particular form of abstinence:

'Scripture indeed does not deny that a person may occasionally abstain from certain meats or from marriage, with advantage to his own spiritual life or the good of the kingdom of God (Matt. vi. 16, 17, xvii. 21, xix. 12; 1 Cor. vii. 32—37). But in such cases the alternative is not put as between a relatively pure and perfect state by the one course, and an impure or defective one by the other; but the one is presented merely as affording opportunities or helps for prosecuting more freely and unreservedly the work of faith than can well be done in the other. If temporary fasting should dispose and enable one to fight more successfully against the lusts of the flesh, or if by abstaining from marriage one could in particular spheres of labour, or in certain conjunctures of the Church's history, more effectually serve the interests of the Gospel than otherwise, then the higher principles of that Gospel, the nobler ends of a Christian calling, will undoubtedly justify the restraint or the sacrifice. But to do this is only to subordinate a less to a greater good: it creates no factitious distinctions in respect to the allowable or forbidden, holy or unholy, in the ordinary relationship and circumstances of life; and calls for a rejection of the natural good in these only when it may be conducive as means to a definite spiritual end.'

6—16. TIMOTHY'S OWN HOLD OF RIGHT DOCTRINE AND RIGHT DISCIPLINE.

6. *in remembrance*] R.V. has **in mind**, the Greek not so strongly implying a re-presentation of these points as a 'representation' in our modern sense; Chrysostom, 'as one giving counsel let him present these things.'

these things] Taking up verse 15 of ch. iii. which introduced the statement following (iii. 15—iv. 5) of **the faith and the good doctrine**. Observe the articles in this latter clause.

Jesus Christ] Again with MSS. transpose, **Christ Jesus.**

nourished] Compare the Prayer-Book Collect for 2nd Sun. in Advent, 'Grant that we may in such wise hear (all Holy Scriptures), read, mark, learn, and *inwardly digest*.' Alford, 'to grow up amongst or be trained in,' comparing Eur. *Phoen.* 368, 'the gymnasia, in which I was brought up.'

whereunto thou hast attained] Rather, **which thou hast always closely followed**: 'hast always' rendering the idea of the perfect, the settled permanent state, better than 'until now' of the R.V.; 'closely'

whereunto thou hast attained. But refuse profane and old 7
wives' fables, and exercise thyself *rather* unto godliness.

rendering the preposition in the compound verb as in the preface of St Luke's Gospel, i. 3, 'having traced the course;' cf. 2 Tim. iii. 10.

7. *refuse profane and old wives' fables*] This clause Westcott and Hort connect by a comma with the preceding rather than the following sentence. Surely to connect so closely the future 'thou shalt be' and the imperative 'refuse' is an unnecessary awkwardness; R.V. taking the same general view of the connexion gives the colon before and the full stop after the clause. It is of less consequence as the subject is continuous either way. If the article with 'fables' points back to the 'doctrines of devils' and the 'lies' of *vv.* 1, 2, yet the 'godliness' and the 'hope in *the living* God who is the *Saviour of all men*' point back also to the 'truth' and the 'mystery' of iii. 15, 16.

refuse] Another of the characteristic words of these Epistles; used as here 2 Tim. ii. 23, and of refusing persons, 1 Tim. v. 11; Tit. iii. 10. In all the other passages of N. T. it has the earlier sense of *deprecor*, 'beg off,' 'decline;' Luke xiv. 18, 'with one consent began to beg off;' Acts xxv. 11, 'If I have committed anything worthy of death I do not beg off from death;' Heb. xii. 19 'they that heard begged off from any word more being spoken.'

profane] As opposed to the godliness of iii. 16, and characteristic of the phraseology of these Epistles; cf. note on i. 9. As 'godliness' is seen to be more and more bound up with a reverent grasp of true doctrine, so the self-willed fancies of heretical teaching are 'profane' as ignoring or denying the present working of the living God.

old wives' fables] For the justification of this epithet see Introd. p. 49; cf. also Appendix, B. The article, the order of the words, and the present tense, have their proper force by rendering the whole sentence, **But those profane and old wives' fables refuse steadily.**

and exercise thyself rather] R.V. omits 'rather' of A.V., connecting with what follows. The conjunction itself admits of being taken either as a stronger contrast with preceding, 'and...rather,' or as a weaker, taking up a somewhat new point following, 'and moreover.' The 'exercising' is taken by most commentators to contain an implied rebuke of the corporeal austerities for religion's sake taught by one school of the earliest Gnostics. But the word has a definitely recognised metaphorical meaning by this time. Cf. the use in 2 Pet. ii. 14, 'a heart trained in covetousness'; Heb. v. 14, 'by reason of use have their senses trained to discern'; Heb. xii. 11, 'them that have been trained by chastening.' And St Paul's use of strong nervous words of command to brace up his younger comrade should make us lay more stress on this word of vigorous metaphor, and less perhaps on godliness; 'do more than acquiesce in correct doctrine and godly dispositions; pursue a vigorous course of training; practise well and widely how to teach both Christian truth and Christian life.' So Theod. Mops. Lat. interprets 'exercitationem' as 'diligentiam doctrinae,'...'ut alios cum omni diligentia ista instruat.' See Appendix, K.

8 For bodily exercise profiteth little: but godliness is profitable unto all *things*, having promise of the life that now is,

8. *bodily exercise profiteth little*] Rather, with R.V., **bodily exercise is profitable for a little**. The Latin of Theod. Mops. gives the straightforward and natural account: 'corporalis exercitatio ad modicum est utilis' (so Vulgate 'ad modicum'): 'qui enim in agone sunt corporali et ad hoc seipsos exercent usque in praesentem uitam, inde solent habere solatium; nam pietatis agon et istius exercitatio ex multis partibus nobis magnum praebet iumentum promittens nobis in futuro saeculo magna praebere; nam secundum praesentem uitam conferre nobis non minima potest.' St Paul, after choosing the strong metaphorical word to enforce the need for a zealous, painstaking ministry, dwells on the metaphor according to his habit. For his fondness for this metaphor see Howson, *Metaphors of St Paul*. Cf. Appendix, K.

godliness is profitable] The 'pietatis agon' affects for good, as Alford puts it, 'not one portion only of a man's being, but every portion of it, bodily and spiritual, temporal and eternal.'

promise of the life] Lit. 'promise of life, that which is life now, and that which will be.' Bp Ellicott and Dr Alford, both after hesitation, interpret 'spiritual happiness and holiness, the highest blessedness of the creature;' but Alford wrongly alters the 'promise' into the 'blessedness promised' instead of giving 'life' its full and proper meaning. Cf. Mk. x. 30 and the extract quoted by Dr Maclear from Lange's *Life of Christ*, III. 459, 'The Christian gains back again already in this world in the higher form of real spiritual essence whatever in the physical and symbolical form of his life he has forfeited; houses enough in the entertainment afforded him by his spiritual associates who receive him; brothers and sisters, in the highest sense of the term; mothers who bless and tend the life of his soul; children of his spirit; lands, of his activity, of his higher enjoyment of nature, of his delights; and all this ever purer, ever richer, as an unfolding of that eternal inheritance of which it is said "All things are yours," in spite of whatever persecutions of the world which dim the glory of these things.' See also Bp Westcott's additional note on 1 John v. 20, where he quotes St Paul's phrase, 'the life which is life indeed.' Observe by the way how there this life needs '*to be grasped and laid hold of*,' as here it is promised to *spiritual training and contest*. Compare also Eph. iv. 18, 'the life of God.'

Both 'the life now' and 'the life to come' are clearly parts of 'eternal life.' Bp Westcott's concluding paragraph is worthy of St Paul in its realisation of what 'the promise' is and its incitement to the necessary 'training.'

'If now we endeavour to bring together the different traits of "the eternal life," we see that it is a life which with all its fulness and all its potencies is *now;* a life which extends beyond the limits of the individual, and preserves, completes, crowns individuality by placing the part in connexion with the whole: a life which satisfies while it quickens aspiration: a life which is seen, as we regard it patiently,

and of that which is to come. *This is* a faithful saying and 9
worthy of all acceptation. For therefore we both labour 10

to be capable of conquering, reconciling, uniting the rebellious discordant broken elements of being on which we look and which we bear about with us; a life which gives unity to the constituent parts and to the complex whole, which brings together heaven and earth, which offers the sum of existence in one thought. As we reach forth to grasp it, the revelation of God is seen to have been unfolded in its parts in Creation; and the parts are seen to have been brought together again by the Incarnation.'

Note the direct bearing of the last sentence on St Paul's doctrine here from iii. 15 to iv. 10.

9. This is *a faithful saying*] R.V. again, **Faithful is the saying**, following the Greek construction. But 'It is a faithful saying,' is equally correct according to English idiom. The A.V. and R.V. end the verse with a full stop, leaving us apparently little liberty to make verse 10 the 'faithful saying.' On the other hand A.V. (Parallel N.T.) gives a colon; and Drs Westcott and Hort alter the colon into a comma, as Conybeare gives it, Faithful is the saying and worthy of all acceptance,—'*For to this end we endure labour &c.*' Bp Ellicott's objection to this, that the 'for' must be the Apostle's and not part of the quotation, is set aside by the undoubted quotation from Cleanthes and from Aratus made by St Paul, Acts xvii. 28, 'For we are also his offspring:' see Aratus' *Phaenomena*:

'We need him all,
For we are e'en his offspring.'

10. *therefore we both labour*] **In view of this**, namely, our hope fixed on the fulness of the blessing of life from the *living* God, a present and a future salvation, 'goodness and loving-kindness to us and to all men, creation, preservation, and all the blessings of this life,' enjoyed to the full only by the faithful, and above all 'the redemption of the world, the means of grace, and the hope of glory' realised with 'a due sense of the inestimable love' only by the faithful; in view of such a glorifying of our being, of all being, any amount of 'toil and moil,' any strain of keenest contest is worth while. We may render the whole 'faithful saying' thus:

'Right well for such a wage and prize
We toil, we wrestle on
Till hope's far goal be won,
Love's full salvation, Life that lies
In God the Living One
For each created son—
Full Life, where Faith to Love replies.'

we both labour and suffer reproach] The balance of MS. authority is for the omission of 'both' and the substitution of 'strive,' 'wrestle,' for 'suffer reproach.' The internal appropriateness which has been

and suffer reproach, because we trust in the living God, who is the Saviour of all men, specially of those that believe.
11 These *things* command and teach.

thought to require the latter seems altogether from the foregoing paraphrase to suit the change: a superficial adaptation of this passage to the somewhat similar 'faithful saying' of 2 Tim. ii. 11, 12 may have caused the reading 'suffer reproach.' But the tone here and in Ep. to Titus is 'work,'—the buoyant tone of one who has been set free to 'labour in the Lord:' in 2 Tim. the deeper shade of 'suffering' has settled on the prison cell. Accordingly in his peroration in ch. vi. 12 St Paul takes up the word and metaphor, 'Fight the good fight of the faith;' while in 2 Tim. iv. 7 he looks back from the prison cell on his own strife as finished, 'I have fought the good fight.' The metaphor had long been a favourite with him, e.g. 1 Cor. ix. 25, where the word is translated in full by R.V., 'Every man *that striveth in the games* is temperate in all things.' See Appendix, E, and K.

we trust] More correctly 'we have hoped and still hope' the 'larger hope,' that God is

'love indeed
And love Creation's final law.'

The perfect expresses a 'Hope that never lost her youth.' The aorist has less MS. authority.

the Saviour of all men] In a lower sense; (1) for the body, in the supply of a present earthly care, and in the blessing of all earth's good gifts, through His living love, the curse being removed through Christ's coming; (2) for the soul, in the supply of the light of Christ to the conscience, such that where revelation has not come, the soul can still live, if it will, the life of God here through Christ unrecognised and hereafter through Christ revealed. 'I am the light of the world,' Joh. viii. 12; 'That was the true light, even the light which lighteth every man, coming into the world,' Joh. i. 9.

specially of those that believe] In a higher sense; (1) through the Christian's quickened enjoyment of all earth's beauties and happinesses, and the transmuting of earthly losses into gains; (2) through the Christian's response of Faith to Love. 'That life which I *now* live in the flesh I live in faith, the faith which is in the Son of God who loved me and gave himself up for me,' Gal. ii. 20; 'He that followeth Me shall not walk in the darkness but shall have the light of life,' Joh. viii. 12. In both cases it is a present salvation that is chiefly in view, both of body and of soul; but in both cases the life that now is, of body and of soul, is only part of the whole life of which the living God is Saviour.

See Lange's and Bp Westcott's notes above. This one last word 'the faithful,' 'baptized believers,' 'holders of the Christian faith,' gathers up the great mystery of Creation, Incarnation, Redemption, from iii. 15 to iv. 11, and sets the great revelation of God in Christ the living Saviour against the 'lies' and 'fables' of men and devils.

Let no *man* despise thy youth; but be thou an example 12
of the believers, in word, in conversation, in charity, in
spirit, in faith, in purity. Till I come, give attendance to 13
reading, to exhortation, to doctrine. Neglect not the gift 14

'Strong Son of God, immortal Love,
Whom we that have not seen Thy Face
By faith and faith alone embrace,
Believing where we cannot prove,—
Thine are these orbs of light and shade,
Thou madest Life in man and brute.'

The more usual interpretation of the verse may be given in Bp Woodford's words: 'God is the Saviour of all, because He willeth the salvation of all and delivered up His Son for us all (Rom. viii. 32). He is in a more complete sense the Saviour of His faithful, because in them His gracious will takes effect through the cooperation of their own freewill with His divine will.' For extracts from Dr Barrow's famous sermons on the text, and for Prof. Birks's view of the passage giving a special aspect of the 'larger hope,' see Appendix, F.

11. *These* things *command and teach*] The link between the paragraphs. 'Lay down against all comers the true Gospel; shew no boyish shrinking; on every side of conduct and character command imitation.'

12. *in conversation*] **In behaviour**; the verb occurs above iii. 15; see note. It is an especial favourite of St Peter's, noun and verb occurring 10 times in his short Epistles. The five words describe five stages, from the most defined external to the most defined internal characteristics—speech, behaviour, love, faith, purity; *love* as it were belonging equally to the inner and the outer self, and combining all. 'The greatest is love.' Yet the special emphasis is on 'purity,' the word itself occurring only here and in v. 2, though another form of the word is used in the similar catalogue, 2 Cor. vi. 6. The same connexion of 'youth' and 'purity' is in St Paul's mind in 2 Tim. ii. 22, 'flee also youthful lusts.' Timothy, at 36 years, was young compared with St Paul and the presbyters. See Introd. pp. 56 sqq. Cf. also the use of the Latin *iuvenis*, for military service up to 40 years; e.g. Liv. i. 43.

in charity, in spirit, in faith] There is no sufficient MS. authority for 'in spirit'; it is curious that A reads 'in spirit' instead of 'in faith' in ii. 7. The phrase, most common in St Paul's earlier Epistles, has left his latest language.

13. *Till I come*] The present indic. (instead of future indic. or aorist subjunctive) is found Luke xix. 13, 'trade ye herewith till I come;' Joh. xxi. 22, 'if I will that he tarry till I come.' The right reading in the former passage, dative of relative with preposition (instead of conjunction), shews how the usage has come; 'during the time in which I am on my way,' 'whilst I am a-coming.'

to reading, to exhortation, to doctrine] The 'public reading' as in the other two places where the noun occurs, Acts xiii. 15, 'after the reading

that is in thee, which was given thee by prophecy, with the
15 laying on of the hands of the presbytery. Meditate upon
these *things;* give thyself wholly to them; that thy profiting

of the law;' 2 Cor. iii. 14 'at the reading of the old covenant;' and similarly 'public exhortation' as in the same verse of the Acts, xiii. 15, 'if ye have any word of exhortation,' cf. also Acts xv. 31, 32; and similarly 'public teaching,' A.V. 'doctrine' in its old sense; cf. Rom. xii. 7, 8, where 'teaching' and 'exhorting' are joined; 'he that teacheth, to his teaching, or he that exhorteth, to his exhorting;' the three parts of the public 'ministry of the Word,' reading, expounding, enforcing. The Bishop's charge in the Ordering of Priests in our Prayer-Book clearly quotes the verse in this sense, '*with doctrine and exhortation taken out of the Holy Scriptures*, and with a life agreeable to the same.'

14. *the gift that is in thee*] The connexion here and round the parallel verse 2 Tim. i. 6 implies a gift for ruling and teaching, distinct from the gift conferred through 'the laying on' of St Paul's hands at Ephesus, Acts xix. 6, the extraordinary gifts of speaking with tongues, &c., from the Holy Spirit; gifts still imparted at this time, as we learn from 1 Pet. iv. 10, 'according as each hath received a gift;' and continued (with change of outward manifestation) uninterruptedly since, as the 'grace of Confirmation or Laying on of Hands.' The gift here is connected with '*prophecy*,' and 'the laying on of the hands of *the presbyters*,' and follows immediately upon the public 'ministry of the word.' The 'prophecy' will naturally be the same as 'the prophecies which went before,' i. 18: and the preposition rendered 'by' in A.V. and R.V. should have the same force as it has in Gal. iii. 19, 'the law ordained through (A.V. 'by') angels,'—a force seen from the synonymous phrase Acts vii. 53, 'who received the law, as it was ordained by angels,' lit. 'unto ordinances of angels'. As angels were the ministrants and attendants of the Great Lawgiver, so the surrounding ratifying witnesses of the bestowal on Timothy of the 'Grace of Orders' were the 'prophecies,' 'going before,' and 'attending,' 'heralds and pursuivants.' Compare the use in 2 Tim. ii. 2, and see note. See Introduction, p. 58.

the presbytery] The word occurs in Lk. xxii. 66 for the body of rulers of the synagogue; and again in Acts xxii. 5, side by side with the use of the word 'presbyters' in connexion with the Christian community, Acts xi. 30, xv. 2, xxi. 18. In the synagogue it included the 'chief priest' as we see from both the passages above; so surely its earliest Christian use here, drawn from that older use still living side by side, *must* include St Paul himself as the chief ruler.

15. *Meditate upon these* things] Rather, to give in our idiom the emphasis of the pronoun in the two clauses, **This life, this work, this gift, be diligent in practising, be wholly given up to them.** Both phrases are classical and are illustrated by the well-known line of Horace *Sat.* I. 9, 2, 'nescio quid meditans nugarum et totus in illis;' where *meditans* refers to the poet's practisings and literary efforts not to mere 'pensive meditation.' So in the compound word Lk. xxi. 14 'not to meditate beforehand what to answer.'

may appear to all. Take heed unto thyself, and unto the 16
doctrine; continue in them: for in doing this thou shalt
both save thyself, and them that hear thee.
Rebuke not an elder, but intreat *him* as a father; *and* 5
the younger *men* as brethren; the elder *women* as mothers; 2
the younger as sisters, with all purity. Honour widows 3

thy profiting] Better, with R.V., **thy progress**, giving to this word its full original force as in 'The Pilgrim's *Progress*.' The Greek word is a late-formed noun belonging to a classical verb, signifying to advance, as an army would do cutting down trees in the way. Cf. Phil. i. 12, 25 and Lightfoot. So Lk. ii. 52, 'Jesus increased.'

16. *the doctrine*] Again, **thy teaching**; 'thyself' sums up verses 12 and 14, 'thy teaching,' verse 13, so that the plural **continue in them** is quite natural. The best punctuation is, with Drs Hort and Westcott, to put only semicolons at the end of *v.* 15 and in *v.* 16, shewing that the reference is the same throughout. It is interesting to compare the version of this passage given in the Prayer-Book (the Form for Consecration of Bishops), to be said by the Archbishop on delivering the Bible: 'Give heed unto reading, exhortation, and doctrine. Think upon the things contained in this Book. Be diligent in them, that the increase coming thereby may be manifest unto all men. Take heed unto thyself, and to doctrine, and be diligent in doing them; for by so doing thou shalt both save thyself and them that hear thee.'

continue in them] Lit. 'abide by them,' 'cling to them.' This is the proper force of the compound verb in St Paul. See Rom. vi. 1; Col. i. 23; Phil. i. 24.

Ch. V. Apostolic Government in regard to Discipline.

1, 2. Timothy's demeanour generally towards his flock.

1. *Rebuke not an elder*] The Greek for 'rebuke' occurring only here in N. T. is a strong word implying roughness and sharpness. Timothy was not to go so far as St Paul went in his rebuke of St Peter, Gal. ii. 11, 'I resisted him to the face because he stood condemned;' much less to copy his rebuke of Ananias, Acts xxiii. 3, 'God shall smite thee, thou whited wall.' See in the Prayer-Book Order for the Consecration of Bishops, the prayer that the new bishop may be 'earnest to reprove, beseech and rebuke, with all patience and doctrine.' This seems exactly to cover the ground held by the next word 'intreat,' again (as in i. 3, ii. 1) to be rendered **exhort**. The word 'elder' is here used of *age*, 'your seniors,' and later of *office*, 'your presbyters,' as the contexts shew.

the younger men *as brethren*] Supply a general verb recalling both the previous verbal notions, such as 'treat,' 'admonish;' cf. Mk. xii. 5, 'and many others (they ill-treated), beating some and killing some,' Rom. xiv. 21, 'It is good not to eat flesh nor to drink wine, nor (to do anything) whereby thy brother stumbleth,' Winer, § 64, I. I. C.

2. *with all purity*] Accurately **in**; the R.V. shews the connexion

4 that are widows indeed. But if any widow have children
or nephews, let them learn first to shew piety at home, and

of the phrase with 'the younger' by a colon instead of comma after 'mothers.' Jerome's rule is well quoted here 'omnes puellas et virgines Christi aut aequaliter ignora aut aequaliter dilige.' There is no simpler safeguard against illnatured remark and gossip than to maintain ***an even level*** of careful courteous intercourse, and what old George Herbert calls 'grave liveliness.'

3—16. TIMOTHY'S DUTIES IN REGARD TO WIDOWS.

Counsel on alms and charities for widows. The natural and obvious view of this passage studied in itself is to present *the Church charities* of this period as having reached an intermediate stage between the common purse or daily ministration of Acts ii. 45, vi. 1, and the order of widows publicly appointed and maintained with specified duties of education, superintendence and the like, which seems to have arisen later, perhaps from a strained interpretation of this passage itself, and which was abolished by the 11th Canon of the Council of Laodicea. 'The women who are called by the Greeks "presbyters," and by us "senior widows," "once-wives," and "churchmothers" ought not to have a position as an ordained body in the Church.' Such a view is exactly parallel with that of *the Church polity* in these Epistles as 'intermediate between the presbyterian episcopacy of the earlier apostolic period and the post-apostolic episcopacy.'

If this is correct, we shall not distinguish, with Bp Ellicott, 'the desolate and destitute widow' of *vv.* 3—8 from 'the ecclesiastical or presbyteral widow' of *vv.* 9—16. More distinct and definite direction is given in verse 10 for the selection of the widows who are described in general terms in verse 5. A generation of Christian life has passed now since the loving undiscriminating 'ministration' of the first days. The very numbers of 'Christian widows' with varying character and circumstances, as well as the reasonableness of the thing itself, require the test of the past conduct, *v.* 10, and the present life, *v.* 5. 'Charity organisation' is the pastor's duty.

3. *Honour widows*] The honour implied is further referred to in *v.* 9; as the honour of *v.* 17 is defined by *v.* 18. So in Acts xxviii. 10 the Melitans 'honoured us with many honours, and when we sailed they put on board such things as we needed.' Cf. Lewin's note there. 'The honours probably included pecuniary aid. *Honor* was often used for money; whence *honorarium* a fee.'

that are widows indeed] So *v.* 16; and in the true text vi. 19, 'the life which is life indeed:' a usage of the article with this adverb peculiar to this Epistle.

4. *children or nephews*] Rather, **grandchildren**, 'nephews' no longer having this meaning as in the time of Jeremy Taylor, who says, 'If naturalists say true, that nephews are often liker to their grandfathers than to their fathers.' Cf. *Bible Word Book*, s.v.

to shew piety] The deeper meaning given to this word above, ii. 2,

to requite *their* parents: for that is good and acceptable
before God. Now she that is a widow indeed, and desolate, 5
trusteth in God, and continueth in supplications and prayers
night and day. But she that liveth in pleasure is dead 6

iii. 8, &c., is not lost here, though it be *practical* godliness. Our Lord's own teaching on this very subject, Matt. xv. 3—6, is just this word, 'writ large.'

to shew piety at home] More accurately **towards their own house.** If it is a little strained to speak of the children learning to shew piety towards their own house when the care of parents or grandparents is meant, it is much more strained to speak of aged widows requiting their parents by the care of their own children or grandchildren. 'Let the children learn,' then it should run. In answer to Bp Wordsworth's objections to this, notice (1) that the Apostle's whole subject is Christian duty *towards* widows, (2) that the repetition in *v.* 16 is only in keeping with other repetitions of the passage, (3) that the word 'learn' here has a clause dependent upon it and so differs in sense from *v.* 13, ii. 11, and 2 Tim. iii. 7, where it is absolute. The plural verb is used, although the subject to be supplied is in the neuter, according to the common N.T. use in the case of persons: e.g. Matt. x. 21, 'children shall rise up.' So the plural verb should be read, 2 Tim. iv. 17, 'that all the Gentiles might hear.' Winer, § 58, 3.

to requite their *parents*] Lit., 'to give due returns to their forbears,' using the old Scotch word, which, as Fairbairn says, exactly corresponds in its including parents and grandparents.

For the phrase 'to give due returns' which only occurs in N. T. here but is thoroughly classical, cf. Eur. *Or.* 467, where Orestes speaks of Tyndareus 'who reared me, kissed me, carried me about,' and then of 'the base returns that I requited him' in slaying his reputed daughter Clytemnestra.

good and acceptable] With R.V. following MS. authority, we should read **acceptable** alone; the addition has been made from ii. 3.

5. *trusteth in God*] The perfect of a continuing settled state, as in ii. 14 'is found in transgression;' so here 'is found with a full hope placed upon God,' **hath her hope set in God.** The same perfect is in iv. 10, taking there however the dative after the preposition, 'we have our hope *resting on* the living God.'

continueth] The same compound, strong, word as in Acts xiii. 43, 'to continue in the grace of God;' its strength is seen in its use, Acts xi. 23, 'that they would *cleave unto* the Lord.'

in supplications and prayers] 'As the words stand, both having the article, prayer is subdivided into its two kinds; if the article were not repeated, prayer and intercession would be taken together as forming one whole,' Winer, § 19, 5, n. See note on ii. 1 for the strict meaning of the two words and for their use in the plural. Compare Acts ii. 42, 'they continued steadfastly...in the prayers.'

6. *liveth in pleasure*] The word occurs only once besides in N.T., James v. 5; where it is coupled with 'living delicately,' and is trans-

7 while she liveth. And these *things* give in charge, that
8 they may be blameless. But if any provide not for his
own, and specially for those of his own house, he hath
9 denied the faith, and is worse than an infidel. Let not a

lated by R.V. 'have taken your pleasure,' consistently with its rendering here 'giveth herself to pleasure.' But surely all the connexion and derivation of the word points to a worse meaning, the rioting of a prodigal; as e.g. its use by the LXX. (as Bp Ellicott points out) in Ezek. xvi. 49, 'this was the iniquity of thy sister Sodom, pride, fulness of bread, and abundance of idleness was in her and in her daughters.' It is reproduced in the cognate 'wax wanton' of *v.* 11. Render perhaps **she that liveth a prodigal's life**. Stress is laid on this being brought out, because St Paul is painting the two pictures, for contrast, in the strongest colours, one all saint, one all sinner.

is dead while she liveth] Has no 'hold on the life which is life indeed,' as urged vi. 19.

7. *these* things *give in charge*] As in iv. 11 and thrice in chap. i.; note on i. 5. The conjunction is **also** rather than 'and'. 'Include the setting of the true life before the widows also in thy charge.'

blameless] One of the key-words of this epistle; of a presbyter iii. 2, of Timothy vi. 14. At the stage reached now by Christianity, the moral life of the believers before the world, 'such as cannot be laid hold of by anyone,' is of vital importance for all ranks equally—for the bishop-apostolic himself, for the clergy, for the poor widows. 'Holiness becometh Thine house' now most especially.

8. *But if any provide not*] The warning is general in form, but taken up *v.* 4 and is again taken up *v.* 16. The negative must be taken closely with the verb **fail to provide**, see note on iii. 5.

for his own] His own relatives and connexions.

According to the best reading there is only one article for the two adjectives, so that it is one phrase rather than two. The R.V. indicates this by omitting the 'for' after 'specially'. By rendering also **his own household** it indicates the full meaning 'relatives and dependents dwelling in the same house.'

he hath denied the faith] The Christian religion based on 'faith that worketh by love,' and so here the Christian's 'rule of life,' briefly described in the earliest days as 'the way,' Acts xxii. 4, &c. There is the same close identification of 'creed' and 'life' in verse 12, where see note.

worse than an infidel] Better, as throughout its use so characteristic of the Epistles to the Corinthians (14 times), **an unbeliever**. It was the technical word for the heathen who had not yet 'professed the faith,' just as its opposite 'faithful' or 'believer' is the term used of all who had been admitted into the Christian body; e.g. Eph. i. 1, and here, verse 16. The clause has no sting therefore such as attaches to 'infidel,' implying the deliberate rejection of religion. They who refuse to minister to the comfort and sustenance of those belonging to them 'are not true to the moral instincts of their own nature and

widow be taken into the number under threescore years
old, having been the wife of one man, well reported of for 10

fall beneath the standard which has been recognised and acted on by the better class of heathens.' Fairbairn.

9. More definite direction is now given as to the honour and the qualification, *Let not a widow be taken into the number.* The position of the word 'widow' at the beginning of the sentence makes it probably part of the predicate, as R.V., **Let none be enrolled as a widow.** A roll or catalogue of widows for whom the alms of the Church were bespoken existed from the very first, Acts vi. and has been the care of each Church and each parish to a greater or less extent to the present day under varying forms and conditions:—the least satisfactory arrangement on a large scale being the provision made by Christian England of 'The House'; the most satisfactory being the pleasant almshouses dotted over the country, and the pension moneys from our Church alms taken month by month as from Christ with delicate attention by our deacon curates themselves to the cottage homes. Those who have had to select from such a list in a parish will have found the hints for selection given here very useful and necessary; (1) ascertained impossibility of support from relatives; (2) good moral character as wife and widow; (3) a defined period for 'old age'; (4) reputation as a good mother, a kind neighbour, a zealous Church worker.

under threescore years old] Lit. 'who is found to be less than 60 years old,' the participle belonging to the previous clause, according to the general usage: cf. Lk. ii. 42, 'when he was twelve years old.'

having been the wife of one man] 'Having been,' if retained should be put as by R.V. in italics, marking it as an English insertion; the phrase 'wife of one man' is precisely the same as in iii. 2, where see note. The clear and indisputable meaning here of the words is that of having been faithful to one husband all his lifetime instead of leaving him for another or adding another, 'no bigamist or adulteress.' She is to be 'enrolled' as such. *Many* of the N.T. exhortations on this point are startling to us as implying even in the circle of Christians very lax principles and habits still. And yet English ministerial knowledge could tell of many startling views and habits that prevail among us now in respect of the sanctity and purity of the married state. It is no 'counsel of perfection' but the plain elementary pledge 'to live together—till death's parting—*after God's ordinance* in the holy estate of matrimony,' that St Paul here commends. And it still needs much commending.

10. *well reported of*] So the word is used of *good* testimony, in the appointment of the deacons, Acts vi. 3, 'seven men of good report;' of Ananias, 'a devout man...well reported of by all the Jews,' Acts xxii. 12.

for good works] Lit. 'in the matter of good works;' the preposition expresses 'the range in which a power acts,' Winer, § 48, 3, a. Cf. 1 Thess. iii. 2, 'God's minister in the Gospel of Christ;' and 1 Tim.

good works; if she have brought up children, if she have
lodged strangers, if she have washed the saints' feet, if she
11 have relieved the afflicted, if she have diligently followed
every good work. But the younger widows refuse: for

i. 18 with note. These good works are not to be limited to such as a widow with means could perform. All were within the reach of the devoted Christian widow, poor as she might be. And pastoral experience can shew similar 'wonderful works' still wrought by 'pious poverty' for the Saviour. The rhythmical structure of the verse is at least characteristic of St Paul's rhetoric, fitted now to incorporate some sacred strain, now to suggest one.

if she have brought up children] R.V. rightly, **if she hath brought up**; 'hath' not 'have' because the moods are indicative, not conditional; 'hath brought up,' not 'brought up,' because the English idiom, in such a retrospect, uses the definite past, while the Greek uses the indefinite aorist: see Revisers' Preface. 'There are numerous cases in which the use of the indefinite past tense in Greek and English is altogether different, and in such instances we have not attempted to violate the idiom of our language by forms of expression which it could not bear.' The bringing up of children most naturally refers to her own home and family, where she has been a nursing mother. This compound verb occurs only here in N.T.; as does the next.

lodged strangers] An ordinary daily incident of both rich and poor life then: and in the days of persecution soon to follow a sacred privilege and necessity.

washed the saints' feet] This special act of Eastern hospitality is singled out doubtless from our Lord's taking the humble service upon Himself at the Last Supper, John xiii. 4—17. Cf. Abraham's reception of the 'three men' at Mamre, Gen. xxviii. 4, 'Let a little water be fetched and wash your feet;' and the designation of Elijah's companion and disciple, 2 Kings iii. 11, 'Elisha the son of Shaphat, which poured water on the hands of Elijah.' 'The saints' is another word used like 'faithful' (v. 8) at the commencement of the Epistles and elsewhere to describe all who have been 'set apart' from the heathen as 'Christ's people' by baptism.

relieved the afflicted] The 'relief' is the same word as in ver. 16, exemplifying the promise 'with what measure ye mete it shall be measured to you again.' To give such relief from small means would not then be harder than now; and it is very striking, when one knows the real life of the poor, to see how much they can and do help one another in trouble, especially when there is 'Christian will' to 'find the way.'

diligently followed every good work] Bp Ellicott rightly seems to point out that the preposition in the compound verb indicates *direction* rather than *diligence*, quoting 1 Pet. ii. 21, 'that ye should follow his steps.' Cf. also Mk. xvi. 20 and verse 24 in this chapter. She might not have been in front rank but she **hath humbly followed** and 'hath done what she could' in every good work.

when they have *begun to* wax wanton against Christ, they
will marry; having damnation, because they have cast off 12
their first faith. And withal they learn *to be* idle, wandering 13

11. *But the younger widows refuse*] There is no article, 'younger' than 60 years; but also more generally, 'comparatively young.' 'Refuse,' i.e. decline to put on the roll of maintenance.

when they have begun to *wax wanton*] Rather, **when they have come to wax wanton.** The aorist subjunctive which has the support of ℵ should be retained, though Alford follows A in reading future indicative. The verb takes up the 'prodigal living' of *v.* 6, seeming to be connected with *strenuus*, 'strong,' and so like 'lusty' and 'lustful' having the idea of wanton licence. The simple verb is used in Rev. xviii. 7 and 9 of Babylon, 'She glorified herself and waxed wanton,' 'the kings of the earth committed fornication and lived wantonly with her.' With the compound form used here may be compared similar compounds, to laugh against, Matt. ix. 24, 'and they laughed Him to scorn;' to witness against, Mk. xiv. 60, 'what is it which these witness against thee?'

against Christ] The only place in the Pastoral Epistles where 'Christ' is used alone, 'Christ Jesus' being the most common title employed.

they will marry] Rather, **they choose marrying.** Their mind is set on husband hunting, with no limitation now of 'only in the Lord.'

12. Corruptio optimi fit pessima; Christ, trust in Christ, the life of Christ, *were* supreme during the former marriage; into the loneliness of widowhood, not safeguarded by age, the flesh and the devil have penetrated, and have dethroned Christ: a rebel's name only can be hers. Cf. *v.* 15.

having damnation] Rather, **condemnation**; a present 'judgment,' of being self-condemned as rebels, deserters: **because they have rejected their first faith**: 'faith' being most naturally used here as above, *v.* 8, the phrase 'their first faith' may thus best refer to their early Christian life, just as in the Epistle to Ephesus (the same Church to which this letter goes) the condemnation is that they 'have left their first love,' and the exhortation is to 'do the first works.' The word 'reject' is the same as in Jude *v.* 8, 'these...defile the flesh and *set at nought* dominion,' where the thought and subject are very much the same, 'turning the grace of our God into lasciviousness, and denying our only Master and Lord, Jesus Christ.' To make the reference to the breaking of a vow or pledge of widowhood seems both inadequate and misleading.

13. *they learn* to be *idle*] Insert 'also'; R.V. **they learn also to be idle.** The position of 'idle' and the stress in the next clause 'not only idlers but' point to this construction, making 'idle' predicate, though no infinitive 'to be,' 'to become,' is inserted. The rendering of Bp Wordsworth, Grimm and others, 'Being idle they are learners running about from house to house,' gives indeed 'an oxymoron—a common figure of speech with St Paul.' But the authority for 'learn' in so

about from house to house; and not only idle, but tattlers
also and busybodies, speaking *things* which they ought not.
14 I will therefore that the younger *women* marry, bear chil-
dren, guide the house, give none occasion to the adversary

absolute a sense is very doubtful, since everywhere, e.g. in 1 Tim. ii. 11. 'let a woman learn in silence,' and 2 Tim. iii. 7, 'always learning and never able to come to the full knowledge,' there is much more in the context of connected *phrase* and *subject*.

wandering about from house to house] Lit. 'the houses' that made up the Christian settlement: so 2 Tim. iii. 6, 'they that creep into our houses.' Compare 3 Joh. 14, 'our friends salute thee.'

tattlers also and busybodies] The first word occurs again only as participle in 3 Joh. 10, 'tattling of us with evil words.' 'Its derivation (connected with *fluere*) points to a babbling *profluent* way of talking.' Bp Ellicott. 'Busybodies,' prying round into other people's business; so 2 Thess. iii. 11, 'not busy, but busybodies.' Hence its use for 'magical arts,' Acts xix. 19. Contrast the epithet of the younger women, Tit. ii. 5 (best MSS.) 'busy at home,' which is not found elsewhere.

14. *I will therefore*] Rather, with R.V. 'I desire;' the stronger verb, as in ii. 8, vi. 9; Tit. iii. 8: and four other passages of St Paul's Epistles: while the weaker verb is used by him more than sixty times, of which four only are in the Pastoral Epistles.

younger women] The passage implies a limitation to widows, as R.V. 'Do not lead the younger widows to expect such help at all as a matter of course. Then those who marry "in the Lord" again will find scope for an active irreproachable Christian life; while,' as he said before, 'those who have been misled, in their trouble, by the world and the flesh, and seek a worldly heathen re-marriage, will not compromise the Church by having had a place on the roll of godly almswomen.'

bear children, guide the house] Compound verbs again, as in verse 10, used only here in N.T., the substantives connected with them however occurring ch. ii. 15 and Matt. x. 25, &c.

to the adversary] The word occurs in three stages in N.T., (1) still retaining its participial force; in Lk. xiii. 17 governing its pronoun, 'those who opposed him,' and 1 Cor. xvi. 9, 'and many (are) opposing,' 2 Thess. ii. 4, 'he that opposeth and exalteth himself.' (2) As abstract adjective in the plural, Phil. i. 28, 'in nothing affrighted by the adversaries,' (3) as abstract adjective in the singular, in this passage. With the use here in the singular, compare Tit. ii. 8, 'That he that is of the contrary part may be ashamed,' and the fifth question in the Order for the Consecration of Bishops apparently echoing both, 'an example of good works unto others, that the adversary may be ashamed.' 'The hostile party, ready to catch hold of anything in the life of Christians, are personified as one,' Fairbairn. St John, in his still later Greek, adopts this singular, 1 Joh. xi. 22, where cf. Bp Westcott: 'the liar, who offers in his own person the sum of all that is false; and not simply *a liar* who is guilty of a particular sin.'

to speak reproachfully. For some are already turned aside 15
after Satan. If any man or woman that believeth have 16
widows, let them relieve them, and let not the church be
charged; that it may relieve them that are widows indeed.
Let the elders that rule well be counted worthy of double 17

to speak reproachfully] Lit. 'on account of,' 'to serve the purpose of abuse,' so tersely R.V. **for reviling**. Compare the similar use, Jude 16, 'shewing respect of persons *for the sake* of advantage.'

15. *some are...turned aside*] Some of the younger widows who had been placed upon the roll had thus been led astray; St Paul was not merely theorising in *vv.* 11—13. The aorist here is rightly rendered 'are turned' according to the account given in *v.* 10.

16. *If any man or woman that believeth*] The balance of authority in MSS. requires us to read with R.V., **If any woman that believeth.**

have widows] Again, **hath widows,** dependent on her. In what precise way we are to understand this verse is not very clear; whether (1) as a general summary of the whole passage, or (2) as a summary of the portion respecting younger widows inculcating such oversight as might anticipate sinful leanings, or (3) as an extension of the charge to more distant Christian relatives than in *vv.* 4 and 8. On the whole, having regard to the way in which the points are put more than once in some fresh aspect, with some degree of repetition, (1) seems best. From 3 to 8 the chief reason given for refusing lavish maintenance is the good of the relatives themselves; from 9 to 15 the good of the widows; in *v.* 16 the good of the Church. Each section is commenced without any introductory particle; and (it may be noticed) in Scrivener's edition is marked by a capital letter.

let not the church be charged] Or, more exactly, **burdened**; the verb is the later Hellenistic form of the strong classical verb 'to weigh down,' 'to oppress.' It is the word used of the apostles' eyes 'weighed down with sleep,' Matt. xxvi. 43; of St Paul's affliction in Asia, 2 Cor. i. 8, 'we were weighed down exceedingly.' Bp Wordsworth quotes Cornelius, bishop of Rome, A.D. 250 (in *Euseb.* VI. 43), as mentioning the existence in the Church of Rome of 'widows and afflicted,' more than 1500 in number. For the N.T. use of 'the Church,' see on ch. iii. 14.

widows indeed] See *v.* 3.

17—25. Timothy's duties in regard to Presbyters.

Timothy's official treatment of the presbyters follows, and his personal bearing as requisite for this. The same general subject runs throughout, though (as noticed above on *v.* 16), the absence of the connecting particles indicates some fresh aspects of it introduced with the more broken style of older age. The dark shading of the picture is dark if it is taken as applying to the *permanent* state of the Church and its clergy. But if we bear in mind that Timothy was not so much the settled Bishop of Ephesus as the authoritative delegate of the apostle for a specific mission, with 'temporary functions which would now be

honour, especially they who labour in the word and doc-
18 trine. For the scripture saith, Thou shalt not muzzle

called episcopal,' so far from stumbling at this view as inconsistent with the praise given to Ephesus in this respect, Rev. ii. 2, 'I know thy works...that thou canst not bear evil men, and didst try them which call themselves apostles, and they are not, and didst find them false,' we shall rather see in it the proof of Timothy's faithful and successful efforts to put down laxness and restore the high ideal of the ministerial office to which he is here urged. This will hold good, whether we take the earlier and more probable date (A.D. 69), or the later (A.D. 96), assigned to the Apocalypse. See Introduction, pp. 19, 20, 66.

17. *the elders that rule well*] The perfect part. with present neuter signification. The verb itself is peculiar to these Epistles, except Rom. xii. 8, 'he that ruleth with diligence,' and 1 Thess. v. 12, 'that labour among you and *are over* you;' and is used of the management 'of a house,' in iii. 4 and 5, 'of children,' iii. 12, and of the mastery 'of good works,' Tit. iii. 8 (where see note) and 14. The word is too general to draw from it the meaning of *ruling* elders as distinguished from *teaching* elders. Doubtless 'government' was the foremost thought in the selection of an 'elder' because *someone* must give orders 'for order's sake.' But the above passage from the earliest of the Epistles, the 1 Thessalonians, shews us the three chief functions of the ministry already blended: (1) that of *the laborious servant*, 'that labour among you,' the same word as here, 'who labour;' (2) that of the *leader and head* in things spiritual, 'are over you,' as here 'that rule;' and (3) that of the *teacher and counsellor*, 'and admonish you,' as here 'in the word and in teaching.' As Bp Lightfoot puts it in his 'Christian Ministry' *Ep. Philipp.*, 'The work of teaching seems to be regarded rather as incidental to than as inherent in the office: "double honour shall be paid......*especially* to such as labour in word and doctrine," as though one holding this office might decline the work of instruction.'

double honour] The word has been defined on *v.* 3; and includes, though it is not confined to, money payment: this is clear from the next verse.

they who labour in the word] The meaning of the Greek word comes out with especial force in 2 Tim. ii. 6, the husbandman *that laboureth*, that really toils 'with honest sweat week in week out.' So Matt. xi. 28, 'Come unto Me all ye that labour,' A.V., where the Prayer-Book in the 'comfortable words' renders 'all that travail.' Surely our word 'labour' has lost some of its strength now since the time when it represented toil and pain like the 'labour pains' of 'a woman in her travail.' It is right therefore to lay stress on the word here in reading the passage.

in the word and doctrine] Rather, **in speech and in teaching.** 'In speech:' the exact phrase has occurred iv. 12, and seems to describe the ordinary intercourse (cf. Col. iv. 6), while 'in teaching' describes the sermon, or lecture, or lesson, the word being characteristic of the present stage of the pastoral office; see note on i. 10.

the ox that treadeth out the corn. And, The labourer
is worthy of his reward. Against an elder receive not an 19
accusation, but before two or three witnesses. Them that 20

18. *the scripture saith*] The quotation is from Deut. xxv. 4, and goes to the end of the clause only, 'thou shalt not muzzle the ox **when he treadeth out** the corn;' or, as Dr Farrar renders, 'thou shalt not muzzle a threshing ox.' The argument from God's care of oxen has been used by St Paul before, 1 Cor. ix. 9, where see Mr Lias's note.

And, The labourer is *worthy of his reward*] Bp Wordsworth prints the Greek of these words in such a way that they are to be included under 'the Scripture saith,' and a common view both in ancient and modern times considers that our Lord's words as recorded Lk. x. 7 are here quoted as Scripture. The R.V. by its full-stop after 'corn' regards the words as the citation only of the proverb, in the same way as it is cited by our Lord 'as a popular and well-known saying.' This is quite a sufficient view, especially since it is more than doubtful whether by this time the Gospels could be thus authoritatively quoted. They are not quoted even in the Apostolic Fathers.

reward] Better, **wages** or **hire**.

19. *Against an elder*] A continuation of Timothy's official duties towards the presbyters, as is indicated by the context. The Mosaic precept here referred to is given in its most general terms, Deut. xix. 15, 'One witness shall not rise up against a man for any iniquity, or for any sin......at the mouth of two witnesses, or at the mouth of three witnesses, shall the matter be established.' So the preposition rendered by A.V. here 'before' is more exactly given R.V. **at the mouth of,** the phrase being given thus in full, Matt. xviii. 16. Winer's *note*, § 47, 9th ed. 'by, with, on the testimony of...witnesses' is more exact than the phrase in his text 'before witnesses.' The reason for being particular here is that in our idiom 'to hear a thing only before witnesses' implies merely sufficient publicity and evidence *of its having been heard*, an entirely different thing from what the Greek conveys *with the context*. The preposition by itself would equally well bear either meaning e.g. (1) in 2 Cor. vii. 14, 'our glorying which I made *before* Titus;' (2) in the common phrase 'of a truth,' Lk. iv. 25, 'of a truth,' i.e. with, on the firm basis of truth, 'I say unto you.' Both meanings come from the proper notion of *superposition*.

but before] Lit. to give an English colloquial pleonasm, 'except unless.' So with more stress than 'but,' **except it be.** The phrase occurs 1 Cor. xv. 2, where R.V. alters 'unless' into 'except.' Cf. the old use of 'but' according to its derivation, 'touch not a cat *but* without a glove,' and Spenser

'But this I read that *but* its remedy
Thou her afford, full shortly I her dead shall see.'

This direction is to be regarded as embodying *the sense* of what St Paul wished to convey under the form of another quotation from O.T., so that we should paraphrase, 'except it be,' in the spirit of

21 sin rebuke before all, that others also may fear. I charge
thee before God, and the Lord Jesus Christ, and the elect

the old precept, 'at the mouth of two or three witnesses,' and so Drs Westcott and Hort print the words. This is the simplest answer to De Wette's question whether Timothy is not to observe this judicial rule in all cases as well as merely in the case of an elder. There is *no question* of the precise observance of this or any other purely ceremonial precepts any longer. The spirit however lives; 'judge, rebuke, but never on ill-supported accusations.'

20. *Them that sin*] A connecting particle has some authority here but not enough for adoption. The absence need not (see note above) make us think the subject is changed from *offending presbyters* to *sinners generally*. This would require more support from the context than is given, the main thought being still Timothy's official and personal bearing towards presbyters. The article with the present participle is nearly the equivalent of a substantive. Cf. Winer, § 47. 7. The same article and present participle occur in 1 John iii. 6, where the force of the present is of the utmost importance. 'It describes a character, "a prevailing habit," and not primarily an act.' Bp Westcott. So here, 'those who are living in sin' among the presbyters. Bp Wordsworth gives a special character to these sins: 'He is speaking specially of Presbyters whose sins, particularly in doctrine, are public and notorious. And this exposition is confirmed by the application of the word "sins" to them here and in *v.* 24, and Tit. iii. 11, where he says of a heretical teacher that he "sinneth being self-condemned." St Paul thus declares the moral guilt of false doctrine.' And he quotes St Paul's prophecy to the Athenian presbyters of such 'grievous wolves,' 'speaking perverse things' among them, Acts xx. 29.

rebuke before all] The word is sometimes 'convict,' sometimes 'condemn.' In its use in these Epistles, here and 2 Tim. iv. 2; Tit. i. 9, 13, ii. 15, it seems always to have reference to *false teaching* and its consequent *evil living*, and to unite the sharp convincing proof of the error and the sharp condemning reproof of the vice.

that others also may fear] Rather, as R.V., **that the rest also may be in fear**; 'the rest,' i.e. those who have heard and perhaps approved of the false teaching and its vicious morals; 'may be in fear,' the longer expression being used to denote the state of abiding 'godly fear.'

21. The solemnity of the adjuration in this verse points to a very definite exercise of the duty imposed, and to expected difficulty in the doing of it, arising perhaps not only from Timothy's diffidence but from the prominence of the 'elders' who are to be 'rebuked.' Cf. Acts xx. 29 as above. Here again as frequently the MS. authority requires us to read '**Christ Jesus**,' not 'the Lord Jesus Christ.' Cf. note on i. 1.

the elect angels] If we compare (1) Jude 6, 'angels which kept not their own principality,' and (2) Jude 14, 'The Lord came with ten

angels, that thou observe these *things* without preferring *one*
before another, doing nothing by partiality. Lay hands 22
suddenly on no *man*, neither be partaker of other *men*'s

thousands of *his holy ones*' coupled with Heb. xii. 22, 'ye are come unto...ten thousands of *angels*,' we may interpret the phrase with Chrysostom of the unfallen angels; and though 'the angels' alone would, as Alford objects, be sufficient to designate the good angels, yet the added epithet has its force in an adjuration against rebel speech and self-will. We may see too with Bp Bull a further appositeness in the adjuration, 'because they in the future judgment shall be present as witnesses with their Lord.' See further on the general meaning of the word 'elect' in N.T. on Tit. i. 1, 2 Tim. ii. 10.

without preferring one before another] More precisely as margin and R.V., **without prejudice**; the word, only occurring here, is exactly the Latin prae-iudicium, a prejudging the case unfavourably. The next clause, 'doing nothing by partiality' or **by preference**, expresses the opposite error of deciding for a favourite apart from the evidence; the substantive only occurring here, though the verb is found Acts v. 36, used of the *partisans* of Theudas, 'to whom a number of men, about four hundred, joined themselves.' The metaphor is seen clearly in Goldsmith's description of the country parson:

'And e'en his failings *leaned to* Virtue's side.'—*Deserted Village.*

22. *Lay hands suddenly on no* man] Better perhaps **hastily**; the adverb has a similar use in the words of the Unjust Steward, Lk. xvi. 6, 'Take thy bond and sit down quickly and write fifty.' Compare the clause in the Litany 'from battle and murder, and from sudden death,' i.e. a death into which we are hurried unawares. The passage has by a large preponderance of ancient and modern commentators been referred to the 'imposition of hands' in ordination; and so the first Ember-Prayer of the English Prayer-Book, 'Guide and govern the minds of thy servants the bishops and pastors of thy flock, that they may lay hands suddenly on no man, but faithfully, &c.' Bp Ellicott's objection that the context only speaks of men ordained is partly met above ver. 17, and is not of so great force as the objections to his own rendering 'No penitent is hastily to be absolved by imposition of hands and readmitted to Church fellowship.' For (1) when the phrase is so brief, it is unnatural to interpret it except in accordance with its clear meaning in the other two places where it occurs in these Epistles, 1 Tim. iv. 14, and 2 Tim. i. 6; and (2) there is no certain proof of the other use of the imposition of hands, i.e. in absolution, so early, although Eusebius, *Hist.* II. 2, calls it 'an old custom.'

neither be partaker of other men's *sins*] **Nor yet be a partner in.** The verb as used in N. T. with a dative implies a fellowship in life and spirit. Compare the simple usage, Lk. v. 10, 'the sons of Zebedee which were *partners with* Simon,' and the derived, 1 Pet. iv. 13, 'ye are *partners in* Christ's sufferings,' and 2 Joh. 11, 'he that giveth him greeting is *partner in* his evil works.' This clause takes up again the dealing truly with the 'error in religion' and 'viciousness in life' of those already

sins: keep thyself pure.
23 Drink no longer water, but use a little wine for thy stomach's sake and thine often infirmities.

ordained; with this fresh thought perhaps; 'the solemn laying on of hands connects you inevitably with the character of those whom you will ordain: but neither can you in your position be free from danger to yourself by laxness in regard to those who are already ordained; *libera animam tuam*; "use the authority given you, not to hurt but to help" your own account before God as well as theirs, by "driving away erroneous doctrine" and evil-living.'

keep thyself pure] This thought follows on: 'there is danger too from your own temptations; see that you "deny all worldly lusts and live soberly" *yourself*.' The order in the Greek is **thyself keep thou pure.** The word here used for 'pure' occurs in that *locus classicus* of 'personal religion,' 1 Joh. iii. 3, where Bp Westcott well distinguishes the three separate Greek words for 'pure,' 'holy' and 'clean.'

Hagnos 'pure,' *hagios* 'holy,' and *katharos* 'clean:' '*hagnos* marks prominently a feeling, the result of an inward effort, and *katharos* a state, coming by the application of some outward means; *hagios* that which is holy absolutely, either in itself (as God) or in idea (as man in virtue of his divine destination). It is in respect of our Lord's human life that He can be spoken of as *hagnos*, and in respect of His true humanity it can be said of Him that "He *is* pure" and not only that "He *was* pure." The result of the perfection of His earthly discipline (Heb. v. 7 ff.) still abides in His glorified state.'

23. *Drink no longer water*] The form of the verb and its tense require the fuller rendering of R.V., **Be no longer a drinker of water.** The connexion seems to be; 'you have, I know, among other means of training and disciplining yourself in "purity," been a water-drinker; but have the courage of a sanctified common sense; this is not the only way, nor even for you the right way, to your end; if your stomach is out of order and your health much enfeebled, take a little wine as medicine, not as indulgence.'

thine often infirmities] 'Infirmities' was a stronger word formerly than now: the Greek word is frequently rendered 'sickness,' cf. Joh. xi. 3, 4, 'He whom thou lovest is sick,' 'this sickness is not unto death,' 'Lazarus is dead.' Two observations may be made on this verse with regard to the question, (1) of temperance, (2) of authorship.

(1) According to the principles of the Church of England Temperance Society the resolution of total abstinence is taken (as it was by Timothy) by those who see in it a discipline in Christian life, or a help in Christian love, and is expressly guarded by the reservation 'except under medical advice;' and the question whether wine and other alcoholic drinks are generally useful in illness is one quite open among C.E.T.S. total abstainers, as among doctors. On a point of medical science St Paul's lay experience will not be claimed as a final settlement.

(2) The verse is so casually introduced that, as Dr Farrar remarks, 'though we see at once how it may have occurred to St Paul's thoughts—since otherwise the former rule might have led to a self-denial still more

Some men's sins are open beforehand, going before to judg- 24
ment; and some *men* they follow after. Likewise also the 25
good works *of some* are manifest beforehand; and they that
are otherwise cannot be hid.

rigid (Rom. xiv. 2), and even injurious to health—it is far too natural and spontaneous, too entirely disconnected from all that precedes and follows it, to have occurred to any imitator. An imitator, if capable of introducing the natural play of thought to which the precept "keep thyself pure" is due, would have been far more likely to add—and especially in an Epistle which so scrupulously forbids indulgence in wine to all Church officials—"and, in order to promote this purity, take as little wine as possible, or avoid it altogether."'

24. It is most natural to regard verses 24 and 25 as a review under a fresh aspect of the two main duties urged upon Timothy in the paragraph; just as in the former paragraph, *vv.* 3—16, verse 16 is similarly related to its preceding context. The meaning thus will be; 'I have bidden you in rebuking your presbyters "to be so merciful that you be not too remiss, so to minister discipline that you forget not mercy"; remember how quickly sometimes error stands "self-condemned," how slow at other times its evil is in working out. Again, in rewarding your presbyters I have bidden you, as a wise and faithful servant, "give to God's family their portion in due season," by deserved promotion and preferment; remember how readily some clerical "good work" comes to the front, while yet the more quiet pastoral service cannot be left in the dark and cold.'

are open beforehand] Better, as R.V., **are evident**; the preposition in the compound adjective only signifies 'at once' 'before one's eyes;' the word is used just as we use 'evident' in geometrical proof, in Heb. vii. 14, 'For it is evident that our Lord sprang out of Juda.'

going before to judgment] The verb is common in the Gospels in its simple sense, e.g. Mk. xi. 9, 'they that went before and they that followed;' here, somewhat metaphorically, it describes the obtrusive forward character of 'advanced' teaching and 'fast' living; cf. 2 Joh. 9, 'every one that goeth forward,' 'that advances in bold confidence beyond the limits set to the Christian Faith' (Bp Westcott). The judgment is that of Timothy and of the Church. The clause seems to recur compressed into one word, Tit. iii. 11, 'such an one *sinneth*, being *self-condemned*' or 'self-judged.' Our metaphors '*patent* error,' '*rampant* vice,' are modern representatives of the two phrases.

some men *they follow after*] More exactly, **some men they only follow after**; the evil consequences and evil repute are slow in attaching themselves.

25. *Likewise also the good works* of some] R.V. excellently, drawing out the double article with substantive and adjective which has the best authority of MSS., **in like manner also there are good works that are evident**. See the interpretation on the previous verse, according to which the more obvious departments in 'the ruling well,' the 'labouring devotedly in speech and teaching,' are here meant.

6 Let as many servants as are under the yoke count their own masters worthy of all honour, that the name of God

they that are otherwise] The **such as are otherwise** of R.V. renders the generalness of the phrase and makes it clear that 'works' not 'men' are meant; such part—often the best part—of the pastor's work of 'ruling well,' and of 'labouring devotedly in speech and teaching,' as does not come before the world.

CH. VI. LAST WORDS ON APOSTOLIC DOCTRINE AND DUTY.

1, 2. TIMOTHY'S DUTIES IN REGARD TO SLAVES.

The last of the four sections of special charge (commenced in the previous chapter) is Timothy's attitude towards Christian slaves. The position taken by Christ and His apostles in regard to slavery and the whole 'social order' of the world is well known. The existing basis of society with its relationships was recognised; while the eternal principles of Christian equality and love were boldly proclaimed, and trusted, as the true solvents of all that was amiss between man and man in God's own time and His own patient way of working both for the material and spiritual world.

The present teaching of St Paul, an echo of similar exhortations (Eph. vi. 5; Col. iii. 22), is in entire harmony with the Divine wisdom of the Master's oracle 'Render unto Cæsar the things which be Cæsar's, and unto God the things which be God's.' Nothing is more wonderful in the life of Christianity than the slow gradual establishment of women's position in the family, and of social and civil freedom in the state, in accordance with the seed-principles of Christ's law; unless it be watching the same growth (hardly yet more than infantile), in the wider sphere of international brotherhood and the signs of a 'Christian conscience' stirring in the intercourse of state with state. See Appendix, J.

1. *as many servants as are under the yoke*] The position of the Greek words and their meaning are against this rendering. There would be no servants (slaves) who would not be 'under the yoke;' but since they were in actual position 'under bondage' as slaves, let them recognise facts. Render with R.V. **as many as are bondservants under the yoke**. 'The yoke of slavery' is applied metaphorically, Gal. v. 1, to the old legal dispensation. The use of the word is derived from the old custom of making prisoners of war pass under a 'yoke' formed of a spear laid crosswise on two upright spears, to denote the yoke of slavery being laid upon them. The reference in Christ's words, Matt. xi. 29, 'take my yoke' is rather to the yoke coupling cattle for drawing.

their own masters] The adjective here rendered 'their own' is in N.T. 'used instead of a personal pronoun by the same kind of misuse as when in later Latin *proprius* takes the place of *eius* or *suus*;' Winer, § 22, 7. As Alford on Eph. v. 22 says, it serves 'to intensify the relationship

and *his* doctrine be not blasphemed. And they that have 2
believing masters, let them not despise *them*, because they
are brethren; but rather do *them* service, because they are
faithful and beloved, partakers of the benefit. These *things*
teach and exhort. If any *man* teach otherwise, and con- 3

and enforce its duties.' We have sixteen instances of the use in these Epistles, e.g. Tit. ii. 9.

his *doctrine*] Again the special **teaching** of the Christian religion, which would be 'evil spoken of' by being supposed to teach a subversive socialism.

2. *rather do* them *service*] Better, **serve them the rather**, all the more zealously.

partakers of the benefit] The article with the participle is clearly subject; and the *masters* are certainly meant. But then divergence arises, Bp Wordsworth making both masters and slaves the benefactors: 'they (i.e. the masters) who take part in the mutual good offices (between masters and slaves) are believing and beloved.' He quotes from Thucyd. ii. 61 for this sense of the verb 'to take hold of with a view to mutual assistance.' Conybeare and Lewin make the slaves the benefactors, quoting from Arist. *Ran.* 777 for the verb 'they who claim their slaves' services.' Grimm, following Chrysostom and Grotius, makes the masters the benefactors, quoting from LXX. Isai. xxvi. 3 for the verb 'they who devote themselves to the kindly care of their slaves.' So far as the usage of the verb in N. T. goes—'to help' 'to succour,' and also of the noun 'the good deed' (to the impotent man), Acts iv. 9 and LXX., the help of the weaker by the stronger is suggested, and so the last view is borne out. Compare too the significant use of the connected noun 'benefactor,' in Lk. xxii. 25, 'they that have authority over them are called benefactors.' Is St Paul using a recognised synonym *honoris causa* for 'lordship,' and, with all the delicate grace natural to the writer of the Epistle to Philemon, lifting it to the height of Christian love? 'Bid them serve their masters all the better. Masters did I say? Nay; own and requite the faith, the love, that makes them set it as their aim to be—not Masters,—no—Brothers of Blessing.'

These things *teach and exhort*] The words have more weight if held to close the whole section from v. 1 than if thought merely to refer to vi. 1 and 2.

3—10. A FURTHER WARNING AGAINST FALSE TEACHERS. THEIR COVETOUSNESS.

From the 3rd verse to the 16th St Paul once again resumes two of the chief topics of the Epistle—false teachers' perverted doctrine, and Timothy's own true unswerving life; in each case with a new thought, (1) of the debasing motive of traffic in godliness, (2) of the inspiring motive of the Master's appearing. He then, *vv.* 17—19, gives one further direction (suggested perhaps by *v.* 10) of pastoral faithfulness towards

sent not to wholesome words, *even* the *words* of our Lord
Jesus Christ, and to the doctrine which is according to
4 godliness; he is proud, knowing nothing, but doting about
questions and strifes of words, whereof cometh envy, strife,

the rich; and in a last abrupt and touchingly natural outburst throws himself upon his son Timothy, and gathers up all his fears and hopes on the one chiefest subject in the brief appeal of *vv.* 20, 21, from which he can no longer keep back the misused name of the monster evil—'knowledge—falsely named, *Gnosis—the Misnomer*,' *vv.* 3—10, unsound teaching, especially for gain.

3. *teach otherwise*] More fully R.V., **teacheth a different doctrine,** but even this does not completely give the force; for the 'different' is not so much 'different from what has just been laid down,' as 'different from the one true deposit, the creed of all my gospel and all your life;' and helps to form the meaning now attached to *heterodoxy*, lit. '*opinions different* from established truth.' The close of the Epistle takes up the opening where this word has occurred before there has been time to lay down any teaching, i. 3. Lewin renders here 'if any man teach what is heterodox.'

wholesome words] Again taking up his opening phrase i. 10, where see note. **Sound** is the best English equivalent, if we do not stay on the most modern and 'cant' sense of the word, but go back to its early vigour, so as to appreciate St Paul's contrast here with the '*sickly* questionings' of the false teacher, *v.* 4. See Appendix, K.

our Lord Jesus Christ] This exact order of the words so familiar to us in St Paul's other writings occurs only here and *v.* 14 throughout these Epistles according to the true text. An imitator would surely, as we see by the various readings so often attempted, have taken pains to make the well-known formula a marked feature. It may be also noted that the aged saint, so near the end of his 'good fight,' does not presume familiarly on his Saviour's intimacy, so as to use the one name 'Jesus' with tripping fluency. It is still 'Christ Jesus,' 'Jesus Christ,' 'The Lord.' See note on i. 1.

the doctrine...according to godliness] Two characteristic words of these Epistles combined in a phrase which might be taken as their keynote—'Holy Truth—True Holiness.' See previous notes on the words and especially the note on the central doctrinal passage iii. 16.

4. *he is proud, knowing nothing*] **'Puffed up,'** R.V. The word occurs only here and iii. 6; 2 Tim. iii. 4; and goes towards composing the *strong* vocabulary of the Epistles: 'filled with a blind "inflated ignorance"' (to quote from Dr Farrar's strong modern vocabulary) may represent the force. The perfect expresses *the state* in which he is; the particular negative his relative, not absolute, ignorance, according to the tendency of N. T. usage.

doting about questions] 'Diseased' or 'mad' on points of subtle disputation. The word in other writers has both meanings, and the opposition to 'sound' would hold equally good with both; but the moral responsibility for this state is clearly implied, and points rather

railings, evil surmisings, perverse disputings of men of cor- 5
rupt minds, and destitute of the truth, supposing that gain
is godliness: from such withdraw thyself. But godliness 6

to the former: 'full of a diseased disputatiousness.' For 'questionings,' see note on i. 4.

strifes of words] Our own derived 'logomachies.' The corresponding verb occurs 2 Tim. ii. 14, 'otherwise only in ecclesiastical writers,' Alford.

railings] Clearly as in Eph. iv. 31, 'anger, and clamour, and railing;' Jude 9, 'durst not bring against him a railing judgment,' not blasphemy against God, but slanderous reviling of one another.

evil surmisings] Our 'suspicions;' this word again is new to N.T. usage. Altogether we have four peculiar words in this verse, *puffed up*, *doting*, *strifes of words*, *surmisings*, indicating the new region of the Church's experience and of the Apostle's feeling.

5. *perverse disputings*] The best attested reading of the Greek word transposes the order of the preposition, and should give us for its meaning 'continual collisions.' This seems the reason for the rendering of R.V. **wranglings**. Compare a similar compound in LXX. 2 Sam. iii. 30, and Jos. *Ant.* x. 7. 5.

of corrupt minds] Lit. **corrupted in mind**. See note on 'mind' Tit. i. 15, and on 'uncorruptness' Tit. ii. 7.

destitute of the truth] Our 'destitute' has almost ceased to have its original proper force 'deprived' of what was once possessed; hence R.V. has rightly substituted, as corresponding with the perf. pass. participle of the Greek, **bereft**.

gain is godliness] A well-known violation by A.V. of the law which places the article with the *subject*. The ending of the Greek noun for 'gain' implies rather a 'trading,' a 'means of profit,' like 'the reaping time' for 'summer.' Hence the twofold correction of R.V. **godliness is a way of gain**. But we lose the emphasis of the subject kept back to the end. Point is gained however in this respect by the omission (required on the authority of the best MSS.) of the next clause, *From such withdraw thyself*. See Appendix, K.

6. So the Pauline paradox comes out strongly; *godliness with contentment* **is** a way of gain, **a great source of gain**. This is spoiled by making the reference to the rewards of heaven. The thought is as in iv. 8, where see the paraphrase quoted of Mk. x. 30. St Paul's 'way to be wealthy' is by the limiting of our wants *and* the limitless realising of Christ's presence and sufficiency;—this being the inmost meaning of this word 'godliness' see ii. 2. The adjective of this word 'contentment' occurs in the noble description of his own disciplined life, 'I have learned, in whatsoever state I am, therewith to be content.... I have all competence in Him that empowereth me,' Phil. iv. 11, 13.

So good George Herbert:

'For he that needs five thousand pound to live
Is full as poore as he that needs but five.'—*The Church Porch.*

7 with contentment is great gain. For we brought nothing
into *this* world, *and it is* certain we can carry nothing out.
8 And having food and raiment let us be therewith content.

And again:

'Teach me, my God and King,
In all things Thee to see,
And what I do in any thing
To do it as for Thee:
* * * *
This is the famous stone
That turneth all to gold,
For that which God doth touch and own
Cannot for lesse be told.'—*The Elixir.*

7. *we brought nothing into* this *world*] A further reason for contentment is drawn; 'the nakedness of our birth and death.' Exactly, **into the world**.

and it is *certain*] Editors are divided as to the authority for this word here: the Revisers and Westcott and Hort omit. Inclining to this view with Codex Sinaiticus, and on the ground that *proclivi praestat ardua lectio*, we have to render the connecting particle that remains 'because;' but need not adopt Alford's strained explanation 'we were appointed by God to come naked into the world, to teach us to remember that we must go naked out of it,' which mars the simple sequence of thought (we should look rather to the looser usage of such particles already beginning to prevail): 'because' may be referred back to the contentment, and so introduce a parallel not a subordinate clause to 'we brought,' **because too we cannot carry anything out**. The verse is linked at the commencement of the Prayer-Book Burial Service with Job i. 21, 'The Lord gave, and the Lord hath taken away; blessed be the name of the Lord,' and so illustrates further the '*godly* content' of the previous verse.

8. *And having food*] Rather, **but**; the opposite, positive view of life. The words for 'food' and 'raiment' are both unused in N.T. except here; both are in the plural, indicating 'supplies of,' for each mouth to be fed, each household to be clothed.

raiment] A rather out-of-the-way word for 'clothing,' if we go by the use found once in Aristotle and once in Josephus, Ar. *Pol.* VII. 17; Jos. *B. J.* II. 8. 5: literally, 'covering;' and so R.V., perhaps merely to keep an *unusualness* of phrase. But the meaning 'shelter,' tent or roof-covering, has been also assigned, from the root word having a more common turn towards this; and 'covering' may have been chosen to include this, if not to express it alone. But the immediate context in *v.* 7 favours the reference to merely *personal* possessions such as dress.

let us be therewith content] The verb is future passive, **we shall be therewith content**, as R.V.; hardly an *implied* exhortation, but 'we shall, if we are godly.' This rendering is preferable to that in the margin of R.V. 'in these we shall have enough' from the similar use

But they that will be rich fall into temptation and a snare, 9
and *into* many foolish and hurtful lusts, which drown men
in destruction and perdition. For the love of money is the 10

of the passive, Lk. iii. 14, 'be content with your wages;' Heb. xiii. 5, 'content with such things as ye have.' The connexion of the word with 'contentment' above should also be maintained.

9. *they that will be rich*] In so wealthy a city as Ephesus the temptation would be very great to the teacher to adapt his 'wares' of doctrine to the popular Asiatic speculations, so as to get and keep name and means; and his hearers would be equally tempted to accept such a compromise. There would be the *genius loci* to whisper 'si possis, recte; si non, quocunque modo, rem;' 'ye know that by this business we have our wealth.' Hence the specially appropriate warning now addressed to **those that are desiring to be rich**, as we must render exactly. Chrysostom's words 'not "*the rich*," for one may have money and dispense it well and disesteem it all the while,' are well quoted here. But G. Herbert's words are still better (*Priest to the Temple*, c. 3), 'The country parson is very circumspect in avoiding all covetousness, neither being greedy to get, nor niggardly to keep, nor troubled to lose any worldly wealth; but in all his words and actions slighting and disesteeming it, even to a wondering that the world should so much value wealth, which in the day of wrath hath not one dram of comfort for us.'

temptation and a snare] There seems no reason to depart from the usual rendering elsewhere of the phrase 'into temptation' as R. V. does 'into a temptation,' because of the words coupled with it; 'a snare' naturally follows, just as 'deliver us from the evil one' follows 'bring us not into temptation,' Matt. vi. 13; it is the thought present to the Apostle's mind at this time; see above iii. 7, 'lest he fall into reproach and the snare of the devil' where the conjunction of words is very similar, and from whence some MSS. have even added here 'of the devil;' and 2 Tim. ii. 26, 'that they may recover themselves out of the snare of the devil.' See Appendix, K.

lusts, which drown men] The lengthened generalised relative here is properly 'of a kind which,' 'which indeed naturally,' so R. V. **such as.** Cf. iii. 15. The simple use of the passive of 'drown' in Lk. v. 7, 'they were being sunk,' is the only other N. T. use of the verb; the noun from which it comes is used by St Paul of his (unrecorded) shipwreck, 2 Cor. xi. 25, 'a night and a day I have been in *the deep.*'

destruction and perdition] The two words give solemnity to the idea of the ruin to be incurred, though it is too much to assign 'ruin of body' to the one and 'ruin of soul' to the other. The compound word is instinctively chosen (see *v.* 8) to complete the terrible picture.

Chrysostom gives many instances of these 'snares and lusts' in his day leading to 'destruction and perdition.' To the example (almost forced upon the memory by the word) from Holy Scripture itself of 'the son of perdition' (Joh. xvii. 12), may well be added G. Herbert's searching words to his brethren; 'they, who, for the hope of promotion, neglect

root of all evil: which while some coveted after, they have
erred from the faith, and pierced themselves through with
11 many sorrows. But thou, O man of God, flee these

any necessary admonition or reproof sell (with Judas) their Lord and Master.' *The Priest to the Temple*, ch. 2.

10. *the love of money*] One word in the original, occurring only here and belonging to the later Greek; the adjective in Lk. xvi. 14, 'the Pharisees, who were covetous,' R.V. 'lovers of money,' and so 2 Tim. iii. 2. 'It differs from the ordinary word for covetousness (e.g. Col. iii. 5) (which does not occur in these Epistles) in denoting rather avarice, a love of money already gained, than an active grasping after more.' Trench's *N. T. Synonyms*, § 24.

the root of all evil] It has been much questioned whether we are to translate this admitted predicate 'a root' or 'the root.' On the general grammatical question, such passages as 1 Cor. xi. 3, 'the head of the woman is (the) man,' make 'the root,' quite correct; if with R.V. we render 'a root,' it *lays a stress* on there being other roots, which is beside the point: the stress surely is on the 'all,' interpreted however in that *rhetorical* sense, if it may be so called, which is common in N. T. as elsewhere (cf. *v.* 17), and is well given in R. V. We may translate **the root of all kinds of evil.** For this use of the plural we may compare 'supplies of food,' *v.* 8.

which while some coveted after] 'Which (love-of-money) some reaching after,' R.V. keeping to the root-notion of the participle. The verb (and its noun) occur four times in N. T. and in each place the Revisers give a different version, 1 Tim. iii. 1 and Heb. xi. 16 in a good sense; here and Rom. i. 27 in a bad sense. 'Desire,' a colourless word, would fit everywhere, but is weak. Bp Wordsworth ingeniously explains the seemingly incongruous desire for the love-of-money thus: 'riches were a proof of divine approbation: love of wealth was a love of God's favour: thus they sanctified *avarice*.' But the relative is only *formally, logically*, in agreement with the abstract 'love-of-money:' all readers of A.V. or R.V. would refer the 'which' to the real antecedent in sense, 'money,' and would be virtually right.

have erred from the faith] R.V. is justified in rendering **have been led astray**. The Greek aorist 'merely represents the action of having occurred, as filling a point of past time' (Winer, III., XL. 45, a). When it stands by itself, as here, with no qualifying word, this force is represented by the English perfect, as giving just in our idiom the past verbal idea merely, with no further stress or point, cf. Ellicott on 1 Thess. ii. 16. The word occurs in N.T. again only in Mk. xiii. 32, 'that they may lead astray, if possible, the elect.' 'The faith' as in i. 19, where see note.

pierced themselves through] Lat. *transfigo;* only here in N.T.

11—16. A FURTHER EXHORTATION TO TIMOTHY. THE LORD'S APPEARING.

Timothy's own true life and bearing are solemnly dwelt upon in contrast to the false and low; see on *v.* 3.

things; and follow *after* righteousness, godliness, faith, love,
patience, meekness. Fight the good fight of faith, lay hold 12

thou, O man of God] Opposed not only to the 'some' of *v.* 10 but to the 'any' of *v.* 3. The phrase 'man of God' occurs also with the same reference to the ministry, 2 Tim. iii. 17, derived probably from the O. T. ministry of the prophets; cf. 2 Pet. i. 21, where the best reading, however, slightly varies the phrase 'men spake from God;' and 1 Kings xvii. 18, 24. It marks the high tone of this final address; and is in keeping with the full dignity of title which in both these last contrasts of the false and the true ministry is given to the great Head of the Church's ministry (and given here only in these Epistles) 'Our Lord Jesus Christ.'

flee these things] 'Unsound words, and ungodly doctrine,' 'questionings and evil surmisings,' 'traffic in godliness and love of money.' These three heads of evil, in the 3rd, 4th, and 5th to 10th verses respectively, are opposed by three pairs of contrasted virtues: 'righteousness and godliness,' 'faith and love,' 'patience and meekness.' In the first pair 'the sound words,' 'the words of our Lord Jesus Christ,' go to the very root of the matter as fully expounded, Rom. vi. 'Baptised into Christ Jesus...dead unto sin, but alive unto God in Christ Jesus...obedient from the heart to that form of teaching...ye became servants of *righteousness*,' and 1 Cor. i. 'We preach Christ crucified...Christ the power of God...of Him are ye in Christ Jesus, who was made unto us wisdom from God and *righteousness*'; all this being but the working out of the very 'words of the Lord,' Matt. v. 6, 'Blessed are they that hunger and thirst after *righteousness*, for they shall be filled.' In the second pair 'faith' is as evidently the antidote to 'ignorance,' 'questionings,' and 'disputes of words,' as 'love' is to 'envy, strife, railings, evil surmisings.' In the third pair 'patient endurance' and 'meekness of heart' are well fitted to produce '*godliness* with *contentment*,' as being the very graces to which 'the words of the Lord' assign the blessings of that 'kingdom of heaven' which *is* 'godliness,' and that 'inheritance of the earth' which *is* 'contentment.' 'Blessed are the poor in spirit,' 'Blessed are the meek.'

meekness] The compound word, **meekness of heart**, a word peculiar here, is to be read. See note on 2 Tim. ii. 25.

12. *Fight the good fight of faith*] St Paul has now mounted above the lower ground in which Timothy was to maintain the true pastor's *rôle* against his rivals. 'The faith,' i.e. the Christian creed, the Christian life, is now a 'fight,' 'a strife,' a 'race,' against time and sense, earth and hell. The metaphor is the most inspiring perhaps to the Apostle himself of all his metaphors as it is also his last; see 2 Tim. iv. 7, 'I have fought the good fight,' 'run the fair race.' Taken from the Greek games, the word 'fight' can be only *mimic* fight, if it be referred to the wrestling or the boxing contest; and if, as 2 Tim. iv. 7, 'I have finished the course' suggests, the running contest is meant, 'fight' is misleading. Not much less so is Farrar's and Alford's 'strive the good strife.' But for the associations which have gathered round our familiar

on eternal life, whereunto thou art also called, and hast
13 professed a good profession before many witnesses. I give

'fight,' and which have prevailed perhaps with the Revisers, we should be surely nearest—for a reader coming fresh to it—with the rendering 'contest.' And the weighty verb, present in tense, placed at the commencement of the sentence, is better represented by Longfellow's '*Be a hero* in the strife' than by keeping too close to the identity of verb and noun. We may render then, **Play thou the man in the good contest of the Faith.**

lay hold on eternal life] More force is given to the intended point by R.V. **the life eternal.** The verb and noun recur *v.* 19, but the epithet is changed to 'the true,' 'the real.' (See note.) And this at once suggests to us that 'eternal life' is not regarded by St Paul here only as 'the prize,' but as *also* the 'straight course' to be *now* vigorously laid hold of; that 'the life eternal' in fact is exactly the same as 'the life which now is, and the life which is to come' of iv. 8, where the metaphor is also of the games. See notes there. Christ is our 'strength' as well as our 'right'; 'the path' as well as 'the prize.' The present imperative refers to the bearing of Timothy through the whole contest; the aorist is, as it were, the voice of the earnest friend standing at a critical corner of the course and rousing him to renewed energy, 'now lay hold.' What Cambridge athlete of the river or the path but knows the value of this? What Christian athlete of the heavenly course? In no way more beautifully could the view now given be expressed than in Dr Monsell's hymn:

'Fight the good fight with all thy might,
Christ is thy strength, and Christ thy right;
Lay hold on life, and it shall be
Thy joy and crown eternally.

Run the straight race through God's good grace,
Lift up thine eyes and seek His Face;
Life with its way before us lies,
Christ is the path, and Christ the prize.'

whereunto thou art also called] Properly, omitting 'also,' **thou wast called** at thy baptism, and, more particularly still, at thy ordination, cf. i. 18, iv. 14. Compare the present language of the Prayer-Book; *Order for Private Baptism*—'Our Lord Jesus Christ doth not deny His grace and mercy unto such Infants, but most lovingly doth *call* them unto Him'; *the Catechism*—'He hath *called* me to this state of salvation,' 'God the Holy Ghost who sanctifieth me and all the *elect* people of God'; *Ordering of Priests*—'Thou hast vouchsafed to *call* these thy servants here present to the same office and ministry.' The direct metaphor is no longer probably continued.

hast professed a good profession] Lit., as R.V. **didst confess the good confession;** 'the good confession' like 'the good contest' with reference to its spiritual character, the faith and obedience of Christ. See next verse.

thee charge in the sight of God, who quickeneth all *things*,
and *before* Christ Jesus, who before Pontius Pilate witnessed
a good confession; that thou keep *this* commandment 14
without spot, unrebukeable, until the appearing of our Lord

before many witnesses] **in the sight of**, the word being taken up in the appeal of the next verse to 'a more tremendous Presence' (Ellicott).

13. *God, who quickeneth*] The word which has the sanction of the MSS. points to God as Preserver of Life, rather than as Creator; but R.V. leaves **quickeneth** in the text because '*New* every morning is the love Our wakening and uprising prove.'

The word is especially suitable, looking back to the charge to 'lay hold strongly of the true heavenly *life*.'

before Pontius Pilate witnessed a good confession] **the good confession**. The meaning may be either (1) 'suffered *under* (i. e. in the time of) Pontius Pilate,' and as the faithful Witness (Rev. i. 5) made that good confession of the Cross, and in it of His Father's love, His own Sacrifice, which has inspired every life of witness and every martyr's death, or (2) '*before* (i.e. before the tribunal of) Pontius Pilate attested the good confession' as 'true King,' i.e. 'very Lord and Christ;' this it is which the oral Gospel must have taught as the basis on which Matt. xxvii. 11; Mk. xv. 2; Lk. xxiii. 3; Joh. xviii. 33—37 were founded; this it is which from St Peter's sermon (Acts ii. 36) to St John's epistles (1 Joh. iv. 14, 15) and thence to every Ordination and every Holy Baptism has been confessed by *Christendom*. Though the whole passage is *more* than polemical, the *form* of 'the charge' is affected perhaps by the thought of that teaching which was beginning to assail the old 'knowledge' and creed about the person of Christ; and so the second which is the sharper, more defined, interpretation may be preferable. The later phraseology seems to take up and draw out more fully the language here, 1 Joh. iv. 14, 15, iii. 23.

'Before' of place and 'under' of time are equally admissible for the preposition: see note on v. 19.

14. *that thou keep* this *commandment*] **the commandment**; this phrase in the singular or plural (as indicated above, *v.* 13) specially characterises St John's first epistle and is closely linked with the confession of the true Christ: and the commandment there is 'love': see e.g. 1 Joh. iii. 23. Again St Paul here, in *vv.* 13, 14, 'I charge thee' &c. is clearly recurring to 'the charge' of i. 5, 'the end' of which is '*love*, out of a pure heart and a good conscience and faith unfeigned.' We have therefore no difficulty as to 'the commandment' here.

without spot, unrebukeable] Both words used of persons only in N.T., elsewhere of things; the latter has occurred iii. 2 and v. 7, and so A.V. apparently here refers them to Timothy; R.V. alters, giving the alliteration and leaving open the question whether they agree with the subject or the object **without spot, without reproach**. The early Greek interpreters take them with 'commandment,' which on the whole the construction favours.

15 Jesus Christ: which in his times he shall shew, *who is* the
blessed and only Potentate, the King of kings, and Lord
16 of lords; who only hath immortality, dwelling in the light
which no *man* can approach unto; whom no man hath
seen, nor can see: to whom *be* honour and power ever-
lasting. Amen.
17 Charge *them that are* rich in this world, that *they* be not

the appearing of our Lord] At His second Advent; lit. 'the Epiphany.' After use in the Apostle's earliest letters, 2 Thess. ii. 8, which dealt directly with the subject, the word has been dormant till now; now in each of the latest letters (here and Tit. ii. 13 and 2 Tim. iv. 1 and 8) it shines out, as is so natural after the 15 years that have made an old man of him:—'Surely the world too is growing old; Timothy may see His coming: yet let it be its own time—no nearer, no further.'

15. *in his times*] R.V. **in its own times**, apparently because sometimes it must be so, e.g. ii. 6; and this would point to a set meaning and quasi-adverbial use. But in Tit. i. 2 inconsistently 'his own seasons.'

the blessed and only Potentate] The 'only,' without being polemical, states the grand truth *positively*, which is the antidote to the *questionings* of the heretical negations. See note on *v.* 13.

King of kings, and Lord of lords] A title given to our Lord, Rev. xvii. 14, as the Lamb; clearly here to God the Father—an addition to the many similar proofs of the Unity of the Godhead. Cf. Pearson, *On the Creed*, Art. 1.

16. *whom no man hath seen*] 'These words as compared with John i. 18 seem to prove decisively that the whole description applies to the Father, not to the Son.' Alford. Between this verse and Matt. v. 8 there is no opposition, the former referring to man with his present bodily powers and iniquities, the latter referring to the 'Beatific Vision' as it has been thence called, the vision of heavenly glory, which was vouchsafed to St Paul, when *translated* into 'the third heaven' (2 Cor. xii. 2), and which will be the portion of the saints perfected and clothed upon with their spiritual bodies, *after* the rest of Paradise.

Verses 15 and 16 have been thought to be part of an early rhythmical Doxology.

17—19. A LAST DIRECTION. THE DUTIES OF THE RICH.

A postscript follows, with an omitted last word for the richer classes at Ephesus. The 'special aspect' under which the last *warning* about false teachers has been viewed by St Paul, and its reflexion in the last *charge* to Timothy, suggests a last addition to the pastoral *directions*. Men and women in their general religious duties, presbyters and deacons and deaconesses in their special offices, family ties and Church charity, the existing problem of slavery, have been pro-

highminded, nor trust in uncertain riches, but in the living
God, who giveth us richly all *things* to enjoy; that *they* do 18
good, that *they* be rich in good works, ready to distribute,

vided for; but the needs of a life free to 'enjoy the world' through the possession of wealth have been as yet untouched. St Paul will add a word of practical guidance here after the grand climax of lofty praise. It is no forger's hand here; but the natural abruptness of old age, and of a St Paul.

17. them that are *rich in this world*] Or more exactly **in the present world**, this being the peculiar phrase of these Epistles equivalent to the general 'this world.' So 2 Tim. iv. 10, of Demas 'having loved the present world;' Tit. ii. 12, 'live soberly...in this present world.' The word 'world' is literally 'age,' having original reference to *time*, and so denoting the physical, social, or spiritual state of things at the given time.

be not highminded] Not as we now speak of a 'noble highminded man,' but as of 'too high and mighty a bearing,' cf. Ps. cxxxi. 1, Prayer-Book, 'Lord, I am not highminded: I have no proud looks.' The compound verb occurs in N.T. only Rom. xi. 20, 'Be not highminded, but fear;' 'do not, because of your Christian standing, assume a lofty superiority over your "broken" Jewish brother;' and the phrase of which it is compounded only Rom. xii. 16, 'Be of the same mind one toward another. Set not your mind on high things, but condescend to things that are lowly.'

nor trust in uncertain riches] It is the same perfect as iv. 10 and v. 5, and the substantive of character; R.V. accurately, **nor have their hope set on the uncertainty of riches.**

in the living God] The MS. authority is against the adjective here, and in favour of the preposition 'upon' rather than 'in,' **but on God.** 'Living' has come in from iv. 10, where (see note) it has its own appropriateness.

all things] Relative or rhetorical, not absolute; as *v.* 10.

to enjoy] Lit. 'for enjoyment'; the word in N.T. recurs only Heb. xi. 25 of Moses at court, 'to have enjoyment of sin for a season.'

18. *that* they *do good*] Another of the many compound words; used however (according to the right reading) of God in providence, Acts xiv. 17, 'in that He did good;' stronger than the ordinary word (e.g. Lk. vi. 9), and taken up in the next clause; render **that they work at doing good.**

rich in good works] The riches are jewels of God's giving, and can be best seen and best enjoyed 'in a setting of fair works.' The two adjectives for 'good' here have a distinction, but not that given by Alford; the first according to a probable derivation signifying what is 'kind and good' in its inner character in a man's conduct towards others, the second what is 'fair and gracious' in outer expression and bearing. The two together came to be used at Athens as one phrase to denote 'a gentleman.' And so such a use of wealth marks 'the Christian gentleman.' For the second word is the one used Matt.

19 willing to communicate; laying up in store for themselves
a good foundation against the time to come, that they may
20 lay hold on eternal life. O Timothy, keep that which is

v. 16, 'let your light shine...that they may see your good works,' and 1 Pet. ii. 12, 'your good works which they behold.' Compare Bp. Westcott's definition, Heb. x. 24 'works which by their generous and attractive character win the natural admiration of men,' and his synonym Heb. vi. 5, 'tasted the goodness—*the beauty*—of the Word of God.' See notes on Tit. i. 16, ii. 7, iii. 8.

ready to distribute, willing to communicate] Again two peculiar compound adjectives. Cranmer's version followed in the Offertory Sentences of the Prayer-Book has 'ready to give and glad to distribute,' giving also the same rendering to the second of our two words in the text from Heb. xiii. 16, 'to do good and to distribute forget not,' where A.V. and R.V. 'to do good and to communicate.' Possibly 'communicate' in such a connexion would have been misunderstood. The corresponding noun is rendered 'distribution' by A.V. in 2 Cor. ix. 13, by R.V. 'contribution.' The 'sympathy' suggested by the margin here of R.V. is certainly implied in the word, which may be said to sum up, in itself, the unity, generosity, and practical piety of the Church, as it worked out, under St Paul (see esp. 2 Cor. viii. ix.), that problem of 'rich and poor together' which the earliest impulses of 'the faith' had solved for the moment only by the short rule of Acts iii. 44, 45, 'all that believed were together and had all things *common*,' —the same word from which our 'willing to *communicate*' comes. The root principle remains the same (2 Cor. viii. 13—15), and this our word conveys, though the practice was not workable for long of selling all into a common stock. G. Herbert seems to express *both* of the present adjectives in

'Joyn hands with God to make a man to live,
Give to all something; to a good poore man,
Till thou change names, and be where he began.'
The Church Porch.

The Christian wealth of England is still far below such a principle; else why the 'weariness and painfulness' known to so many of our clergy in begging appeals for 'good works' of piety and charity?

19. *laying up in store*] The compound verb, again peculiar, is another example of the law of later Greek explained *v.* 8. Here we have the riches in the form of 'good works' laid *away* as a solid foundation in and *from* which the building rises. This 'building up,' if the full explanation of the verse given on iii. 13 be sound, is of the spiritual life both here and hereafter. The rich cannot 'lay hold of' any true higher life, if they neglect the plainest duty, lying first and lowest, of using their wealth for 'God who provided all.' So in iv. 8 the life is only to be grasped by spiritual 'training.'

that they may lay hold] The same tense and voice as the 'lay hold' of *v.* 12, and the interpretation is similar.

on eternal life] The MS. authority is strongly in favour of the

committed to *thy* trust, avoiding profane *and* vain babblings,
and oppositions of science falsely so called: which some 21

adverb 'really' in place of 'eternal,' with the article; as R.V. **the life which is life indeed**; and nothing could be better than such a phrase to describe the 'heavenly' or 'spiritual' or 'eternal' life, in its two parts on this side and on that side the grave, as explained above on *v.* 12 and iv. 8; 'the life worth living.'

20, 21. A LAST APPEAL. THE KEEPING OF THE DEPOSIT.

20. See the summary above at *v.* 3. This brief *résumé*, at the close, of the main anxiety of the whole Epistle is like the corresponding *résumé*, *v.* 16, of the rule for widows, and *v.* 24 of the visitation of presbyters.

O Timothy] Previously, and in 2 Tim., when the address is less intense and solemn, 'my child,' 'my child Timothy.'

keep] The stronger word **guard**. Compare 1 Joh. v. 21, 'Little children, guard yourselves from idols.'

that which is committed to thy *trust*] The MSS. favour the simpler noun, compounded with only one preposition, here and in the only other places where the word occurs in N. T., 2 Tim. i. 12, 14, the latter place being exactly parallel. What is this 'deposit?' It has been thought to be (1) grace for his own spiritual life, 'the commandment' above *v.* 14, (2) grace for the office of superintending the Church at Ephesus, 'the charge' above *v.* 17 and elsewhere; and these *are* the two subjects pressed most closely upon Timothy, *next to the great, the recurring and now all absorbing anxiety*, that he may have (3) grace to maintain sound doctrine; the 'charge' of i. 3, 18, iv. 6, 16, vi. 3; 2 Tim. i. 13, 14, ii. 2, 16. The words which follow are alone sufficient to make (3) the certain reference. In effect, to use the words quoted from St Vincent of the island-school of Lerins (the author of the famous canon of Christian doctrine 'quod semper quod ubique quod ab omnibus'), St Paul says to Timothy 'Depositum custodi: *catholicae fidei talentum* inviolatum illibatumque conserva.'

avoiding profane and *vain babblings*] Lit. **turning away from the profane babblings**; the article with 'babblings' and not with 'oppositions' shews that both go together, with 'knowledge.' 'Babblings' is another of the 'Pastoral' compounds recurring in 2 Tim. ii. 16. The word is literally 'empty voicings,' vox et praeterea nihil, windbag; speculations and errors which are the complete opposite of the solid Church truth on its firm foundation and rock, 'Thou art the Christ.' For the accus. after this verb, cf. Winer, § 38, 2, 6.

oppositions of science falsely so called] Rather, as R. V. **the knowledge which is falsely so called.** 'The knowledge falsely so called' is in the Greek the well-known *Gnosis*, only used here in N. T. with direct reference to the heretical teaching, though the allusions, both with substantive and verb, imply that assumptions of superior knowledge were among the claims of the new theology. The 'oppositions' meant are probably the *dualistic* oppositions between the good and evil principle, see Introduction, pp. 45, 46; though some explain them as the dialectical

professing have erred concerning the faith. Grace *be* with thee. Amen.

¶ The first to Timothy was written from Laodicea, which is the chiefest city of Phrygia Pacatiana.

niceties and subtle rhetorical antitheses of the teachers. See Dr Hort's interpretation, Appendix B. This peculiar 'Pastoral' word goes to make the Apostle's biting 'aculeus in fine.'

21. *which some professing*] 'Which,' this misnamed Gnosis. '*Professing*' has occurred in this sense ii. 10.

have erred] Lit., 'missed the mark,' as i. 6 and 2 Tim. ii. 18; aorist as *v.* 10.

the faith] As above, *v.* 10.

Grace be *with thee*] MS. authority gives the plural **with you**, as at the end of 2 Tim. and Titus; the Apostolic benediction being sent through the delegate episcopus to his Church.

There is, of course, no sufficient authority for the Subscription, which (like the Subscriptions to the other epistles of St Paul) is ascribed to Bp Euthalius (5th cent.) and is therefore later than the best MSS. The Alexandrian and Sinaitic MSS. read only FIRST EPISTLE TO TIMOTHY. Its statement that the letter was written from Laodicea is supposed to be drawn from Col. iv. 16. See the paraphrase of Erasmus: 'vicissim vos legatis epistolam quae Timotheo scripta fuit ex Laodicensium urbe.' But Bp Lightfoot, *Coloss.* p. 343, gives strong reasons against this identification; (1) that St Paul had not ever been at Laodicea, indeed had been long a prisoner either at Cæsarea or Rome, when he wrote to the Colossians; (2) that 1 Timothy bears many proofs of having been written elsewhere than at Laodicea, and of being separated by an interval of some years at least from the Colossian letter.

THE SECOND EPISTLE OF PAUL THE APOSTLE

TO

TIMOTHY.

PAUL, an apostle of Jesus Christ by the will of God, 1
according to the promise of life which is in Christ Jesus,

TITLE.

The best MSS. give, as for the first Epistle, the shortest title, **Second Epistle to Timothy**.

CH. I. APOSTOLIC GIFTS AND RESPONSIBILITIES.

1, 2. THE SALUTATION TO TIMOTHY.

1. *an apostle of Jesus Christ*] Read with the MSS. **Christ Jesus**, and see note on 1 Tim. i. 1 for the frequency of this order of the words.

by the will of God] This phrase with the preceding words in precisely the same order commences the Ep. to Colossians and Ep. to Ephesians, followed in the former by 'and Timothy our brother.' The phrase also introduces both 1 Cor. and 2 Cor. The use here shews that there is no asserting of impugned authority intended by it; but rather there is a going back to the first calling and sending by God, from no personal merit, but by His purpose of mercy alone; and **apostle through the will of God** is a short phrase for the full statement of Gal. i. 15, 16, 'it was the good pleasure of God, who separated me even from my mother's womb and called me through His grace, to reveal His Son in me, that I might preach Him among the Gentiles.'

according to the promise of life] This, *for Timothy*, is the sphere of his apostleship as of his life. 'To me to live is Christ.' 'If any man be in Christ, he is a new creation.' 'Lay hold on the life which is life indeed.' For the apostleship in regard to *Titus* and the Cretans see note on Tit. i. 1. Render, with R.V., **the promise of the life**, the article with 'in Christ Jesus' making 'life' definite at once; while according to regular use no article is required in the Greek prepositional phrase on which 'life' depends, 'according to the promise,' from the nature of the word 'promise.' Compare the usage in 1 Tim. iv. 8, 'having the promise of the life which now is and which is to come.' That passage and 1 Tim. vi. 12 give the clue to the choice of the phrase here. Timothy there is exhorted to train himself in the godliness which has the promise of 'the divine life' and to

2 to Timothy, *my* dearly beloved son: Grace, mercy, *and*
peace, from God the Father and Christ Jesus our Lord.
3 I thank God, whom I serve from *my* forefathers with pure
conscience, that without ceasing I have remembrance of

'lay hold of it' (see notes). So here his spiritual father recalls his own experience and assurance to encourage his son—the free love of God which had laid hold of him and given him work as the seal of pardon, and (in the doing of that work) 'life in Christ Jesus,' begun here to be perfected hereafter in spite of persecution. The greater the sense of sin, the stronger the sense of rescuing 'grace and mercy,' and the clearer the assurance of 'peace,' the crown of blessings.

2. my *dearly beloved son*] Or **my beloved child**. 'Child' as in 1 Tim. i. 1; 'beloved' in place of 'mine own,' but surely not a weaker word, when we remember its use to express 'the only begotten,' Matt. iii. 17.

mercy] Omitted in the greeting to Titus is in both the letters to Timothy, and may imply St Paul's inner oneness with his 'beloved child' in the feeling 'he shewed me *all* the mercy as he shewed me *all* the sin.' Cf. note 1 Tim. i. 2. All is 'writ large' in *vv.* 8—12.

3—7. Timothy's Inheritance of Personal Faith and Ministerial Gifts a double ground of Appeal.

From what St Paul was himself follows now the first appeal to Timothy, based on his affectionate remembrance of the son's likeness to his spiritual father, (1) in the personal faith forged with links of natural piety, (2) in the ministerial gift transmitted as a spiritual heritage. With his usual fine tact St Paul hints a connexion between his own and Timothy's early experiences, to emphasize his depth of feeling towards him.

3. *whom I serve...with pure conscience*] The verb 'serve' with its noun 'service' was specially used to render the worship of Jehovah by the covenant people; it is the same as in St Paul's profession before Felix, Acts xxiv. 14, 'after the way which they call a sect so serve I the God of our fathers,' and again before Agrippa, Acts xxvi. 7. The service of the old covenant was true and real service so long as it was with a pure conscience and until the conscience was enlightened. Hence the force of the verb with its qualifying clauses in the very similar passage, Rom. i. 9, 'God is my witness whom I serve in my spirit in the Gospel of His Son.' The old service of sacrifice and ceremonial ('the giving of the law and the service,' Rom. ix. 4) has given place to the 'living sacrifice, the reasonable or spiritual service,' Rom. xii. 1. Cf. Phil. iii. 3.

that without ceasing I have remembrance] A.V. follows the Vulg. which has 'quod habeam tui memoriam.' R.V. better, 'how unceasing is my remembrance,' the construction being similar to Rom. i. 9, 'God is my witness how unceasing.' It is objected to this that 'the importunity of Paul's prayers for Timothy could not have been the occasion

thee in my prayers night and day; greatly desiring to see 4
thee, being mindful of thy tears, that I may be filled with

of his solemn thanksgiving to God.' But though the *formal construction* may seem to limit the object of the thanks, yet it is really more in accord with St Paul's manner of thought *and* speech to take all the clauses to the end of *v.* 5 as making up his thanksgiving. The structure of the chapter is evidently, 'I am thy dear father in life and work; I am very thankful to have a dear son in my desolateness—to remember thee at all hours, and most and best in my prayers,—to count the days and nights till I shall see thee—to think of thy tears when I left thee—and so to hope for refreshing news of thy true and trusty faith, learnt like my own, at a mother's knee. By all this that is between us—and yet more, by that gift of gifts to thee, the Grace of Orders, when these hands of mine were laid upon thy head, and my work was thine, O Timothy my son, play the man, the minister; the man of God, God's minister; with me and after me.'

in my prayers] More precisely, **in my supplications.** See note on 1 Tim. ii. 1, from which we see that this word indicates a felt 'want' and a petition for its supply. St Paul sorely *wanted* strength and support for the last struggle, and Timothy could help him; so he prayed, not *in Timothy's behalf* so much as for Timothy to come *in his behalf*.

night and day] Variously taken, with 'my prayers,' as A.V., or with 'longing to see thee' (as R.V.). The phrase in the accusative, Luke ii. 37, closes the sentence; in the genitive, as here, and 1 Thess. ii. 9, iii. 10, introduces it; in these latter passages the participles equally with 'longing' require emphasis and do not lose it by 'night and day' preceding; so that Dean Alford's objection to following these here as precedent seems needless. 'Greatly desiring' seems a fair rendering of the verb alone, the preposition indicating in this case not 'greatly,' but 'towards,' 'yearning towards.' Render the clause **night and day longing to see thee.**

4. *being mindful of thy tears*] At the close we must suppose of the visit paid him by St Paul in accordance with the intention expressed 1 Tim. iii. 14. It seems very awkward to insert this clause as a subordinate parenthesis 'with a faint causal force,' 'longing to see thee, as I remember thy tears in order that I may be filled with joy'; but this must be the effect of R.V. rendering. And again there is difficulty in either rendering of the participle in *v.* 5 with this construction; (1) A.V. 'when I call to remembrance' present, whereas we ought to read the aorist (2) R.V. 'having been reminded,' implying that there had been some occasion or messenger to give such news, of which we have at least no other hint. It is better to follow Drs Westcott and Hort in putting a comma after 'tears' and joining verses 4 and 5 thus, 'that I may be filled with joy in being reminded.' The thought underlying this phrase 'to be filled with joy,' 'to have one's joy fulfilled,' is, as Dr Westcott puts it in 1 Joh. i. 4, that the fulfilment of Christian joy depends upon the realisation of fellowship. This fellowship may be *with* bodily presence, as 2 Joh. 12; Joh. iii. 29; or

5 joy; when I call to remembrance the unfeigned faith that is
in thee, which dwelt first in thy grandmother Lois, and thy
6 mother Eunice; and I am persuaded that in thee also. Where-

without, as Joh. xv. 11, xvi. 24, xvii. 13; 1 Joh. i. 4, 'these things we write that our joy may be fulfilled.' The joy of the apostle is secured by his 'little children' realising full fellowship. Similarly the thought here is an echo of St Paul's feelings expressed 5 or 6 years before to his Philippian 'beloved ones,' and the expressions are an echo too. Through that letter ran the theme 'gaudeo: gaudete'; in that, with a wonderful tenderness and delicacy St Paul shews them that 'unity,' 'brotherly love,' is 'the one thing lacking' to perfect their joy: the one thing that to hear of or see in them will fulfil *his* too. Compare Phil. i. 3—8, ii. 1, 2, iv. 4. Through this letter runs the theme 'fidem servavi: serva'; and with the same considerate love St Paul makes the appeal to his timid son to be 'strong in the faith' turn first on the *fulfilment of his own joy* which will result.

The final conjunction 'in order that' depends then formally on 'I give thanks in my supplications,' really on the whole affectionate yearning and praying spirit of *vv.* 3 and 4.

5. *remembrance*] The noun occurs only 2 Pet. i. 13, iii. 1, besides in N. T.; the verb Tit. iii. 1, where see note, 2 Pet. i. 12, &c.

the unfeigned faith that is in thee] 'Unfeigned,' 'true and trusty.' Contrasted with that of Phygelus and Hermogenes and Demas, i. 15, iv. 9. The word is applied to 'love,' Rom. xii. 9, and to 'wisdom,' James iii. 17. It has been used with 'faith,' 1 Tim. i. 5.

which dwelt first] The pronoun may be rendered **a faith such as**, 'the which faith,' as it is rendered 1 Tim. i. 4. Cf. also 1 Tim. iii. 15. 'Dwell in,' the verb, is used (in quotation) in 2 Cor. vi. 16 of the indwelling of the Almighty, in Rom. viii. 11, 2 Tim. i. 14 of the indwelling of the Holy Spirit, in Col. iii. 16 of the indwelling of 'the word of Christ,' the nearest passage to this; where however Bp Lightfoot explains it of 'the presence of Christ in the heart as an inward monitor'; as Dr Westcott explains 1 John ii. 14 'ye are strong and the word (of God) abideth in you,' 'the natural endowment of energetic vigour is consecrated to a divine end by a divine voice.' Here too, then, 'faith' is personified. Like 'Heavenly Wisdom' she 'dwelt in' these pious Jewesses from the first, in their early hold of the promises made to Israel, before 'the glad news' of Jesus Christ the 'glory of his people Israel.' Then, in a larger room, a clearer light within them, the Faith of their fathers in a pure conscience was 'transfigured' into the Unclouded Faith of Christ Jesus their Saviour and dwelt within them, and the light and love from that pure presence there passed over into the breast of son and grandson.

thy grandmother Lois] The non-Attic word is used. Eunice is referred to Acts xvi. 1 as 'a Jewess which believed.'

and I am persuaded that in thee also] A.V. following the Greek idiom of ellipse; R.V. 'and, I am persuaded, in thee also,' following the English idiom of ellipse.

fore I put thee in remembrance that *thou* stir up the gift of
God, which is in thee by the putting on of my hands. For 7
God hath not given us the spirit of fear; but of power, and

Prof. Reynolds quotes here 'the celebrated mothers of Augustine, of Chrysostom, of Basil, whose life sincerity and constancy became vicariously a glorious heritage of the universal Church.' We may add the mother of the Wesleys.

6. *Wherefore I put thee in remembrance*] More decidedly **For which cause.** It will break the whole delicacy and tenderness of the exhortation, unless the cause be taken as the thankful recognition of Timothy's living faith and likeness to his spiritual father.

put thee in remembrance] See note on the last verse. Timothy had been sent himself to 'put the Corinthians in remembrance of St Paul's ways that were in Christ,' ten years before, and was then his 'child beloved and faithful in the Lord.' See the same word 1 Cor. iv. 17, the only other use in N.T. in the active.

that thou *stir up the gift of God*] The verb may be rendered fully, dwelling on the metaphor, 'kindle the glowing embers of the gift of God,' or as margin of R.V. 'stir into flame.' The 'live coal from the altar' had 'touched his lips' at his ordination; the 'lightening with celestial fire' from 'the anointing Spirit' in His 'sevenfold gifts' had taken place, as it has ever been invoked and bestowed at 'The Ordering of Priests,' cf. v. 14. According to the view taken of Timothy's greater or less despondency and slackness, the stress may be either on the verb or on the preposition with which it is compounded; either '*re*kindle' or 'kindle *into flame.*' Perhaps we may best adopt Dr Reynolds's interpretation of the position. 'We ought not to infer more than that Timothy's work had suffered through his despondency arising from the peril and imprisonment of his master. He may have been ready to despair of the Church. The special *charisma* needed therefore in his case was *parrhesia* or a clear bold utterance of the faith that was in him.'

by the putting on of my hands] Rather, **through the laying on.** See note on 1 Tim. iv. 14, where the character of this 'laying on of hands' is shewn. 'My hands' here is not inconsistent with 'the hands of the presbytery' there. St Paul of course was chief among the presbyters. But *there* the largeness of the attendant testimony, the fulness of the circle of ordaining elders, is put forward as a reason for every nerve being strained to run the race: since he is compassed with so great a cloud of witnesses, let him give all heed that his 'progress may be manifest unto all.' *Here* one chief figure, the closest and the dearest, fills all the view: 'for *my* sake, my son.'

7. *For God hath not given us*] Rather, **gave us**; i.e. both St Paul and Timothy, at the time of their 'setting apart' for the ministry; this gift is of special grace for special work, more particularly the proper temper and character formed in them by the Holy Spirit; and this **not a spirit of cowardice,** 'a spirit' being preferable to 'the spirit' of A.V. as more plainly indicating this character, the spirit we are of in regard to ministerial work, than 'the spirit,' which though written with s, not S,

8 of love, and of a sound mind. Be not thou therefore ashamed

is still liable to be mistaken by the listener or reader as though the Holy Spirit were meant. This indeed Bp Ellicott wishes, needlessly making two classes of passages, one like Eph. i. 17, and this, where the reference to the gift from God is very near, and one like Gal. vi. 1, where it is not. But all the passages in effect suppose the working of the Holy Spirit on our human spirit so that we have a certain spirit, temper, character, resulting.

Some MSS. and Versions (and so Clement and Chrysostom) have confused this verse with Rom. viii. 15 and read instead of *deilias*, 'cowardice,' the word that is used there in the totally different connexion, *douleias*, 'slavery.' And similarly we have there the variant *deilias*, 'cowardice.' It is quite natural that the new phrases coined for the new needs should echo the very ring of the older at times, and at times be (as we have seen) fresh-minted altogether. The *noun* 'cowardice' occurs only here in N.T.; the verb and adjective belonging to it occur only as used *by our Lord Himself*, 1 John xiv. 27, 'let not your heart turn coward'; Matt. viii. 26, 'why are ye cowards, O ye of little faith' (so Mk. iv. 40); Rev. xxi. 8, 'for the cowards and unbelieving... their part shall be in the lake that burneth with fire.' This striking usage emphasises the warning that follows not to be 'ashamed of the *testimony of our LORD*.'

but of power, of love, and of a sound mind] '*power*—yes, for surely not in vain is spoken over us the consecrating word; not in vain do we go forth bearing authority from Christ... We "preach Christ crucified,"—"the power of God."' Bp How, *Pastoral Work*, c. vi; who also well describes the '*love*' as 'a simple, self-forgetting, self-sacrificing love' that can lay itself out to win even 'the uninteresting, the hard, cold, rude, ignorant, degraded'; but for '*sound mind*' gives a less convincing quotation from Keble's preface to the *Christian Year*, 'a sober standard of feeling in matters of practical religion.' The R.V. gives 'discipline,' and in the margin as the exact rendering of the Greek, 'sobering,' *sôphronismos* differing from *sôphrosynê* 'soberness,' as *logismos*, 'reasoning,' differs from *logos*, 'reason.' But as the word is the noun of the verb rendered Tit. ii. 4 'train in purity,' and its root is the word *sôphrôn* rendered 1 Tim. iii. 2 and elsewhere in these epistles 'pure' (see notes), 'training in purity' would seem the exact force here. And though the verb (note on Tit. ii. 4) and therefore its noun seems in general usage to mean only 'train,' 'discipline,' yet here too, thinking of the keywords in these epistles, we shall believe that St Paul is *raising* the word back to its proper level of '*moral* discipline.' So St Gregory treating of the life of the Pastor (*Pastoral Charge*, Pt. ii. c. 2) makes this the first qualification; 'Rector semper cogitatione sit mundus —quia necesse est ut esse munda debeat manus quae diluere sordes curat.' Then we find, as we should expect, that these three brief notes of the ministerial character of Timothy are expanded through the next chapter: *power*, ii. 14—19, *moral discipline*, ii. 20—22, *love*, ii. 23—26.

of the testimony of our Lord, nor of me his prisoner: but be
thou partaker of the afflictions of the gospel according to the
power of God; who hath saved us, and called *us* with a 9

8—12. Appeal to Timothy to be a brave Champion both of the saving work of Christ and of the suffering witness of St Paul.

8. *Be not thou therefore ashamed*] Omit 'thou' here, and in 'be thou partaker;' the stress is on the 'shame' and 'suffering,' and no pronoun is expressed in Greek.

the testimony] For, in behalf of, the Cross of Christ, recalling the very words of Christ, when He first declared 'the Cross,' Lk. ix. 26, 'whosoever shall be ashamed of me.' 'Testimony' is the neuter word as in 1 Tim. ii. 6 (see note). Here with gen. objective, though in 2 Thess. i. 10 with gen. subjective 'our testimony unto you.'

our Lord] The phrase occurs only here and in 1 Tim. i. 14, in St Paul; but is used also by St Peter, 2 Pet. iii. 15, 'the longsuffering of our Lord,' and in Heb. vii. 14, 'our Lord sprang out of Juda.'

Both quasi-imperative and imperative are *aorist*, and contrasted with *present* imperatives imply the *taking up* or *not taking up* a particular line of action in contrast with the continuing or not continuing some course. Whether or not Timothy had as yet shewn shame or cowardice, this exhortation delicately looks only to the future. Winer, § 56 b.

me his prisoner] See Introduction, p. 44.

partaker of the afflictions of the gospel] Vulg., Th. Mops. (true reading), 'collabora Euangelio.' R.V. **suffer hardship with the gospel.** The exact form occurs ii. 3 with no case attached: the thought in both places is the same, and is again elaborated in the rhythmical refrain of ii. 11, 12. Fellowship with Christ, with the Gospel, with St Paul—it is all one and the same thing. 'With the Gospel' is more natural than 'for the Gospel,' which would need a preposition, 'in behalf of,' 'for the sake of,' 'in' or 'unto' according to N.T. usage. For the personifying, which is quite in St Paul's manner, compare Tit. ii. 5, 'that the word of God be not blasphemed;' Rom. x. 16, 'they did not all obey the Gospel;' Phil. iv. 14, 'ye had fellowship with my affliction;' and especially Phil. i. 27, 'with one soul striving together with the faith of the Gospel.'

according to the power of God] Looks back to *v.* 7; God, who giveth, *hath* power.

9. *who hath saved us*] Rather, **who saved us**; the 'saving' and 'calling' should both be referred to the same point of time—viz. Baptism; and verses 9 and 10 are compressed by the Prayer-Book Catechism into the sentence 'he hath *called me to this state of salvation* through Jesus Christ our Saviour.' See note 1 Tim. ii. 4.

us] Not limited to Paul and Timothy, but as in the parallel passage, Tit. iii. 5, embracing all the baptised, all who have 'the faith of God's elect.' See generally the note there. The 'holy calling' here answers, in its twofold aspect of privilege and duty, to the 'heirs of eternal life,' and the 'maintaining of good works,' there.

holy calling, not according to our works, but according to
his own purpose and grace, which was given us in Christ
10 Jesus before the world began, but is now made manifest by
the appearing of our Saviour Jesus Christ, who hath abolished
death, and hath brought life and immortality to light through

not according to our works] More exactly, Tit. iii. 5, 'not by virtue of works, works in righteousness, which we did,' **but in accordance with His own purpose and free gift given to us in Christ Jesus in eternal times gone by**; see note on the parallel clause Tit. i. 3, where the phrase 'eternal times' is explained, and the preposition 'before.' Theod. Mops. gives well the connecting thought which carries St Paul here from his appeal for boldness into another of his exulting Gospel anthems. 'Take,' he says in effect, 'take great pains, bear long pains —for a gift so great, so age-long.'

10. *is now made manifest*] **but manifested now**; the opposition thus put between the 'given' and the 'manifested' implies that the gift had been, in the phrase of the other parallel passage, Rom. xvi. 25, '*kept in silence* through times eternal.' Compare 1 Tim. iii. 16, 'who in flesh was manifested.'

by the appearing] The one use of the substantive 'epiphany' for the Incarnation, and so the authority for our use of it in the Church's season of Epiphany. See notes on 1 Tim. vi. 14 and Tit. ii. 13. *The verb*, with this reference, occurs again Tit. ii. 11 and iii. 4.

our Saviour Jesus Christ] Again, with the best MSS., **Christ Jesus**; the title now especially frequent, see note 1 Tim. i. 1.

who hath abolished death] More exactly, **abolishing death, as he did, and bringing into light instead life and immortality**. The verb for 'abolish,' lit. 'to make useless, powerless,' is used here of the Incarnation; in Heb. ii. 14, of the Atonement; in 1 Cor. xv. 26, of the Second Advent, as effecting this victory; at each stage the victory is assured. To us the Incarnation and the Atonement are extended through union with Christ in Holy Baptism. Compare Dr H. Macmillan, *Two Worlds are Ours*, p. 22. '*Naturally*, we are the creatures of days and months and years that vanish, regulated by sun and moon and stars that will perish. But, born anew in Christ, we enter into a sphere where time has no existence, where one day is as a thousand years, and a thousand years as one day; we lay hold on eternal life.'

hath brought...to light] Vulg., Th. Mops., 'illuminavit,' i.e. 'shed over them a full mid-day light.' The use of the corresponding substantive 2 Cor. iv. 4, 6, shews the force best, *the illuminating power of the Gospel of the glory of Christ*. 'Life,' 'the life that is truly life,' 1 Tim. vi. 19, the spiritual life, which is 'immortality;' see notes on 1 Tim. vi. 12, 19; iv. 8. The Ember hymn well expresses the present glory of this 'life' thus illuminated,—'our glory meets us ere we die.'

through the gospel] Added to the second half of the clause, as coming back to the thought of verse 8, where 'the gospel' personified

the gospel: whereunto I am appointed a preacher, and an 11
apostle, and a teacher of the Gentiles. For the which cause 12
I also suffer these *things*: nevertheless I am not ashamed:
for I know whom I have believed, and I am persuaded that
he is able to keep that which I have committed unto *him*
against that day. Hold fast the form of sound words, which 13

represents the saving work of the Lord and the suffering ministry of St Paul as here.

11. *whereunto I am appointed a preacher*] Rather, **for which I —remember—was appointed a herald.** St Paul 'magnifies his office' here in the same terms as in 1 Tim. ii. 7; but there to assert his authority for ruling, here to commend his example in suffering: see note.

12. *For the which cause I also suffer these* things] R.V. places 'also' after 'suffer' that the emphasis may belong as much to 'these things' as to 'suffer' according to the order of the Greek; and substitutes **yet** for 'nevertheless,' which is too emphatic for the Greek word.

am not ashamed] The reference to ver. 8 is obvious, as 'these things' are the chains and dungeon of 'the Lord's prisoner.' Cf. Rom. i. 16.

I know whom I have believed] Rather with R.V. **him whom,** because it is the relative not the interrogative pronoun that is used.

to keep that which I have committed unto him] R.V. places in the margin the alternative sense, according to its rule when the balance of authority is nearly even, 'that which he hath committed unto me'; and gives the literal Greek 'my deposit.' The genitive of the personal pronoun rendered 'my' may be either subjective here or objective; hence the uncertainty, which the context does not clear up entirely. On the whole, looking to the speciality of the phrase and its use in 1 Tim. vi. 20, and below ver. 14 of Timothy's guarding of the sound doctrine handed on to him, *and here only besides,*—it seems most probable that St Paul is adopting, to describe God's commission to him, the same words in which he describes the same commission to Timothy. And by a change very characteristic of St Paul, when we might have expected the phrase to run 'am persuaded that I shall be enabled to guard' it is made to run 'am persuaded that he is able to guard.' Cf. '*yet not I, but Christ liveth in me*' Gal. ii. 20. The guarding, thus, is exactly the same, viz. God's, in the 14th verse, 'guard *through the Holy Ghost which dwelleth in us.*' Compare Rom. vii. 24, 25 with viii. 9. See note on 1 Tim. vi. 20, for a fuller account of the 'deposit' itself, as the commission to hand on sound doctrine. If at the end of the first epistle this had become the Apostle's chief absorbing anxiety, much more is it so now, in the very hour of his departure.

against that day] With a view to, in readiness for, that day; cf. Jude 6, 'angels...he hath kept...unto the judgment of the great day.'

thou hast heard of me, in faith and love which is in Christ
14 Jesus. *That* good thing which was committed unto *thee*

13, 14. The double ground of Appeal is also the double line of Responsive Action.

13. *Hold fast the form of sound words*] Rather, **Hold to the model;** the word for 'form' has occurred in 1 Tim. i. 16. As Bp Lightfoot points out, Clem. *ad Cor.* c. v. *fin.*, the compound signifies the first roughly modelled block in the sculptor's art; just as in the sister art the similarly formed compound *hypogrammos* is the pencil drawing to be traced over in ink, or the outline to be filled in and coloured. Cf. 1 Pet. ii. 21, 'leaving you an example that ye should follow his steps.' **Hold to or keep to** rather than 'hold fast,' because it is the simple not the compound verb.

sound words] Here opposed to the gangrene of Hymenæus and Philetus, ch. ii. 17, see notes on 1 Tim. i. 10; Tit. i. 9. Add the following from Dean Vaughan on '*The Wholesome Words of Jesus Christ*,' Cambridge 'University Sermons' of 1866. 'Never before through the whole volume of his letters has St Paul applied that term to the Gospel. Now it is almost his only epithet for it....New experiences make new expressions....St Paul himself saw the first symptoms of this morbid action of the Gospel; alternations of hectic flush and deadly pallor; of a pulse now throbbing, now torpid; of lost appetite and broken sleep; of deformed excrescence and palsied limb....Each falsehood in religion is some overstrained onesided or isolated truth. Either free grace or free will—either faith or duty—either truth or charity—either dependence or responsibility—either the Humanity or the Divinity—not both, not all—this has been in all time the oscillation, the ebb and flow, of human doctrine; and the Gospel has been not healthy, not well, but sickly, at times almost dying, in consequence. The *wholesome words* are known by this sign—that in them every part of the truth is equally present, every function of the life equally vigorous. Health is the balance of the powers: a healthy Gospel is one which holds in exact equilibrium opposite forces—excluding nothing that is good, yet suffering no one good thing to engross and swallow up the whole.'

which thou hast heard of me] 'Of' in the sense of **from**, the Latin *a* not *de;* so very frequently in A.V. representing the other meaning of *a*, 'by'; cf. 1 Cor. xi. 32 'chastened of the Lord.'

in faith and love which is in Christ Jesus] The faith and the love are both 'in Christ Jesus,' and are, as Fairbairn puts it, 'the spiritual element or frame of mind in which the pattern of things exhibited to him should be remembered and applied.' The clause belongs to 'keep,' not (as Alford) to 'heard.' So A.V. and R.V., by the insertion of the comma. St Paul had as *his* secret of activity and endurance the present sense of a present Saviour, and he longs for Timothy too to possess it as constantly. See note on ii. 1.

14. That *good thing which was committed unto* thee] **The good**

keep by the Holy Ghost which dwelleth in us. This thou 15
knowest, that all they which are in Asia be turned away from
me; of whom are Phygellus and Hermogenes. The Lord 16
give mercy unto the house of Onesiphorus; for he oft re-

deposit as in *v.* 12 and 1 Tim. vi. 20, *catholicae fidei talentum;* see notes on both verses.

keep by the Holy Ghost which dwelleth in us] **Guard through the Holy Ghost.** The indwelling of the Holy Ghost is 'the gift of God' in verse 6, the 'Grace of Holy Orders' for the office and work of a priest; cf. Acts xiii. 2, 4.

15—18. A SAD WARNING AND A BRIGHT EXAMPLE.

The connexion is: 'Many faithless ones failed me; be thou faithful all the more:—the faith and practice of an Onesiphorus may surely be thine.'

15. *all they which are in Asia be turned away*] Omit 'be'; the tense describes a definite act, not a continuing state. We are left to conjecture when and where this desertion took place. 'They which are in Asia' implies the residents in Asia, but the desertion may have been either in Asia, between the first and second imprisonments, or in Rome: perhaps the former more probably, on the ground that Timothy's knowledge of it is appealed to, as also is his knowledge of Onesiphorus' service *at Ephesus*, while the help rendered by Onesiphorus at Rome is spoken of independently. The 'Asia' meant is the Roman province according to most Commentators (Howson, *Dict. Bib.*) which embraced Lydia, Mysia, Caria, and Phrygia, as distinguished from 'Asia Minor' commonly so called and from the continent of Asia. Lewin however (*Life and Epistles of St Paul*, I. p. 190) identifies the Asia of N.T. with Lydia alone, i.e. from the Caicus to the Mæander, with the plain of the Cayster within it, which Homer calls 'the Asian Meadow,' cf. *Il.* II. 461, Virg. *Georg.* I. 383, 'Asia...prata Caystri'; and he makes three strong points: (1) that the 'Mysia' of Acts xvi. 6 seems clearly separated there *from* 'Asia'; (2) that '*the* seven churches which are in Asia' on this hypothesis just cover the whole district; (3) that 'the dwellers in Asia' of Acts ii. 9 heard their own language, not *three* languages, Lydian, Mysian and Carian. Prof. Ramsay, the most recent authority on the geography of Asia Minor, appears to support this latter view.

of whom are Phygellus and Hermogenes] The MSS. favour the form **Phygelus**, but nothing is known of him; or yet of Hermogenes.

16. *The Lord give mercy*] The phrase 'give mercy' does not occur elsewhere in N.T. As the use of the word 'mercy' with 'grace and peace' in the salutation to Timothy in both epistles marks the special intimacy and tenderness of sympathy between St Paul and his 'son in the faith,' so here the 'friend in need' is the 'friend indeed.'

the house of Onesiphorus] The natural though not necessary inference from this phrase here and in iv. 19, and from the prayer in ver. 18, is that Onesiphorus himself was dead.

17 freshed me, and was not ashamed of my chain: but, when
he was in Rome, he sought me out very diligently, and found
18 *me.* The Lord grant unto him that *he* may find mercy of

he oft refreshed me, and was not ashamed of my chain] That is, '*in Asia*, before I came to Rome this last time' or 'when on my way hither bound.' The clause which follows seems to prevent our referring this to anything *at* Rome e.g. the *libera custodia* of the first imprisonment Acts xxviii. 20; Eph. vi. 20, where the word is used, as here, in the singular. But we may refer it to a similar *libera custodia*, which was exchanged on arrival at Rome for that close confinement which needed Onesiphorus' 'zealous' seeking out.

17. *when he was in Rome, he sought me out very diligently*] It is the simple verb, and, according to the best MSS., the positive not the comparative adverb, **he sought me diligently**. What 'close confinement' could be under the Emperor Tiberius we see from Suet. *Tib.* 61 (quoted by Lewin) 'quibusdam custodiae traditis non modo studendi solatium ademptum sed etiam sermonis et colloquii usus.' What it could be under Nero's lieutenant Tigellinus, who succeeded Burrus as *praefectus praetorii* A.D. 63, we learn from Tacitus, who says of him (*Hist.* i. 72) 'crudelitatem mox deinde avaritiam et virilia scelera exercuit corrupto ad omne facinus Nerone.'

Where did Onesiphorus find St Paul? Nero to screen himself had given the word for the most virulent animosity against the Christians (Tac. *Ann.* XV. 44). When St Paul then was brought prisoner to Rome, he must have been known as one of their chief leaders, and as such would be confined now not in any 'hired house,' not in any 'guard house' of the *praetorium*, or any minor state prison, such as that of Appius Claudius if it still existed, or even the 'Stone Quarry Prison,' *lautumiae*, at the furthest north-west corner of the Forum, but (we may believe) in the Carcer itself, the Tullianum or 'Well-Dungeon,' at the foot of the Capitol. This last with its chill vault and oozing spring was the worst, as we gather from Seneca *Controv.* IX. 3. where one Julius Sabinus asks to be removed from the 'Carcer'—the Prison *par excellence*—to the *lautumiae*. See Burn, *Rome and the Campagna*, p. 80, and his fuller account of the 'Carcer' in Excursus.

18. *The Lord grant unto him that* he *may find mercy of the Lord in that day*] The repetition of 'the Lord' arises apparently from the use of two clauses together which had become customary separate phrases in intercessory prayer. In its first use, as in ver. 16, with the article, understand 'our Lord' as in the Epistles generally, cf Winer, Pt. iii. § 19*a*; and in its second use 'God the Father' (Bp Ellicott). For a somewhat similar English use cf. Coll. for 4 S. in Advent 'O LORD, raise up (we pray thee) thy power and come among us...through the satisfaction of thy Son our Lord.' The sentence should be regarded, as by Revisers, as a parenthetic prayer forced from him as he recalls the love that persevered to find him 'in the lowest pit'; though he is chiefly bent on completing the tale of benefits for Timothy's good; 'go thou' he would imply 'and do likewise.'

the Lord in that day: and in how many *things* he ministered *unto me* at Ephesus, thou knowest very well.

Thou therefore, my son, be strong in the grace that is in 2

and in how many things *he ministered* unto me] Omit with the best MSS. 'unto me'; the statement is general of ministry to the Church, but the context gives a special suggestion of ministry to St Paul in his 'overseer's' office there. The Greek words would well bear rendering **how fully he played the deacon**; but anyhow the work is more prominent than the office, that of attending to bodily needs; as St Paul uses the word *diakonein* of himself when carrying the alms to Jerusalem, Rom. xv. 25 'now I say I go unto Jerusalem ministering unto the saints,' and of Onesimus with himself at Rome 'whom I would fain have kept with me, that in thy behalf he might minister unto me in the bonds of the gospel.' Philem. 13.

thou knowest very well] Lit. 'better' i.e. than that I should need to dwell upon it.

Ch. II. Apostolic Zeal and Purity.

1—7. Personal and Ministerial Zeal enforced by Parables from the Life of the Soldier, the Athlete and the Farmer.

The Apostle resumes the main thread of exhortation to Christian courage. After its enforcements by Timothy's inherited grace (i. 5) and the grace of his 'laying on of hands' (i. 6), by the free gift of the Saviour's own life with all its love and light (i. 9, 10), by his own apostleship (i. 11—13), the defection of false friends (i. 15), the refreshing zeal of Onesiphorus (i. 16—18), he plies his scholar with new illustrations yet of the old lesson. Courage to hold the torch up and hand the torch on (ii. 1, 2) is to be drawn from the soldier's life (ii. 3, 4), the athlete's (ii. 5), the farmer's (ii. 6); and our Lord Himself, the Great Teacher by parables, will point their moral for him (ii. 7).

1. *Thou therefore, my son, be strong*] Rather render **my child**, as in 1 Tim. i. 2 where the difference is explained, and **be strengthened**, 'be emboldened,' because the verb is of the same class in Greek as our English verbs with the ending -en. It occurs again in the active iv. 17 'the Lord stood by me and strengthened me.' So the Vulg. here has the Low Latin 'confortare,' whence our own 'comfort' and 'comforter.'

in the grace that is in Christ Jesus] 'Christ Jesus' here and in ver. 3 according to the order of the words as they framed themselves on the aged Apostle's lips in these last years. See note on 1 Tim. i. 1. 'In the grace,' strengthened, that is, in those virtues and spiritual powers which in their fulness are in Christ. 'The grace *that is in* Christ Jesus,' as distinguished from 'the Grace of Christ' appears to be used only here. We have had 'life that is in Christ Jesus' 2 Tim. i. 1; then 'faith and love that are in Christ Jesus,' the first two movements and powers of that life, i. 13; and now the full 'grace,' all the developed activities of strong life. As a matter of *language* the prepositional phrase 'that is in Christ Jesus' may mark progress towards

2 Christ Jesus. And *the things* that thou hast heard of me
among many witnesses, the same commit thou to faithful
3 men, who shall be able to teach others also. Thou therefore
4 endure hardness, as a good soldier of Jesus Christ. No *man*

the adjectival phrase which we should use now, 'the Christian life,' 'the Christian graces'; see note on 1 Tim. i. 2. But we may rejoice that the changing phrase was (as it were) crystallised for us here at a stage that shews so plainly how inward sanctification is nothing but continued and increased vital personal union with Christ.

2. the things *that thou hast heard of me among many witnesses*] 'Of' in the sense of **from** as in i. 13; '**among**,' i.e. 'in the presence of' according to the well-known use of the same preposition in Gal. iii. 19 '(the law) ordained *through* angels,' i.e. 'in the presence of,' 'amid the pomp of.' Cf. Winer III. § 47 i., 'intervenientibus multis testibus.' We are most probably to understand the presbyters who assisted at Timothy's ordination. See 1 Tim. iv. 14; and note the similar form of the statement there 'amid the pomp of prophesying' with the similar use of the preposition.

the same commit thou to faithful men, who shall be able] Lit., 'who are of such a class that they will be able,' as 1 Tim. i. 4, &c. St Clement of Rome, St Paul's contemporary, thus further defines the rule of this apostolic succession, *ad Cor.* c. xliv. 'The Apostles appointed the above-named priests and deacons, permanence being afterwards given by them to the office in order that on the death of the first-appointed other reputed men should succeed to their ministry. Those then who were appointed either directly by the Apostles or in the second generation by other approved heads with the consent of the whole Church... we do not think can be rightly ejected from office.' See Lightfoot's emended text, p. 136.

3—6. The three illustrations follow of the soldier, the athlete, the farmer, with the common point of *persevering pains*. They are all familiar to St Paul. That of the soldier has occurred already, 1 Tim. i. 18, where see references.

3. *Thou therefore endure hardness*] The best MSS. give one compound verb instead of pronoun conjunction and simple verb, **take-part-in-suffering-hardship**. As our A.V. stands, the words may seem hard and severe, with little allowance for difficulty and weakness. But the phrase in the Greek is a volume of tenderness and yearning confidence, of a father's claim to loyal imitation. 'Take your share in the enduring of hardness. Take up my mantle. I say not—go and brave hard fighting in the trench, hard words, hard deeds, for Christ your Master. I rather say—being such an one as Paul the aged—come with me, come after me, be one with us all who war the good warfare. My own son in the faith, I crave (strange though it seem), to nerve me for my last crowning effort, the sight of your young heroism. The standard that must fall from my failing hands you will grasp will you not?'

4. *No* man *that warreth*] More literally **no one on service**, as in Luke iii. 18 'men on march' came to St John Baptist. Carr, however,

that warreth entangleth himself with the affairs of *this* life;
that he may please him who hath chosen *him* to be a soldier.
And if a man also strive for masteries, *yet* is he not crowned, 5

there quotes instances from the classics for the absence of the article, Eur. *Ion* 639, *Med.* 68, as shewing that possibly it may be used irregularly as a substantive, 'no fighting man.'

entangleth himself with the affairs of this *life*] The verb occurs only here and in 2 Pet. ii. 20; the noun only here: 'affairs,' in the sense in which we speak of a 'man of affairs' skilled in public business; the word has been debased since the writing of A.V. and of Shakespeare's

'There is a tide in *the affairs* of men
Which taken at the flood leads on to fortune.'

And now we use the word chiefly of 'the affairs of every-day life' and the like. The Vulg. has well 'implicat se negotiis secularibus.'

For the word 'life' cf. Trench, *N. T. Syn.* § 27.

who hath chosen him] Rather, **who enrolled him**; the word is only here in N.T., a later Greek word.

5. *And if a man also strive for masteries*] The 'also' is placed by R.V. before 'a man' instead of after as A.V.; correctly, though awkwardly; as implying not that a man may perhaps beside soldiering also contend in the games, which is the proper inference from the position of 'also' in A.V., but that 'there is first the case of a soldier, and there is *also* the case of an athlete.' The verb, from which comes our 'athlete,' occurs here only in N.T., though the substantive in the derived sense of 'conflict' occurs in Heb. x. 32, 'a great conflict of sufferings.' Render, **and if again a man contend in the games**. We have had the illustration from the race-course and its 'games' in 1 Tim. vi. 12, and shall have it again lower down, ch. iv. 7. As Eph. vi. is the chief soldier's illustration, so 1 Cor. ix. 25 sqq. is the chief athlete's, in St Paul. The foot-race is used very strikingly also, Heb. xii. 1. Cf. Appendix, K.

except he strive lawfully] **Except he have kept the rules of the contest.** 'The six statues of Jupiter at Olympia were made from the fines levied on athletes who had not contended lawfully.' Pausan. v. 21. (Bp Wordsworth.) Among the rules of the Olympic games were the following; competitors had to prove to the judges that they were freemen, of pure Hellenic blood, not disfranchised, or convicted of sacrilege, and that they had gone through the ten months' preparatory training; they, their fathers, brothers, and trainers had to take oath that they would be guilty of no misconduct in the contests; and they had then a month's preliminary exercises in the gymnasium at Elis under the superintendence of the judges. The 'games' included longer and shorter foot-races for men and for boys, chariot-races, horse-races, wrestling, boxing; the *pentathlon*, a combination of leaping, flat-racing, discus-throwing, spear-throwing, and wrestling; and the *pancration*, a union of boxing and wrestling. 'Without interruption for upwards of a thousand years the full moon after the summer solstice every fourth year witnessed the celebration of these games. B.C. 776—A.D. 394.' Wordsworth, *Greece*, p. 315.

6 except he strive lawfully. The husbandman that laboureth
7 must be first partaker of the fruits. Consider what I say;
8 and the Lord give thee understanding in all *things*. Remember that Jesus Christ of the seed of David *was* raised

6. *The husbandman that laboureth*] This third illustration is well known from St Paul's use, 1 Cor. iii. 6—9, where the substantive corresponding to 'farmer' or 'husbandman' occurs. 'Ye are God's husbandry'; lit., 'God's farmed, tilled, land.' The stress of meaning lies on the participle 'that laboureth' and we must give the old full sense to the English word; as the Vulgate putting the participle in the emphatic first place in the sentence 'laborantem agricolam oportet primum de fructibus percipere.' See the bearing of the same word, 1 Tim. iv. 10, and especially v. 17 where see note. It is true, as the Wise man says, 'the profit of the earth is for all,' Eccl. v. 9, and the laziest vagabond can claim from the Poor-law his 'right to live.' But the husbandman who has 'toiled with honest sweat,' putting sinews, brains, and conscience into his work, must **be the first to partake of the fruits**, as the R.V. rightly renders, more clearly shewing the point. If the Christian knight wishes for any prize worth having, the farmer's, as well as the athlete's and the soldier's life, will say 'no pains no gains':

'For more of wisdom, health, or wealth,
We'll trust and labour on;
They come to neither life by stealth,
No cross no crown.'

7. *Consider what I say*] 'Apply the parable'; **for our Lord**—the Great Teacher of parables—**shall give thee understanding**. The MS. authority requires the future indicative instead of aorist optative. The verb belonging to our substantive here 'understanding' is used by our Lord in Matt. xiii. 51, after all His parables of the kingdom of heaven, 'Have ye understood all these things?' and the corresponding adjective in Matt. xv. 16 'And Peter answered and said unto Him, Declare unto us the parable. And He said, Are ye also even yet without understanding?'

8—13. A YET HIGHER ILLUSTRATION FROM GOD'S OWN PLAN OF SALVATION—THE CROSS BEFORE THE CROWN.

Just as in the first chapter St Paul appeals first to Timothy's sympathies and experiences of an earthly kind to brace him up—his own strong feelings moved even to tears, his mother's and grandmother's faith and piety, the touch of the vanished hand in the solemn rite of ordination (*vv.* 4—7), and then paints for him 'the power of *God*,' 'the appearing of our Saviour Christ Jesus who abolished death,' as the chief and strongest motive for keeping up heart and hope, since *His* must be the winning side, *He* must be able to keep that which is committed to Him (*vv.* 8—12): so now, after the appeal to earthly analogies and common human experiences as to the necessity and the reward of pains and perseverance, he rises from the earthly to the

from the dead according to my gospel: wherein I suffer 9
trouble, as an evil doer, *even* unto bonds; but the word

heavenly, from the human to the Divine. 'Remember, God's plan—even the old, old promise to "the seed of the woman"—came out complete in the fulness of time. Jesus Christ of the seed of David bruised the old serpent's head when He rose "victor over the tomb." True, I, or any one of us His humble servants, may for a time seem trodden under, but 'tis only for a time; the salvation, the eternal glory, is assured in His power; if we endure we shall also reign with Him. This is the motive of motives to play the man; this is indeed being strengthened in the grace *that is in Christ Jesus*.'

8. *Remember that Jesus Christ of the seed of David* was *raised*] The force of the participle and the true order of the phrases require the rendering **Remember Jesus Christ risen from the dead, of the seed of David.** In the other N.T. places where the accusative follows this verb 'remember,' it is of a thing not a person, Matt. xvi. 9; 1 Thess. ii. 9; Rev. xviii. 5. And this use is really followed here; it is 'Jesus risen—a historic fact' which is set before Timothy. '**Risen**,' not 'raised,' according to the ordinary usage of the passive, as e.g. Matt. xi. 11, Mark xvi. 14, and suiting best the idea prominent here of Christ's own power. The force of the clause 'of the seed of David' is seen in the paraphrase above.

according to my gospel] The gospel entrusted to me to teach, as in 1 Tim. i. 11; 'a solemn way of speaking, identifying these truths with the preaching which had been the source of Timotheus's belief.' Alford.

9. *wherein I suffer trouble, as an evil doer*] **Hardship** rather than 'trouble,' the same word as in *v.* 3; **malefactor** rather than 'evil doer,' the same word as of the thieves on the cross, Lk. xxiii. 32, these being the only N.T. occurrences.

even *unto bonds*] 'Even' need not have been italicised in A.V., much less omitted by R.V.; for the force of the preposition is more fully given with than without it. In the similar passage, Phil. ii. 8, the 'obedient unto death' of A.V. has actually been altered by R.V. into 'obedient *even* unto death.' Vulg. 'usque ad.'

'Over the blackened ruins of the city (the firing of which had been falsely set down to the Christians) amid the squalid misery of its inhabitants, perhaps with many a fierce scowl turned on "the malefactor" he passed to his gloomy dungeon. There as the gate clanged upon him, he sat down, chained night and day, without further hope, a doomed man. His case was far more miserable than it had been in his first imprisonment, two or three years earlier. He was no longer permitted to reside "in his own hired room." He was in the custody, not as before of an honourable soldier like Burrus, but of the foul Tigellinus, whose hands were still dripping with Christian blood.' Farrar, *Messages of the Books*, p. 388.

but the word of God is not bound] Not his own preaching power, but the power of the Gospel at large. The Church is more than the in-

10 of God is not bound. Therefore I endure all *things* for the elects' sakes, that they may also obtain the salvation which

dividual, however eminent. The perfect passive tense here represents the state, 'is not in a bound state,' is not 'cribbed, cabin'd and confined'; according to the proper force of the perfect, as in 1 Tim. vi. 17, 'nor have their hope set on,' 2 Tim. iv. 8, 'who have their love set on his appearing.'

10. *Therefore I endure all* things] Therefore, because 'pains bring gains'; therefore, because (vv. 3—9) as with Christ, so with His Church;

'If the cross we meekly bear,
Then the crown we shall wear.'

Bengel and others do not go far back enough, trying wrongly to find the reason in the last clause alone. Alford seeing this turns 'therefore' into 'for this reason,' and joins it to what follows 'that they may obtain,' alleging the Apostle's usage of the phrase in favour of this. But the passages he quotes, 1 Tim. i. 16, and Philem. 15, have both got other particles connecting with the preceding. And here we have none except 'therefore' itself. And St Paul just as frequently uses 'therefore' for the past; cf. Eph. v. 17 'wherefore be ye not foolish,' vi. 13 'wherefore take up the whole armour of God.'

The Greek word rendered 'endure' is our Lord's word in His charge to the Seventy, Matt. x. 22, and in His discourse of the last things, Matt. xxiv. 13; Mk. xiii. 13 'He that endureth to the end the same shall be saved.' St Paul has used the verb before twice only, cf. Rom. xii. 12 'rejoicing in hope, patient in tribulation,' 1 Cor. xiii. 7 'Charity...hopeth all things, endureth all things'; both which noble passages fully bear out the significance assigned to the word by Ellicott on 1 Thess. i. 13 'It does not mark merely the *endurance*, the "sustinentiam" Vulg., or even the "patientiam" (Clarom.), but the "perseverantiam" the *brave* patience with which the Christian contends against the various hindrances, persecutions and temptations that befall him in his conflict with the inward and outward world.' It occurs again iii. 10.

for the elects' sakes] For the sake of the Church; see note on Tit. i. 1, where the words used at first for 'Christians' are discussed. The general purport is as in Col. i. 24, where Lightfoot paraphrases 'I cannot choose but rejoice in my sufferings. Yes, I Paul the persecutor, I Paul the feeble and sinful, am permitted to supplement—I do not shrink from the word—to supplement the afflictions of Christ. My flesh is privileged to suffer for His body—His spiritual body, the Church'; and explains that this supplementing of Christ's sufferings is 'not in their sacrificial efficacy but their ministerial utility.' 'The Church is built up by repeated acts of self-denial in successive individuals and successive generations.' So we see the old fire of the first captivity is burning up still more ardently as the end draws near. 'The salvation which is in Christ Jesus' is for him at hand; the faith is kept. What still he can, that he will, do and bear, that their salvation also may be assured; and *that* Timothy *his son* will surely also both practise and preach.

sakes] R.V. gives 'sake,' perhaps better as the interest of the whole

is in Christ Jesus with eternal glory. *It is* a faithful saying: 11
For if we be dead with *him*, we shall also live with *him:* if 12
we suffer, we shall also reign with *him:* if we deny *him*, he

Church 'the one body' was one and the same. Otherwise, the plural may still be used, as e.g. in 'for all your sakes.' 'Sake' is the same as the German 'sache,' 'res,' 'thing,' 'account,' 'cause at law.' Cf. the phrase 'for old sake's sake.'

that they may also obtain] The 'also' is intended in the English of A.D. 1611 to qualify 'they' as well as the verb; in the more precise English of A.D. 1881 R.V. writes 'they also.' So the looser use of 'also' has been altered Matt. xxvi. 71, 'this fellow was also with Jesus,' into 'this man also was with Jesus.' The more exact use two verses later 'thou also art one of them,' shews that the A.V. translators exercised a literary freedom in the matter. The O.T. revisers have left Zech. viii. 21 'I will go also.' The N.T. revisers who have altered Mk. ii. 28, Joh. v. 19, 1 Cor. ix. 8 have not ventured to alter Joh. xii. 26, xiv. 3.

with eternal glory] The thought is the same as in 2 Cor. iv. 17; *the affliction*, light and *for the moment*, worketh *glory*, an *eternal* weight of glory.

11. It is *a faithful saying*] Literally, **Faithful is the saying**, as in 1 Tim. i. 15, iii. 1, iv. 9; Tit. iii. 8. See note on the first passage and Appendix, E. To close the argument, this rhythmical, perhaps liturgical, strain is quoted. It is introduced by 'for,' as is the quotation in Acts xvii. 28. The R.V. by printing 'For' in the text and 'for' in the margin thus incline to regarding the conjunction as part of the quotation. If it be not part, it will still have quite a fitting sense, as often in classical Greek 'indeed' or 'in fact' gives a better translation than 'for'; cf. Donaldson's *Greek Grammar*, p. 605.

For if we be dead with him] Read, **For if we died with him.** It is most natural to refer this to the dying with Christ in Baptism, Col. ii. 20, iii. 3, where the aorists are equally to be observed. This would be the thought in the original framing of such a Christian hymn as this may have been. But St Paul's baptism was no old ceremony and out of date; he was 'always bearing about in the body the dying of Jesus' 2 Cor. iv. 10; just as the English Prayer Book Service bids Christians after their baptism 'die from sin, continually mortifying all evil and corrupt affections.' Hence he can well use the phrase so as to cover his 'hardship even unto bonds,' and his 'daily dying' to 'fill up the sufferings of Christ.'

we shall...live with him] in the 'eternal glory.'

12. *if we suffer*] Rather **endure** with brave and manly submission; ver. 10. The submission is followed by sovereignty, as death by life. Cf. Matt. xix. 28 'ye which have followed me......shall sit on twelve thrones.'

if we deny him] The MS. authority requires the future **if we shall deny him**, cf. Matt. x. 32, 33. The future there and here indicates 'ethical possibility,' i.e. what can and may take place, viewed speculatively. Is it not possible that this very phrase of the 'Oral Gospel' embodied

13 also will deny us: if we believe not, *yet* he abideth faithful:
he cannot deny himself.
14 Of these *things* put *them* in remembrance, charging *them*

in Matt. x. 33 may have already found a place in this earliest of hymns?

13. *if we believe not*] R.V. **if we are faithless** giving both the play of words in the contrast 'he abideth faithful' and the stronger force required for the climax; as 'sovereignty' is better than 'life,' so a 'faithless rejection' is worse than 'the denials of our weaker moments,' a Judas than a Peter. The word 'seems always in the N.T. to imply not 'untrueness,' 'unfaithfulness,' but definitely 'unbelief.' Ellicott. Cf. Mark xvi. 11, 16.

he abideth faithful] To His covenant and promise, cf. Rom. iii. 3. We should insert with MSS. the conjunction, to connect the final clause with this; **for he cannot deny himself.** The balance of probability is strongly in favour of this clause being part of the quotation, if only from the rhetorical weakness of *adding* such a tail piece, however true and weighty. The aorist infinitive represents the idea of the verb in itself simply and absolutely, free from any limit or condition of time; 'for deny Himself—He cannot.' So in Mk. xv. 31 'save Himself—He cannot.'

We may render the passage thus, to shew its balanced force and rhythm:—

'If with Him we died,
Life with Him we shall have won;
If we suffer at His side,
We shall share His throne;—
With Him—Yes, here and ever.

If we Him deny,
We shall be by Him denied;
If we leave Him faithlessly,
Faithful doth He bide;—
Deny Himself—No, never.'

14—26. THE ESPECIAL SPHERE OF BOTH PERSONAL AND MINISTERIAL ZEAL IS (1) PURE DOCTRINE, (2) A PURE LIFE.

The proper connexion is to be sought in the earlier part of the previous passage, particularly ver. 2. For the whole of the paragraph now opening has reference to Timothy's dealing with the teachers he is to appoint and train, and to his own bearing as an example for them. The 'striving about words' is clearly opposed to '*teaching* the truth,' as in the similar use of the word 1 Tim. vi. 3, 4, where it is he 'that teacheth a different doctrine' who is 'doting about disputes of words.' 'These things' then will take up the same word 'these' of ver. 2, and the object after the verb will be the 'faithful teachers' 'able to teach others.' And the train of thought in chaps. i. and ii. is this: 'Be brave and true yourself like me; be faithful to the truth as I have been; suffer for the truth's sake as I have done; choose teachers too

before the Lord that *they* strive not about words to no profit,
but to the subverting of the hearers. Study to shew thyself 15
approved unto God, a workman that needeth not to be

with the same pure doctrine, the same pure life; twin seals these are of God's firm foundation; false doctrine leads to vicious life; the pastor's holy living goes far to draw men off from Satan.'

14. *Of these* things *put* them *in remembrance*] See note on Tit. iii. 1 for this verb, and on i. 5 for its noun.

charging them *before the Lord*] Or **in the sight of.** The MS. authority for 'God' instead of 'the Lord' is insufficient to justify the change.

The verb to 'charge' is properly 'to bear solemn witness,' the preposition giving intensity; hence the two meanings to 'preach' and to 'charge.' St Paul uses it in the latter sense three times with 'in the sight of' in these Epistles, 1 Tim. v. 21, 2 Tim. iv. 1 and here; and in 1 Thess. iv. 6 in the former. It occurs eight times in the Acts, and in Luke xvi. 28, where the construction is the same as here, and where we may equally well render 'that he may charge them not to come also themselves into this place of torment.'

that they *strive not about words*] The infinitive; the MS. authority is now known to be against the imperative which was the reading of the Vulgate 'Noli contendere verbis.' The original is one word, occurring only here; its noun only in 1 Tim. vi. 4, from which our own 'logomachy' has come.

to no profit] Lit. 'a course useful for nothing,' a neuter accusative in apposition to the sentence, somewhat as in 1 Tim. ii. 6 'the testimony to be borne.'

but *to the subverting of the hearers*] Omit 'but'; this clause expresses the result of the word wrangling,—viz. subversion, lit. catastrophe; a turning upside down of all right reason and sound morality. The word only occurs besides in 2 Pet. ii. 6 'condemned them (Sodom and Gomorrah) *with an overthrow*.'

15. 'Let your own example back your precepts to your teachers.' The stress therefore is to be laid on 'thyself.'

Study to shew thyself] **Take pains to present thyself**; both verbs are aorists, because that tense gives *the verbal idea* always, and the force intended here is 'Have for your ideal in work and aim "thorough."'

approved unto God] Or 'one who has stood God's testing'; so the substantive in Phil. ii. 22 'ye know the proof,' i.e. the approved character 'of Timothy.' In one respect, that is, the Philippians had themselves tested Timothy, viz. how he had served with St Paul in furtherance of the Gospel. The opposite word, 'unable to stand the test' occurs Tit. i. 16 where see note; and ch. iii. 8.

a workman] Implying zeal and activity, as, in a bad cause, Phil. iii. 2.

that needeth not to be ashamed] Only here in N.T.; in Joseph. *Antt.* xviii. 7. 1 in the same sense 'nor think that one should-not-be-ashamed to be inferior.' In classical Greek 'shameless' 'impudent' is the force

16 ashamed, rightly dividing the word of truth. But shun pro-
fane *and* vain babblings: for they will increase unto more
17 ungodliness. And their word will eat as *doth* a canker: of

of the cognate word. Both senses come from the proper meaning of the verbal ending 'that which cannot be made ashamed.' Vulg. 'operarium inconfusibilem.'

rightly dividing] This is the literal meaning, whether we refer the dividing to the sacrificial division of victims or to the distributing of bread or to the cutting of a road; or better, with R.V. apparently, take Theodoret's interpretation 'we praise those husbandmen who cut their furrows straight,' and so get for our second rendering 'holding a straight course in the word of truth' (R.V. margin) and for our third (R.V. text) **handling aright the word of truth.** The word does not occur again in N.T. or classical Greek; but in LXX. Prov. iii. 6, xi. 5, 'he shall direct thy paths,' 'the righteousness of the perfect shall direct his way.' Vulg. 'recte tractantem.'

the word of truth] The facts, the doctrines, the creeds, through which God's true work and will for man are revealed.

16. *shun*] The word is the same as in Tit. iii. 9 where reasons are given for rendering it **avoid**. The present tense here and in ver. 14 are all the more forcible for the aorists which come in between. 'Be ever putting in remembrance' 'ever avoiding.' The article before 'profane babblings' points to a well-known theme, 'these false teachers and their talk.' 'Let your teachers and yourself handle truth aright; but the false teachers and their profane babblings avoid.' Hence there is no real ambiguity about the subject to the next clause; though R.V. leaves us in doubt. 'For these false teachers will only proceed further in ungodliness.' The pronoun in the next verse refers back to them.

profane and *vain babblings*] **Profane babblings**; 'babblings' is sufficient rendering of the word without the addition of 'vain': the word only occurs here and 1 Tim. vi. 20; see note there.

they will increase unto more ungodliness] Lit. **they will proceed further on.** The verb corresponds to the word for 'progress' in 1 Tim. iv. 15 where its usage is noted. As Bp Ellicott points out, the future shews that the error of the false teachers had not yet 'appeared in its most developed state.'

17. *their word*] As opposed to 'the word of truth' above, the fictions and heresies in which the Gnostic scheme expressed itself.

will eat] Lit. 'will have pasture.' The word occurs Joh. x. 9 'will find pasture.' Cf. Latimer *Serm.* p. 525 quoted in the *Bible Word Book* 'In another place St Paul compareth their doctrine unto a sickness which is called a canker; which sickness, when she once beginneth at a place of the body, except it be withstood will run over the whole body, and so at length kill.'

as doth *a canker*] Or more exactly **a gangrene** or 'eating sore,' the root notion of 'gangrene' as of the common word 'grass' being 'to devour' 'to eat.' Galen defines it as a tumour in the state between inflammation and mortification.

whom is Hymeneus and Philetus; who concerning the truth 18
have erred, saying that the resurrection is past already; and
overthrow the faith of some. Nevertheless the foundation 19

of whom is Hymeneus and Philetus] Or 'among whom'; the partitive genitive. Hymenæus is probably the same as in 1 Tim. i. 20; see note. Philetus is not mentioned elsewhere.

18. *who concerning the truth have erred*] More exactly, **men who concerning the truth erred by maintaining**. For the compound relative indicating the class see on Tit. i. 11; for the verb 1 Tim. i. 6, vi. 21. The present participle, with the aorist verb, may indicate the repetitions of their 'saying' and so their 'maintaining,' and leads the way to the following verb being present.

that the resurrection] The MS. authority for the omission of the article is hardly strong enough to be followed, though R.V. notes the variant in the margin by the rendering 'a resurrection.' Curiously, in Acts xvii. 32, where there is no article, R.V. still renders 'when they heard of the resurrection,' there evidently intending the rule to apply that 'the article is omitted before many abstract nouns.' Why not here also? So that the retention or omission of the article will make no difference in translation. Winer has no notice of either passage in his full chapter on this, Pt III. § xix.

is past already] Some identified the resurrection with the soul's spiritual renewal by the doctrine of the Gospel causing it 'to burst forth from the sepulchre of the old man'; others with the departure of the soul from the body, the world in their view being only the habitation of the dead. See Fairbairn. Irenæus and Tertullian both allude to the former error, which may well have been the view here referred to.

and overthrow] Better **are subverting**; for the word see note on Tit. i. 11.

19. *Nevertheless the foundation of God standeth sure*] R.V. alters into the less strong 'howbeit'; the same conjunction, which St Paul does not use elsewhere, occurs five times in St John's Gospel, and is rendered by R.V. 'nevertheless,' in xii. 42 (but with another conjunction added), 'yet' in iv. 27, xx. 5, 'howbeit' in vii. 13, xxi. 4. The adjective 'sure' or 'firm' from its position must be attribute not predicate, **the firm foundation**. What is this 'firm foundation'? St Paul's thought is still of Timothy as chief teacher, of his true teachers, and of the false teachers; not (except by the way) of private believers or the whole Church. The passage then is parallel to 1 Tim. iii. 14, 15, 16, where we have seen the Church is called the 'pillar and ground of the truth' with reference to the way in which office bearers 'ought to behave themselves,' 'holding the mystery of the faith in a pure conscience,' and avoiding 'the snare of the devil.' The foundation is therefore the Church built on apostolic doctrine, 'strong in the strength which God supplies through His eternal Son'; cf. 'on this rock—the apostolic confession of a true faith—I will build my church,' Matt. xvi. 18. And we may paraphrase, 'Nevertheless the holy Apostolic church continueth stedfast, having these two marks of a faithful ministry, the Apostles' teaching and the Apostles' fellowship, a pure doctrine and a holy life.'

of God standeth sure, having this seal, The Lord knoweth
them that are his. And, Let every one that nameth the
20 name of Christ depart from iniquity. But in a great house
there are not only vessels of gold and of silver, but also of
wood and of earth; and some to honour, and some to
21 dishonour. If a man therefore purge himself from these,

this seal] The Lord's acknowledgment of His true ministers; 'God knoweth His own, not Korah, Dathan, and Abiram, but Moses, the servant of the Lord,' Num. xvi. 5; and His warning to unholy teachers; 'Ye shall knock at the door, saying, Lord, Lord, open to us; and he shall say to you, I know not whence ye are; depart from me all ye workers of iniquity,' Luke xiii. 27. The former quotation is exact from LXX., with the alteration of 'the Lord' for 'God'; the latter freely turns St Luke's record into a maxim, adopting precisely the same Greek words for 'depart' and for 'iniquity'. This is the more natural, as we recall the solitary pair of friends the inspired historian and the inspired correspondent, interchanging 'comfortable words' in that prison cell at Rome. 'Only Luke is with me,' ch. iv. 11. Cf. ver. 26 note on 'taken captive.'

Alford justifies the adding of a 'seal' in this metaphor of the 'foundation' by regarding it as 'probably in allusion to the practice of engraving inscriptions over doors (Deut. vi. 9, xi. 20) and on pillars and foundation stones (Rev. xxi. 14).'

the name of Christ] The MS. authority is almost unanimous for **the Lord** instead of Christ; and this fits in remarkably with the above passage in St Luke.

20. The connexion is; 'False teachers may do great damage; but the real truth, the strong main structure, is uninjured and stable, while at the same time there may be some bad work in it as well. And to turn from the structure to the furniture, we must distinguish similarly between the good and the bad portions, the valuable and the worthless.'

But in a great house] **Though** is better than either 'but' A.V. or 'now' R.V. Wordsworth explains well of the 'imperfections and blemishes which exist in the Visible Church on earth,' and quotes Augustine 'in congregatione Christiana,' *Serm.* 15; where 'congregatio' is in the large sense in which St Jerome for example uses it 'Ecclesia enim congregatio vocatur' (*in Proverb.* c. xxx.), and in which 'congregation' is used in our English version of the XXXIX. Articles 'Ecclesia Christi visibilis est coetus fidelium.' Our Lord's parable of the Drag-net is the best parallel to this description of the 'mixed and imperfect condition of the Church on earth,' Matt. xiii. 47.

21. *If a man therefore purge himself from these*] That is, as Bengel puts it, 'if any one shall by purifying himself have gone out of their number.' The compound verb 'purge out' only occurs besides in 1 Cor. v. 7 where the preposition gives the force 'purge out from your houses the old leaven.' Wordsworth forcibly notes here; 'a man may *at one time* of his life be numbered among vessels to dishonour, and yet *may*

he shall be a vessel unto honour, sanctified, and meet for
the master's use, *and* prepared unto every good work. Flee 22
also youthful lusts: but follow righteousness, faith, charity,
peace, with them that call on the Lord out of a pure heart.
But foolish and unlearned questions avoid, knowing that 23

become a vessel to honour, by cleansing himself out from their number and condition. Mark this assertion of Free Will.' And again, 'a Christian man may not *go out* of the *great house* which is the Visible Church of God: he cannot separate himself wholly from sinners, but he must cleanse himself from them *as sinners;* that is, he must not communicate with them *in their sins.*'

sanctified] Or perhaps better 'purified.' 'Sanctified' belongs to metaphor, the implied Christian life and service; but *in form* the sentence remains a *simile* to the end. Hence R.V. rightly renders **the master's use**, i.e. the master of the house, not with some printed copies of A.V. 'the Master's,' which would imply an immediate reference to God. 'Meet for use' is the same word as in iv. 11 'serviceable,' and in Philem. 11, where Onesimus formerly 'unprofitable' is 'now profitable.'

prepared] This word and 'sanctified' are both perfect passive participles, and are more expressive than our English can shew of the resulting final state reached. See note on verse 26.

22. *Flee also youthful lusts*] Here, as in ver. 16, and again below ver. 23, the article has a certain emphasis, bringing forward again and again the different parts of the old theme 'the false teachers, their errors of doctrine, their viciousness of life.' 'Be a different man yourself, flee the lusts of the younger men.' On Timothy's age see note 1 Tim. iv. 12.

but follow] Rather **and**, not because the conjunction does not express an opposite to the preceding clause; but because *the verbs* are placed so as to have the main emphasis together, and '*but*' here would draw us away from this. We may render: 'Beware their bad life—those lusts of life's prime—flee from them, and follow after righteousness.'

follow] Add **after**, in order to give the proper force of *active pursuit*. The whole passage is a reminiscence of 1 Tim. vi. 11, where see note on the virtues named. 'Peace' seems added here to the three selected because the immediate context is different. Here the strife arising from the false teachers' words and ways is already in St Paul's mind, and suggests the turn given to what follows. The comma after 'peace' of R.V. has been inserted rightly; its omission (as in A.V. of A.D. 1611, though many printed copies have inserted it,) unites 'peace' entirely with what follows, and denotes, as Ellicott puts it, 'not merely "peace" in the ordinary sense but "concordiam illam spiritualem" (Calvin) which unites together all who call upon (1 Cor. i. 2) and love their Lord'; but it makes an unbalanced and ugly sentence; and loses the very significance of the clause as following on ver. 21. It is the whole life of the man of God, in his pursuit of each virtue, which is to be lived apart from sinners and in the communion of saints. See also notes on 1 Tim. i. 5; Tit. i. 15.

23. *But foolish and unlearned questions*] **But those foolish and**

24 they do gender strifes. And the servant of the Lord must
not strive; but be gentle unto all *men*, apt to teach, patient,
25 in meekness instructing those that oppose themselves; if

ignorant questionings steadily refuse; as above 'beware their bad doctrine; their foolish questioning decline.'

unlearned] The word occurs nowhere else in N.T., its meaning 'indoctus' and then 'ineptus' is seen in Prov. viii. 5, 'Ye *fools*, be ye of an *understanding* heart.' Hence its appropriate union here with 'foolish.' 'Ignorant' has a shade of moral fault very frequently, which makes it a better rendering than 'unlearned.' Cf. Ps. xlix. 10, 'the ignorant and foolish' (Pr.-B. V.).

questions] 'Questionings,' see note on 1 Tim. i. 4.

avoid] 'Decline,' see note on 1 Tim. iv. 7 where the form of the sentence is very similar to ver. 22.

knowing] Seems to require some such addition as 'as thou dost' to render the original; 'knowing that' being a weak and colloquial phrase by itself.

24. *And the servant of the Lord*] The conjunction here is exactly parallel in its force to 'and follow after' in ver. 22. 'The servant,' not 'a servant,' the emphatic position of 'servant' at the beginning is best rendered by the definite article. 'Servant,' that is, 'bondservant' or 'slave,' the title by which St Paul frequently describes himself as 'a minister of Christ.' Cf. Tit. i. 1.

gentle] The word only occurs in N.T. here and 1 Thess. ii. 7, denoting 'an outward mildness and gentleness, especially in bearing with others,' Ellicott; who connects it with one of the Greek roots for 'speak,' so that it would have originally meant 'kind of speech.'

apt to teach] See 1 Tim. iii. 2.

patient] A compound adjective more exactly 'patient of wrong,' and so better **forbearing**. The first part of the word is the same as 'tolerable' in Luke x. 14.

25. *in meekness instructing*] Meekness, gentleness of heart, the feeling as separate from the demeanour: still more clearly brought out by the use of the compound word 1 Tim. vi. 11. The corresponding adjective is used by 'the Lord' Himself of Himself, 'I am meek and lowly in heart,' Matt. xi. 29. See note on Tit. iii. 2. A very interesting passage where it occurs is Gal. v. 22, where Bp Lightfoot divides the nine fruits of the Spirit into three sets of three, and shews how each of the first two triads is arranged in an ascending scale, (1) love, joy, peace, (2) patient endurance, kindly feeling, active beneficence. May not the third triad be similarly arranged thus, (3) a childlike trust, a woman's meekness, a man's self-mastery?

instructing] The word is explained 1 Tim. i. 20 and Tit. ii. 12; in all but two of the thirteen places where it occurs in N.T. the sense of 'correction,' 'discipline' is clear; and in those two, Acts vii. 22, xxii. 3, the instruction is that of school or college, and 'schooled' will best express it. So here 'correcting,' **bringing under discipline**.

those that oppose themselves] Lit. 'that are becoming contentiously

God peradventure will give them repentance to the acknow-
ledging of the truth; and *that* they may recover themselves 26
out of the snare of the devil, *who are* taken captive by him
at his will.

disposed'; the usage of the middle is *disponere aliquid*, not *disponere se*; hence 'oppose themselves' must not be taken as at any rate a literal version; the word corresponding to the *perfect* of this verb is the well known 'adversaries' 1 Cor. xvi. 9, used also 1 Tim. v. 14.

if God peradventure] Lit. 'if God might perchance at some time,' Lat. 'si forte aliquando.'

will give] The optative not subjunctive mood has the best authority. The exact force then is 'You must discipline them, in case God may give them repentance, as we wish and pray.'

repentance] The word occurs only four times in St Paul's Epistles, though frequent in St Luke's Gospel and Acts. Cf. Trench, *N. T. Syn.* p. 247, who defines it as 'a change of mind, taking a *wiser* view of the past, a regret for the ill done in that past, and out of all this a change for the better.'

to the acknowledging of the truth] Better, **unto the full knowledge**; 'unto' expresses the state into which repentance is designed to bring them, as Acts xi. 18, 'hath God granted repentance unto life'; 'full knowledge' as in 1 Tim. ii. 4, where see note.

26. *and* that *they may recover themselves*] Omit 'that,' the verb depending on 'if perchance.' The verb 'recover themselves' is literally 'return to soberness.' Constructed with the preposition 'out of' it has the pregnant force very frequent in Greek 'become sober and escape out of.' Cf. Winer, *Gr.* § 66, 2, p. 547. The simple verb occurs ch. iv. 5 'be sober'; another compound in 1 Cor. xv. 34 'awake out of' drunkenness 'righteously.' This compound is only here in N.T.

the snare of the devil] Has occurred 1 Tim. iii. 7, where, as here, it is the snare laid by the devil, a state of proud self-will morally and intellectually, the very opposite to a state of obedience to God's will.

who are *taken captive by him at his will*] The A.V. rendering is a mere enlargement of the idea of 'snare,' requires the aorist part. and refers the two different pronouns to the devil. But (1) St Paul's use of the perfect passive participle, **held captive**, is very strongly in favour of a reference to *the final state* of 'recovery,' not to the previous state of 'entanglement.' The final clause in ver. 21, where this participle ends the sentence, expresses the final state of 'the vessel unto honour.' The final clause in iii. 5 where the false teachers are described, has the same participle to shew their permanent rejection of vital godliness. The final clause in iii. 17, where the man of God is described, is ended in the same weighty form, 'for every good work in a state of perfect preparedness.' Hence the force of the perfect participle (as distinguished from the aorist) required here is 'that they may recover themselves out of the snare of the devil, continuing in the state of willing captivity into which they have been brought,' 'held willing captives.'

(2) St Paul's use of the first pronoun here, rendered 'by him,' is

3 This know also, that in the last days perilous times shall
2 come. For men shall be lovers of their own selves, covetous,

strongly in favour of a reference to the 'servant of the Lord.' A certain person or thing is in his mind as his chief subject; and he refers to him or it after an interval, short or long, merely with this pronoun. Cf. 1 Tim. iv. 16, 'continue in them'—the words of the faith and of the good doctrine; Tit. iii. 1, 'Put them in mind'—the aged men and women, the younger men and servants of ch. ii.; 2 Tim. ii. 17, 'their word will eat'—'those who strive about words,' ver. 14.

(3) St Paul's use of the preposition 'unto' for 'into a state of,' 'into conformity with' is strongly in favour of the last clause being intended to express the resulting state and condition; cf. 'unto honour,' 'unto every good work,' ver. 21; 'unto full knowledge,' ver. 25.

Render, therefore, **held willing captives henceforth by their deliverer** (the servant of the Lord) **to do the will of God**. So substantially the R.V. The participle is from a verb to 'capture alive.' Cf. Luke v. 10 the only other N.T. passage where the word occurs, and see Farrar's note, 'The word seems to imply the contrast between the fish that lay there glittering in *dead* heaps, and men who should be captured not for death (Jas. i. 14) but for life.' Both places refer to the evangelising work of the ministry.

CH. III. APOSTOLIC LIFE AND DOCTRINE.

1—5. APPEAL TO TIMOTHY FOR PURE LIFE IN VIEW OF THE WORSE DAYS AND LIVES TO COME.

The same three thoughts are still in St Paul's mind, viz. (1) his own life's work and suffering now closed, (2) Timothy's life and teaching as the pattern still for other ministers, (3) the false teachers to be shunned and stopped. They are blended in an old man's artless way as each is uppermost, (3) vv. 1—5; (2) 5; (3) 6—9; (2) 10; (1) 10—12; (3) 13; (2) 14—17. But the main central thought—anxiety for Timothy—comes in, after the others, three times.

The connexion with chap. ii. seems to be: 'do your best to win back those who are only in the first stage of opposition (see ii. 25, 'those that are setting themselves contentiously'); there will be men ere long too far gone for this in evil living and false teaching; from these there is no help for it but *to turn away*.'

1. *This know also*] Lit., 'take notice of this,' the present tense. Our Lord in Luke xii. 39 has the same formula.

in the last days] 'Not only the very last days, towards the end of the world, but in general (according to the Hebrew phrase) *the days to come*, or *the future time*, whether nearer or afar off. He supposeth this would begin to happen in the age of Timothy, ver. 5 *from such do thou* (thou, Timothy) *turn away* and avoid them,' Bp Bull, *Serm.* XV. init. So Calvin, 'universum Ecclesiae Christianae statum.'

perilous times shall come] Lit. 'difficult,' **grievous**; the meaning is well seen from the only other place where it occurs in N.T. Matt. viii. 28, 'two possessed with devils exceeding *fierce*,' i.e. difficult to deal with,

boasters, proud, blasphemers, disobedient to parents, un-
thankful, unholy, without natural affection, trucebreakers, 3

'so that no man could pass by that way.' 'Shall come,' lit., **will set in.** Vulg. 'instabunt,' 'will be upon us,' 'will be present.' In Gal. i. 4 the perfect participle is used, 'this present evil world.'

2. *For men shall be lovers of their own selves*] 'The article is generic; the men who shall live in those times,' Alford. **Self-lovers, money-lovers**; the first pair of adjectives in the description go naturally together; the first of the words occurs only here in N.T., the second only in Luke xvi. 14, 'the Pharisees also who were lovers of money.' The first and an almost exact synonym of the second occur together in Ar. *Pol.* II. v. where Plato's question is being discussed whether there ought to be private property or not. 'It is clear then that the better plan is for the property to be held separately while the produce is common. Besides even for the pleasure of the thing it makes an unspeakable difference to regard a piece of property as one's own. Indeed it is probably no mere chance that makes each of us hold himself first in his regard. It is human nature. But being a self-lover is rightly blamed. By this is not meant loving oneself, but doing so too much; just as we speak of the man who is a money-lover, since all love what belongs to them. But to support and succour friends or guests or comrades is a very delightful thing and this requires our having property of our own. The "community" idea robs us of the virtue of generosity in the use of property.' See note on 1 Tim. vi. 10.

boasters, proud, blasphemers] R.V. better, **boastful, haughty, railers.** Theophrastus (*Characters* c. 23) describes 'boastfulness' to be 'an endeavour to pass for a man of greater consequence than one really is.' In the next chapter he describes 'haughtiness' to be 'a contempt for every one but a man's self.' The climax is (1) a spirit of vain glory in themselves, (2) an overweening treatment of others, (3) actual abuse and reviling of others. The first word describes a man who sins against truth, the second a man who sins against love, the third a man who sins against both. Cf. Rom. i. 30; 1 Joh. ii. 16 (and Westcott's note); Trench, *Syn.* § 29. For this general meaning of 'railers' rather than 'blasphemers,' cf. 1 Tim. vi. 4 'envy, strife, railings.'

disobedient to parents] Or, in one word, **unfilial**; this with 'unthankful, unholy,' makes another triad: breakers of the fifth commandment go on to be breakers of the tenth; and thus throwing aside the second table go on to throw aside also the first, 'unfilial, unthankful, unholy.' The word for 'unthankful' occurs elsewhere only Luke vi. 35 in the Sermon on the Mount. For 'unholy' see notes on 1 Tim. i. 9.

3. *without natural affection, trucebreakers, false accusers*] Or, **unloving, unforgiving, slanderers**, another triad which starts from another breach of the same fifth commandment, the rending of the family ties of love, and advances to a breach of the sixth commandment in a refusal to make peace, and further of the ninth commandment in calumnious attacks and slanders. The threefold contrary spirit is in the same Sermon on the Mount, Luke vi. 27, '*love* your enemies, *do good* to them that hate you,

false accusers, incontinent, fierce, despisers of *those that are*
4 good, traitors, heady, highminded, lovers of pleasures more
5 than lovers of God; having a form of godliness, but denying

bless them that curse you.' The word for 'unloving' occurs only in Rom. i. 31, the other similarities of which seem to suggest that St Paul may have it in his mind, and be sadly tracing the decline and fall of Christian men back to the old heathen state. The word for 'unforgiving,' means 'unwilling to make a truce,' the opposite of 'peacemakers,' Matt. v. 9. It has been wrongly introduced in Rom. i. from this place where only in N.T. it is found, though an ordinary classical word.

incontinent, fierce, despisers of those that are *good*] **Vicious or uncontrollable, unapproachable, unkindly to all good**, a descending triad, in which the characters of the libertine, the churl, the worldling are painted. The three words occur nowhere else in N.T. But the exact opposites are found together in Tit. i. 8, 'temperate, a lover of hospitality, a lover of good.'

4. *traitors, heady, highminded*] The last triad again descending, **false and forward and full of conceit**, the spirit of one who 'with a light heart' (1) betrays old friends, and (2) rushes headlong on new faiths, and (3) remains to the end impenetrably wrapped in clouds of self-esteem. The second word only occurs Acts xix. 36, 'to do nothing rash'; the third has been explained 1 Tim. vi. 4; cf. 1 Tim. iii. 6; a purely 'pastoral' phrase in N.T., though thoroughly classical. Note the weight and force of the perfect participle closing the list of epithets. Cf. ii. 25. The A.V. 'highminded' has entirely changed its meaning, as Rom. xi. 20 shews, 'be not highminded, but fear.' Cf. Lightfoot, *Revision of N. T.* p. 175; and see note on 1 Tim. vi. 17.

lovers of pleasures more than lovers of God] Both compounds only occurring here, like the similar compounds 'self-lovers' and 'money-lovers' with which the passage opens. The word for 'pleasures' is always in a bad sense in N.T., Luke viii. 14 'choked with...pleasures of this life.' So Jas. iv. 1, 3; 2 Pet. ii. 13.

5. *having a form of godliness*] The word for 'form' is strictly 'formation,' its ending implying process rather than result, the producing of the form; hence in Rom. ii. 20 'thou hast the ideally perfect presentation of knowledge and truth.' 'The Jew believed that he had in the law the sole embodiment, the forming, of knowledge and truth, that he could give to knowledge and truth their right form, and so was the proper teacher of the world.' Gifford. So here **holding to a presentment of godliness**; full 'profession' though there is little enough of the substance; 'still making out that there is the real nature of godliness.' The stress lies on the making out, the representation, whether as here the inner reality is absent or as Rom. ii. 20 present. Similarly 'a professor of divinity' is credited with exhibiting real truth and knowledge; not so 'a religious professor.' Compare too our Lord's 'I will profess to you I never knew you,' Matt. vii. 23, with the account of 'the defiled and unbelieving' who 'profess that they know God, but by their works they deny him,' Tit. i. 16. The Greek word for

the power thereof: from such turn away. For of this sort 6
are they which creep into houses, and lead captive silly
women laden with sins, led away with divers lusts, ever 7
learning, and never able to come to the knowledge of the

'form,' of which our word is the causative process, means 'embodied substance,' standing between 'unclothed essence' and 'unsubstantial appearance'; see Lightfoot, *Revision of N.T.* p. 77.

denying the power thereof] The power lies in the production of 'works' as in Tit. i. 16. Cf. Bp Bull 'to deny the power of godliness is for a man by indecent and vicious actions to contradict his outward show or profession of godliness' *Serm.* xv. p. 376 (Oxf. 1846). The force of the perfect pass. participle is noted ii. 25 **living in denial of its power.**

from such turn away] The conjunction emphasises the 'such,' but not without affecting also the verb 'turn away,' cf. ver. 9; 'offenders of the first degree try to win back; but *from these men*, hardened in error, make it your habit to *turn away*,' see ver. 1. In harmony with this direction is the conduct of St John at Ephesus some 10 or 15 years later, according to the tradition. 'John, the disciple of the Lord, going to bathe at Ephesus, and perceiving Cerinthus within, rushed out of the bathhouse without bathing, crying out, "Let us fly, lest even the bathhouse fall on us, because Cerinthus the enemy of the truth is within" (*Iren.* III. iii. 4). Epiphanius substitutes Ebion for Cerinthus. Both Cerinthus and the Ebionites denied the reality of the Incarnation.' Plummer, *St John* (Gosp.), Introduction, p. 15.

6—9. Appeal to Timothy for pure doctrine in view of the worse doctrines to come.

6. *For of this sort*] **For of these,** the reason of the warning; the mischief has begun.

which creep into] The verb occurs only here in N.T., but is classical.

lead captive] For the primary sense cf. Luke xxi. 24; for the derived, Rom. vii. 23; 2 Cor. x. 5.

silly women] The neuter gender and the diminutive ending of the word here indicate the degraded contemptible state to which they have come. Vulg. 'mulierculas'; 'womanlings,' Farrar.

laden with sins] The simple verb occurs only Rom. xii. 20, where it is quoted from LXX., Prov. xxv. 22 'thou shalt heap coals of fire'; the compound verb in iv. 3. Why such women especially? Their burdened conscience lays them open to any proselytisers who promise relief.

led away with divers lusts] Apparently the meaning is (not 'lusts of the flesh' but rather) as in iv. 3, which Wordsworth explains of persons 'who in their prurient craving for something new, to stimulate and gratify their diseased appetite, accumulate to themselves a promiscuous heap of self-chosen teachers.' 'Led' belongs to 'women'; it occurs with the same construction, Rom. viii. 14.

7. *never able*] The negative used indicates the class of persons conceived of.

8 truth. Now as Jannes and Jambres withstood Moses, so do
these also resist the truth: men of corrupt minds, reprobate
9 concerning the faith. But they shall proceed no further:

the knowledge of the truth] **The full knowledge**, a 'decisive and stable apprehension,' Alford. See note on 1 Tim. ii. 4. Cf. Lightfoot, *Revision N.T.* p. 61, where he defines our word as 'the advanced or perfect knowledge which is the ideal state of the true Christian,' and quotes 2 Cor. vi. 9 'as unknown and yet well known.'

8. *Now as Jannes and Jambres*] **And like as**; the conjunction should be translated 'now' only when there is more of a fresh departure; the present is only a small additional paragraph. Jannes and Jambres are mentioned here only in Scripture. The Targum of Pseudo Jonathan inserts their names in Ex. vii. 11, Mambres which the Vulgate reads here being sometimes a later form for Jambres in the Jewish Commentaries. They were held to be the magicians who first imitated the wonders wrought by Moses and Aaron (see ver. 13 'impostors' or 'magicians') but afterwards failing confessed that the power of God was with those whom they had withstood. Pliny, *Hist. Nat.* XXX. i. 2, mentions their story 'est et alia magices factio a Mose et Jamne et Jotape Judæis pendens.' He could not have derived his information from St Paul. There must have been an oral tradition or a lost book of Israelitish early history. Mr Poole (Art. *Dict. Bib.* from which this account is mainly taken) inclines to the latter supposition as more likely to preserve the exact names. That they are exact he thinks probable; since (1) the termination in Jambres or Mambres is like that of many Egyptian compounds ending with RA "the Sun," as Men-kau-ra, (2) Jannes appears to be a transcription of the Egyptian name Aan, that of a king of the 15th dynasty who was probably the second predecessor of Joseph's Pharaoh, and the most prevalent names among the Egyptians were those of kings then reigning or not long dead. The Rabbins state that Jannes and Jambres were sons of Balaam, and prophesied to Pharaoh the birth of Moses, and were authors of much mischief, subsequently perishing either in the Red Sea or in the tumult over the golden calf.

resist the truth] Rather, **withstand**, keeping the word.

of corrupt minds] Implies too much a *natural* viciousness; the perfect passive participle implies 'having come to a corrupt state and remaining in it' as above. *In itself* the word 'corrupt' from the Latin participle (cf. the Vulg. 'corrupti mente)' should have just this force, but in usage it is a mere adjective; render **corrupted in mind**.

reprobate] Just as in Tit. i. 16, where see note.

9. *But they shall proceed no further*] The same words as in ii. 16, where their advance is predicted. Here the future beyond that advance is seen. The adverbial phrase with the verb lends itself to this double meaning, being in the comparative and so capable of being rendered there 'still farther' and here 'not very far.' So in St Luke's usage, Acts iv. 17, 'that it spread no further'; but xx. 9, 'while Paul was very long discoursing'; xxiv. 4, 'that I may not weary thee at great length';

for their folly shall be manifest unto all *men*, as theirs also
was. But thou hast fully known my doctrine, manner of 10
life, purpose, faith, longsuffering, charity, patience, persecu- 11

cf. 1 Tim. iii. 14, 'quite shortly'; 2 Tim i. 18, 'very well'; Acts xvii. 22, 'somewhat superstitious.'

manifest] Lit. 'thoroughly manifest,' a strong classical compound occurring only here in N.T.

their folly] The noun occurs only here and Luke vi. 11, where R.V. renders 'madness'; Ellicott, 'wicked as well as insensate folly'; Trench, 'the foolishness which is akin to, and derived from wickedness' (*N.T. Syn.* § 75); for the adjective see note on Tit. iii. 3.

as theirs also was] R.V. literally, **came to be**; the conjunction emphasises pronoun and verb as in ver. 5.

10—17. THE APPEAL FOR PURE LIFE AND DOCTRINE IN VIEW BOTH OF ST PAUL'S OWN PAST AND THE EVIL FUTURE.

The connexion is: 'You were trained to a life the opposite of all this, in learning to copy me, in learning to rest all upon the Scriptures; see that you live the life.'

10. *But thou hast fully known my doctrine*] The MS. authority on the whole favours the aorist, which suits also the aorists of ver. 14 and does not assert, as the perfect would, the certainty of Timothy's settled continuance in 'following.' The perfect may have come in from 1 Tim. iv. 6, where it is more appropriate in connexion with the present participle 'being continuously nourished.' On the meaning of the word see note there: **thou didst closely follow.**

my doctrine, manner of life] Again, **teaching**; cf. 1 Tim. i. 10. 'Manner of life' is a word occurring here only in N.T., a substantive derived from the verb used above 'led' ver. 6 and Rom. viii. 14, which shews how **conduct** is the natural derived sense; cf. Gifford's note 'all who are moved and guided by the Spirit and follow His guidance.' The word is classical in the general sense of 'guidance,' 'course,' 'training'; and occurs Ar. *Eth. N.* x. vii. 3, as here.

purpose] In i. 9, and wherever else it is used in St Paul's epistles, refers to God's purpose and plan of salvation. It occurs four times in N.T. to render 'the *shew*-bread.' But in Acts xi. 23 it is used of Barnabas who 'exhorted them all that *with purpose of heart* they would cleave unto the Lord,' and this is exactly the force here.

faith] In the same general and usual sense as in ii. 22; 1 Tim. vi. 11, where 'love' and 'brave patience' also occur; for this last see also note on ii. 10.

longsuffering] Occurs with 'brave patience' or 'endurance' in Col. i. 11, where Lightfoot distinguishes thus: 'While "endurance" is the temper which does not easily succumb under suffering, "long-suffering" is the self-restraint which does not hastily retaliate a wrong. The one is opposed to *cowardice* or *despondency*, the other to *wrath* or *revenge* (Prov. xv. 18).' In 1 Tim. vi. 11 this 'endurance' is coupled with 'meekness of heart' which is rather the opposite of 'rudeness,' 'harshness.' See ii. 25, and note.

tions, afflictions, which came unto me at Antioch, at Iconium,
at Lystra ; what persecutions I endured : but out of *them* all
12 the Lord delivered me. Yea, and all that will live godly
13 in Christ Jesus shall suffer persecution. But evil men and

charity] As throughout N.T., **love**.

11. *afflictions, which came unto me*] It is better to make the 'afflictions' go with the preceding, and make a new clause commence with the relative. So R.V. **sufferings; what things befell me; what persecutions.**

The Antioch meant is that in Pisidia, originally planted by the Magnesians. Seleucus the son of Antiochus re-settled it, and called it Antioch after the name of his father: which name it kept, though under Augustus made a colony with the additional name of Cæsarea. Plin. *N. H.* v. xxvii. 24 'Pisidæ...quorum colonia Cæsarea, eadem Antiochia.' Its ruins are still to be seen, one of the most striking objects being a very perfect aqueduct of twenty-one arches. See Lewin, *Life of St Paul*, I. 137. For the work and sufferings at Antioch see Acts xiii. 14—50. The place usually understood by Antioch would be the large and important city of Antioch in Syria; but in writing to Timothy, whose home was in that district, St Paul would use the word with its well-known local meaning.

Iconium lies S.E. of Antioch at a distance of sixty miles, on the dusty highroad connecting Ephesus with Antioch of Syria. It is still called Cogni, and, like Damascus, is an oasis in the desert, by the dry plains of Lycaonia. See Acts xiii. 51—xiv. 6.

Lystra lies about forty miles to the south of Iconium, on the same road, in a hollow, on the north side of which rises Kara Dagh or the Black Mountain. Its ruins remain and are called 'the thousand and one churches,' it having been an episcopal see under the Byzantine emperors. This was Timothy's birth-place. See Acts xiv. 6—20.

St Paul mentions these places and his sufferings there, (1) because they were the first, in his first period of ministry, (2) they were well known to Timothy and may well have led him to cast in his lot with the Apostle. See Introduction, pp. 57, 59, 62.

but out of them *all*] Rather, **and**, yet with an ascending force which marks a contrast, so that 'and yet' is hardly too strong; though the more exact rendering is to lay stress on 'all' and on 'delivered,' cf. Winer, III. § 53, 3.

12. *Yea, and all*] The force of the two conjunctions is shewn in note on 1 Tim. iii. 10.

that will live godly] **Whose will is**, compare Luke xvi. 26, 'they whose will is to pass from hence to you.' 'In Christ Jesus.' The whole phrase is nearly the equivalent of 'to lead a godly and a Christian life' (Baptismal Service, Pr.-Bk.).

13. *But evil men and seducers*] The word 'seduce' in A.V. occurs nine times in Old and New Testament always in the general sense of 'lead astray'; everywhere except here it is used to represent the Greek word for this cognate to the English word 'planet' 'the wanderer,' (cf. Jude's

seducers shall wax worse and worse, deceiving, and being
deceived. But continue thou in *the things* which thou hast 14
learned and hast been assured of, knowing of whom thou
hast learned *them;* and that from a child thou hast known 15
the holy scriptures, which are able to make thee wise unto

'wandering stars') and almost immediately following here 'deceiving,' cf. 1 Tim. iv. 1 and note. R.V. in these places varies between 'seduce' and 'lead astray.' The word so rendered here is properly 'enchanter,' from the cries of incantations used. So 'magicians,' and more generally 'impostors.' Compare for the general sense, the most probable here, the use of the verb by Plato, *Phæd.* 81, 13, 'the soul having served and loved the body and been *bewitched* by it through desires and pleasures.' Some think there may be a reference to the magic arts, such as those of Jannes and Jambres; and certainly Ephesus had an evil repute in this respect itself, cf. Acts xix. 13, 19. 'Ephesian letters' was a common expression for charms made up of magic words and worn as amulets.

shall wax worse and worse] The same verb as in ver. 9. The 'progress' is a 'rake's progress,' step after step **leading and being led astray**. Compare Rev. xviii. 23, 'with thy sorcery were all the nations *deceived*,' 2 Joh. 7, 'many *deceivers* are gone forth into the world...this is the *deceiver* and the antichrist.'

14. *But continue thou*] 'Thou' emphatic; 'continue,' better **abide**, i.e. make no downward progress, go not astray: the construction of the next clause illustrates the brevity of the Greek use of the relative; lit. 'in those things which thou didst learn, and as to which thou wert fully persuaded.' The last verb occurs here only in N.T. But it is a good classical word.

which thou hast learned] The three past tenses of this verse are aorists, and should be rendered **didst learn, wert assured, didst learn.** A definite time is implied when the learning and the assurance came, in that early youth.

knowing of whom] 'Knowing as thou dost' as in ii. 23. The plural 'of what persons' should be read. Lois and Eunice must be understood, as in i. 5.

15. *from a child*] Lit. **from a babe**; the word occurs four times in St Luke's 'Gospel of the Infancy,' ch. i. and ii., and again xviii. 15; Acts vii. 19.

thou hast known] Lit. 'thou knowest,' the perfect having this present force, and the Greek idiom in a phrase like this using the present where we use the perfect definite. The meaning is that there has been a continued knowledge present always 'from a babe' and present now. So in Joh. xv. 27, 'ye are, i.e. have been, with me from the beginning,' cf. Winer, III. § 40.

the holy scriptures] Lit. 'the sacred writings' of the Old Testament. It was a requirement of the Rabbis that a child should begin to learn the Law by heart when five years old. 'Raf said to Samuel, the son of Schilath, a teacher, "Do not take the boy to be taught before he is six years old, but from that year receive him, and train him as

16 salvation through faith which is in Christ Jesus. All
scripture *is* given by inspiration of God, and *is* profitable

you do the ox, which, day by day, bears a heavier load." Philo, a contemporary of our Lord, says, "They are taught, so to speak, from their very swaddling clothes by their parents, masters and teachers, in the holy laws, and in the unwritten customs, and to believe in God, the one Father and Creator of the world," (*Legat. ad Caium*, § 16). At the age of thirteen he became a "son of the Law," and was bound to practise all its moral and ritual requirements.' Geikie, *Life of Christ*, I. 173.

The original word for 'scriptures' is used of Moses' writings Joh. v. 47, where Westcott well points out that it 'appears to mark the specific form rather than the general scope of the record' which is denoted by the word used in ver. 16.

which are able] Present participle, in harmony with the *present* sense of 'thou hast known,' and marking the abiding continuous power of the Holy Scripture.

to make thee wise] The verb occurs here only in N.T.; its participle in 2 Pet. i. 16, 'cunningly devised'; the tense is *aorist* according to the proper use of the aorist, to give the idea of the verb in its most general form, 'the scriptures have this capacity of making wise.'

through faith which is in Christ Jesus] See note on 1 Tim. iii. 13; the clause belongs to the verb 'make wise,' not to the noun 'salvation.' The doctrine and scheme of Christianity is required to illuminate the precept and history of the Old Testament. 'In vetere Testamento latet novum, in novo vetus patet.' Ellicott quotes Hooker, *Eccl. Pol.* i. 14. 'The Old did make wise by teaching Salvation through Christ that should come, the New by teaching that Christ the Saviour is come.' Cf. also Art. VII. in the English Prayer Book, 'The Old Testament is not contrary to the New; for both in the Old and New Testament everlasting life is offered to mankind by Christ.'

16. *All scripture*] The word for 'Scripture' occurs fifty-one times in N.T., always, except 2 Pet. iii. 16, of the recognised Old Testament Scriptures, the Law, the Prophets, and the Hagiographa, or of one or more of them; in 2 Pet. iii. 16 the reference is to St Paul's epistles and to 'the other Scriptures.' The A.V. of A.D. 1611 is therefore not wrong (though many printed copies have altered it) in rendering the word as 'Scripture' with a capital S; for it is by itself the recognised technical term.

We should translate **Every Scripture** probably, as is the proper rendering when there is no article. The word 'Scripture' is without the article also in Joh. xix. 37; 1 Pet. ii. 6; 2 Pet. i. 20. Those who retain the rendering 'All Scripture' with A.V. would lay stress on the technical use of the word shewn above, so that it may be treated as a proper name, comparing Acts ii. 36, 'all (the) house of Israel.' But this is unnecessary, especially as the three places where the word occurs without the article in the singular have the meaning 'a Book or passage of Scripture' and they are in date as late as or later than this Epistle.

for doctrine, for reproof, for correction, for instruction in 17
righteousness: that the man of God may be perfect,
throughly furnished unto all good works.

given by inspiration of God] One word in the original, a passive verbal, occurring only here in N.T., and meaning 'filled with the breath of God' so as to be 'living oracles,' Acts vii. 38. Cf. 2 Pet. i. 21, 'holy men of God moved by the Holy Spirit.' Compare also the following passage written about A.D. 95, at the same time as the last N.T. book, St John's Gospel: 'Search the Scriptures, the true Scriptures, the Scriptures of the Holy Ghost: ye know that there is nothing unrighteous, nothing counterfeit written in them.' Clem. Rom. *ad Cor.* c. 45.

There are two ways of taking this adjective, either as an attribute (so R.V.) or a predicate (so A.V.); either 'Every Scripture, inasmuch as it is inspired of God, is also useful &c.' or 'Every Scripture is inspired and is profitable &c.' In the latter case the second predicate comes in tamely. In the one case inspiration is assumed, in the other it is asserted.

profitable for doctrine] **For teaching.**

for reproof] The noun occurs only Heb. xi. 1, 'the proving of things not seen.' The corresponding verb is used five times by St Paul in these epistles, e.g. iv. 2.

correction] Only here in N.T. though a good classical word, cf. Dem. *c. Timocr.* 707, 7 'they shall lose their promotion to the Areopagus for putting down the amendment of the laws.'

for instruction in righteousness] Lit. **discipline which is in righteousness**; the verb 'disciplining' has occurred, 1 Tim. i. 20; 2 Tim. ii. 25, where see notes. It occurs with 'reprove' in the letter to the church at Laodicea, Rev. iii. 19, where R.V. 'chasten.' 'Which is in righteousness' just as 'faith which is in Christ Jesus' above; the definite article indicates the definite sphere of exercise for the discipline and the faith. See note on 1 Tim. i. 2, where *without the article* the preposition and its case are shewn to be very nearly equivalent to an adjective. Ellicott well sums up the meaning 'that Holy Scripture *teaches* the ignorant, *convicts* the evil and prejudiced, *corrects* the fallen and erring, and *trains in righteousness* all men, especially those that need bringing to fuller measures of perfection.'

17. *the man of God*] As in 1 Tim. vi. 11.

perfect] In the sense in which, for example, Confirmation is sometimes said to make 'a perfect Christian,' i.e. one perfectly equipped and supplied with the full measure of gifts and graces through the Holy Spirit. The word for 'perfect' here occurs nowhere else in N.T. It is derived from an adverb meaning 'exactly,' and so occurs in Homer, *Il.* XIV. 92, of speaking 'exactly to the purpose,' in Theophrastus *H. P.* 2. 5. 5, of being 'full-grown.' **Complete**, then, as R.V. renders, is more correct than A.V. So when the word is compounded with hand, foot, mind, we get 'perfect of hand,' 'of feet,' 'sound of mind,' &c.

throughly furnished] The perfect participle again expressing the

4 I charge *thee* therefore before God, and the Lord Jesus
Christ, who shall judge the quick and the dead at his
2 appearing and his kingdom; preach the word; be instant

resulting and abiding state; the verb is from the same root as the adjective; hence R.V. rightly preserves the play upon the words by rendering **furnished completely.** It only occurs again in Acts xxi. 5, 'we had accomplished,' completely finished, the days. Another compound occurs Luke vi. 40, 'Every one, when he is perfected, shall be as his master.'

CH. IV. APOSTOLIC SUCCESSION AND FELLOWSHIP.

1—8. THE LAST APPEAL. THE SAME WARNING. THE OLD EXAMPLE.

The three main thoughts (see iii. 1) recur, but with added intensity, in this last brief *appeal*, and *warning*, and *example*. Similarly in 1 Tim. vi. 20 observe the 'aculeus in fine.' 'Play the man thyself; beware the lives and tongues of error; see how the old warrior dies.'

1. *I charge* thee *therefore*] Read **I charge thee**, omitting the pronoun and conjunction. The stress is on the verb itself, more marked and solemn because placed quite abruptly; almost therefore, 'I adjure thee.' For the meaning and use, see on ii. 14.

and the Lord Jesus Christ] The best MSS. have **and Christ Jesus**, see note on 1 Tim. i. 1.

who shall judge] The thought of 'Christ the Judge,' which was the subject of St Paul's earliest letters to the Thessalonians fifteen years before, recurs now in this last warning word. So too the word 'appearing,' *epiphany*, which is a characteristic of the 'Pastorals': see note on 1 Tim. vi. 14.

at his appearing] The better authorities read 'and' for 'at'; 'his appearing' is to be taken therefore as the accusative of the object appealed to in the solemn adjuration; as the same verb is used LXX. Deut. iv. 26, 'I call *heaven and earth* to witness against you'; the first construction being equivalent *in sense* to 'I call God to witness, and Christ Jesus,' the second is added as if it had been so, 'and I call to witness His appearing.' So the uncompounded verb is constantly used with the accusative. Cf. Mk. v. 7.

and his kingdom] 'His *coming*, at which we shall stand before Him, His *kingdom* in which we shall hope to reign with Him.' Alford.

2. *preach the word*] The *unconnected* aorist is emphatic; so is the *aorist*, to indicate the 'verb thought' standing out with prominence; 'I adjure thee, remember—preaching, persisting, reproving, rebuking, rousing,—to it, in God's name!' If the tenses had been present, the stress would have been different; 'Go on with each, keep on at it, form the habit of it.'

be instant] The other uses of the word in N.T. are either in the sense (of person) 'coming and standing by' or (of time) 'being present,' cf. Acts xvii. 5; as below ver. 6. Here the sense is the classical one of 'giving attention,' 'applying oneself' to a thing. Compare Dem. *De Cor.*,

in season, out of season; reprove, rebuke, exhort with all
longsuffering and doctrine. For the time will come when 3
they will not endure sound doctrine; but after their own
lusts shall they heap to themselves teachers, having itching

305. 7, 'what means and resources our country possessed when I entered on the administration, what *when I applied myself to it* I collected for her.'

in season, out of season] An oxymoron, not to be pressed literally any more than the familiar *nolens volens*, but implying, as we should say, '*constant* application.' Vulg. 'opportune,' 'importune.'

reprove] The same word as in iii. 16, 'reproof'; less strong than the following 'rebuke,' which St Paul has nowhere else; it is frequent in the Gospels, and occurs Jude 9.

exhort] Or here perhaps 'rouse'; see note on 1 Tim. v. 1. The order of the verbs in some MSS. is 'reprove, rouse, rebuke'; so Vulg. 'argue obsecra increpa in omni patientia et doctrina,' which the English Prayer-Book follows in the last prayer for the consecration of a Bishop 'that he may be earnest to reprove, beseech and rebuke with all patience and doctrine.'

longsuffering] See 1 Tim. i. 16; 2 Tim. iii. 10.

doctrine] Rather **teaching**; this word only occurs in Tit. i. 9 besides, of the Pastoral Epistles, though it is used by all the Evangelists and by St Paul four times in his other Epistles. The distinction, drawn Tit. i. 9, holds equally here between this word and the word translated 'doctrine' in ver. 3.

3. *sound doctrine*] **The sound doctrine** as in 1 Tim. i. 10, where see note.

but after their own lusts] Vulg. 'ad sua desideria,' in opposition to the healthful doctrine. Compare the same phrase in the singular, James i. 14, 'Each man is tempted when he is drawn away by his own lust and enticed.' R.V. still retains 'lusts'; this word in the age of the A.V. had also the wider sense of 'strong desire' not being restricted as now to one passion only. 'Lust' in Ps. xcii. 10, Pr. Bk., is 'desire' in A.V. and R.V. But the word here denotes *a corrupt will* leading both to corrupt doctrine and corrupt life. See note on iii. 6. Trench, *N.T. Syn.* § 87, quotes Cicero's definition of the word here rendered 'lust'; 'immoderata appetitio opinati magni boni rationi non obtemperans,' *Tusc. Quæst.* iii. 11. It is sometimes 'concupiscence' Rom. vii. 8; very rarely in a good sense 'desire,' Phil. i. 23.

shall they heap to themselves] A compound form of the verb used in ch. iii. 6 for 'laden.'

having itching ears] An ambiguous rendering in A.V.; but the original is clear, the nominative case shewing that it is the pupils not the teachers who have the itching ears. R.V. corrects this by transposing the clause to the commencement of the sentence; but this gives up the close proximity of the two words for 'ears'; **because they have itching ears** should be the rendering. The participle is middle, lit.

4 ears; and they shall turn away *their* ears from the truth,
5 and shall be turned unto fables. But watch thou in all
things, endure afflictions, do the work of an evangelist,
6 make full proof of thy ministry. For I am now ready to be

'scratching themselves,' as Arist. *H. A.* ix. 1, 18. Out of a prurient longing for novelty and excitement, 'instead of receiving those Teachers who are authorized by Christ to instruct them and have a regular call and mission from Him to execute their sacred office, and preach by the Rule of Faith, they will stray away from their Pastors and from their own proper Fold and will raise up for themselves a confused heap of Teachers.' Wordsworth.

4. *shall turn away* their *ears*] Better **will**. The word for 'ears' here and above is literally 'the hearing'; it is used in classical Greek for 'ear' when there is reference to the act of hearing, not merely as a member of the body. See Alford on Heb. v. 11, who quotes Philo i. 474, 'they have ears but no *hearings* in them.' Hence the exact propriety of our word in the plural, Mk. vii. 35, and the significance of Bengel's comment, 'non unus in aure meatus.'

shall be turned unto] The verb is 2nd fut. passive, but middle in sense, 'will turn themselves aside.' So with R.V. **will turn aside**. The aor. pass. from which this future is formed has occurred 1 Tim. i. 6, v. 15, the pres. part. vi. 20, the last with an accusative of the object turned from. Cf. Winer, *Gr.*, § 38. 2, b; § 38. 4.

unto fables] The article has the same force as above, ii. 22, 23, 'these fables' which are now being invented and circulated. Cf. Tit. i. 14.

5. *But watch thou*] Exactly and fully, **but thou, be thou watchful and sober,** combining A.V. and R.V., and emphasising the pronoun. The proper force of the verb is certainly 'sobriety' literal and then metaphorical. See note on the adjective, 1 Tim. iii. 2. The metaphorical sobriety is in effect 'watchfulness,' though not from 'wakefulness' so much as from 'wariness,' cool-headedness. Hence the proverb, 'the tongue of the drunkard, but the heart of the sober.' The present tense is plainly most suitable to this *state* of calm sober consideration in everything; while the aorists which follow as suitably express the going to and taking up 'hardship,' 'preaching,' 'ministry,' just as in ver. 1.

the work of an evangelist] Not here that of any separate class, but that which belonged to Apostles and the humblest Evangelists proper, equally. See the Prayer in the Form of Consecration of Bishops (Eng. Pr.-Bk.), 'that he may evermore be ready to spread abroad thy gospel, the glad tidings of reconciliation with thee.'

make full proof] Or **fulfil**, i.e. fully perform, the same meaning of the word as is most probably to be assigned to Luke i. 1, 'those matters which have been fulfilled among us.' Vulg. 'ministerium tuum imple.'

6—8. 'I have appealed to you by the *warning* of the evil times and teachers that will be: I appeal to you now by the *example* of the good times and the good teacher that have been. Let my mantle fall on you, my days are numbered.'

6. *For I am now ready to be offered*] The present tense is still more

offered, and the time of my departure is at hand. I have 7
fought a good fight, I have finished *my* course, I have kept

vivid, and so the personal pronoun **for as to me—I am already being offered**; and the Greek word means 'am being poured out as a drink-offering.' St Paul recalls the thought and very phrase of his letter to Philippi in the first captivity; what was then a possibility is now a certainty; Phil. ii. 17, 'If I am required to pour out my life-blood as a libation over the sacrificial offering of your faith, I rejoice myself and I congratulate you all therein.' See Bp Lightfoot, who quotes the similar metaphor recorded of St Paul's great heathen contemporary Seneca when on the point of death, 'respergens proximos servorum addita voce, *libare se liquorem illum Jovi liberatori*.' Tac. *Ann.* xv. 64.

my departure] Another thought and phrase from the same time and letter, Phil. i. 23, 'I am hemmed in on both sides, my own desire tending towards this, to depart and to be with Christ.' The metaphor of verb there and noun here is of a journey either by land or sea—loosing tent-cords, or weighing anchor, *for starting up to depart*; this latter part of the meaning belongs to the preposition. So in Luke xii. 36, 'he will return from the wedding' ought to be rendered 'he will depart.' The servants look out eagerly not merely at the moment of his return being due, but from the moment of his *departure from* the feast being due. Clement of Rome connects this word, used for 'death,' with 'journey,' used for life. 'Blessed are the elders who have taken the journey before us, in that they had their departure in mature and fruitful age' (*ad Cor.* c. 44). The corresponding words for *arrival* at the end of a stage in the journey are the same verb and noun compounded with the preposition 'down' instead of 'up': for verb see Gen. xix. 2, where Lot asks the angels to 'tarry all night,' and Luke ix. 12, '*lodge* and get victuals,' xix. 7, 'He is gone in to *lodge* with a man that is a sinner'; for noun Luke ii. 7, 'no room for them in *the inn*,' xxii. 11, 'where is the *guest-chamber?*' The original meaning of the word would be 'to loose the beasts of burden for *settling down to rest*.' Our word here has become an English word, *analysis*, from the cognate sense of 'breaking up' or analysing the component parts, *e.g.* of a sentence.

is at hand] Rather with R.V. **is come**, lit. 'stands by' me, cf. Acts xxiii. 11, 'the Lord *stood by* him and said.' It is altogether a word of St Luke's, being used eighteen times by him; by St Paul above, iv. 2, and 1 Thess. v. 3, and nowhere else in N.T.

7. *a good fight*] **the good fight**, see 1 Tim. vi. 12, where the metaphor is discussed; the second clause here, 'I have finished the course,' certainly suggests that the foot-race is to be the chief thought in the 'games contest,' 'the fair race—'tis run; the course—'tis finished; the faith—'tis kept' may represent the perfect tense used: 'per effectus suos durat,' Poppo. The aspirations of Acts xx. 24, Phil. iii. 12, have now been realised; the Christian athlete is all but 'emeritus.' 'He stands almost alone under the shadow of an impending death; but it is the last effort of a defeated and desperate

8 the faith: henceforth there is laid up for me a crown of righteousness, which the Lord, the righteous judge, shall give me at that day: and not to me only, but unto all them also that love his appearing.

cause: the victory is already gained....With the assured conviction that the object of his life was fully accomplished, he might well utter these words on which seventeen centuries have now set their indisputable seal.' Stanley, *Apostolic Age*, pp. 169—170.

the faith] In the same objective sense as so often throughout these Epistles, the sacred deposit of historic truth and teaching, cf. 1 Tim. vi. 20, 21, &c.

8. *henceforth*] Or, 'it remains only that' as in Matt. xxvi. 45, in the Garden of Gethsemane 'it remains only for you to sleep on,' 'there is nothing else to be done.' St Paul commonly uses the word (with and without the article) to introduce the closing words of exhortation in his Epistles, 2 Cor. xiii. 11; Eph. vi. 10; Phil. iii. 1, and again after a digression iv. 8; 2 Thess. iii. 1. It seems unnecessary to have recourse to the sense in which Polybius uses the word, 'accordingly,' 'proinde,' 'itaque.' In construction it is a neuter adjective used adverbially.

there is laid up] Cf. Luke xix. 20, 'laid up in a napkin,' Col. i. 5 'the hope which is stored up for you in the heavens.'

a crown of righteousness] **The crown**; the genitive 'righteousness' is similar to the genitives of the particular contests in which the crown was won; *e.g.* Pind. *Nem.* v. 9, 'Pytheas, broad-shouldered son of Lampo, won the crown of the double-contest (wrestling and boxing) at the Nemean games.' 'Righteousness' then is the 'race' of the Christian life. So in 1 Tim. vi. 11; 2 Tim. ii. 22, 'follow after righteousness,' and in ch. iii. 16, 'the discipline which is in righteousness,' the word is instead of a volume. The genitives in James i. 12, 'the crown of life,' 1 Pet. v. 4, 'a crown of glory,' are similar to the genitives of the particular material of which the crown was made; *e.g.* Pind. *Nem.* vi. 18, 'He too was victor at Olympia and first won himself the crown of olive for the Æacidæ from Alpheus.' The crown at the Pythian games was of laurel leaves, at the Nemean of parsley, at the Isthmian of ivy.

shall give] **Award**; the word has occurred 1 Tim. v. 4, where see note. This and the well-known passages Luke xix. 8, 'I *restore* fourfold,' xx. 25, '*Render* unto Cæsar the things that are Cæsar's,' Rom. xiii. 7, '*Render* to all their dues,' shew the force of the compound verb here 'give the due award.'

> 'A pound of that same merchant's flesh is thine;
> The court *awards* it and the law doth give it.'

The same word is used by Christ of the judgment, 'then shall he *reward* (R.V. render) every man according to his works' Matt. xvi. 27.

unto all...that love his appearing] The perfect part.; the sense is fully given by **who have their love set on**, as R.V. well renders the similar perfect, 1 Tim. iv. 10, 'we have our hope set on the living God.'

Do thy diligence to come shortly unto me: for Demas 9, 10
hath forsaken me, having loved *this* present world, and is
departed unto Thessalonica; Crescens to Galatia, Titus

For the special force of this higher word *agapân* for 'to love' see Trench, *N. T. Syn.* § 12 'a word born within the bosom of revealed religion,' and Westcott, Joh. xxi. 15, 'St Peter lays claim only to the feeling of *natural love* of which he could be sure; he does not venture to say that he has attained to that *higher love* which was to be the spring of the Christian life.'

his appearing] As in ver. 1, of the second coming; to which all the six occurrences of the substantive in N.T. refer. The verb in Luke i. 79 and Tit. ii. 11, iii. 4 refers to the first Epiphany.

9—18. THE SCATTERING OF FRIENDS. ENTREATY FOR TIMOTHY'S PRESENCE. ASSURANCE OF THE LORD'S PRESENT HELP.

The connexion is: 'Do your best to come to me—to come with all speed—to come before the winter stops you—lest it be too late. But for Luke, I am all alone. One by one they of Asia have left me. Yet I am not alone. I can still do all things through Him that enables me.'

9. *Do thy diligence*] The same verb as in Tit. iii. 12 and below ver. 21. 'Make an earnest effort,' 'do thy best.' Compare the use in Gal. ii. 10, 'this was my own heartfelt desire.'

shortly] Further defined ver. 21.

10. *Demas*] Very likely a shortened form of Demetrius; two persons of the name occur in N.T., Acts xix. 24, the silversmith of Ephesus, and, 3 Joh. 12, the bearer possibly of that letter, one to whose character all bore testimony, which St John himself ratified. The Demetrius or Demas here seems to occupy a middle place; a Christian believer and follower, who however had lost 'his first love,' and forsook the Apostle in his hour of trial, to attend to the business of the world. He had been with him in the first imprisonment, Col. iv. 14.

hath forsaken] **Forsook,** so in ver. 16. The same strong compound verb and tense occur Matt. xxvii. 46, where the rendering 'why hast thou forsaken me?' is more correct, because the aorist is used there of what is just happening, cf. Phil. ii. 28, Gal. vi. 11.

having loved] 'Because he loved'; this verb is chosen in half-conscious irony of contrast to ver. 8 and the love set on the future appearing of the Lord.

this *present world*] Lit. 'age'; cf. note on 1 Tim. vi. 17. The other world, the world of eternity, is under the Eternal God the King of the ages, 1 Tim. i. 17. Cf. Luke xx. 35, xviii. 30. 'The Apostles speak of themselves and their generation as living on the frontier of two æons, the Gospel transferring them across the border. The distinction of time between the two becomes lost in the moral and spiritual conception.' Bp Lightfoot on Gal. i. 4.

unto Thessalonica] Why, is not known, except so far as this place suggests either home or business.

Crescens to Galatia] Before the Christian era and for two centuries

11 unto Dalmatia. Only Luke is with me. Take Mark, and

afterwards the form Galatia (Galatæ) is almost universally used by Greek writers to the exclusion of Gallia (Galli), when they do not employ Celtice (Celtæ), whether speaking of the people of Gaul properly so called, or of the Asiatic colony. And 'Galatia' here was traditionally interpreted of European Gaul. It is thus explained by Eusebius *H. E.* III. 4 'Of the other followers of St Paul, Crescens is recorded as having been sent to Gallia,' and by others. It is so taken also by those MSS. which read *Gallian* for *Galatian*, for the former reading may be regarded as a gloss. The Churches of Vienne and Mayence both claimed Crescens as their founder. Weight is also to be attributed to this tradition in favour of western Gaul because it is not the *prima facie* view. From the language of Clement *ad Cor.* c. v. 'having taught righteousness through the whole world and having come to the boundary of the west' it appears that St Paul's intention to visit Spain (Rom. xv. 24) was fulfilled, and it is not improbable that this western journey included a visit to Gaul, which would make a visit of Crescens to it afterwards as natural as the visit of Titus to Dalmatia, with which it is linked. The above, representing substantially the view of Bp Lightfoot (*Galatians*, pp. 2, 31, *Clement*, p. 50) is further illustrated in Introduction, pp. 42, 44.

Titus unto Dalmatia] Dalmatia was part of the Roman province of Illyricum on the east coast of the Adriatic, now *Herzegovina* or *Bosnia*. Its capital was Salona (now *Spalatro*) to which place the Emperor Diocletian retired. St Paul had preached in the neighbourhood 'round about unto Illyricum,' possibly near Dyrrachium, now *Durazzo*, the scene of the great contest between Cæsar and Pompeius, and the port from Macedonia into Italy. The mission of Titus would naturally connect itself with some such labours, which still formed a part of the 'care of all the churches,' see Introduction, 'Life of Titus.'

11. *Only Luke*] Lucas is a contraction of Lucanus, which occurs frequently in inscriptions, and may indicate the position of a *libertus* or freedman: many such, we know, were the house physicians, the profession, as such, being in very little esteem. See Plaut. *Menæchm.* v. 3—5, and cf. Bekker's *Gallus*, p. 207. St Luke is distinguished from 'they of the circumcision,' Col. iv. 14, and so cannot be identified with Lucius St Paul's 'kinsman,' Rom. xvi. 21. He first appears as a companion of St Paul, Acts xvi. 1, at a time very nearly that of an attack of the Apostle's constitutional malady or 'thorn in the flesh,' Gal. iv. 13; and the words in Col. iv. 14 'the beloved physician' seem to breathe a feeling of personal gratitude and obligation. St Luke travelled with the Apostle on his last journey to Jerusalem (Acts xxi. 1) and also, two years later from Jerusalem to Rome (Acts xxvii. 2). The absence of his name from the greetings in Philippians may be due to his having then left Rome for a time; but he was again with him before the close of the two years, Col. iv. 14, Philem. 24; and is now at his side 'alone' in his last hours. See Introd. p. 44. After St Paul's death, according to Epiphanius *cont. Hær.* LI. 11, St Luke 'preaches first in Dalmatia and Gallia; in Italy and Macedonia, but first in Gallia;

as Paul himself says of some of his companions in his epistles "Crescens in Gallia," for we are not to read "in Galatia" as some mistakenly think, but "in Gallia."' Bithynia and Achaia are named as the place of his martyrdom somewhere between A.D. 75 and A.D. 100.

For a striking comparison drawn between St Luke and Demas see Keble's Poem on St Luke's Day (*Christian Year*):

'Two converts, watching by his side,
  Alike his love and greetings share;
Luke the beloved, the sick soul's guide,
  And Demas, named in faltering prayer.

Pass a few years—look in once more—
  The Saint is in his bonds again;
Save that his hopes more boldly soar,
  He and his lot unchanged remain.

But only Luke is with him now!—
  Alas! that even the martyr's cell,
Heaven's very gate, should scope allow
  For the false world's seducing spell.'

Take Mark] A.V. varies between 'Mark' and 'Marcus' in the different passages where the name occurs. R.V. rightly throughout 'Mark' (Lightfoot, *N. T. Rev.*, p. 157). 'Marcus' was the Latin surname for John (Johanan, the Grace of God) the son of Mary, who lived at Jerusalem, apparently with good means (Acts xii. 12), and 'cousin' of Barnabas of Cyprus (Col. iv. 10). He and his mother must have been well known to St Peter, who went to her house straight from the prison; and the phrase 'Mark my son' 1 Pet. v. 13 makes it probable that he was converted by that Apostle. Compare a similar phrase in 1 Tim. i. 2, 18. He was 'minister' to Paul and Barnabas on the first missionary journey through Cyprus, but left them at Perga (Acts xiii. 5, 13), possibly to escape the dangers of Asia Minor; and for this reason St Paul declined to have his help on the second journey (Acts xv. 38) though at the cost of breaking with St Barnabas, who took St Mark again to Cyprus. A reconciliation must have taken place before we next hear of him, as he is reckoned by St Paul in the first imprisonment at Rome as one of his 'fellow labourers unto the kingdom' who have been 'a comfort' unto him, Col. iv. 10. After this he seems to have joined St Peter at 'Babylon' (1 Pet. v. 13) whence he must have returned to Asia Minor, so that Timothy could now 'take him up.' After St Paul's death he is said to have laboured in Egypt and to have died by martyrdom. His Gospel must have been written between A.D. 63 and A.D. 70; according to Irenæus, after the deaths of St Peter and St Paul; according to Jerome, 'Peter relating and Mark writing.' See Maclear's Introduction to St Mark's Gospel, pp. 14, 15, &c. As especially in keeping (by undesigned coincidence) with what we have seen above of St Mark's own fall and restoration and his slow advance to settled power as a 'fellow labourer unto the kingdom' and 'profitable to the ministry,' we should observe (if it has not been noticed in this connexion before) what significance the two parables and the one miracle have which are recorded only by St Mark. They are the

bring *him* with thee: for he is profitable to me for the
12, 13 ministry. And Tychicus have I sent to Ephesus. The
cloke that I left at Troas with Carpus, when thou comest,

healing of the deaf and dumb man at Decapolis, with the *five stages* in his gradual cure (vii. 31), the healing of the blind man at Bethsaida, with the *four* successive stages (viii. 22), and the parable of the seed growing secretly and slowly, '*first the blade, then the ear, after that the full corn in the ear*' (iv. 26). Among the many lessons learnt from Christ, through St Peter, *this* laid hold of St Mark; it fitted his need, gave him good hope and heart that he could indeed 'rise on stepping-stones of his dead self' to a new and higher life; and what he thus found so true in his own case he could not but put on record, to be a 'profitable ministry' through the Holy Spirit to very many 'feeble-hearts,' who like him have become 'great-hearts' and 'lion-hearts' for Christ.

> 'Companion of the Saints! 'twas thine
> To taste that drop of peace divine,
> When the great soldier of thy Lord
> Call'd thee to take his last farewell,
> Teaching the Church with joy to tell
> The story of your love restored.'
>
> *The Christian Year*, 'St Mark's Day.'

profitable...for the ministry] Lit. **serviceable for ministering**. Observe the emphatic position of the verb 'for he is,' almost implying 'whatever he once may have been': primarily this ministering would be to himself, as Erastus and Timothy are designated 'ministers unto him,' Acts xix. 22.

12. *Tychicus*] The accent of the word shews it to be formed from the noun for 'chance'; as with us a common surname is Chance.

Tychicus, a native of proconsular Asia (Acts xx. 4), went with St Paul on the third missionary journey to Jerusalem, perhaps as a delegate from his own Church; was with him towards the close of the first imprisonment at Rome (Col. iv. 7); after the release was again with him on the way to Nicopolis (Tit. iii. 12); and now just before his death is sent to Ephesus. From St Paul's reference to him in Col. iv. 7 as his 'beloved brother and faithful minister' we see the naturalness of his going on with the Apostle and St Luke to Rome.

have I sent] Rightly, if we take the tense (as is most probable) to be the epistolary aorist. Instances of this in St Paul are 2 Cor. viii. 18, 22, ix. 3, Gal. vi. 11, Eph. vi. 22, Col. iv. 8, Phil. ii. 25, 28, Philem. 11. St Paul then is sending Tychicus with this letter to take Timothy's place at Ephesus; he had therefore finally decided to send Artemas, not Tychicus, to Crete when he wanted to have Titus with him, Tit. iii. 12. See Introduction, pp. 43, 44.

13. *The cloke*] Vulg. 'penulam.' The oldest use of the word is traced back beyond the Latins nearly to the time of Alexander the Great, in a fragment of a Doric poet, Rhinthon (Julius Pollux *Onomast.* vii. 60). Hence the Latin must have adopted it from the Greek, not

bring *with thee*, and the books, *but* especially the parch-
ments. Alexander the coppersmith did me much evil: the 14

vice versa. The Roman *paenula* was a travelling cloak, long, and thick, and sleeveless, made generally of wool, sometimes of leather. Cf. Mart. xiv. 145 *paenula gausapina*, xiv. 13 *paenula scortea*. Dr Farrar suggests that 'perhaps St Paul had woven it himself of that *cilicium*, the black goats' hair of his native province, which it was his trade to make into tents. Doubtless the cloke was an old companion. It may have been wetted many a time with the water-torrents of Pamphylia, and whitened with the dust of the long roads, and stained with the brine of ship-wreck. Now, shivering in some gloomy cell under the Palace, or it may be on the rocky floor of the Tullianum, with the wintry nights coming on, he bethinks him of the old cloke and asks Timothy to bring it with him.' He quotes also the letter of Tindale, the translator of the English Bible, from his prison in the damp cells of the Vilvoorde: 'I entreat your Lordship, and that by the Lord Jesus, that, if I must remain here for the winter, you would beg the Commissary to be so kind as to send me, from the things of mine which he has, a warmer cap...I feel the cold painfully in my head....Also a warmer cloke, for the one I have is very thin....He has a woollen shirt of mine, if he will send it. But most of all...my Hebrew Bible, Grammar and Vocabulary, that I may spend my time in that pursuit. William Tindale.' There is some foundation for the interpretation 'a book-case' or 'portfolio,' which the Syriac versions support: none for the meaning 'a chasuble,' the passages of Tertullian and Chrysostom, quoted in favour, being really conclusive for the meaning 'travelling cloak.' There is no certain case of the use of the term in this technical sense before the time of Germanus, patriarch of Constantinople in the 8th century. See Dr Sinker's Article, *Dict. Christ. Antiq.*

at Troas] We do not know when this was; Farrar suggests that 'he left them behind, with Carpus, to take care of them, in his hasty arrest at Troas.' But see Introduction, p. 43.

and the books] The papyrus books; 'perhaps poems of Aratus, a Cilician like himself, or pamphlets of Philo or the Wisdom of Solomon.' See Bp Bull, Sermon x. p. 242.

the parchments] Writings on vellum; *membrana*, the Latin word, of which the Greek is a transcript, is properly a feminine adjective with which *cutis* is supplied, 'the skin covering the limbs (membra).' Hence *membrana Pergamena* was the thin sheep or calf skin sheet invented by Eumenes of Pergamus; of which *membrana* supplies the Greek word, and *Pergamena* has been corrupted into 'parchment.' Our 'vellum' is said to be from the French vélin, calf skin. Bp Bull, Sermon x. p. 245, takes these 'parchments' (after Estius) to be St Paul's *adversaria* or commonplace books 'wherein he had noted what he thought might be of use to him out of the many books he had read.' Farrar suggests 'a document to prove his rights as a Roman citizen' or 'any precious rolls of Isaiah or the Psalms or the lesser Prophets.'

14, 15. Dr Farrar's suggestion for the link of connexion is possible, that St Paul's second arrest took place at Troas, and that such an one

15 Lord reward him according to his works: of whom be thou
16 ware also; for he hath greatly withstood our words. At
my first answer no *man* stood with me, but all *men* forsook

as Alexander the coppersmith could easily have procured his arrest, and when suddenly seized by the lictors at Troas he could have had no time to take away his possessions. On 1 Tim. i. 20 we have seen that there is no particular reason to identify this Alexander with the one mentioned there. Rather the addition of 'coppersmith' as a distinguishing title suggests the opposite. 'The smith' would be perhaps more certainly correct; the word being quite as commonly used for 'blacksmith.'

14. *did me much evil*] The Greek word has a technical meaning, 'impeached,' 'indicted,' and so it is sometimes rendered here 'laid many grievous things to my charge'; but it is in the simpler sense, '*shewed me* much mischief,' that the verb is used nine times by St Paul. Cf. 1 Tim. i. 16, Tit. ii. 10, iii. 2.

the Lord reward him] The aorist optative has less weight of MS. authority than the future indic. **will render**, which tense of the same verb has occurred ver. 8.

15. *hath greatly withstood*] The aorist should be read for the perfect, **he withstood.** There is apparently an antithesis intended between Alexander's 'works' of mischief and the Apostle's 'words.' It does not seem to be false teaching that is referred to therefore, but (we may conjecture) evil *action*, by stirring up opposition to St Paul's preaching from Ephesus perhaps to Troas, scheming to bring him into trouble, finally rousing the Roman authority, which since the Roman fire no longer regarded Christianity as a *religio licita*, so as to bring about his arrest. There might be thus a special point in the warning given to Timothy, lest Alexander should be on his track as he set out for Rome.

16—18. 'Then came my first trial at Rome; Alexander was as nothing compared to "the lion"; I was alone, yet "not alone"; the Lord delivered me; and He will deliver me, even through and out of death—Safe home, safe home, in port.'

16. *At my first answer*] This should not be referred to any preliminary trial at Ephesus or elsewhere, but to the 'prima actio' of the main case at Rome before Nero or his representative; 'if the matter was one of difficulty the hearing might be adjourned as often as was necessary: such respite was called *ampliatio*.' See Dict. Ant. *judex*.

stood with me] The simpler compound is the better supported by MSS., **took my part,** was my 'advocatus.' Under the emperors this word signified a person who in any way assisted in the conduct of a cause, our 'solicitor,' and was sometimes equivalent to 'orator' or 'patronus,' who made the speech for the client, our 'counsel' or 'barrister.' See Dict. Ant. *advocatus*. The verb here is generally in N.T. without any case following, in the sense of 'to come,' and is especially used by St Luke, occurring twenty-nine times in the Gospel and the Acts, against nine times elsewhere in N.T. The meaning of 'support,' with the dative, is quite classical. Cf. Æsch. *Eum*. 309.

me: *I pray God* that it may not be laid to their charge.
Notwithstanding the Lord stood with me, and strengthened 17
me; that by me the preaching might be fully known, and
that all the Gentiles might hear: and I was delivered out
of the mouth of the lion. And the Lord shall deliver me 18
from every evil work, and will preserve *me* unto his heavenly
kingdom: to whom *be* glory for ever and ever. Amen.

all...forsook me] As in ver. 10.

laid to their charge] More exactly **to their account**, lit. 'reckoned to them.' So the line of Martial, which has been adopted as a motto for sundials and clocks, 'horae pereunt et imputantur,' 'are put to our account.'

17. *the Lord stood with me*] Again **took my part**.

strengthened me] 'Infused strength into me.' Cf. 1 Tim. i. 12; Phil. iv. 13.

the preaching might be fully known] Lit. '**the message** preached,' as in Tit. i. 3. The neuter form of the noun requires this. Cf. 1 Cor. i. 21 'through the foolishness of the preaching,' where R.V. has only altered 'preaching' into 'the preaching.' Accordingly A.V. may stand here. 'Fully known' is the same word as in ver. 5, 'fully performed'; indeed thus was made the proclamation of the name of Christ 'before the Gentiles and kings' (Acts ix. 15) in the world's capital, before its highest magistrates, on a supreme trial of life and death.

out of the mouth of the lion] R.V. rightly **lion**. The phrase comes from Ps. xxii. 21 and therefore has no *defined limit* of reference such as 'the lion of the amphitheatre,' or 'Nero,' or 'Satan,' though, it is true, the popular cry against the Christians later was 'Christianos ad leonem,' Tertull. *Apol.* c. 40; and the phrase used of the death of Tiberius earlier was 'the lion is dead,' Jos. *Ant.* xviii. 6. 10; and Satan going about to frighten the saint out of his 'good confession' is called 'a roaring lion,' 1 Pet. v. 8. 'The lion's mouth' is each and all of these; the evil within and the evil without, 'all adversities which may happen to the body, and all evil thoughts which may assault and hurt the soul' (Collect 2nd S. in Lent).

18. *And the Lord shall deliver*] The 'and' is omitted in the better MSS. The Apostle for the last time 'goes off abruptly' at the word 'deliver,' and breaks into a final song of 'faith, hope and love.' The preposition after the verb is changed to suit the noun it goes with.

every evil work] Substantially the same in reference as above, 'the mouth of the lion'; 'Fightings and fears within, without.' It has been thought that the Apostle had the Lord's Prayer in his mind, giving faith's application of the clause 'deliver us from the evil'; and if so it is interesting to observe his interpretation, not 'from the evil one,' *masculine*, but 'from the evil,' *neuter*. The phrase 'his heavenly kingdom' which does not occur elsewhere, and the ascription of the 'glory,' may also be a reminiscence of the doxology; which must in that case have been already in use, as an addition to the prayer.

19 Salute Prisca and Aquila, and the household of Onesi-
20 phorus. Erastus abode at Corinth: but Trophimus have I

And this is what we should expect from its occurrence in Matt. vi. 13 in so large a proportion of MSS. and versions; see Carr *in loco.*

preserve me *unto*] lit. **save me into**, 'bring me safe unto.' Cf. ii. 25. The same construction is found in classical writers. Cf. Soph. *Philoct.* 311.

19—22. Last words of salutation, entreaty, benediction.

He takes up the thought of *vv.* 9—12, weaving in with it the new thought of his last greetings.

19. *Salute Prisca and Aquila*] Prisca, or Priscilla, and her husband Aquila of Pontus had been driven from Rome with the Jews by the edict of the Emperor Claudius (Acts xviii. 2); they were staying at Corinth with St Paul 'because they were of the same trade' (ver. 3); they accompanied him 18 months later to Ephesus (ver. 18) where they 'further instructed Apollos' (ver. 24); were still there when St Paul wrote his first letter to Corinth (1 Cor. xvi. 19); afterwards were again at Rome 'cessante edicti saevitia,' perhaps on business; their house became a place of assembly for the Christians, and they endangered their lives for St Paul (Rom. xvi. 3). Now they seem settled at Ephesus. Dr Howson quotes Priscilla as the example of what the married woman may do for the general service of the Church, in conjunction with home duties, as Phœbe is the type of the unmarried servant of the Church or deaconess; and cites Archdeacon Evans as to her usefulness to Timothy at Ephesus. 'In his dealings with the female part of his flock which in that time and country required peculiar delicacy and discretion, the counsel of the experienced Priscilla would be invaluable. Where for instance could he obtain more prudent and faithful advice than hers in the selection of widows to be placed upon the eleemosynary list of the church and of deaconesses for the ministry?' Dict. Bib. *Priscilla.*

the household of Onesiphorus] See i. 16—18 and notes.

20. *Erastus abode*] 'Stayed at his post'; the verb suggests certainly that he had been commissioned by St Paul for some duty which he courageously fulfilled; if therefore it is unlikely that the Erastus who was chamberlain or treasurer (Oeconomus) of Corinth could be a fellow minister with Timothy to Macedonia (Acts xix. 22), it is equally unlikely that he could have been *set on duty* at Corinth, as is implied here. In which case we may identify the Erastus of Acts xix. 22 with the Erastus here, and regard the 'chamberlain' as a different person. See sketch of last journeys of St Paul and his companions in the Introduction, p. 43.

Trophimus] An Ephesian and Gentile, who was with St Paul at Troas on the third missionary journey (Acts xx. 4) and accompanied him to Jerusalem, causing a disturbance there because he was a Gentile (Acts xxi. 29). The only natural way of placing this event is at some

left at Miletum sick. Do thy diligence to come before 21
winter. Eubulus greeteth thee, and Pudens, and Linus,
and Claudia, and all the brethren. The Lord Jesus Christ 22
be with thy spirit. Grace *be* with you. Amen.

¶ The second *epistle* unto Timotheus, ordained the first bishop of the church of the Ephesians, was written from Rome, when Paul was brought before Nero the second time.

visit to Miletus after the close of the Acts, see Introduction, p. 43. *Miletum* must be a misprint of A.V. as there is no authority anywhere for a neuter form.

21. *before winter*] '*The motive* (rather *a motive*) of the letter is the desire for Timothy's presence, Haste! Come! iv. 9 "*Haste to come quickly*," iv. 21 "*Haste to come* before winter," iv. 13 "when thou comest," i. 4 "*Yearning* to see thee," iv. 5 "my *death is near* at hand."' Farrar, *Message of the Books*, p. 397.

Eubulus] Of him nothing is known.

Pudens...and Claudia] The identity of these two members of the Church at Rome with the Pudens and Claudia of Martial is discussed in Appendix, H.

Linus] According to general testimony bishop of Rome. Cf. Iren. iii. 3, § 3 'Peter and Paul, when they founded and built up the church of Rome, committed the office of its episcopate to Linus.' Cf. also Euseb. *H. E.* III. 2 'of the church of the Romans after the martyrdom of Paul and Peter the first to be appointed to the office of bishop was Linus, of whom Paul makes mention at the end of his letter to Timothy.' Eusebius also gives the length of his episcopate as twelve years A.D. 68—80.

22. The closing benediction is peculiar being twofold, first 'with thy spirit' and then 'with you,' i.e. 'thee and thine.'

The Lord Jesus Christ] The MS. authority is in favour of 'The Lord' alone. Observe how often this one brief name of his Saviour and Master has fallen from his pen in these closing paragraphs, taking the place of the full special title Christ Jesus (see 1 Tim. i. 1) used through the Pastorals; five times in the last fifteen verses, *vv.* 8, 14, 17, 18, 22, is the 'Master's' presence and aid claimed and acknowledged by one whose highest title of honour as an Apostle had been 'the Lord's servant,' 'the Master's bond-slave.' We are reminded of pious George Herbert, who at his induction to his sacred charge at Bemerton made his resolve and prayer that his humble and charitable life might so win upon others as to bring glory, he said, 'to my JESUS whom I have this day taken to be my Master and Governor; and I am so proud of this service that I will always observe and obey and do His will; and always call Him JESUS my Master, and I will always contemn my birth, or any title or dignity that can be conferred upon me, when I shall compare them with my title of being a priest and serving at the altar of JESUS my Master'; and who could in his last hours of suffering answer his wife's anxious enquiry with the reassuring certainties of that Master's presence; 'he had passed a conflict with his last enemy and had overcome him by the merits of his Master JESUS.' Walton, *Life of George Herbert.*

The subscription has no sufficient authority; see note on subscription to 1st Epistle, p. 152. But its statements are in this case more nearly correct. See, as to Timothy's charge at Ephesus, Introduction, p. 66. For St Paul's appearances before Nero see note above, ch. iv. 16; and Introduction, p. 44.

The oldest MS. authority gives for subscription only SECOND EPISTLE TO TIMOTHY.

THE EPISTLE OF PAUL TO

TITUS.

PAUL, a servant of God, and an apostle of Jesus Christ, 1
according to the faith of God's elect, and the acknow-

TITLE.

The oldest known form is the briefest, TO TITUS. So also the subscription to the Epistle should run.

CH. I. THE APOSTOLATE. ITS SCOPE AND METHOD.

1—4. APOSTOLIC GREETING.

1. *Paul, a servant of God*] **A bond-servant** (as R.V. margin) or **slave of God**; in St Paul's other uses of this word as his title it is 'slave of Jesus Christ.' The variation has been well pointed to as an evidence of genuineness; 'a forger would not have made a deviation so very noticeable.' The reason for the variation is probably the same as for the phrase 'God our Saviour' here and through these epistles; see note 1 Tim. i. 1. Here in the Salutation itself we have 'God's slave,' 'God's elect,' 'God who cannot lie,' 'God our Saviour.' Paul is the minister of the One Personal Eternal God; it is 'faith in *Him*,' full knowledge of *Him* that is wanted where, as Lewin remarks was the case in Crete, 'Judaism and then Gnosticism, its offspring, had corrupted the Word, and the Gospel had become so disfigured by strange phantasies that its features could scarcely be recognised.'

and an apostle of Jesus Christ] The 'and' is in Vulgate 'autem' not 'et' or 'sed,' the exact force being almost 'and so as a consequence.'

'Jesus Christ' is here the right order, as Tischendorf 8th ed. admits, though in 1 Tim. i. 1; 2 Tim. i. 1 'Christ Jesus' should be read. See notes there. It is natural enough that the new order of the words should sometimes be displaced by the older and more familiar.

according to the faith] Vulg. 'secundum'; and the R.V. keeps **according to** rightly enough in spite of all modern commentators who wish for the meaning 'with a view to' as in Phil. iii. 14, 'I press on *toward* the goal,' and think that 'according to' must imply that the faith and knowledge is the rule or *norma* of the Apostle's office. But surely the word is not so narrow. Its common use, e.g. in 'The Gospel *according to* St Matthew,' gives a wider sense, 'in the sphere

2 ledging of the truth which is after godliness; in hope of

of,' 'on the side of truth where St Matthew stands and sees and teaches.' And this sense is of course directly derived from the proper meaning of the preposition 'along,' 'throughout.' So here, the faith and full knowledge of the Cretan Christians is the sphere within which he is to execute this commission from Jesus Christ as an apostle *to them*. His apostleship might have other spheres for other times and other Churches. Calvin says of St Paul's commendation of his apostleship here 'indicat *ecclesiae* magis quam *unius Titi* habitam a Paulo rationem.'

God's elect] Among the N.T. words corresponding to the universal later use of the word 'Christians,' 1 Pet. iv. 16, are 'those who are being saved,' 'the called,' 'the chosen' or 'elect,' 'the consecrated' or 'saints,' 'the faithful' or 'believers.' The first chapter of St Peter's first epistle touches all; 'to the *elect* who are sojourners of the Dispersion' *v.* 1—'receiving now the *salvation* of your souls,' *v.* 9—'like the Holy One which *called* you, be ye yourselves also *holy*' *v.* 15—'who through him are believers in God' *v.* 21. Cf. 2 Pet. i. 10 'make your *calling* and *election* sure,' i. 1 'who have *obtained faith*,' ii. 21 'the *holy* commandment delivered,' cf. Rev. xvii. 14 '*called* and *chosen* and *faithful*.' The name 'faithful' evidently means 'those who have been made partakers of and received the faith'; and *all* the names describe a present state of privilege and sonship and grace, the same as that assigned to the baptized in the Catechism, 'he hath *called* me to this *state of salvation*'—'the Holy Ghost, who *sanctifieth* me and all *the elect people of God*,' and in the Baptismal Services, 'Grant that this child, now to be baptized therein, may receive the fulness of thy grace and ever remain in the number of thy *faithful* and *elect* children,'—'walk answerably to your *Christian calling*.'

the acknowledging of the truth] Rather, **the full knowledge**, in opposition to the 'knowledge falsely so called' of Gnostic teachers; see *v.* 16 and note on 1 Tim. ii. 5.

after godliness] The old English use of 'after,' **according to**; cf. Heb. v. 6, 'a priest for ever after the order of Melchisedec.' The same preposition being used and in the same sense as just above 'according to the faith.' 'The truth' is not speculative but moral truth, affecting the life—that they 'may learn the Creed, the Lord's Prayer and the Ten Commandments, and all other things which a Christian ought to know and believe *to his soul's health*.' Pr.-Bk. Baptismal Service. For 'godliness' see note on 1 Tim. ii. 2.

2. *in hope of eternal life*] The force of this phrase 'in hope' in N.T. is seen best from 1 Cor. ix. 10, 'to plow in hope—to thresh in hope of partaking,' or Rom. iv. 18, 'who in hope believed against hope.' It stands strongly by itself with a verb of some *other* strong feeling or action, equivalent to *summa spe*. The force of Acts xxvi. 5, 6 comes out far more clearly if we keep 'in hope' there too, and understand St Paul to say 'All the Jews know me; from a boy I have been a strict Pharisee; and today **I** am living *in hope* of the promise to

eternal life, which God, that cannot lie, promised before the 3
world began; but hath in due times manifested his word

our fathers as I stand here on my trial—the hope to which our twelve tribes look; and about this very hope I am called to account.' Comparing the structure as well as the subject matter of that verse, we may well connect 'in hope' here with 'Paul the Apostle' before, and with 'the message wherewith I was entrusted' after. St Paul is still magnifying his office, as the emphatic *ego* shews. 'My commission is threefold, and ranges from (1) the first spiritual life and gifts of those who have been chosen by God, through (2) the growing life of the true man of God thoroughly furnished, to (3) all the hope of glory; how your people in Crete may be justified, sanctified, glorified, is in the message wherewith I was entrusted; against this no Judaic formalism, no Gnostic spiritualism can hold: *I* have taught you (1) of the Holy Catholic Church; (2) of the Communion of saints and the Forgiveness of sins; (3) of the Resurrection of the body and the Life everlasting: and you are my true child after this common faith.'

God, that cannot lie] See verse 1; 'God's promise, and mine as His messenger, is very different from the Cretan teachers' word' (*v.* 12). The epithet is unique in N.T.

promised before the world began] R.V. literally, 'before times eternal'; A.V. from Vulg. 'ante tempora saecularia.' The parallel passages are 2 Tim. i. 9 'his own purpose and grace which was given us in Christ Jesus *before times eternal*,' Rom. xvi. 25 'the mystery which hath been kept in silence *through times eternal*,' 1 Cor. ii. 7 'which God foreordained *before the worlds*,' Vulg. 'ante saecula.' The last passage shews the meaning of the Vulgate, 'before the times of the world's history,' which is definite and accepted by R.V. there, though rejected here and in 2 Tim. i. 9 in favour of a bare and indeed meaningless phrase. It is better to import no extraneous definiteness into *aionios*, and also to recognise the proper idiomatic use of the preposition as to times and dates, of which 2 Cor. xii. 2 is an instance, 'fourteen years ago,' not 'before fourteen years.' Render **in eternal times gone by**. There is no difficulty as to the fact here or in 2 Tim. i. 9; with God to purpose, to promise, to give, are all one.

3. *but hath in due times*] See note on 1 Tim. vi. 15: and compare Gal. vi. 9. The phrase may well be thought the Hellenistic equivalent of the more classical form with preposition and substantive alone, John v. 4; Rom. v. 6 'in due season Christ died,' in accordance with the growing use of *idios*, which occurs fifteen times in the Pastoral Epistles.

manifested his word] Bp Wordsworth follows Jerome in understanding this directly of Christ 'manifested His Word'; but such an usage has no proper support in St Paul. 'To understand with modern interpreters "*the Gospel*," he says, is a feeble tautology.' But Col. i. 26 gives us 'to fulfil (i.e. to preach fully) *the word of God*, even the mystery which hath been hid...now *manifested*...which is Christ in you, *the hope of glory*, whom we proclaim.' Compare also Rom. xvi. 25 quoted above. So Vulg. and Theod. Mops. Lat. 'manifestavit verbum suum.'

through preaching, which is committed unto me according
4 to the commandment of God our Saviour; to Titus, *mine*
own son after the common faith: Grace, mercy, *and*
peace, from God the Father and the Lord Jesus Christ our
Saviour.

through preaching] Rather, as R.V. margin, **in the proclamation**, to define the mode of manifestation—a historic creed, 'declaring God's mind not by dark intimations merely or distant promises but in great facts.' For such a 'proclamation,' the earliest written 'Gospel,' see 1 Cor. xv. 1—8. Cf. also 1 Tim. iii. 16 and the note.

which is committed unto me] More exactly as R.V., **wherewith I was intrusted**, as in 1 Tim. i. 11.

according to the commandment] Better, as in 1 Tim. i. 1, where see note, **by authority from**. And therefore Titus is to 'reprove with all *authority*,' ch. ii. 15.

of God our Saviour] The same phrase with the same force as in 1 Tim. i. 1 (see note), and again in this Epistle ii. 10, iii. 4. The reference is to God the Father, compare the Prayer for Peace and deliverance in the Prayer-Book, 'that Thou art our Saviour and mighty Deliverer,' while in the next verse the same title is given to God the Son. But observe the *order* here, as in 1 Tim. ii. 3, **our Saviour God**; the closing emphasis on the word 'God' expresses still more forcibly than 'God our Saviour' the thought explained in verse 1.

4. *to Titus*, mine *own son*] With R.V. render **my true child**, as in 1 Tim. i. 2, where the force of the phrase is drawn out. On the connexion of Titus with St Paul see Introduction, p. 67 sqq.

after the common faith] The insertion of 'the' implies 'the faith common to the Church, to believers generally': as the words stand without an article, it is rather the faith common to St Paul and Titus, **in a common faith**, or 'in communion of faith;' see note on 1 Tim. i. 2.

Grace, mercy, and *peace*] The MSS. authority is against the insertion of 'mercy' here, though occurring in the salutation of both the letters to his other 'true child' Timothy. If the reason for the insertion in Timothy's case suggested on 1 Tim. i. 2 be true, its absence is appropriate here in the case of Titus. Though true son and trusted colleague, he had not been, like Timothy, the constant companion and the *alter ego* of one who, while 'fain to serve the best,' was ever 'conscious most of wrong within.'

from God the Father] The later form in these Epistles for 'our Father,' cf. 1 Tim. i. 2; 2 Tim. i. 2.

For the sense of the 'Father' see Bp Westcott, add. note on 1 Joh. i. 2. 'St John does not use the Pauline phrase "our Father" in his own writings; in the Epistles he uses uniformly the absolute title "the Father" without any addition; and in the Apocalypse "his (my) Father" but not "the Father." "The Father" suggests those thoughts which spring from the consideration of the moral connexion of God and man in virtue of the creation of man "in the image of God"; "my Father" points to those which spring from the revelation of the connexion of the Incarnate Son

For this cause left I thee in Crete, that thou shouldest 5
set in order the *things* that are wanting, and ordain elders
in every city, as I had appointed thee: if any be blameless, 6

with God and with man, "the Son of God," "the Christ." In his latest writings S. John regards the relation of the Divine Fatherhood in its eternal, that is, in its present realisation—"the Father" from its absolute side.'

and the Lord Jesus Christ] This fullest and most emphatic title, according to the true text, occurs only in 1 Tim. vi. 3 (note there and on 1 Tim. i. 1) and vi. 14. Read here, **Christ Jesus**.

our Saviour] See note on 1 Tim. i. 1 for this title given to Christ in the Pastoral Letters and in St Peter. It occurs not seldom in the Prayer Book, though much less often than 'Jesus Christ our Lord'; e.g. in the 2nd and 3rd Collects for Evening Prayer, Collect for 2nd S. in Advent, Septuagesima, Easter Even, Prayer of Consecration, &c.

5—9. Commission of Titus, generally, and in regard to Bishops or Presbyters.

5. The salutation, which has laid down emphatically the principle of apostolical authority, is followed at once by an uncompromising assertion of the authority delegated to Titus, and its chief exercise by him in ordination. Notice how this is strengthened (1) by the right reading, **I left thee behind,** (2) by the compound **that thou mightest further set in order,** (3) by the using of the pronoun *ego*, **as I myself gave thee charge.** '*I* began it all; let none thwart *you* in continuing my work as my delegate.'

As to the occasion of St Paul's visit to Crete here referred to, see Introduction, pp. 73—75.

the things *that are wanting*] Jerome paraphrases 'rudimenta nascentis Ecclesiae.' Cf. 'dispensatio erga credentes ita ut et ad consensum instituerentur per ordinationes ecclesiasticas.' Theod. Mops. Lat.

ordain elders in every city] On the word 'elders' see notes on 1 Tim. iii. 1; 'in every city,' i.e. from town to town, in no way implying any direction as to there being one or more than one. R.V. alters 'ordain' into 'appoint' as the simple meaning of the Greek, without the modern special sense now attaching to ordain. The meaning of 'ordain' in English of A.V. date is seen in 1 K. xii. 32; Ps. vii. 13; Dan. ii. 24, where the O. T. revisers give respectively 'ordain,' 'prepare,' 'appoint.' Cf. Hakluyt, *Voyages*, II. 455, 'He *ordeined* a boat made of one tree' (*Bible Word-Book*, p. 440).

as I had appointed thee] Is misleading, being open to the interpretation 'do you appoint *others* as I have appointed you,' whereas the sense intended was of course, as in the similar use of the same word Acts vii. 44, 'as he had appointed speaking unto Moses,' i.e. 'appointed for thee to do.' Cf. also Acts xxiv. 23, A.V. 'he commanded a centurion,' R.V. 'he gave order to the centurion.' In N. T. usage there is little if anything of the sense wished for by Bp Ellicott (after the Vulg. 'disposui'), 'not only bid but taught him how to do it.'

the husband of one wife, having faithful children not
7 accused of riot or unruly. For a bishop must be blameless,
as the steward of God; not self-willed, not soon angry, not

The verbs 'further set in order,' and 'gave thee charge,' are in the middle voice, because the 'ordering' and 'arranging' is not literal and primary, as of chairs and tables, but secondary and transferred to mental thought, to moral action. Winer distinguishes these meanings as 'physical' and 'metaphysical,' *Gr.* Pt. III. § 38, 2, b. Cf. note on 1 Tim. i. 7.

6. *if any be blameless, the husband of one wife*] 'Blameless'; the word has occurred 1 Tim. iii. 10, to the same effect as 'without reproach' in 1 Tim. iii. 2, that word describing a character 'such as cannot be laid hold of,' this denoting a life 'such as cannot be called in question,' Vulg. 'sine crimine.' For the importance of this primary qualification see note on 1 Tim. v. 7. It fits exactly with the next, 'husband of one wife.' This also was what the ordinands were to be *before* they were appointed presbyters; hence 'husband of one wife' refers to the prevalent polygamy, and has nothing to do with prohibition of a second marriage *after* ordination. We see in this here as elsewhere in the Pastoral Epistles (see note on 1 Tim. iii. 2) 'a solemn demand for purity and blamelessness in the marriage relation amid widespread concubinage and licence.' Dr Reynolds, *Expositor*, Vol. VIII. p. 74. Technically, 'not a bigamist.'

having faithful children] 'Faithful' is ambiguous, implying either 'trustworthy' or 'believing'; no doubt the latter is intended; the presbyter's household must not be one where the influence and teaching have been such that the children have still remained heathen; nor yet one where 'faith' and 'duty' have been severed; for they must also be neither **chargeable with riotous living** nor **unruly**, but living 'in temperance, soberness and chastity,' and submitting themselves 'to all that are put in authority.' 'Riotous living' is perhaps better than R.V. 'riot' (which is also substituted for the A.V. rendering of the same word 'excess' in Eph. v. 18), as recalling the typical instance of the character in the '*Prodigal* Son,' Luke xv. 13. 'The *prodigal* is one who cannot save or spare, to use Spenser's word, 'scatterling.' The word forms part of Aristotle's ethical terminology, the truly liberal man being one who keeps the golden mean between the two extremes, *prodigality* on one side and *stinginess* on the other.' Trench, *N.T. Syn.* § 16.

7. *For a bishop must be blameless*] Or, as R.V., **the bishop.** Both are correct and idiomatic; note on 1 Tim. iii. 2. 'Bishop' here is admitted to refer to the 'presbyter' of verse 5, 'bishop' describing the nature of the duties assigned, viz. superintendence and pastoral oversight, while 'presbyter' refers rather to station and character; the one is *official* the other *personal.* See note on 1 Tim. iii. 1, Introduction, pp. 15—19, and Appendix, C. Bp Wordsworth well paraphrases here, 'For he who has the oversight of others ought to be blameless.'

as the steward of God] 'The director of the house of God;

given to wine, no striker, not given to filthy lucre; but a 8
lover of hospitality, a lover of good *men*, sober, just, holy,

Timothy had been told how he was to conduct himself in "the house of God," and now Titus is told that every bishop or elder has similar responsibilities.' Dr Reynolds. Cf. 1 Cor. iv. 1, 2; 1 Pet. iv. 10. An approved settled Christian life was essential, because recent converts from heathenism might endanger the Christian Church by bringing into it the relics of their heathen life. Even in the 4th century Chrysostom complains that men came to the Holy Communion hustling and kicking one another.

not self-willed, not soon angry] 'Self-willed,' 'headstrong,' 'unfeeling,' occurs only here and 2 Pet. ii. 10 in N.T. Theophrastus (*Char.* XV.) describes the character in a way which shews the idea conveyed by the word to be worse than our English 'self-willed' implies. He describes it as 'A certain roughness that shews itself in a man's whole conversation and behaviour. Ask one of this savage temper if he has seen such a person lately, he answers you, *Prithee, friend, don't be impertinent.* If you desire to know the price of anything he has to sell, he grows surly, and asks *what fault you find with it?* He is inexorable upon the slightest offence; do but chance to tread upon his foot, or push him with your elbow, and he'll never forget you as long as he lives. If a friend desires to borrow some money of him he at first gives him a flat denial, but upon second thoughts brings it to him, and throwing it down in a churlish manner, *Well, here 'tis,* says he, *but I never expect to see it again.* If he stumbles against a stone in the street, he looks back and falls a cursing it.' Burgell's Trans. 'Soon angry,' 'irascible,' 'choleric,' only here in N.T., not as Theod. Mops. 'reminiscentem iram et per longi temporis spatia tenentem,' i.e. 'bearing malice.' The form of the word denotes rather 'liable to,' 'with frequent fits of.' So the word occurs in the *Teaching of the Twelve Apostles*, iii. 1, 'Be not soon angry, for anger leadeth to murder.' The word for 'jesting,' Eph. v. 4, is from an adjective of similar form, 'quick at banter.'

not given to wine, no striker] As in 1 Tim. iii. 3, **not quarrelsome over wine, no striker**; see notes there.

not given to filthy lucre] As of the deacons in 1 Tim. iii. 8, where see note; elsewhere in N.T. only the adverb, 1 Pet. v. 2. Vulg. 'non turpis lucri cupidum.' Bp Ellicott (following Huther) refers it especially to 'dishonesty with the alms of the Church, or any abuse of a spiritual office for purposes of gain.' The similarly formed word 'filthy communication,' Col. iii. 8, is in R.V. 'shameful speaking'; and it would be clearer to render here **not given to unfair gains**. '*Fair* gains' are the parson's right for fair pains, 1 Tim. v. 18; 2 Tim. ii. 6. The phrase 'filthy lucre' has come to bear a meaning as if, according to a right and high standard, money *per se*, rents, tithes, and fees, were all 'of the earth' worldly, and unfit to be pressed for by any clergyman who professed to set an example.

8. *a lover of hospitality*] As in 1 Tim. iii. 2, where its appropriateness to the times is explained.

9 temperate; holding fast the faithful word as *he* hath been
taught, that he may be able by sound doctrine both to
10 exhort and to convince the gainsayers. For there are

a lover of good men] An adjective occurring only in N.T. suggested by the similar compound preceding, as with the similar play of words 2 Tim. iii. 4, 'lovers of pleasure rather than lovers of God.' The contrast there of 'thing' and 'person' as the object of affection increases the probability of the neuter 'good' being intended here rather than the masculine 'good men;' but 'lover' should be kept as having suggested the phrase, **a lover of hospitality, a lover of good.**

sober, just, holy, temperate] Rather, **pure, righteous, holy, temperate**. On the distinction between 'pure' and 'temperate' see 1 Tim. iii. 2; on that between 'righteous' and 'holy' see 1 Tim. ii. 9. The generally drawn distinction of 'doing one's duty to man' ('righteous'), and 'to God' ('holy'), would mislead there, and so does R.V. following A.V. here in rendering 'just,' though substituting 'righteous' in such striking passages as Matt. i. 19, 'Joseph, being a righteous man;' 1 John i. 9, 'he is faithful and righteous to forgive us our sins.' See Dr Westcott's note on this last verse, 'The essence of righteousness lies in the recognition and fulfilment of what is due from one to another. Truth passing into action is righteousness.' On man's part therefore 'righteousness' is duty done to God *and* to man *for* God's sake. So in effect Trench, *N.T. Syn.* § 88, 'The second great commandment is not coordinated with the first greatest, but subordinated to and in fact included in it.'

9. *holding fast the faithful word*] Or, **the faithful saying**, keeping the connexion with the technical phrase of these Epistles, 1 Tim. i. 15. 'Though no one "faithful saying" is quoted, yet it may be used comprehensively of them all, and is here guaranteed by "the teaching" of the Apostle himself.' Dr Reynolds.

as he *hath been taught*] The grammar requires, as R.V., **which is according to the teaching**. *The Teaching of the Twelve Apostles* is the title of a newly discovered manuscript of very early days placed by Bp Lightfoot 'somewhere between A.D. 80—110.' But its title is not intended to suggest its authorship. We may accept it as the private venture of someone who desires to set forth his views on moral conduct and Church order, believing them to represent the mind of the Apostles. See Introduction, pp. 22, 23. Similarly then 'the teaching' here meant is the oral Gospel and Instruction of St Paul.

able by sound doctrine both to exhort] Accurately with R.V. (the position of the verb in the clause being noted) **able both to exhort in the sound doctrine**. 'Exhort' has nothing to do with 'gainsayers' but refers to the building up by exhortation and comfort of believers. Compare 1 Tim. v. 1, where see note. The 'Pastoral' phrase 'the sound doctrine' is examined 1 Tim. v. 10, where 'the doctrine' is seen to be the equivalent English word, as it is passing into technical use. *Didachê* on the other hand remains untechnical, 'teaching.'

and to convince the gainsayers] R.V. **convict**. See note 1 Tim. v. 20.

many unruly and vain talkers and deceivers, specially they
of the circumcision: whose mouths must be stopped, who 11
subvert whole houses, teaching *things* which *they* ought not,
for filthy lucre's sake. One of themselves, *even* a prophet 12

10—16. THE UNRULY RIVAL TEACHERS ARE TO BE REPRESSED.

10. *many unruly*] Add **men**, leaving the pair of attributes to go together, as in the Pauline usage, **empty talkers and deceivers of the mind**. Both compounds occur only here in N.T.; but the substantive, meaning *vaniloquentia*, has occurred 1 Tim. i. 6, where the meaning is defined in what follows, 'though they understand neither what they say, nor whereof they confidently affirm;' and the verb, meaning *seducit*, is used Gal. vi. 3 and defined by the context 'if a man thinketh himself to be something when he is nothing.' Peile translates 'self-deceivers,' i.e. visionary enthusiasts, comparing Is. xliv. 20 and James i. 26.

specially they of the circumcision] Judaizing Christians. Jews from Crete are named among the visitors to Jerusalem Acts ii. 11, and the Christianising of the island cannot have been quite recent, even from *v.* 6, 'having faithful children.'

11. *whose mouths must be stopped*] The verb is so used in classical Greek often; the 'stopping' must have reference to the 'convict' of verses 9 and 13. Compare the use of 'to muzzle' in the Gospels, e.g. Mk. iv. 39, 'Peace, *be still*,' and 1 Pet. ii. 15, where the 'ignorance of foolish men' is 'to be muzzled' by 'well-doing.'

who subvert whole houses] As R.V. **men who**, the compound relative implying the class to which they belong, and so the conduct for which they should be silenced; hence almost, 'seeing that they.' Cf. 1 Tim. i. 4, 'the which.' Render **subvert whole households**. Why should the Revisers give up the Latin word 'subvert,' which the A.V. has rendered familiar, and which gives the *metaphorical* overthrow more clearly?

teaching things *which* they *ought not*] The negative used implies *the general class* of wrong teachings rather than any definite and specific facts or views. The effect is a *less* positive statement than if the other negative had been used; and the rendering 'things which they ought not to teach and which they know they ought not' is impossible. It should be 'things of a class which *I* think improper to be taught.'

for filthy lucre's sake] Rather, **for the sake of unfair gains**, see verse 7. Bp Ellicott quotes a striking passage from Polybius, *Hist.* VI. 46. 3, with respect to the Cretan character; 'and generally their character as to unfair gains and covetousness is of this kind—they are the only nation in the world among whom no sort of gain is thought unfair.'

12. *One of themselves*] Rather, **one of them**, there being nothing to indicate emphasis till the next two words come, **a prophet of their own**; the force is, 'there is a Cretan saying—and by a prophet of their own:' for the adjective see *v.* 3.

Epimenides was a poet priest and prophet of Gnossus in Crete,

of their own, said, The Cretians *are* alway liars, evil beasts,
13 slow bellies. This witness is true. Wherefore rebuke them

who was invited to Athens about 596 B.C. to purify the city after the pollution of Cylon, and is said to have died at Lacedaemon soon after, aged 150 years. This hexameter verse is from his 'Oracles,' and the first part was quoted by Callimachus in his 'Hymn to Zeus'—

'"Cretans are always liars"; *thy grave* has been claimed by the Cretans,
Thine, O King immortal, who livest and reignest for ever.'

Peile quotes Calvin's Latin hexameter rendering

'Mendax, venter iners, semper mala bestia Cres est,'

and it would run in English

'Cretans are always liars, are wild beasts, do-nothing gluttons.'

Their general character was well known from the proverb of 'The three worst Ks, Kretans, Kappadocians, Kilicians,' and from the word which meant 'to play the Cretan' coming to mean 'to play the cheat and liar,' as 'to play the Corinthian' was 'to play the prodigal and libertine.'

For their ferocity and greed and falseness cf. Polyb. VI. 46, 47, 'The Cretans, on account of their innate avarice live in a perpetual state of private quarrel and public feud and civil strife . . . . and you will hardly find anywhere characters more tricky and deceitful than those of the Cretans.'

In favour of the Cretans may be said that they sacrificed to their stern mentor Epimenides as a god, and that Titus, who was to adopt and enforce this severe censure of St Paul, has been honoured to this day as the apostle of Crete. See Pashley's *Travels in Crete*, vol. I. p. 175. Cf. Appendix, I.

13. *This witness is true*] Not to be taken, as Dr Farrar says, *au pied de la lettre*, as though the Cretans were indiscriminately wicked. Nor to be taken as authority for 'scolding' in the modern sermon. The *spirit* of St Paul and of Titus must be taken with the *letter:* and the counsel of Bp Wilberforce remembered, 'speak straight to them, as you would beg your life, or counsel your son, or call your dearest friend from a burning house, in plain, strong, earnest words' (*Ordination Charge*, 1846).

rebuke them sharply] As above, **convict** or **confute**, *v.* 9. R.V. loses much by 'reprove,' which is even weaker than 'rebuke' and quite unequal to the burden of 'confute and condemn.' The substantive corresponding to 'sharply' occurs Rom. xi. 22, in the metaphor of the *cutting out* of the evil branches from the olive tree, 'the goodness and *severity* of God;' and the adverb itself in 2 Cor. xiii. 10 in reference to the severe measures to be taken by St Paul at Corinth, 'that I may not when present deal sharply.' Dr Reynolds puts the drift well: 'a sharp knife, firm handling, free incisions, are needed for some poisonous and putrefying sores; and as in former days Titus had to shew the Corinthians how to purge out the old leaven, to deliver

sharply, that they may be sound in the faith; not giving 14
heed to Jewish fables, and commandments of men, that
turn from the truth. Unto the pure all *things are* pure: 15
but unto them that are defiled and unbelieving *is* nothing
pure; but even their mind and conscience is defiled. They 16

wicked persons to Satan, to rebuke pretentious Sciolism, so once more out of sheer kindness he was commanded not to spare them.'

that they may be sound in the faith] Again 'healthy,' 'healthful,' keeping up, with this 'Pastoral' word, the metaphor of health in the body corporate of the Cretan Church. Compare Prov. xv. 4, 'A wholesome tongue—Heb. the healing of the tongue—is a tree of life' with verse 10, and 1 Tim. vi. 3, 'if any man teacheth a different doctrine and consenteth not to sound—wholesome—words.'

14. *not giving heed to Jewish fables*] See note on 1 Tim. i. 4 and Introduction, pp. 45 sqq. 'The old Judaism got itself entangled in a new Platonism. Those *endless genealogies* which had always charmed the Israelite, as he traced his own pedigree from Seth and Abraham and David, were now beginning to soar into higher heights of speculation, till at length they dealt with angelic relationships and lost themselves in interminable mazes of celestial emanations.' Dr Vaughan, *The Wholesome Words of Jesus Christ*, p. 7.

commandments of men] See note on 1 Tim. iv. 3 and Introduction, pp. 46, 48, 50; 'erga escarum insumptionem scrupuloso agere videbantur,' Theod. Mops. The addition of the participial clause *without the article* leaves more emphasis on 'men' as opposed to God the true lawgiver; the participle is only formally in agreement with *men*; the real stress is on the thought 'desertion of the truth,' '*human* commandments with the truth abandoned.' Compare i. 6, where the main attribute to 'children' is 'believing' and 'not in accusation &c.' is secondary. Winer, Pt. III. § 20, 4. The translation of A.V., by putting the comma after 'men' and rendering '*that* turn away' as the more general relative, seems nearer to this force of the Greek than the R.V. 'men who turn.'

15. *Unto the pure all* things are *pure*] To the same effect as 1 Tim. iv. 3, 4, 5. Cf. Matt. xv. 2, 11 for the 'wholesome words of Jesus Christ' on the same point. The *true* principle of lawful Christian abstinence is given (with the same phrase) Rom. xiv. 20. 'The "all things" are those which in themselves have no *moral character*, food, marriage, business, pleasure, daily life, Sabbatic observance, and social freedom; that vast region of conduct to which Jewish pedantry and oriental asceticism had applied the vexatious rules Touch not, taste not, handle not.' Reynolds.

defiled and unbelieving] As 'the pure' here corresponds to 'them that believe and have full knowledge of the truth' in 1 Tim. iv. 3, so impurity of life and unsound doctrine go together.

but even their mind and conscience] Rather, **nay, there is defilement of both their mind and their conscience.** Nothing is pure, and indeed those very organs to which we look for instilling purity are defiled. Cf. Matt. vi. 22, 23, 'The lamp of the body is the eye; if thine eye be evil,

profess that *they* know God; but in works they deny *him*, being abominable, and disobedient, and unto every good work reprobate.

2 But speak thou *the things* which become sound doctrine:

thy whole body shall be full of darkness.' The 'mind' in N.T. is more than '*reason*' and '*intellect*,' including also '*the will*' and '*the feelings*,' 1 Tim. vi. 5; Rom. i. 28 'God gave them up to a reprobate mind.' The 'conscience,' *suneidêsis*, is the '*moral sense*,' or 'self-consciousness,' pronouncing intuitively by a spiritual instinct on our acts, 1 Tim. iii. 9; Rom. ii. 15. 'The two united represent the stream of life in its flowing in and flowing out together.' Cf. Appendix, A, iii. 1, and D.

is defiled] R.V. 'are defiled,' our modern idiom differing from the Greek, which has the singular verb agreeing with the nearer only of the two nouns. In old English also two substantives when closely allied in meaning not uncommonly are followed by the singular verb, e.g. 'Destruction and unhappiness is in their ways.'

16. *They profess that* they *know God*] Vulg. 'confitentur'; 'profess' is retained by R.V., though its modern sense is more generally 'pretend': the Greek is 'openly acknowledge,' and the word is used of those Books of the Bible which are 'homologoumena,' 'fully acknowledged.' This sense of 'profess' remains in our 'Professor' or Public Teacher. Cf. Matt. vii. 23 'then will I profess unto them.'

being abominable, and disobedient] Vulg. 'cum sint abominati.' Compare Rev. xxi. 8 'the fearful and unbelieving and abominable,' 27 'anything unclean or he that maketh an abomination and a lie.'

unto every good work reprobate] The first of six occurrences of the phrase 'good' or 'fair' 'work' in this Epistle, cf. ii. 7, 14, iii. 1, 8, 14. So in 1 Tim. it occurs six times and twice in 2 Tim. For the force of this particular word for 'good' see note on 1 Tim. i. 18. The application of sound doctrine to daily life is the natural and necessary object of the Apostle at this stage of progress in the Christian Church. See Introduction, pp. 32—34. 'Reprobate' comes from the Vulg. 'reprobi'; the Greek is lit. 'unable to stand the test,' 'tried and found wanting.' It occurs again 2 Tim. iii. 8. Its best known use is in 1 Cor. ix. 27 'lest after I have preached to others I myself should be rejected.' **Worthless** here gives the force.

CH. II. THE APOSTOLATE; ITS EFFICIENCY AND ITS SPHERE.

1—3. WHAT STANDARD OF HOLY LIVING IS TO BE MAINTAINED; FIRST, FOR ELDER MEN AND WOMEN.

After these instructions to Titus for the appointment of presbyters and the repression of false teachers in chap. i., St Paul proceeds to lay down for him the standard of Christian life (*v.* 1), in old men (*v.* 2), old women (*v.* 3), young women (*vv.* 4, 5), young men, including Titus himself (*vv.* 6—8), slaves (*vv.* 9, 10); based on the gifts of God's grace in Christ and the hope of God's glory (*vv.* 11—14); this standard to be authoritatively maintained (*v.* 15).

that the aged men be sober, grave, temperate, sound in 2
faith, in charity, in patience. The aged women likewise, 3
that they be in behaviour as becometh holiness, not false

1. *sound doctrine*] See on i. 9, 1 Tim. i. 10.

2. *the aged men*] Better, **aged men**; here of the ordinary life of the older men, as the comparative is used in 1 Tim. v. 1 'rebuke not an elder'; not 'elders' or 'presbyters.' St Paul is himself four or five years older than when he wrote to Philemon 'being such an one as Paul the aged' (*v.* 9).

sober, grave, temperate] Render **sober, grave, pure**, in preference to R.V. 'temperate, grave, sober-minded,' which are too nearly allied in modern significance; R.V. has the restricted modern sense of 'temperate' here (of use in drink), when in i. 8 it has been used in the large and proper sense. Bp Wordsworth for 'grave' suggests 'reverend,' 'worshipful.' 'Sober' in regard to 'strong drink,' see note on the word 1 Tim. iii. 2; 'grave' in all 'propriety of demeanour,' see note on the corresponding substantive 1 Tim. iii. 4; 'pure' in respect of 'unclean thought and desire,' see notes on the word 1 Tim. iii. 2; below ver. 4.

sound in faith, in charity, in patience] The articles seem intentionally prominent, **sound in their faith, their love, their patience**; 'these are recognised essentials of Christian character, but be careful that you have the real wholesome graces, without anything spurious or diseased.' The article is used throughout the emphatic enumeration of these and other Christian virtues, 2 Pet. i. 5—7, where R.V. translates with italics 'in *your* temperance patience,' &c. There 'faith' is the first and 'love' the last. The 'patience' is especially seen in tribulation, cf. Rom. xii. 12.

3. *The aged women likewise*] **That aged women**, not of any order of women corresponding to that of 'elders'; though this exact word is used of such an order in the 11th Laodicean Canon, 'those that are called elder women, to wit those that preside in the church, must not be ordained'; cf. Neander, *Ch. Hist.* III. 305 sqq.; and in Apocryphal Acts and Martyrdom of Matthew, Tisch. *Act. apocr. apost.*, p. 187. It undoubtedly arose later, based upon this passage, see note on 1 Tim. v. 3—16.

be *in behaviour*] Vulg. here 'in habitu sancto,' and in 1 Tim. ii. 9 'in habitu ornato,' but the Greek word here more *properly* corresponds to the classical sense of habitus '*settled* ways and bearing,' (comp. 'behaviour'), while the Greek word there fits its Low Latin sense 'raiment' ('*arrayment*'), (comp. 'riding *habit*'). The translation by the earlier English versions, Wiclif 'habite,' Tindale, Cranmer 'raiment,' makes it likely that the sense of the Vulgate was the *later* sense of 'habitus' and therefore here inadequate. R.V. rightly **demeanour** as covering more than the modern sense of 'behaviour,'—Jerome's 'incessus, motus, vultus, sermo, silentium.'

as becometh holiness] One word, an adjective, in the Greek, for which R.V. gives **reverent**, Alford 'reverend,' with a difference of meaning

accusers, not given to much wine, teachers of good things;
4 that they may teach the young *women* to be sober, to love

intended, though 'reverent' had once the sense of 'reverend,' e.g. *Homilies*, p. 345, 'partakers of his reverent Sacraments.' But 'reverent' now implies 'with a certain dignity of sacred decorum,' to use Jerome's words. 'Reverend' occurs in English Bible only in Ps. cxi. 9, 'holy and reverend is his name,' and 2 Macc. xv. 12, 'a virtuous and a good man, reverend in conversation.'

The Greek means literally 'as becometh a sacred office,' and, as the simple word and its derivatives are used especially of the priesthood, well expresses a reverential spirit of consecration, mindful of the Christian believer's priesthood and its requirements. This passage and 1 Tim. ii. 9 'that women adorn themselves...which *becometh* women *professing godliness*—through good works,' taken with 1 Pet. ii. 9, 'a royal *priesthood*, a holy nation, a people for God's own possession,' and Tit. ii. 14, 'a people for his own possession, zealous of good works,' seem to supplement and explain one another. The phrase finds full recent appropriation in Miss F. R. Havergal's lines:

'Keep my life, that it may be
Consecrated, Lord, to Thee.
Keep my feet, that they may be
Swift and 'beautiful' for Thee.
Keep my lips, that they may be
Filled with messages from Thee.
Keep myself, that I may be
Ever, *only*, ALL, for Thee.'

Who that has known the happiness of help for Christian living from the example and service of such an elder saintly woman among his own kinsfolk or acquaintance, but will bless St Paul as Founder and Patron, through the Holy Spirit his Inspirer, of the best women's rights, although he 'suffered not a woman to speak in the church'?

not false accusers] As 1 Tim. iii. 11, A.V. and R.V., **not slanderers**; see note.

not given to much wine] Lit. with R.V. **nor enslaved to much wine**, cf. Rom. vi. 16—18, where however the Revisers leave the weaker 'servants'; lit. 'ye were enslaved to Righteousness.' Cf. 2 Pet. ii. 19, 'slaves of corruption, for of whom a man is overcome to the same is he also enslaved.' The use of the word rendered 'temperate' in 1 Tim. iii. 11 in conjunction with 'not slanderers,' and corresponding to our phrase here, defines its meaning in these Epistles as strictly literal—'*sober*, as to strong drinks;' see ver. 2.

This character of women generally for intemperance is satirised in *Anthology*, XI. 297, 1:

'Mother, how is it thou lovest the wine
More than thou lovest this son of thine?'

their husbands, to love their children, *to be* discreet, chaste, 5
keepers at home, good, obedient to their own husbands,

And XI. 298, 1—5:

'The thirsty boy begs mother for a draught;
But, like her sex, quite overcome with wine,
Still drinking deep and turning just her head,
"I can't—'tis such a drop, dear laddie mine,
This flagon holds but thirty pints," she said.'

teachers of good things] The only other N.T. compound with this word for 'good,' 'fair,' 'beautiful' is in 2 Thess. iii. 13, 'be not weary in *well-doing*.' The adjective, used with 'works,' is specially characteristic of this Epistle; below *vv.* 7, 14, iii. 8, 14. The emphatic repetition in iii. 8 further shews that we are right in interpreting the compound here **'teachers of good works.'** Compare the passages quoted above on 'reverent.' The contrast in these last four phrases of high calling and low falling is precisely parallel to that in 1 Tim. iii. 2, and strictly in accord with the early Church history of grand saintliness and gross sin. It strengthens the argument for the literal meaning there of 'husband of one wife.'

4, 5. THE STANDARD OF HOLY LIVING FOR YOUNG WOMEN.

4. *that they may teach the young* women *to be sober*] A.V. 'teach to be sober' (i.e. pure) gives the full meaning of the verb, but not its grammatical force **train in purity to be lovers of their husbands, lovers of their children.** The verb has in Philo and other authors come to have hardly more than the force 'school,' 'train,' but surely St Paul is here restoring and raising it. The verb is only here, and the subst. only in 2 Tim. i. 7, where see note.

5. to be *discreet, chaste*] The 'expulsive power of the new affection' for husband and for child would lead them on best to be wholly **pure** (note above on ver. 2 and on 1 Tim. iii. 2) in mind and spirit, and **chaste** in look, and word, and act.

keepers at home] Rather, we should read with R.V. **workers at home**, following MS. authority though with no support from the older versions. Vulg. 'domus curam habentes.' The word, which appears not to be found elsewhere, is formed similarly to the word for 'malefactor,' which in N.T. occurs only 2 Tim. ii. 9, and Luke xxiii. 32, 33, 39: and to that used of the younger widows, 1 Tim. v. 13, 'prying round into other people's work.' The verb occurs with the same variation of reading, Clem. Rom. *ad Cor.* I. 1, the Alexandrine MS. reading 'workers' as here; 'And ye taught them to be grave workers at home, keeping to the due limits of subjection, wholly pure minded;' an evident reminiscence of this passage.

good, obedient to their own husbands] Vulg. excellently, 'benignas,' **kindly**, 'amiable,' 'good,' as we say 'a good man is good to his beast'; so it is used evidently of masters towards slaves in union with 'gentle,' i.e. 'considerate,' 1 Pet. ii. 18, 'in subjection to your masters,

6 that the word of God be not blasphemed. Young *men*
7 likewise exhort to be sober minded. In all *things* shewing
thyself a pattern of good works: in doctrine *shewing* un-

not only to the kindly and considerate, but also to the churlish.' Render the next clause, which is identical in 1 Pet. iii. 1 and 5, **in subjection to their own husbands.** This participial phrase is almost proverbial apparently at this time. The word and thought 'subjection' occurs prominently in Titus and St Peter; Tit. ii. 5, 9, iii. 1; 1 Pet. ii. 13, 18, iii. 1, 5, v. 5.

that the word of God be not blasphemed] Better, **be not evil spoken of**; the word of God is here 'the Gospel' in the sense of 'the Christian religion;' in 1 Tim. vi. 1 called 'the name of God,' and 'the doctrine.' For 'the word of God' cf. Rev. i. 2, 9, vi. 9. St Paul's earlier usage connects itself more with *the preaching* of the Gospel, 1 Cor. xiv. 36; 2 Cor. ii. 17, iv. 2; Col. i. 25. The clause belongs to the whole instruction. 'If Christians profess to be influenced by a supernaturally strong and sacred motive, and then fail to do what lower and ordinary motives often succeed in effecting, the world charges the failure on the lofty motive itself, and Christ bears once again the sins of His people.' Dr Reynolds.

6—8. THE STANDARD OF HOLY LIVING FOR YOUNG MEN.

6. The younger women in Crete were to be placed under the guidance of elder women, though in Ephesus Timothy was himself to instruct them. The young men are to have the special care of Titus.

Young men *likewise exhort to be sober minded*] Rather, **the younger men...pure minded.** The verb occurs in Mk. v. 15, Lk. viii. 35, of the 'possessed of devils' being restored to sound reason; and in Rom. xii. 3, 2 Cor. v. 13, of sober, reasonable judgment; but here, from the context, and from the use of the cognate verb ver. 4 and its context, and of the corresponding adjectives, 1 Tim. iii. 2; Tit. i. 8, ii. 2, 5, it seems limited to 'purity of mind and spirit.' In the somewhat similar exhortation to Timothy, 1 Tim. v. 22, the word is different, 'keep thyself chaste,' as above in ver. 5 'chaste' is joined with 'pure'. 'Chaste' is suitable there because sins, actual sins, are the contrast rather than an impure spirit and state of mind.

7. *shewing thyself*] The middle participle and the reflex pron. for emphasis; Winer, III. 38, 6.

a pattern of good works] The simple word—our 'type'—here with the thing, as in 1 Tim. iv. 12 with the person. So the compound with the thing, 2 Tim. i. 13, with the person, 1 Tim. i. 16. The latter is the first rough model of the sculptor; the former, the model when worked over afterwards with care. So in the sister art, the compound (1 Pet. ii. 21) and the simple word (whence our 'graphic') are the 'pencil drawing' and the 'painting.' See Bp Lightfoot on Clem. Rom. *ad Cor.* I. 5, 'the greatest example of patience.'

The phrase 'good works' is perhaps the most striking of the charac-

corruptness, gravity, sincerity, sound speech that cannot 8
be condemned; that he that is of the contrary *part* may be
ashamed, having no evil *thing* to say of you. *Exhort* 9

teristic phrases of the Epistle. See note on ver. 3 and on 1 Tim. vi. 18. Its exact force in St Paul's mind seems to be an echo of Matt. v. 16, 'let your *light shine*...that they *may see* your good works (*kalos*) and *glorify your Father*.' The word *kalos* is 'good to view as well as good within,' *agathos*, 'good in itself.' Hence the two are joined to describe 'a gentleman.' The Christian religion was felt to be by this time on its trial before the world, and its works must be 'fair and white' in the fierce light of ill-wishing scrutiny, which 'blackens every blot.'

in doctrine shewing *uncorruptness*] 'Shewing' is to be supplied from 'shewing thyself' as a second clause; again, **the doctrine**, as 1 Tim. i. 10, &c.

'Uncorruptness' joined with 'gravity' points to the absence of corruption 'from the intrusion of a lower motive' in the teacher; 'with no doubtful motive and no doubtful manner.' For this sense of 'uncorruptness' compare 1 Tim. vi. 5, 'men corrupted in mind and bereft of the truth, whose motive in religion is gain.' For 'gravity' as before compare 1 Tim. ii. 2. The word rendered 'sincerity' in A.V. should be omitted from lack of MS. authority.

8. *sound speech*] For the 'Pastoral' word 'sound' cf. 1 Tim. i. 10, vi. 3; 2 Tim. i. 13. From the union in this counsel of 'speech' and 'doctrine' we must understand 'sound speech' to be part of the public teaching function of Titus. 'That cannot be condemned,' Vulg. 'irreprehensibile'; cf. 1 Tim. vi. 14 for the similar formation and sense 'that cannot be laid hold of.'

may be ashamed] The active is 'to shame,' 1 Cor. iv. 14 (present). Cf. the subst. 'to your shame,' 1 Cor. vi. 5. The middle pres. and imperf. with 2 fut. pass. are 'to shame myself at,' 'to take shame at'; Luke xviii. 4, 'regard not man;' Heb. xii. 9, 'gave them reverence'; Matt. xxi. 37, 'they will reverence my son.' The 2 aor. pass., which occurs here and 2 Thess. iii. 14 without an object, should be classed with these, rather than be regarded (as by Bp Ellicott) as a passive 'be shamed.' His quotation from Ps. xxxv. 26 is quite inconclusive; for the aor. pass. of the verb, with which our tense is there coupled, has clearly a middle sense in 1 John ii. 28, where Bp Westcott renders 'that we may not shrink with shame.' **Be ashamed** is therefore correct, as A.V. and R.V.

having no evil thing *to say of you*] i.e. 'since he has, and finds that he has.' The reading 'us' for 'you' should be adopted with the best MSS. St Paul identifies himself with Titus and all Church teachers and workers. So St John with his 'children' 1 John ii. 1, 'we have an advocate'; ii. 28, 'that we may have boldness.' The word for 'evil' is not common in N.T.; twice in St John's Gospel, R.V. 'doeth ill,' 'they that have done ill'; twice in St Paul besides, R.V. 'good or bad'; once in St James, R.V. 'confusion and every vile deed.' 'Worthlessness is the central notion,' Trench, *N.T. Syn.* § 84,

servants to be obedient unto their own masters, *and* to
10 please *them* well in all *things;* not answering again; not
purloining, but shewing all good fidelity; that they may

'nequam,' 'naughty,' originally 'light' and 'slight.' Contrasted is the 'positively evil' or 'mischief working,' 'deliver us from the evil,' Matt. vi. 13. The point of the word is here then 'he should have nothing mean, contemptible, good for nothing, to taunt us with.' The 'good' above and the 'evil' here find (as does the thought) apt illustration in Shakespeare's

'So *shines* a *good* deed in a *naughty* world.'

9, 10. THE STANDARD OF HOLY LIVING FOR SLAVES.

9. Exhort *servants*] The verb is supplied from ver. 6. The phrases and the necessary limits of Christian counsel to slaves are touched on in notes 1 Tim. vi. 1, 2. Lewin well observes here 'at that time slavery was a civil institution, which Christianity without any civil power could not disturb.' The more special counsel here may have been suggested by some particular cases of insubordination among the restless Cretans. See above on i. 12.

The *Teaching of the Twelve Apostles* gives a still stronger admonition 'Ye servants shall be in subjection to your masters *as to a figure of God* in reverence and fear.'

to be obedient] As R.V. **to be in subjection**, cf. ver. 5. The adjective **well pleasing** is frequently used by St Paul, but (except here) with 'God'; so the verb and adverb in Ep. to Hebrews. Vulg. 'in omnibus placentes.' The context suggests as most natural the addition of **to them** to complete the sense.

not answering again] Vulg. 'contradicentes,' **not gainsaying**, i.e. withstanding, cf. i. 9; John xix. 12, 'speaketh against,' margin R.V. 'opposeth Cæsar'; Rom. x. 21, 'a disobedient and gainsaying people'; Heb. xii. 3, 'him that hath endured such gainsaying of sinners against themselves'; Jude 11, 'perished in the gainsaying of Korah.' The Old Eng. 'withsay' is a curious link between 'gainsay' and 'withstand'. Compare the German *wider* and *gegen*.

The *Bible Word-Book*, p. 280, quotes from Gower:—

'There may no man his hap *withsain*.'

10. *not purloining*] Old French *purloigner*, i.e. pour-loin, *to convey far*, to 'make away with,' rendering the adverb in the Greek 'afar,' 'apart.' The verb only occurs in N.T. here and Acts v. 2, 3, '*put away* part of the price.'

But 'purloin' has come to have so petty a meaning as to narrow unduly the thought here. Almost all trades arts and professions were at this time in the hands of slaves; and so all tricks of trade, all mercantile or professional embezzlement and dishonesty, are covered by the word; just as 'all good fidelity' 'covers the whole realm of thought, of speech temper and gesture, as well as embraces the sanctity of covenants, the sacredness of property, and the dignity of mutual relations.'

adorn the doctrine of God our Saviour in all *things*. For 11
the grace of God that bringeth salvation hath appeared to

all good fidelity] The weight of MS. authority is in favour of this reading, though 'all love' has strong support.

God our Saviour] God the Father, as above, 1 Tim. i. 1, &c.; render **our Saviour God**. The phrase fits with the thought, 'quo vilior servorum conditio eo dignior Deus Salvator, dignior Dei redemptio.' Dr Reynolds quotes Chrysostom, 'The Greeks judge of doctrines, not from the doctrine itself but from conduct and life; women and slaves may be, in and of themselves, teachers,' and adds, 'God gets his highest praise from the lips of little children, his robes of glory from the faithfulness honour and simplicity of bondslaves.' See Appendix, J, on *St Paul and Slavery*.

11—15. The sphere of the Apostolate—to claim all Life for God, through His Grace, and for His Glory.

11—14. The first of the two Evangelical outbursts of that 'spring of living water' in St Paul's own heart which kept his life and teaching always green and fresh. It corresponds with the passage in 1 Tim. i. 11, 12, where see note, but is (as we should expect from St Paul's less close and tender relation to Titus) more general. Coming to the end of the plain practical counsels for men and women, old and young, whether free or slaves, he 'goes off at a phrase,' one which he has used several times, but the full significance of which he now allows himself to dwell on—'our Saviour God.'

Upon this he enlarges fervently, bringing out of it at the same time the true springs of holy living for all alike; these are, as the General Thanksgiving of the Prayer Book puts it, (1) the grateful appropriation of the 'inestimable Love in the redemption of the world by our Lord Jesus Christ,' (2) the thankful realisation 'of the means of grace,' and (3) the joyful anticipation 'of the hope of glory'; all three being really but one—Christ Jesus, for us, and in us.

Thus (1) ver. 11. The grace of God appeared in Christ, 'who for us men came down from heaven' bringing salvation to all. (2) ver. 12. It guides us daily—to 'true repentance and His Holy Spirit'—that we may 'live a godly, righteous and sober life.' (3) ver. 13. So living we look for the appearing again with power and great glory, 'when we shall be made like unto Him.' In other words, ver. 14—He gave Himself for us, 'that we may dwell in Him and He in us,' a people for His own possession now and evermore.

'Live your creed,' says St Paul, 'adorn your doctrine, as indeed you well can. Work *from* Life; let doctrine inspire duty. *This is* the doctrine of our Saviour God; God the Father Almighty, who made all men and hateth nothing that He made, really did, as a past fact of history, manifest His love by sending His only Son to redeem all men; that love really does as a present fact of experience give us the life of His Son through His Spirit; that love really will as an equally certain fact in the future manifest the glory of His Son

12 all men, teaching us that denying ungodliness and worldly lusts we should live soberly, righteously, and godly, in

as God, and give us the fulness of Divine Life, the fruition of His glorious Godhead. And the Father's love is the Son's; He gave Himself to redeem us, He gives Himself to purify us, to possess us, that we may be zealots for the ideal, the Divine, life, whose glory is "my Father worketh hitherto and I work." Claim, then, all life for Him.'

11. *For the grace of God*] 'Grace' is well defined as '*Love* imparting *itself* and producing its own image and likeness.' Hence the fitness of the three words in the Apostolic Valediction which is also a Benediction: 'The *Grace* of our Lord Jesus Christ, and the *Love* of God, and the *Communion* of the Holy Ghost,' 2 Cor. xiii. 14. The stress, from the order of the words, is on 'appeared' and 'to all men'; and the article before 'bringing salvation' should now (owing to the additional authority of Cod. Sin. against it) be omitted, making the adjective into a predicate. **For the grace of God was truly manifested, bringing salvation to all men.** The verb occurs iii. 4 and Luke i. 79, 'the dayspring from on high shall visit us, *to shine upon* them that sit in darkness,' from which hymn the word may well have been taken. 'The hymn of prophecy became the fact of history.' The light of God's Grace dawned on the world at the birth of Christ. The aorist marks the certainty of the event itself, that it took its place in history.

12. *teaching us that*] Rather, 'training us'; and the present participle implies a continued training, **putting us under discipline;** this form of the word is explained on 1 Tim. i. 20. The comma should be before 'that,' which has its proper meaning **in order that.** This 'training,' 'discipline,' 'education,' is through the means of grace. 'The moral aim of the disciplining in question is expressed first in the negative then in the positive form.' Fairbairn.

denying ungodliness and worldly lusts] Better, **having renounced,** though R.V. keeps 'denying', and Alford urges that the aorist participle and aorist verb cover the same extent, the whole life. This no doubt is a thoroughly *correct* use of the participle, but not a necessary use; and the position of the participle at the very beginning and the verb at the end of the clause suggests rather the other equally legitimate use of the participle, to express the priority of the renunciation. So 'I renounce the devil, the world, the flesh' is the first act in the first of the 'means of grace,' holy baptism.

ungodliness] The opposite of 'godliness,' see notes 1 Tim. i. 9, ii. 2. Our present word and its connexions occur three times in the Pastoral Epistles, three times in St Peter, three times in St Jude; otherwise only in Ep. to Romans.

worldly lusts] The adjective 'worldly' is only used once besides in N.T., in Heb. ix. 1, of the sanctuary in the wilderness, 'a sanctuary of the world.' Here the phrase covers the ground of 1 John ii. 16, 17, where see Bp Westcott's full note. 'The desire of things earthly as ends in themselves comes from the world and is bounded by the world. It is therefore incompatible with the love of the Father....In

this present world; looking for *that* blessed hope, and the 13
glorious appearing of the great God and our Saviour Jesus

themselves all finite objects, "the things that are in the world," are "of the Father." It is the false view of them which makes them idols....The three false tendencies which S. John marks cover the whole ground of "worldliness," the desire to set up the creature as an end.' This word 'worldly' occurs in the *Apostolical Constitutions*, VII. 1, 'abstain from fleshly and worldly lusts,' apparently combining this passage and 1 Pet. ii. 11, though its original, *The Teaching of the Twelve Apostles*, has 'fleshly and bodily,' I. 4.

we should live soberly, righteously, and godly] The clause is adopted to describe a true Christian life in the Pr.-Bk. 'General Confession' and 'Baptismal Service for Adults.' See above and ver. 11. Bp Ellicott rightly; 'Christian duties under three aspects, *to ourselves, to others*, and *to God;* but not to be too much narrowed, though the *order* and the *meanings* point to this;' and see notes on 1 Tim. ii. 9; Tit. i. 8.

this present world] See note on 1 Tim. vi. 17.

13. *looking for* that *blessed hope*] **The blessed hope,** cf. Rom. viii. 24, where it is both the hope and the object of the hope; Col. i. 5, '"for the hope," i.e. looking to the hope *which is stored up;* the sense of "hope," as of the corresponding words in any language, oscillates between the subjective feeling and the objective realisation.' Bp Lightfoot. Cf. 1 Tim. i. 1.

and the glorious appearing] So A.V., considering the two nouns as a Hebraism for a noun and an adjective; but R.V. better, literally, **and appearing of the glory**; this substantive, from the verb 'hath appeared' of ver. 11, is limited in N.T. use to St Paul, who has it six times, and always, except 2 Tim. i. 10, of the *future* appearing of Christ (see note on 1 Tim. vi. 14). It comes three times in St Paul's last letter, 2 Tim. The word has been adopted for *all* the epiphanies of the Son of God in O.T. days, as the angel of the covenant, at Bethlehem, to the Gentiles with 'the doctors,' in His miracles and parables, in the 'infallible proofs' of the 'forty days,' in 'the powers of Pentecost,' in the life of His Church and of each Christian soul by faith, until His 'coming with power and great glory.'

the great God and our Saviour] So A.V., Winer, Alford, Conybeare, on the ground that St Paul's usage is against 'our great God Jesus Christ.' Alford rightly says that it can be no objection to this that St Paul's usage is also against 'the manifestation of the Father God,' because it is the appearing *of the glory* that St Paul speaks of, and this glory is certainly the Father's *and* the Son's, Matt. xvi. 27 compared with Matt. xxv. 31, 'come in His Father's glory,' 'come in His glory.' Nor can the rule that the one article indicates the one subject, and that therefore the two expressions refer to one personality, be too strongly relied upon as decisive against this view. Bp Ellicott who opposes this A.V. rendering yet admits this, 'there is a *presumption* in favour of it on this account, but on account of the defining genitive "of us," nothing more;' and in *Aids to Faith* (quoted

14 Christ; who gave himself for us, that he might redeem us from all iniquity, and purify unto himself a peculiar

in Winer, III. § 19, 5, note), 'the rule is sound in principle but in the case of proper names or quasi-proper names, cannot safely be pressed.' The usage in 2 Pet. i. 1, and in Jude 4, is also doubtful: R.V. which renders there 'our God and Saviour,' 'our only Master and Lord,' but adds the marginal 'Or, our God and *the* Saviour,' 'Or, the only Master, and our Lord,' here too gives **our great God and Saviour**, but adds in the margin, 'Or, of the great God and our Saviour.' The early Fathers are with R.V. Ignatius, *ad Ephes.* i., seems to quote it 'according to the will of the Father and Jesus Christ our God.' See Bp Lightfoot's note. Chrysostom asks 'Where are they who say that the Son is less than the Father?' Jerome, 'Magnus Deus Jesus Christus salvator dicitur.' Compare the long list in Bp Wordsworth's note; Calvin, Ellicott, Fairbairn, &c. among moderns. The objection raised on the ground of St Paul's usage will be less felt, when the strong language of 1 Tim. iii. 15, 16 with the reading 'He who,' and of Phil. ii. 6, 7, Col. i. 15—20 is weighed; and when the connexion of this Epistle in its language and thought with St Peter and St Jude is remembered, it may well seem that the later mode of speaking of Christ, in the now settled faith and conviction of the Church, is beginning to find place.

14. *who gave himself for us*] Dr Reynolds well gives the connexion '*who*—in this lofty and august majesty, and because He was possessed of it—*delivered up Himself*—His whole unique personality—*on our behalf*.'

that he might redeem us] By the payment of a ransom price; see note 1 Tim. ii. 6 for the origin of this image and its place among the metaphors of the Atonement. Compare Norris, *Rudiments of Theology*, pp. 168, 169, 173, 216. St Peter, 1 Pet. i. 18, calls the slavery, from which 'ye were redeemed,' 'your vain manner of life handed down from your fathers'—writing to the Jewish Christians, who as Jews had had at least a certain moral standard. St Paul, thinking of the Cretans and their sunken state of morals, defines the slavery as **all iniquity**, a word which St Peter keeps for 'the lascivious life of the wicked' by which righteous Lot was sore distressed. Compare 1 Tim. i. 9. Rom. ii. 14, 15 describes that 'moral law of nature,' the breaches of which make the 'iniquity' of Rome, and Ephesus, and Crete, and England, irrespective of the more defined written law.

and purify unto himself a peculiar people] 'Purify' is the word constantly used of Christ in the days of His flesh 'cleansing' the lepers. Cf. Matt. viii. 3. His object in His great gift of Himself was that He might say to leprous souls 'I will, be thou cleansed.'

a peculiar people] 'Peculiar' in its old sense from 'peculium,' the property which a son or slave was allowed to possess as his own, cf. Exod. xix. 5. 'Ye shall be a peculiar treasure unto me above all peoples.' So Deut. vii. 6, where the Septuagint has the same Greek word. 'But the Percies affirmyng them to be their owne propre prisoners and

people, zealous of good works. These *things* speak, and 15
exhort, and rebuke with all authority. Let no *man* despise
thee.

their peculiar praies, and to deliver them utterly denayed.' Hall, *Hen. IV.*, fol. 19 *b*. *Bible Word-Book*, p. 454.

The Greek word means 'one who remains over to me,' 'my acquisition,' and so the parallel phrase 1 Pet. ii. 9, 'a people for a possession,' interprets it. Vulg. 'acceptabilis,' and so Theod. Mops. *Latin Text*, but the Latin commentary. shewing Theodore's own interpretation, far better 'ut proprium sibi populum adquireret.' For a full account of the word see Bp Lightfoot, *Revision of the N. T.*, p. 234 sq. '*People*' is itself the proper word for the chosen, select, people; in the original phrase in O. T. therefore the Israelites, now the Church Catholic.

zealous of good works] The force of this word can be seen in Luke vi. 15, 'Simon who was called the Zealot,' Acts xxi. 20, 'and they are all zealous for the law, xxii. 3, 'being zealous for God, even as ye all are this day;' what the 'Zealot' party which set itself up for extra loyalty and strictness to the Law as a nationalist badge was to the nation at large; what the Jewish Christians were to their better instructed Gentile brethren, and Jews generally to Christians, in respect of the old ritual observances: this Christ would have His Church be to the rest of the world in respect of good works shining before men, 'zealots of goodness, charged with the genius of goodness—the passion for godliness:' Dr Reynolds. So St Peter again has the word 'who is he that will harm you, if ye be zealots of goodness?' 1 Pet. iii. 13. But may we not also say here is the true 'enthusiasm of humanity,' the very purpose, mark, of the Incarnation and Atonement; that we may be zealots of philanthropy, charged with the genius of social regeneration, the passion for practical piety? This aim and scope of the Saviour's work makes the 'Faithful saying' of the next chapter iii. 8 rise plainly to the level of the other 'Faithful sayings' of 1 Tim. and 2 Tim.

15. *These* things *speak, and exhort, and rebuke*] The three verbs rise as a climax, describing the degrees of earnestness and intensity to be put forth according to the occasion; 'these things,' all from ii. 1.

with all authority] The word looks back to the 'authority' of St Paul's own commission i. 3, and implies its delegated fulness. So 1 Tim. i. 1, where see note.

Let no man *despise thee*] 'Do not thyself disesteem and cheapen thy authority.' This is the exact force of the Greek verb used for 'despise.' Cf. 'it is naught, it is naught, saith the buyer,' Prov. xx. 14. 'Believe,' as we might say now, 'in the grace of holy orders.' 'Believe there is something in the faithful pastor's, the faithful priest's, visit to the sick or whole, different from and beyond the faithful layman's. Foster this belief for your people's sake. Their faith in this matter will have much to do with their healing.' Cf. Bridges, *Christian Ministry*, c. x, 'Expect great things—attempt great things. This expectation is the life of faith—the vitality of the Ministry—that which honours God, and is honoured by God.'

3 Put them in mind to be subject to principalities and

Ch. III. The Apostolate—its Ministry of Goodwill and Good Works.

The last verse of chap. ii., in gathering up the previous counsels, also makes a link for passing to the further consideration of *social and civil duties generally*. So the R.V. in printing the verse as a separate paragraph. Westcott and Hort connect entirely with chap. iii.

The duty is laid down in verses 1 and 2 of living 'in the bond of peace,' ('even if tyrannical' is implied, but with Pauline tact *not* expressed), and 'in dutiful allegiance to the constituted authority.' This is enforced (verses 3—5) by the motive of God's saving love to men 'even when they were enemies,' and (verses 6, 7) of the *power*, conveyed through the gift of the Spirit, for such a spiritual life. The appeal to this high calling closes the last of the special counsels in practical duty; as a similar lofty strain closed the last but one, ver. 14. St Paul, in drawing to an end, recapitulates (as at the end of the first letter to Timothy) the main points of the letter, viz., (1) the practical issues of religion in all the duties of life, in verse 8; a summary of ii. 1—iii. 7; the silencing of false teachers through his appointment of good and sound elders, and his own vigorous soundness, in verses 9—11; a summary of i. 5—16. The chapter and letter then close with personal directions (ver. 12—14), and salutations (ver. 15).

1—7. The duty of living in peace from a sense of God's love and through the Spirit's power.

1. *Put them in mind*] 'Them' must be 'the Cretan Christians' generally: St Paul is gathering all up in his mind for his final counsel. The verb for 'put in mind,' and its substantive, occur twice in St John, once in St Luke, but in St Paul only in the Pastoral Epistles three times; in St Peter's Epistles three times; and once in St Jude's. Joh. xiv. 26 shews the full construction, accus. of person and of thing, 'He shall bring all things to your remembrance.' The A.V. in 3 John 10, 'I will remember his deeds,' is surely in the old sense of 'remember,' which survives in our valedictory request 'remember me to all your circle;' R.V. 'bring to remembrance,' cf. note on the similar compound 2 Tim. i. 6.

to be subject to principalities and powers] Rather, more fully as R. V. **to be in subjection**. Elsewhere in St Paul's Epistles the phrase 'principalities and powers' refers to spiritual and angelic powers, good or evil, cf. 1 Cor. xv. 24; Eph. iii. 10; Col. i. 16. But the word in its old sense (see *Bible Word-Book*, p. 477) was used of any 'chief place,' as in 2 Macc. iv. 27 of the office of high priest. And the meaning here is the same as in the two places where it occurs in the Gospels, Luke xii. 11, where our Lord prophesies that His disciples shall be brought before 'the rulers and the authorities,' and xx. 20, 'so as to deliver him up to the rule and to the authority of the governor.' There is not sufficient warrant for the connecting 'and' here; render **to rulers to authorities**. Both words illustrate the idiom 'res pro persona.'

powers, to obey magistrates, to be ready to every good
work, to speak evil of no *man*, to be no brawlers, *but* 2
gentle, shewing all meekness unto all men. For we our- 3

Vulg. 'potestates' from whence the Italian *podestà* a magistrate. The difference between the two words is that the former expresses a governing *de facto*, whether also *de jure* or not, the latter a governing *de jure*, a duly constituted authority. 'They who rule' occurs with 'the authorities' in the *locus classicus*, Rom. xiii. 1, where, however, R.V. has retained 'power,' apparently because *from that passage* the phrase 'the powers that be' has become an English household word in the sense of 'lawful authority.' The other household use of 'powers' in the phrase 'The Great Powers,' seems to belong rather to the synonym *dynamis* as expressing material force. In Matt. xxviii. 18 the change from 'power' to 'authority' in R.V. enhances the kingly office and prerogative.

to obey magistrates] The word only occurs Acts v. 29, 32; xxvii. 21, where a dative follows; and so it may be here, if we join it with the preceding; but it seems more Pauline to add the verb absolutely. From note on ii. 5 we should expect it to differ from the preceding clause, in being more specific in its reference to the official system of government; render perhaps **to obey their rules**, 'to obey state laws.' Fairbairn refers to the earlier history of the island and a 'known tendency on the part of the Cretans to insubordination and turmoil,' quoting from Polybius VI. 46, 'constantly upset by seditions and murders and tribal wars.'

to be ready to every good work] This takes us on a step still further; first a general submission, then a loyal acceptance and execution of public orders, then the learning and labouring truly to get one's own living and to do one's duty, domestic, social and civil. That 'the good work' has such a reference is implied in Rom. xiii. 3. The 'ready' is exactly 'whatsoever ye do, do it heartily unto the Lord,' cf. Col. iii. 23. 'The true workman never shirks when the overseer is not by; he has not one rule for work done for himself, and another for work done for his master. There is a work that is mean and pitiful; all grudging unwilling toil, all 'scamped' work, fair to the eye but second rate in reality, is mean and pitiful; it is like work done by the slave at the whip's end, or like the labour of the convict in gaol; it is forced and unwelcome and as badly done as possible.' M. A. Lewis, *Faithful Soldiers and Servants*, p. 58.

2. *to speak evil of no* man] Cf. 1 Tim. i. 20, vi. 1; Tit. ii. 5. In the first place used absolutely 'to blaspheme,' as Acts xxvi. 11, 'I strove to make them blaspheme.'

to be no brawlers, but *gentle*] Better, as R.V., **not to be contentious**; the word only occurs in N. T., 1 Tim. iii. 3, where it is joined, as here, with 'gentle' or 'forbearing'; see note there.

shewing all meekness] The compound form of the word has occurred 1 Tim. vi. 11, coupled with 'patience,' see note. The distinction between 'gentleness' above and 'meekness' is given by Aquinas (quoted in *N. T. Syn.* p. 152), as twofold, (1) 'gentleness,' *clementia*, is 'lenitas superioris ad inferiorem'; meekness, *mansuetudo*, is 'cuiuslibet ad quemlibet': (2) 'gen-

selves also were sometimes foolish, disobedient, deceived, serving divers lusts and pleasures, living in malice and

tleness' is in outward acts, 'est moderativa exterioris punitionis'; 'meekness' is in the inner spirit, 'proprie diminuit passionem irae.' But besides its separateness of force in combination with 'gentleness,' the 'meekness' here is especially fitted to lead on to the argument of the next verse from its own proper sense. 'It is an inwrought grace of the soul; and the exercises of it are first and chiefly towards God, when we accept His dealings with us without disputing. He that is meek indeed will know himself a sinner amongst sinners; or if there was One who could not know Himself such, yet He too bore a sinner's doom and endured therefore the contradiction of sinners, Matt. xi. 29, "I am meek and lowly of heart;" and this knowledge of his own sin will teach him to endure meekly the provocations with which they may provoke him, and not to withdraw himself from the burdens which their sin may impose upon him (Gal. vi. 1; 2 Tim. ii. 25).' *N. T. Syn.* p. 150.

3. *For we ourselves also were sometimes foolish*] 'Sometimes' in the old sense of 'sometime,' Eph. ii. 13, 'ye who sometimes were afar off.' Cp. Shaksp. *Rich. II.* 1. 2. 54 (*Bible Word-Book*, p. 551):

> 'Farewell, old Gaunt: thy *sometimes* brother's wife
> With her companion grief must end her life.'

The position and tense of the verb and particle justify our rendering **For there was a time when we too were foolish.** 'Foolish'; 'in this word there is always a moral fault lying at the root of the intellectual,' *N. T. Syn.* § 75; as in Lk. xxiv. 25, 'O foolish men and *slow of heart*,' and Gal. iii. 1 'O foolish Galatians, who did *bewitch* you?' so 'wanting in spiritual sense,' 'blind'; cf. 1 Tim. vi. 9; 2 Tim. iii. 9.

disobedient, deceived] **disobedient**, as i. 16, 2 Tim. iii. 2, and all other N.T. passages; 'insuadibiles,' Theod. Mops. Lat.; 'inobedientes,' Jerome; not as Vulg. 'increduli,' 'distrustful;' **going astray**, rather than 'deceived;' the verb is no doubt used in both passive and neuter sense, but compare the use of the pres. part., Matt. xviii. 12, 'doth he not leave the ninety and nine...and seek that which goeth astray?' and 1 Pet. ii. 25, 'For ye were going astray like sheep;' where the argument for patience from a sense of having erred and strayed is just the same. May not St Peter have taken up this very force of the word, and so been led to the quotation from Isai. liii.? It is a question whether even in 2 Tim. iii. 13 'leading astray and going astray' would not express the antithesis better than 'deceiving and being deceived.' There is no stress on their 'being deceived,' which might furnish rather an excuse than an aggravation.

serving divers lusts and pleasures] The Greek is stronger, **being the slaves of,** as Luke xvi. 13 'to be God's slave and Mammon's slave' and elsewhere. 'Divers' is only used by St Paul in these 'Pastoral' letters; of diseases, Luke iv. 40: twice in Heb., twice in St Peter, once in St James. But the compound is used of 'wisdom,' Eph. iii. 10. 'Pleasures' in the N.T. use is stronger than our English word. It only occurs James iv. 1, 3 of lusts and adulteries, 2 Pet. ii. 13 of day-revels and

envy, hateful, *and* hating one another. But after that the 4
kindness and love of God our Saviour toward man appeared, 5
not by works of righteousness which we have done, but

debauchery, and Luke viii. 14 of their 'choking' effect, along with carking care and riches.

living in malice and envy] 'Malice' is the 'evil habit of mind' which manifests itself in positive evil and harm-doing, see note on ii. 9 and Trench, *N. T. Syn.* § 11. It comes between a state of envy and the actual working of ill to a neighbour.

hateful, and *hating one another*] Vulg. 'odibiles odientes invicem'; 'hateful' in the particular form of the Greek word here does not occur elsewhere in N. T., but is formed just as 'abominable' in Tit. i. 16. The full sense is well seen in the compound 'hateful to God' (not as A.V. 'haters of God') Rom. i. 30.

The whole verse seems an echo, in brief, of the fuller description of heathen life written ten years before in Rom. i. 18—32. As in ii. 12, St Paul identifies himself with the Cretans in self-condemnation, and divine mercy; exemplifying the 'meekness' he inculcates.

4. The contrast is striking; God hated the sinners' sins, and the sinners hated one another, but God loved all the sinners through it all, and at the right time let His 'loving kindness' 'appear.' Render: **When the kindness of our Saviour God and his love toward man appeared.** 'Kindness' is the word in Eph. ii., the passage of which the present seems a reminiscence; there its colleague is the Pauline 'grace,' ii. 5, 7, 8. The proper force of the word is well given *N. T. Syn.* § 63 'Wine is *chrestos* which has been mellowed with age, Luke v. 39; Christ's yoke is *chrestos*, as having nothing harsh or galling about it, Matt. xi. 30.' Jerome's definition from the Stoics is quoted, 'Benignitas est virtus sponte ad benefaciendum exposita.' Abp Trench adds: 'This *chrestotes* was so predominantly the character of Christ's ministry that it is nothing wonderful to learn from Tertullian (*Apol.* 3) how 'Christus' became 'Chrestus,' and 'Christiani' 'Chrestiani,' on the lips of the heathen—with the undertone, it is true, of contempt.' In N.T. usage the word is peculiar to St Paul. 'Love toward man'—our 'philanthropy'—occurs Acts xxviii. 2, and the adverb xxvii. 3, 'shewed us no common kindness,' 'treated Paul kindly.' But St Paul, as with many other words, elevates it to a higher height than that of man's kindness to man, and 'philanthropy' is thenceforth even in its ordinary sphere transfigured with the brightness of the character of God. The best Christian should be the best philanthropist.

God our Saviour] As before, so frequently, of the Father; while below the same title is given to the Son, ver. 6; as in chap. ii. 10, 11 followed by 13.

5. *not by works of righteousness*] The exact grammatical form is rendered by **not by virtue of works, works in righteousness which we did.** We should read the neut. accus. of the relative with the best authorities, rather than the genitive here. Bp Wordsworth well explains the reason of the clause: that when those false teachers were asked what was their ground of hope of salvation, they would reply

according to his mercy he saved us, by the washing of

'The works wrought in righteousness which we did'; but St Paul would answer 'God's mercy.'

he saved us] Vulg. 'salvos nos fecit.' Compare the aorist tenses in Col. ii. 13—15. Bp Lightfoot thus brings out the force (*Revision of N.T.* p. 85): 'St Paul regards this change from sin to righteousness, from bondage to freedom, from death to life, as summed up in one definite act of the past; potentially to all men in our Lord's Passion and Resurrection, actually to each individual man when he accepts Christ, is baptized into Christ.' 'It is the definiteness, the absoluteness of this change, considered as a historical crisis, which forms the central idea of St Paul's teaching, and which the aorist marks.' See also note on 1 Tim. ii. 4.

by the washing of regeneration] Properly **through the washing** or **through the laver**; the preposition expresses the channel or means through which; the 'washing' or 'laver' 'of regeneration' is evidently one phrase for the sacrament of Holy Baptism. The genitive marks 'the attribute or inseparable accompaniments,' Winer § 30 2 B, who quotes Mk. i. 4, 'repentance-baptism.' Cf. Col. i. 22, 'his flesh-body,' i.e. His material, natural body, distinguished from the mystical body before mentioned. Cf. also 'the fire of testing,' *Teaching of the Twelve Apostles* xvi. 5.

Should we render here 'washing' or 'laver'? It has been usual among English commentators as Wordsw., Alf., Conybeare, Ellicott, to render 'laver,' and to understand the baptismal font, on the ground that the Greek word 'means always a vessel or pool in which washing takes place.' So no doubt the form in *tron* properly signifies, as e.g. *arotron* a plough, *alabastron*, an ointment-bottle. But classical usage is *in the plural* 'a bath,' Hom. *Il.* xviii. 489, Æsch. *Ag.* 1080; *in the sing.* 'the act of washing,' Hes. *Op.* 755, 'expiatory libations,' Soph. *El.* 84, 'water for washing,' *Œd. Col.* 1599; Aristoph. *Lys.* 378. The Septuagint usage is only in the sing., Jer. xxxi. 25, 'A man baptized from the death of sin, and again taking hold of it, what does he gain from his washing?' Cant. iv. 2 'Thy teeth are like a flock of ewes that are newly shorn, which are come up from the washing.' The N.T. usage is only in the sing., Eph. v. 26, 'having cleansed it (the Church) by the washing of water with the word,' R.V., with margin 'Gr. laver,' and the present passage where R.V. gives 'washing,' with margin 'Or, laver.' According to R.V. rules this inconsistency neutralises its verdict. For in Eph. v. 26 it is implied that 'laver' is more *exact;* in Tit. that 'washing' is more, and 'laver' less likely, as the meaning of the Greek. On the whole the classical usage, the A.V. and R.V. text, support the rendering 'washing.' As to the form of the word, the Greeks may have been at liberty to divert it from its proper meaning, having the kindred form *loutêr* for 'a bath,' which, according to analogy, should be 'a bathing man.' Somewhat similarly having *astêr* for 'a star' they used *astron* for 'a cluster of stars.'

regeneration] '*Palingenesia* is one of the many words which the Gospel found, and, so to speak, glorified.' Abp Trench, who ad-

regeneration, and renewing of the Holy Ghost; which he 6

mirably draws out the enlargement here, *N.T. Syn.* § 18. The word had been used by the Pythagoreans, in the doctrine of transmigration of souls, for their reappearance in new bodies; by the Stoics for the periodic renovation of the earth in spring; in Cicero it describes his restoration to his dignities and honours after his return from exile; in Josephus the restoration of the Jewish nation after the captivity. The word does not occur in the Septuagint; and in N.T. only here and Matt. xix. 28. 'In our Lord's words there is evident reference to the new birth of the whole creation (Acts iii. 21), which shall be when the Son of Man hereafter comes in His glory; while St Paul's "washing of regeneration" has to do with the new birth not of the whole travailing creation, but of the single soul, which is now evermore finding place....The *palingenesia* which Scripture proclaims begins with the *microcosmus* of single souls; but it does not end there; it does not cease its effectual working till it has embraced the whole *macrocosmus* of the universe.'

But if, as seems most consistent with the whole chapter, and with St Matthew's grand aim to paint a present 'kingdom of the heavens,' the reference of Matt. xix. 28 is to *the Church*, Catholic and *Apostolic*, then 'regeneration' in both passages refers to the same act and epoch, when our Lord having 'overcome the sharpness of death' opened the Kingdom of Heaven to all believers, and on the day of Pentecost 3000 souls said to Peter and the rest of the Apostles 'Brethren, what shall we do?' and were baptized by them 'unto the remission of their sins,' and 'continued stedfastly in the apostles' teaching and fellowship.' In our Lord's words and in St Paul's the setting up of this kingdom, the entrance into it, is life from the dead, a second birth; and Joh. iii. 3, 5 'Except a man be born anew, he cannot see the kingdom of God; Except a man be born of water and of the spirit, he cannot enter into the kingdom of God,' (summed up in *palingenesia* Matt. xix. 28) explains and is explained by Eph. v. 25, 26, 'Christ loved the church and gave himself up for it, that he might cleanse it by the washing of water with the word' (summed up in *palingenesia*, Tit. iii. 5).

and renewing of the Holy Ghost] R.V. keeps this rendering of A.V. which necessarily makes 'renewing' depend like 'regeneration' on 'the washing'; giving in the margin as a good, but not so good, construction 'and through renewing,' where the government is carried back to the preposition. It is only a question of the naturalness of the order of words, and of the doctrine that 'renewing' or 'renovation' depends on Baptism being expressly stated or left to be inferred. The doctrine itself cannot but be true, as *life* must precede *growth*, and *growth* must depend upon *life*. Compare Eph. v. 26, where the purpose of Christ giving Himself up for the Church is stated to be, *first* that He might cleanse it by the washing of water through the word (as above), and *then* that He might *sanctify* it, till there should be no spot nor blemish; and Rom. xii. 2, 'Be ye transformed (present tense) by the renewal of your mind;' see that the gradual restoration of the Divine image be ever going forward. No nobler commentary on the phrase has been written than the ancient 'Veni Creator.'

shed on us abundantly through Jesus Christ our Saviour;
7 that being justified by his grace, we should be made heirs

6. *which he shed on us abundantly*] More closely in R.V. **which he poured out upon us richly**; the verb is the same, in the same tense, as in Acts ii. 33, 'he hath poured forth this'; the aorist there being used according to Greek idiom of what has just happened, here of God's objective act once for all, in which all His successive giving was potentially included.

through Jesus Christ our Saviour] 'As its channel and medium,' Alford. 'All the spiritual Blessings of the New birth, and of the New life, are represented as flowing down to us from and out of the one fountain and well-spring of the love of God the *Father;* and are all derived to us *through* God the Son, God and Man, Who is the sole channel of all grace to men; and are applied to us personally by the agency of God the Holy Ghost. All these Blessings come to us through the Incarnation of God the Son, Who took our nature and died for us, and washed us from our sins by His blood. And the Incarnation is, as it were, the point of contact at which the Channel of Filial Grace joins on to the Well-spring of Paternal Love. And the point of contact at which the living water of Grace, which flows from the Well-spring of Paternal Love through the Filial channel of Grace, is poured forth into our souls is in the laver of our New Birth in Baptism.' Wordsworth.

7. *being justified...be made heirs*] The word 'justifying' and 'justification' occur 25 times in the great group of Epistles, written 10 years before this to the Romans, Corinthians, Galatians, whose subject is 'Christ the Redeemer,' 'Christ for us.' It has not been used in the next great group written five years before this, to the Ephesians, Colossians and Philippians, whose subject is 'Christ the Life,' 'Christ in us,' 'Christ our Sanctification.' 'Righteousness,' however, that right relation between God and man, the restoration to which *is* justification, occurs seven times against 50 times in the former group. So in Eph. v. 26 (already quoted as parallel in form and sense to our present passage), 'the cleansing' *is* the justifying, and the 'sanctifying' follows, as here 'being heirs' follows. This verse then, in its two clauses, repeats, with reference to God the Son, what in verse 5 was said with reference to God the Father as to the twofold saving mercy; just as in the former 'Gospel' passage, ii. 11—14, 'renunciation' and 'obedience' are both spoken of, first as the work of God the Father's grace (11, 12), and then as the result of God the Son's gift of Himself (14). The justification by God the Father's grace—the regeneration—effected potentially once for all by Christ through His death, resurrection and outpouring of the Holy Spirit, and appropriated individually by Faith (expressed or implied) in Baptism, is to be followed by a 'life of heirship' or 'sanctification'; so the Latin translation of Theod. Mops. 'ut heredes efficiamur,' and the comment, 'at segregavit nos in ditissimam quam nobis bonorum praestitit fruitionem,'—the third of the Baptismal Blessings, 'inheritors of the kingdom of heaven,' with a right and title to receive now 'the fruits of the Spirit.'

according to the hope of eternal life. *This is* a faithful 8
saying, and these *things* I will that thou affirm constantly,
that they which have believed in God might be careful to

according to the hope of eternal life] (1) In A.V. and R.V. it is implied that these words are to be taken together and 'made heirs' left absolute; then this last clause finds an eloquent expansion in Eph. v. 27 (see above), and 'glorification' crowns 'sanctification,' as sanctification followed justification. (2) The R.V. margin gives 'heirs, according to hope, of eternal life.' In this case 'eternal life' must most fittingly be interpreted as usually in St John, and 1 Tim. iv. 8, vi. 12, 19, 'the spiritual life that is and is to come;' 'according to hope' will be as Eph. iv. 4, 'called in one hope of your calling,' and 1 Tim. i. 1, 'Christ Jesus our hope,' where this life's state of salvation must be included in the object of hope; and 'justification' and 'sanctification' will be the only two objects named of the Spirit's outpouring. But the phrase in Tit. i. 2, as there interpreted, favours (1).

8—14. THE ABIDING PRACTICAL HOLINESS OF GOOD WORKS.

8. See summary at the beginning of the chapter, and note in Appendix E on *The Faithful Sayings*.

This is *a faithful saying*] Render as 1 Tim. i. 15, where see note, **Faithful is the saying.** We begin a new paragraph embodying 'another of the compendious fruitful utterances,' thus uniting the wisdom of many, the wit of one, of God's prophets. As in the other cases, it is to be referred to the following clause, and here to that which comes after the parenthesis, **see to it that they which have believed God may be careful to maintain good works.** So Bp Wordsworth, 'a formula *introducing* a solemn asseveration which declares the *practical* character of the doctrine of Regeneration by Baptism...the teaching of St Paul in the Pastoral Epistles on the necessity of good works,' 1 Tim. ii. 10, v. 10, vi. 18; 2 Tim. ii. 21; Tit. i. 16, ii. 7, 14, iii. 14...'they who have been born anew in baptism have entered into a solemn covenant with God, by which they obliged themselves to a *new* and holy *life*.' The particle 'in order that' may be taken as part of the quotation, as Conybeare suggests, and as used with the subjunctive for an imperative; cf. Eph. v. 33, 'and (let) the wife (see) that she fear her husband;' Mark v. 23 '(I pray thee), that thou come and lay thy hands on her;' Cic. *Fam.* 14, 20, 'ibi ut sint omnia parata.' See Winer § 43, 5, a.

these things] should be rather, **concerning these things.**

affirm constantly] Rather, the compound implies **affirm confidently.** The word is only (in N.T.) here and 1 Tim. i. 7; the middle as there and Tit. i. 5.

they which have believed in God] Lit. **believed God**, the least emphatic of the constructions with 'believe,' that is, the earliest and simplest form of faith, the personal going out of the soul to the personal God and Father, that 'takes Him at His word.' So how natural, at the end of a life's experience which built up the Christian Creed, is St Paul's return to the simplest elements of the personal trust which

maintain good works. These *things* are good and profitable
9 unto men. But avoid foolish questions, and genealogies,
and contentions, and strivings about the law; for they are
10 unprofitable and vain. A man *that is* a heretick, after

has underlain the life and doctrine all the time (perfect tense as here) 'I know whom I have believed and do believe,' 'I know who is my trust.' 2 Tim. i. 12; cf. Acts xvi. 34.

might be careful] **May make it their study**; nowhere else in N.T. but frequent in LXX., e.g. 1 Sam. ix. 5, 'leave caring for the asses and *take thought* for us,' and in classical Greek.

to maintain good works] Lit. to 'stand forward,' in N.T. only in St Paul, as in 1 Tim. iii. 4, v. 17, of 'presiding over' 'ruling'; so in LXX.; but in classical Greek in the sense here, 'to be master of,' 'practised in,' as a secondary sense, as well. Here the word carries further the thought in the Greek of 'good;' the good works are not only to be good in themselves, but seen to be good; Christians are not only to do such good works, but to let their light shine, to be to the front, in doing them. The corresponding word for a wrong zeal is used by St John: 2 John 9, 'Whosoever goeth onward and abideth not in the teaching.' The use of these two verbs in their special sense, and the order of the words for evident special emphasis, confirm the view taken here, as by Bp Wordsworth and others (A.V. certainly, R.V. probably), that this clause is the 'Faithful saying.' We may perhaps render it as such, and try to mark the several points noted, in a proverbial couplet;—

'Is God thy trust? Then make the study thine
In all good works to let thy candle shine.'

These things *are good*] As is St Paul's way, the word 'good' from the immediately preceding context, serves to make the transition to another point. 'Good works' are necessary, all these practical counsels in fact are good and will bring their profit to men; for positive teaching of plain duties is the best safeguard against error.

9. The summary of the other chief topic of the letter; the dealing with the false teaching and evil living of the day. See note above.

avoid foolish questions] The Greek puts the errors first in stronger contrast to the good; 'questions' should be 'questionings' as in 1 Tim. i. 4. See note there; where also 'genealogies' is considered. 'Genealogies' would be a special and prevailing theme of the 'questionings,' and 'fightings about the law,' of the 'contentions,' as Bp Ellicott points out, following Wiesinger. Cf. 1 Tim. vi. 4; 2 Tim. ii. 23; and Introduction on the Gnostic heresy. Keeping the A.V. **avoid** we may give it the due emphasis at the close, as we cannot with 'shun' of R.V. 'Avoid' from Fr. *vuider*, *vider*, 'to make empty,' is used intransitively and transitively, exactly as the Greek word here is also used to 'give a wide berth,' 'to stand off and make a circuit.' Cf. 1 Sam. xviii. 11, where R.V. still has 'David avoided out of his presence twice;' Prov. iv. 15, 'walk not in the way of evil men: avoid it, pass not by it.'

unprofitable and vain] 'Vain' is added to intensify 'unprofitable';

the first and second admonition, reject; knowing that *he* 11
that is such is subverted, and sinneth, being condemned of
himself.

from its use here then it should mean 'vain' in its results, and be opposed to 'good,' which is 'seen to be good' above. So in 1 Cor. xv. 17, 'your faith is vain, *ye are yet in your sins.*' While above, ver. 14, 'our preaching is void; your faith also is void: we are found false witnesses;' there is no true basis of fact for preaching or faith; the word there being different. See Bp Ellicott's note, and references.

10. This and the next verse seem to close the last instruction; St Paul reviews the counsel given as to doctrine and discipline; similarly at the close of 1 Tim. See summary at beginning of ch. vi.

A man that is *a heretick*] This being so, it would be unnatural if the epithet here were required to have the definite narrowed meaning which we now give to the word 'heretic'. The *internal* consideration favours a meaning which covers quarrelsome opinionative controversy and speculation, contentiousness in faith *and* morals. The *external* consideration is from St Paul's usage of the word and its substantive. Prof. Reynolds misrepresents Bp Ellicott as saying 'St Paul uses the word for contentious conduct, not heterodox opinions: divisions, not doctrinal error.' His words are, 'the word does not imply specially the open espousal of any *fundamental* error in 1 Cor. xi. 18, 19; Gal. v. 20; but more generally, "divisions in church matters," possibly of a somewhat maturer kind.' In that early day the 'self chosen divergence,' which is the essence of the word, included *both* religious belief *and* practice. Theod. Mops. Lat. Comm. defines '*haereticum*—illum qui ea quae contraria sunt pietatis praeelegit.' And Augustine's definition was exact, 'haeresis schisma inveteratum.' It was not till later that Jerome's distinction held good, 'haeresis perversum dogma habet; schisma propter Episcopalem dissensionem ab ecclesia separatur.' This distinction as to *doctrine* and *discipline* found illustration in the Council of Nicæa, Arius being condemned as a heretic for maintaining that Christ was a Divine being but created, Meletius as a schismatic for ordaining bishops without the authority of his metropolitan or consent of his fellow bishops in the province of Egypt. Here the R.V. by its rendering **heretical** and its marginal 'factious' adopts this more general meaning for the word.

after the first and second admonition, reject] **A first and second admonition.** Cf. Eph. vi. 4, 'nurture them in the chastening and admonition of the Lord.' 'Discipline' or 'chastening' (see the verb ch. ii. 11) is *per poenas*, 'admonition' is *verbis*, encouraging or reproving words according to the occasion. Here the reference must be to i. 13, the reproof of confutation and condemnation. 'Reject' should be rather **refuse**, as in 1 Tim. iv. 7 where see note; and (of the widows) v. 11; refuse, that is, to argue with, or to countenance. St Paul's use is against the interpretation which has classical support, 'exclude' from Church membership, as in Lucian of divorcing a wife. But his use is *for* a stronger meaning than 'avoid.'

11. he that is *such is subverted*] **Is perverted**, the word is used by

12 When I shall send Artemas unto thee, or Tychicus, be
diligent to come unto me to Nicopolis: for I have deter-
13 mined there to winter. Bring Zenas the lawyer and

Lucian for 'turning inside out,' in LXX. for 'a very froward generation,' Deut. xxxii. 20. Vulg. has 'subversus,' but Theod. Mops. Lat. 'perversus.' It does not occur again in N.T., the usual compound being with the preposition 'through and through' instead of 'out and out.' Cf. Acts xx. 30 'speaking perverse things,' Phil. ii. 15 'in the midst of a crooked and perverse generation.' It cannot, as Professor Reynolds thinks, describe 'the effect of the isolation' recommended, but is rather the state of obstinate *wrongheadedness* (to use a similar English metaphor), which, after two chances of enlightenment rejected, becomes *wilful sin*. The present tense should have its full force, **is a wilful sinner**. Cf. Eph. iv. 26 'Be ye angry and sin not,' 1 Joh. iii. 6 'Whosoever abideth in him sinneth not,' is not a sinner in wilful purpose and habit.

being condemned of himself] **Self-condemned**, as such, by callousness to the two approaches of God's minister: the word does not occur again in N.T.

12—14. Personal directions. As to the conjectural chapter of biography of which we have traces here, see Introduction, pp. 40–44. We may suppose that the object of the sending Tychicus or Artemas was to take the place of Titus during his stay with St Paul. From 2 Tim. iv. 12, Tychicus would seem to have been sent to Ephesus, so that Artemas may have been finally chosen for Crete. Of him nothing is known. Tychicus is one of the most valued of the 'fellow helpers,' 'the beloved brother and faithful minister and fellow-servant in the Lord,' entrusted with the Ephesian and Colossian letters, and the 'comfortable words,' five years before, in the enforced absence of the first imprisonment at Rome, Eph. vi. 21; Col. iv. 7.

12. *When I shall send*] Lit. 'when I shall have sent,' aor. subj.: Vulg. 'cum misero.' Titus would of course wait for his deputy's arrival.

to Nicopolis] The town of that name *in Epirus* most probably, since 'there was a large population, a good harbour, and numerous opportunities of coming into contact with old friends from the churches of Achaia.' The Nicopolis in Cilicia has nothing to recommend it; that in Thrace is preferred by the Greek commentators; compare too the subscription at the end of the Epistle 'Nicopolis in Macedonia.' But this has no authority; and the supposed better fitting in of *this* Nicopolis with the last journey west (cf. 2 Tim. iv. 10) is too uncertain to have weight against the evident fitness of a well-known post as the *rendezvous* for the winter, and a base of further operations.

for I have determined there to winter] Shewing that St Paul was at liberty; that is, between (as may be safely assumed) the first and second imprisonment. Cf. Introduction, p. 44.

13. *Bring Zenas the lawyer and Apollos on their journey*] The verb 'bring on their journey' is literally 'send forward,' and so Vulg. here 'praemitte'; but in the other eight places of its use in N.T. 'deduco' is used, that is, 'conduct,' 'take them a certain part of the way.' So in old

Apollos on their journey diligently, that nothing be wanting
unto them. And let ours also learn to maintain good 14

provincial English 'I will send you a mile,' meaning 'accompany you.' R.V. in four places has 'bring on the way,' in five, 'set forward on the journey;' but in only one, Acts xxi. 5, does the context *require* that the 'accompanying' should be prominent, 'they all with wives and children brought us on our way till we were out of the city.' Here **set forward** with less thought of bringing (A.V.) seems sufficient.

Zenas the lawyer and Apollos] Zenas is the Greek form of Zenodorus, as Apollos of Apollodorus, Artemas of Artemidorus. Nothing is known of him, but the phrase itself suggests that he was one of the class of Jewish scribes or lawyers, i.e. experts in Jewish law who were especially numerous among the Pharisees. On his conversion he may have retained the name, as Simon the Zealot and Matthew the publican did theirs. As his class had for their fuller title 'teachers of the law,' 'doctors,' Luke ii. 46, v. 17, he would be especially fitted to become one of the order of the Christian 'teachers'; cf. Eph. iv. 11, 'some to be apostles, some prophets, some evangelists, some *pastors and teachers*.' Apollos, on the other hand, was recognised as an apostle. He was an Alexandrian by race, a learned (or eloquent) man, mighty in the Scriptures, instructed in the way of the Lord, to whom Priscilla and Aquila 'expounded the way of God more carefully' (Acts xviii. 26) at Ephesus. He became a most successful evangelist in Achaia and at Corinth, and was regarded by St Paul as a brother apostle, independent in will and action, 1 Cor. xvi. 12, but preaching and serving an undivided Christ, 1 Cor. i. 12, iii. 22, 23. From this passage we may infer, not that they had been resident in Crete, which introduces an unnecessary complication with the official authority of Titus, but that they had undertaken such a 'pastoral mission' there as St Paul had invited Apollos to undertake to Corinth, 1 Cor. xvi. 12; perhaps, with Mr Lewin, that they were on the way from Corinth to Alexandria, and were the bearers of this letter to Titus.

This visit of 'an apostle' and 'a teacher,' and the hospitality to be exercised towards them by Titus, are to stimulate, St Paul adds, the zeal and liberality of the whole body of Christians, the Cretan Church.

diligently] Vulg. 'sollicite' Theod. Mops. Lat. 'velociter'; but the following clause 'that nothing be wanting unto them,' favours 'attention' rather than 'speed,' and implies provision for the journey as part of the sympathetic attendance; so in 3 Joh. 6 'set forward on their journey *worthily of God*,' i.e. with supplies worthy of their service to God, the following verses making this clear, 'we therefore as fellow Christians ought to give them hospitable support.'

14. *let ours also learn*] More clearly as R.V. **and let our people also learn.** Theod. Mops. excellently, because Titus (as a poor person) could not be expected to do all, 'teach,' he says, 'your people to attend carefully to the support of their religious teachers.' St Paul quotes again half of the 'Faithful saying' of ver. 8, 'maintain good works,' and gives this as a most important and primary application of the general law for a practical Christian life, by adding 'for such necessary wants'

15 works for necessary uses, that they be not unfruitful. All that are with me salute thee. Greet them that love us in the faith. Grace *be* with you all. Amen.

¶ It was written to Titus, ordained the first bishop of the church of the Cretians, from Nicopolis of Macedonia.

for the needful wants of the ministry. The article requires this interpretation; these well-known and existing wants that are inevitable, when your ministers have to spend their time in saving, not money, but men's souls. For the usage of this word (in the plural) always as 'wants,' not 'uses,' cf. Acts xx. 34 'these hands ministered unto my necessities,' Rom. xii. 13 'communicating to the necessities of the saints.'

This passage recording the visit of an 'apostle' and a 'teacher,' and dwelling on the support of the ministry, finds a striking illustration in the *Teaching of the Twelve Apostles*, which dwells with especial prominence on the work of travelling and resident *apostles*, and *prophets*, and *teachers*, and on their support. It is noticeable too how in the twenty or thirty years which probably elapsed between this Epistle and the '*Teaching*' the large-hearted law here laid down had been liable to abuse, and required guarding. Three out of the sixteen chapters, xi., xii., xiii., are occupied with this subject. See Introduction, pp. 22—24.

15. Closing Salutation.

15. *All that are with me salute thee*] The companions of his journey or sojourn, cf. Gal. i. 2; Col. iv. 7—14. They are not specified and would be changing, as his needs and their feelings changed, cf. 2 Tim. iv. 9—12.

Greet them that love us in the faith] Rather: **salute them that love us in faith,** 'in faith,' as 1 Tim. i. 2 'my true child in faith,' i.e. spiritually, where see note. The phrase marks the gradual crystallising of the word 'faith,' somewhat as 'our Christian friends' has become a modern formula: cf. Tit. i. 4 'in communion of faith.'

Grace be *with you all. Amen*] The shortest form of the Benediction, the fullest being at the end of 2 Cor. 'An inclusive benediction that comprehends the *episcopus* and those committed to his oversight, Titus and all the faithful in Crete.' Bp Ellicott; who rejects the final 'Amen,' as at the end of both the letters to Timothy, though the MS. authority for it is stronger here, on the ground that accidental omission seems less probable than insertion. The end recalls the beginning; the Apostle, whose sphere of ministry was the faith and full knowledge of the Cretan Christians, prays for 'grace' to be with them 'all.'

The subscription given above has no sufficient authority; see note at end of 1 Tim.; and for 'Macedonia' note above, *v.* 12. The best supported subscription here is simply To Titus.

APPENDIX.

A. CHRISTOLOGY OF THE PASTORAL EPISTLES.

IN this Note the attempt is made to arrange systematically the references scattered through Liddon's *Divinity of our Lord*, but to retain mainly his own description of the passages, to supplement them where necessary, and to combine with them the statements of Pearson *On the Creed*.

I. The distinguishing character of these epistles is the stress they lay upon the vital distinction between heresy and orthodoxy.

The true faith is to the soul what the most necessary conditions of health are to the body; it is
'the healthful doctrine,' 1 Tim. i. 10; Tit. i. 9, ii. 1;
'healthful speech,' Tit. ii. 8, 2 Tim. i. 13.

The orthodox teaching is styled
'the good doctrine,' 'the doctrine,' 1 Tim. iv. 6, vi. 1.

Any deviation is self-condemned as being such;
'not to teach a different doctrine,' 1 Tim. i. 3, vi. 3.

The heretic prefers his own self-chosen private way to the universally received doctrine;
'heretical,' Tit. iii. 10;
he is to be cut off after two admonitions from the communion of the Church;
'a man that is heretical after a second admonition refuse,' Tit. iii. 10,
on the ground that he
'is perverted and sinneth, being self-condemned,' Tit. iii. 10.

Heresy is spoken of by turns as a crime and a misfortune;
'made shipwreck concerning the faith,' 1 Tim. i. 19;
'have been led astray from the faith,' 1 Tim. vi. 10;
'concerning the truth have erred,' 2 Tim. ii. 18.

Deeper error is characterised in severer terms;
'giving heed to seducing spirits and doctrines of devils...branded in their own conscience,' 1 Tim. iv. 1, 2.
Cf. 2 Tim. iii. 8, iv. 4.

Heresy is said to destroy the spiritual body like a gangrene;
'their word will eat as doth a gangrene,' 2 Tim. ii. 17.

II. What then *is* orthodoxy in these epistles?

To hold 'the Faith,' the objective body of truth, 1 Tim. i. 19, iii. 9, iv. 1, 6, v. 8, vi. 10, 21; 2 Tim. iii. 8, iv. 7; Tit. i. 13, ii. 2.

And the Church is

'the pillar and ground of the truth,' 1 Tim. iii. 15.

This truth, which the Church supports, is already embodied in

'the pattern of sound words which thou hast heard from me,' 1 Tim. iii. 15.

Cf. 1 Tim. i. 15, iii. 16; 2 Tim. ii. 12; Tit. iii. 4.

To hold 'the Faith' is to rest the soul upon a support which guarantees its safety; that support is Christ;

'believe *on* him unto eternal life,' 1 Tim. i. 16.

To hold 'the Faith' is to have entered into an atmosphere which encircles and protects and fosters the growth of the spiritual life; that atmosphere is Christ;

'the faith which is *in* Christ Jesus,' 1 Tim. iii. 13; 2 Tim. iii. 15.

To hold 'the Faith' is to accept God's salvation by the washing of regeneration and renewing of the Holy Ghost

'*through* Jesus Christ our Saviour,' Tit. iii. 5.

To hold 'the Faith' is to believe in Christ's Person as being the Centre of the New Dispensation;

'He was believed on in the world,' 1 Tim. iii. 16.

To hold 'the Faith' is to believe Christ's own guarantee of the truth of the whole object-matter of faith;

'I know him whom I have believed, and I am persuaded that he is able to guard that which he hath committed unto me against that day,' 2 Tim. i. 12.

To hold 'the Faith' is to have all hope, all trust, all love, all life, centred in Christ;

'Christ Jesus our hope,' 1 Tim. i. 1;

'trust and love which is in Christ Jesus,' 2 Tim. i. 13;

'live godly in Christ Jesus,' 2 Tim. iii. 12.

III. Who then is the Christ? What is the body of truth about the Person of Christ, indicated in these epistles?

(1) He is 'perfect man, of a reasonable soul and human flesh subsisting';

'*himself* man, Christ Jesus,' 1 Tim. ii. 5, 6.

What makes up the complete human being, the 'perfect man'? Human nature is divided sometimes into body, soul and spirit, sometimes into body and soul; in the latter case 'soul' includes both the natural affections and emotions and desires, and also the reason and will and conscience.

'He who was manifested in the flesh was justified in the spirit,' 1 Tim. iii. 16.

For a fuller understanding of these brief phrases of the earliest creed, compare the general statements of Holy Scripture respecting these elements of Christ's human nature, as thus given by Bp Pearson (*On the Creed*, Art. iii.); "As then man consisteth of two different parts, body and soul, so doth Christ: He assumed a body, at His conception, of the blessed Virgin. 'Forasmuch as the children are partakers of flesh and blood, he also himself likewise took part of the same' (Heb. ii. 14). The verity of His body stands upon the truth of His nativity, and the actions and passions of His life show the nature of His flesh.... And, certainly, if the Son of God would vouchsafe to take the frailty of our flesh, He would not omit the nobler part, our soul, without which He could not be man. For 'Jesus increased in wisdom and stature' (Luke ii. 52); one in respect of His body, the other of His soul. Wisdom belongeth not to the flesh, nor can the knowledge of God, which is infinite, increase; He then whose knowledge did improve together with His years must have a subject proper for it, which was no other than a human soul. This was the seat of His finite understanding and directed will, distinct from the will of His Father, and consequently of His divine nature; as appeareth by that known submission, 'Not my will, but thine, be done' (Luke xxii. 42). This was the subject of those affections and passions which so manifestly appeared in Him: nor spake He any other than a proper language when before His suffering He said, 'My soul is exceeding sorrowful, even unto death' (Matt. xxvi. 38). This was it which on the cross, before the departure from the body, He recommended to the Father, teaching us in whose hands the souls of the departed are: for 'when Jesus had cried with a loud voice, he said, Father, into thy hands I commend my spirit: and having said thus he gave up the ghost' (Luke xxiii. 46). And as His death was nothing else but the separation of the soul from His body; so the life of Christ as man did consist in the conjunction and vital union of that soul with the body. So that He which was 'perfect God, was also perfect man, of a reasonable soul and human flesh subsisting.' Which is to be observed and asserted against the ancient heretics (Arians and Apollinarians), who taught that Christ assumed human flesh, but that 'the Word,' or His Divinity, was unto that body in the place of an informing soul."

Again, He is a 'sinless man';

> 'was justified (lit. was proved righteous) in his spirit,' 1 Tim. iii. 16.

Compare 2 Cor. v. 21, and especially Rom. v. 18, 19, where the corresponding noun is used, 'one lifelong mighty act of righteousness.'

Further, He is more than 'a sinless man'; He is 'man.' 'Christ's manhood is representative of the human race...and it is in virtue of His manhood that He is our Mediator, our Redeemer.'

> 'One mediator also between God and men, himself man, Christ Jesus, who gave himself a ransom for all,' 1 Tim. ii. 5.

'Great stress indeed does St Paul lay upon the Manhood of Christ as the instrument of His mediation between earth and heaven, as the channel through which intellectual truth and moral strength descend from God into the souls of men, as the Exemplar wherein alone human nature has recovered its ideal beauty, as entering a sphere wherein the Sinless One could offer the perfect world-representing sacrifice of a truly obedient will.'

(2) He is 'perfect God,' 'very God of very God.' 'Jesus Christ, the Saviour and Messias, is the true, proper and natural Son of God, begotten of the substance of the Father,...the only Son of God, the true Jehovah, who hath that being which is originally and eternally of itself,

and on which all other beings do essentially depend' (Pearson, *On the Creed*, Art. ii.).

He is the Source of ministerial power;

'putting me into the ministry,' 1 Tim. i. 12;

'a good minister of Jesus Christ,' 1 Tim. iv. 6.

Cf. 1 Tim. v. 11; 2 Tim. ii. 3.

He is the Sun and Centre point of orthodox truth; moral, social and religious;

'the words of our Lord Jesus Christ,' 1 Tim. vi. 3;

'the Lord shall give thee understanding,' 2 Tim. ii. 7.

He is the Redeemer of the whole world, not as the humanitarian heresies would suggest of races or classes;

'who gave himself a ransom for all,' 1 Tim. ii. 6.

He is the Awarder of indulgence and mercy and judgment;

'that in me as chief might Jesus Christ shew all his longsuffering,' 1 Tim. i. 16; cf. ver. 13.

Cf. 2 Tim. i. 18; iv. 1, 8, 14.

He is invisibly present among angelic attendants;

'I charge thee in the sight of God and Christ Jesus and the elect angels,' 1 Tim. v. 21.

Cf. vi. 13; 2 Tim. iv. 1.

He is ready at hand to aid in trouble;

'out of them all the Lord delivered me,' 2 Tim. iii. 11.

Cf. iv. 17, 18, ii. 1, 10.

He is the object of prayer and thanksgiving;

'I thank Christ Jesus our Lord,' 1 Tim. i. 12;

'them that call on the Lord,' 2 Tim. ii. 22.

He was pre-existent before the Incarnation;

'who was manifested in the flesh,' 1 Tim. iii. 16;

'Christ Jesus came into the world,' 1 Tim. i. 15.

He has the same titles as God the Father. In Ep. to Titus the epithet 'Saviour,' given four times to God the Father, is given four times also to Jesus Christ; one of these passages, according to the truer rendering, expressly speaks of Him as God;

'our great God and Saviour Jesus Christ,' Tit. ii. 13.

Cf. Tit. i. 3, 4, ii. 10, 11, 13, iii. 4, 6.

IV. We see then in conclusion from these epistles, as is plainly to be seen from all his former letters, that 'St Paul insists with particular earnestness upon the truth of our Lord's real humanity.' But we see equally that 'to suppose that he believed Jesus Christ to be merely a man is a paradox which could be maintained by no careful reader of his epistles. Take St Paul's doctrine as a whole and it must be admitted to centre in One who is at once and truly God as well as Man.'

And at the same time, in spite of the dogmatic form in which the truth is to be held, and along with all the resulting moral counsels of 'good works,' St Paul's fervour of thought and expression makes us understand fully, no less from his latest letters than from the rest, that, as Bp Lightfoot puts it (*Philippians*, p. viii.), 'though the Gospel is capable of doctrinal exposition, though it is eminently fertile in moral results, yet its substance is neither a dogmatic system nor an ethical code, but a Person and a Life.'

B. JUDAISTIC CHRISTIANITY.

IT is only right to draw attention to the important view taken by Dr Hort of the passages in these Epistles bearing on heresy and false teaching. See his Lectures on 'Judaistic Christianity' delivered in A.D. 1887, but published since his death, in A.D. 1894. Bp Lightfoot's opinions on the subject as published in *Biblical Essays* in A.D. 1893 were expounded in his Lectures of A.D. 1865, attended by the present writer, but are in entire harmony with the line followed in the Introduction to the Colossians, A.D. 1875. In contrast to the view he takes (see above, Introd. pp. 46—53) Dr Hort sees *only* Judaistic teaching in the false doctrine condemned. This will be seen from the following interpretations given by him of some of the chief phrases.

'*To teach a different doctrine*,' 1 Tim. i. 3, vi. 3, he explains as merely 'unfitness and irrelevance of teaching,' and compares Heb. xiii. 9.

'*Fables and endless genealogies*' he describes as merely 'the rank growth of legend respecting the patriarchs and other heroes of early Mosaic history, which had grown up among the Jews both in Hebrew and Greek before the time of the Apostles...included in the Haggada, extant still in the Talmud, much more in the Midrash, partly also in Philo and Josephus; we can perhaps form a still better conception of it from the Book of Jubilees (extant only in translations) the legends of which are strung upon a basis of numbered generations.'

'*Oppositions*,' 1 Tim. vi. 20, he explains as only 'the endless contrasts of decisions founded on endless distinctions which played so large a part in the casuistry of the Scribes as interpreters of the Law; it would thus designate frivolities of what was called the Halacha as the 'myths' and 'genealogies' designate frivolities of the other great department of Jewish learning, the Haggada.'

'*Knowledge which is falsely so called*,' 1 Tim. vi. 20, he defines as 'the barren traditionalism which 'the lawyers' called 'knowledge' and of which they boasted themselves to have the key; cf. Luke xi. 52...the distinctive lore of a class of canonists and casuists' which 'lies behind the familiar exclamation "this multitude which *knoweth* not the law" are accursed.'

Dr Hort thus thinks, with Weiss, that the duty laid on Timothy and Titus is not that of refuting deadly errors, but of keeping themselves clear, and warning others to keep clear, of barren and mischievous trivialities usurping the office of religion. But surely this is to neglect or minimise the force and bearing of the many weighty passages set out in the previous note (Appendix A), and which deal with much more vital and solemn questions than need be, if mere 'barren and mischievous trivialities' were alone in question. If it were not for this, the meaning of the words and phrases might be sufficiently exhausted by the Jewish usages quoted. Neither is it contended that the words have any full philosophic technicality, for which contemporary evidence should exist; but that they are the old Jewish phrases, with some of their old meaning, but with a new oriental meaning also, to express the new oriental speculations; which is the earlier literary stage, to be followed later by the defined technical use. And Dr Hort admits Cerinthus to have flourished at a date not more than 25 years later, as 'a Judaistic Christian at last, if indeed he can rightly be called a Christian who was at the same time in the conventional sense a Gnostic.' See Appendix I (3).

C. THE CHRISTIAN MINISTRY.

THE following passages from Bp Lightfoot's essay, *Philippians*, pp. 264—6, give clearly his conclusions on some points connected with the Christian ministry.

'According to the broader meaning of the sacerdotal office the priest may be defined as one who represents God to man, and man to God. It is moreover indispensable that he should be called by God, for no man "taketh this honour to himself." The Christian ministry satisfies both these conditions. The threefold ministry can be traced to Apostolic direction; and short of an express statement we can possess no better assurance of a Divine appointment or at least a Divine sanction....The Christian minister is God's ambassador to men: he is charged with the ministry of reconciliation; he unfolds the will of heaven; he declares in God's name the terms on which pardon is offered; and he pronounces in God's name the absolution of the penitent....Throughout his office is representative not vicarial....Again, the Christian minister is the representative of man to God—of the congregation primarily, of the individual indirectly as a member of the congregation. The alms, the prayers, the thanksgivings of the community are offered through him.... His acts are not his own but the acts of the congregation.'

Compare also his latest judgment on the organisation of the early Church given in *The Apostolic Fathers*, Pt. II. vol. i. p. 390.

'The whole subject has been investigated by me in an Essay on the Christian Ministry: and to this I venture to refer my readers for further information. It is there shewn if I mistake not that though the N.T. itself contains as yet no direct and indisputable notices of a localized Episcopate in the Gentile Churches, as distinguished from the moveable Episcopate exercised by Timothy in Ephesus and by Titus in Crete, yet there is satisfactory evidence of its development in the later years of the Apostolic age; that this development was not simultaneous and equal in all parts of Christendom; that it is more especially connected with the name of S. John; and that in the early years of the second century the Episcopate was widely spread and had taken firm root, more especially in Asia Minor and Syria. If the evidence for its extension in the regions east of the Ægean at this epoch be resisted, I am at a loss to understand what single fact relating to the history of the Christian Church during the first half of the second century can be regarded as established; for the testimony in favour of this spread of the Episcopate is more abundant and more varied than for any other institution or event during this period, so far as I recollect.'

We may add from *The Church and the Ministry*, pp. 265 sqq., some of Canon Gore's conclusions from his investigation of the Gospels and Epistles.

(1) *The Apostolate.* The Apostles are empowered by Christ and inspired by the Spirit as the primary witnesses of Christ's resurrection, stewards of the divine mysteries, ambassadors and ministers of the effected reconciliation of man to God. Their function is the ministry of the word. It involves also a ministry of grace. The Apostles appear as the ordainers of an official clergy in the Churches, by communicating to them through the laying on of hands an empowering gift of the Holy Ghost.

(2) The apostolate is not a localized but a 'general ministry of the word.' We recognise an extension of the apostolic function in some of its main features (*a*) to prophets, (*b*) to apostolic men like Timothy and Titus, known probably as 'teachers' and 'evangelists,' who, without as far as we know, sharing miraculous power had yet imparted to them by the laying on of apostolic hands what was essentially apostolic authority to guard the faith, to found and rule Churches, to ordain and discipline the clergy.

(3) *Presbyter-bishops.* Under this general ministry of the Apostles and their fellow-workers we find a local ministry of 'presbyters' or 'bishops' who are appointed by the Apostles and ordained by the laying on of hands to share in some particular community the pastorate and stewardship which Christ instituted in His Church. They are the local ministers of discipline—this being the function which was attached of old to the Jewish presbyterate—but they are as well the 'superintendents' in general of local affairs, the administrators of the Churches; and as the Churches are spiritual societies, so their function is spiritual. These local pastors are called also 'teachers' in the Epistle to the Ephesians, and we have no reason to suppose that they were not from the first, in a sense, 'ministers of the word' though in subordination to apostles, prophets and teachers. Again, since the earliest sub apostolic writers speak of 'the offering of the gifts' or the ministry of the Eucharist as the special function of the 'bishop,' and St James presents the presbyters to us as exercising a ministry of healing, both physical and spiritual, we need not hesitate to regard them as having been from the first the ministers of the sacraments.

(4) *Deacons.* We are also presented with a subordinate ministry of deacons. If their primary function was to administer alms, yet they are also presented to us as baptizing and teaching—at least when they were endowed with qualifying gifts—though probably this function did not belong to their office. Besides we find a female 'diaconate' as well as instances of 'prophetesses' in the Church, who however do not seem to have exercised any public ministry. We also hear of other leading Christians who specially addicted themselves to works of mercy and received a corresponding authority.

D. ST PAUL AND CONSCIENCE.

FOLLOWING up the Interpretation of 'Conscience' given in the Note on 1 Tim. i. 5, as drawn from its derivation, we may add the Definitions given on the side of moral philosophy by Bp Butler and Dr Whewell, and the Exemplification furnished in St Paul's own case.

Bp Butler in his *Dissertation on Virtue*, speaks of 'a moral faculty; whether called *conscience, moral reason, moral sense*, or *divine reason;* whether considered as a perception of the understanding, or as a sentiment of the heart; or, which seems the truth, as including both.' And Dr Whewell's teaching agrees with this in describing Conscience as 'the Faculty or Habit of referring our acts to a moral standard; as an authority not ultimate or supreme, but depending, for its validity, upon its coincidences with the supreme rule; the supreme rule being one which requires the exercise of reason for its discovery and application.' See *Elements of Morality*, 3rd ed., Art. 262 &c. Butler's phrase 'the natural *supremacy* of Conscience' over Appetite, Desire and Affection (see his *Second Sermon on Human Nature*) should be understood as 'the natural *authority*'; since 'Conscience has not, according to his own view, a *supreme* authority, but is herself subject to the Supreme rule which enjoins all virtue and duty and which is in reality the Law of God. Hence arises the correctness of the two apparently inconsistent maxims:—that *to act against one's conscience is always wrong;* but that *to act according to one's conscience does not ensure being right.* For the Conscience may be darkened or misled or perverted in various ways, and so may lead men into error and even into crime; but still Conscience, however erroneous, is superior to mere appetite and desire, and is in the right when she controls those inferior springs of action' (Whewell).

In A.D. 58, some 20 years after his conversion, St Paul began his speech before the Sanhedrim: 'I have lived in all good conscience (whether blinded or enlightened) before God until this day' (Acts xxiii. 1). He said to Felix, 'Herein do I *exercise myself* (by an open strict enquiring intelligence) to have always a conscience void of offence toward God and toward men' (Acts xxiv. 16). Two years later he tells Festus and Agrippa of his persecuting days, 'I thought that I *ought* to do many things contrary to the name of Jesus.' The painful enlightenment of his blinded conscience he refers to by quoting Christ's own word 'it is hard for thee to kick against the goad.' The following his conscience then on the right path he speaks of as being 'not disobedient to the heavenly vision.' See Acts xxvi. 9—19.

Nine years passed; but, as John Bunyan says of him, 'Paul was like the nightingale with his breast against the thorn.' He begins his last letter with nearly the same words, 'I thank God whom I serve from my forefathers with pure conscience' (2 Tim. i. 3). In their light we see the force of what he had said the year before in 1 Tim. i. 13, that 'blasphemer, persecutor, injurious' as he had been, yet he obtained mercy *because* he 'did it *ignorantly* in unbelief.' Even then he had not disobeyed his conscience, though of its blinded state with the resulting sin he speaks with the deepest self-condemnation and penitence. It is

30 years since his conversion, but he has an abiding sense of being still 'the chief of sinners.' Conscience in itself he did not regard as a sufficient standard: compare 1 Cor. xv. 9; Gal. i. 13. Howson, who draws this subject out as above at some length in his *Character of St Paul*, pp. 97—107, quotes Bp Sanderson, 'the error was in his understanding: that erroneous judgment poisoned all,' and adds, 'in what degrees the error was caused by want of candid enquiry into the facts of Christianity, by prejudice in the study of the Old Testament, by the pride which sought to satisfy God's law by mere legal obedience and by the indulgence of the passion of bigotry, we cannot ascertain.'

We do not wonder that from such a personal experience should come the last repeated earnest warnings and appeals; 'the end of the commandment is charity out of a good conscience' (1 Tim. i. 5), 'hold fast faith and a good conscience, which some having put away have made shipwreck' (ver. 19), 'the mystery of the faith in a pure conscience' (1 Tim. iii. 9), 'consciences seared with a hot iron' (1 Tim. iv. 2), 'mind and conscience defiled' (Tit. i. 15).

E. THE FAITHFUL SAYINGS.

THESE occur five times in these Epistles; and if, according to the view taken in the Notes, the formula refers in all cases to the sentences following, we may briefly describe them according to their subject-matter as way-marks of the earliest Christianity, sign-posts of 'The Way' (Acts ix. 2), witness-stones of Him Who is 'The Way' (Joh. xiv. 6).

Thus we have:—

(1) Christ's Coming—the way of sin's forgiveness: 1 Tim. i. 15.
(2) Christ's Ministry—the way of noble service: 1 Tim. iii. 1.
(3) Christ's Life—the way of spiritual progress: 1 Tim. iv. 9.
(4) Christ's World—the way of honourable work: Tit. iii. 8.
(5) Christ's Strength—the way of successful suffering: 2 Tim. ii. 11.

Dr Cox (*Expositions*, 3rd Series, p. 231) gives a clear account of the probable origin of these Sayings as due to the teaching of the New Testament Prophets; and of the special force arising from the circumstances of the time, and from the truths enshrined, which may well have been at work, to make them win their way as Faithful Sayings.

These accounts may be summarized briefly.

"These Faithful Sayings are in all probability *prophetic* sayings, sayings first uttered by the prophets of the Church (cf. 1 Cor. xii. 28, 'God hath set some in the church, first apostles, secondly *prophets*, thirdly teachers'). Obviously St Paul quotes them from some other lips than his own, adducing them in proof or confirmation of his own words. Obviously too from the very tone in which he cites them, they were well known and widely approved, sayings which carried authority in many or even in all the churches of the time;—words which were found to be so apt and simple and terse that they spread from church to church and were tossed from lip to lip, as proverbs are at this day, until they became 'household words' at least in the 'household of faith.' And if we remember that these sayings are found only in the Pastoral Epistles, and that these Epistles were not written till more than 30 years after the Day of Pentecost, i.e. after the Christian prophets had commenced their work, we shall at least admit that there had been ample time for some of their sayings to have crept into common use, to have won general acceptance as true, trustworthy and most happy expressions of the fundamental truths of the Gospel."

(1) Christ's Coming—the way of sin's forgiveness:—

1 Tim. i. 15. *It is a faithful saying and worthy of all acceptation that Christ Jesus came into the world to save sinners.*

"That 'Christ Jesus *came*—Christ Jesus *advented—into* the world' could be said of none but Him. For it implied that His coming, His advent, was a conscious and voluntary act, a self-determining effort of His will. It implies His pre-existence in some other world;—the eternal being and the incarnation of the Divine Word and Son, God manifest in the flesh. For Who is this that comes into the world, not by the decree of a Will higher than His own, but by His own act and deed? Who is this if not God Himself?

"No doubt this Saying won universal acceptance in the Church and was commended as a faithful saying by St Paul, partly because it thus met the test by which the Apostles had demanded that all 'spirits' and all utterances should be tried. But we may well believe that the Apostolic Church loved and adopted it not so much for its opening as for its closing words, that Christ Jesus *came into the world* was much; but that He came into the world *to save sinners*;—God in Christ came into the world, not, as a Jew would have expected of Him, to succour and reward His faithful servants, not, as a Greek would be prepared to believe, to indulge His caprice and lust, or aid and rescue His devotees;—but *to save sinners*, to bless His enemies, to redeem 'this people that is accursed,' and 'the foolish and wretched herd, debarred from wisdom'—this was the pathetic surprise, *this* the mystery of grace, which broke men down into tears of penitence and love and rapture."

(2) Christ's Ministry—the way of noble service:—

1 Tim. iii. 1. *It is a faithful saying, If a man desire the office of a bishop, he desireth a good work.*

"That which gave vogue and acceptance in the primitive Church to the words 'if a man seek the pastorate, he craves an honest occupation' or an occupation morally honourable and beautiful, was the fact that in that early time, surrounded by an hostile world, the pastors of the Christian congregations filled an arduous and perilous position. The post of danger is the post of honour. And they were exposed to danger of many kinds. The first to suffer, when all suffered for the Faith, they had to risk, and commonly to endure the loss of all things dear to the natural heart....Any pastor who scruples to call his work an honest occupation or to confess that it can bring no honour to him save as he closely dedicates himself to its duties, delights in them and throws himself into them, lacks the mind that was in Christ, Who 'emptied Himself,' and humbled Himself to manhood, to death, to the cross. It is to *a work* that he has been called; and by his work he will be judged. The more profuse and lofty his claims, the sorrier is the figure he presents, if his toil and pains do not correspond with his claims."

(3) Christ's Life—the way of spiritual progress:—

1 Tim. iv. 9. *It is a faithful saying and worthy of all acceptation, For therefore we both labour and wrestle on, because we have our hope set on the living God, who is the Saviour of all men, specially of the faithful.*

"The God Who had long been known as the Redeemer of the Jews was now revealed to faith as the Redeemer of the whole world. To men who had lived so separate a life as the Jewish members of the Church, and had begun to feel that their singularity and isolation was a barrier and a hindrance, if also a privilege; to its Gentile members, who had been divided from each other by rival divinities, by different customs and creeds, and who were beginning to suspect that 'Great Pan' with all the other *immortals* 'was dead'—the conviction that there was but *one* God for all men—a *living* God, over Whom time and the changeful thoughts of men had no power—a *Saviour* Who could really help them where they most needed help by taking away that brooding sense of sin and that awful looking for of judgment, by which the prophetic soul of the world was then oppressed; this Catholic and reconciling conviction could not fail to be most welcome to every generous and aspiring spirit, whether of Jew or Gentile.

"St Paul's application of this Saying is plain in connexion with his exhortation to Timothy to 'exercise'—*gymnasticise*—himself unto godliness. For this, viz. to attain the godliness he had been enforcing, those who have this hope in God 'toil and wrestle,' as in the gymnasium, labour even to weariness and strive even to agony. This is the worth of 'godliness,' its power to build up, to train and to develop the energies of the spiritual life."

For the incidental bearing of the passage in its closing phrases on the 'larger hope' see Appendix.

(4) Christ's World—the way of honourable work:—

Tit. iii. 8. *It is a faithful saying and these things I will that thou affirm confidently, that they which have believed in God may be careful to maintain good works, honest or honourable occupations and callings.*

"What gave the Saying its authority and acceptance in the Apostolic Church was the feeling that life, not words, was wanted; in the Rabbinical schools Judaism had run to mere words which had no influence on life and conduct; in the academies of the Sophists philosophy had also run into mere words which bred only intellectual questionings and strifes; pure examples were wanted, not windy speculations, loving and helpful service, not new theories of ethics. And the Church acted on the faithful saying. For hardly 40 years after St Paul wrote this epistle, the accomplished Roman statesman Pliny wrote a letter in which he gave the earliest description which has come down to us from a non-Christian source of the very Churches which the Apostle had founded; how they assembled on certain stated days before it was light, and repeated in alternate verses with one another a hymn or form of prayer to Christ as to some God, *binding themselves by a sacrament*—not for any criminal purpose but—*to abstain from fraud, theft and adultery, from falsifying* their word, and from retaining what did not belong to them."

(5) Christ's Strength—the way of successful suffering:—

2 Tim. ii. 11—13. *It is a faithful saying: For if we died with him, we shall also live with him; if we endure, we shall also reign with him: if we should deny him, he also will deny us; if we are faithless, he abideth faithful, for he cannot deny himself.*

"This Faithful Saying fits into St Paul's general course of thought. The husbandman, the athlete, the soldier, Timothy, Paul himself, all help to illustrate it and prove it worthy of all acceptation. No Cross, no Crown. To the early disciples just redeemed from ignorance, superstition and vice, the substance of the Gospel thus expressed in terse, winning and memorable forms would be most precious. *We* forget how large, impressive and wonderful a fact the death of the Cross must have been to men who might any day be hung on a Cross like that of Christ, simply because they believed on His name. And the words 'we died with Him' would also recall the most sacred and momentous act of their lives. Baptism was to them far more than it is or can be to us. To them it was putting on Christ in face of a hostile world; it was avowing a faith for which they had to risk the loss of all things, even of life itself. Again, how could they be exhorted to endure and not recall all that was most heroic and yet most tender and pathetic in the Man of Sorrows, all that they might have to bear for His sake? Any one of their assemblies might be broken up by the mob or the legionaries. At any moment an envious rival, a morose servant, a delator who lived by his base trade, might denounce them to the Roman magistrates. They might be called to fight with gladiators or wild beasts in the arenas; or to see wife, sister, child torn or trampled to death on its sands. And what if there were some who shrank even then, as afterwards, from leaving all for Christ's sake and the Gospel? What if with trembling hand and averted eyes they should throw a few grains of incense on the altar of the reigning Cæsar and thus renounce Christ and salvation?

"A Saying such as this would be true and faithful indeed to such lives; would strike the profoundest chords in the memories and hearts of men to whom these facts, these scenes, these prospects, were the very stuff of daily experience, and on which, as they held, their very life and the life of the world depended."

F. ST PAUL AND THE LARGER HOPE.

DR ISAAC BARROW, the famous Master of Trinity College, Cambridge, has four well-known Sermons on Universal Redemption, in which, taking 1 Tim. iv. 10 for his text, he adopts the position maintained by the *Apology* of Robert Barclay "(1) that God, Who out of His infinite love sent His Son our Lord Jesus Christ into the world, Who tasted death for every man, *hath given to every man*, whether Jew or Gentile, Turk or Scythian, Indian or barbarian, of whatsoever nation, country or place, a certain day or time of visitation, during which day or time it is possible for them to be saved and to partake of the fruits of Christ's death. (2) That for this end God hath communicated and given unto every man a measure of the light of His own Son, a measure of grace, or a measure of the Spirit. (3) That God, in and by this light and seed, invites, calls, exhorts and strives with every man, in order to save him, which, as it is received and not resisted, works the salvation of all, even of those who are ignorant of the sufferings and death of Christ and of Adam's fall."

He sums up, in reference to the passage in 1 Tim. iv. 11;—"Since we are plainly taught that our Lord is the Saviour of all men, and it is consequent thence that He hath procured grace sufficiently capacifying all men to obtain salvation, we need not perplex the business or obscure so apparent a truth by debating how that grace is imparted, or by labouring overmuch in reconciling the dispensation thereof with other dispensations of Providence" (Serm. 72).

And again;—"The undertakings and performances of our Saviour did respect all men, as the common works of nature do; as the air we breathe in, as the sun which shineth on us; the which are not given to any man particularly, but to all generally, not as a proper enclosure, but as a common; they are indeed mine, but not otherwise than as they belong to all men" (Serm. 74).

See further Plumptre, *The Spirits in Prison*, p. 178.

A different interpretation of the passage is put forward by Prof. Birks (*Victory of Divine Goodness*, p. 190):—

"The Apostle, again, declares of the living God, that 'he is the Saviour of all men, specially of them that believe.' This name of God will be most fully and completely revealed in the future happiness and glory of believers alone. But He is also 'the Saviour of all men.' Can this apply to temporal benefits alone, which will wholly cease, and are to be wholly followed by total absolute destruction and ruin? Can it be satisfied with conditional benefits made wholly void through the perverseness of the sinner? How will this agree with our Lord's reasoning on another Divine title 'the God of Abraham, Isaac and Jacob'? Such a name, He then teaches, implies no transient, but an enduring relation. Here, too, it would seem that the same law of reasoning must apply. Unbelievers are not saved from judgment, from righteous punishment, from the second death, from shame and everlasting contempt, from everlasting fire. Is there any sense in which they may still be saved, consistently with the inflexible truth of these solemn messages of God? They will be saved from bodily corruption 'for as in Adam all die, even so in Christ shall all be made alive.' They will be saved from the curse of hopeless vanity, from that first death, in which the creature is self-ruined and God Himself is not glorified, but for ever blasphemed. They will be saved from the abyss unfathomable and unsearchable in its depth and darkness, when 'death and hell are cast into the lake of fire.' Will they not also be saved from that utter hopeless misery, where no ray of light or comfort breaks in on the solitude of everlasting despair? Will they not be saved, in a strange mysterious sense, when the depth of their unchangeable shame and sorrow finds beneath it a still lower depth of Divine compassion, and the creature, in its most forlorn estate, is shut in by the vision of surpassing and infinite love?"

G. THE N.T. USE OF 'MYSTERY.'

THE derivation and classical usage of the word are explained in Note upon 1 Tim. iii. 9. A fuller understanding of what took place at the Eleusinian Mysteries will guide us in following the N.T. use of the phrase. Preller in his account of Eleusis and the Mysteries, p. 399 sqq. has summed up the performance as consisting of the following elements:—hymns, sacred dances, musical scenes, sudden apparitions, with solemn utterances and precepts to accompany them. He regards it as certain that the crowning and consummation of the whole celebration at Eleusis consisted in certain representations of a dramatic character, mysteries or miracle plays, which were acted in the sacred meeting-hall and which contained the revelations to be made to the initiated. 'A ceremony,' he adds, 'affects people by its symbolism, and each man interprets the symbolism according to the state of his heart and his belief. Of dogmatic teaching there was none at Eleusis; only pleasing sights to remain in the imagination, and short enigmatical sentences to be stored in the memory, all likely to recur to the mind at the critical moments of life, and whenever that state of nervous exaltation recurred which had existed when they were first received at Eleusis.'

Following this guidance we may trace in the N.T. use of the word 'mystery' (1) a narrower and (2) a wider conception of its meaning.

(1) The narrower conception seems to be found in the Gospels, the Revelation and the earlier usage of St Paul.

(2) The wider conception is limited to St Paul's later usage.

(1) We seem to have, as the proper idea connected with the word, *a symbol conveying a truth.*

(*a*) In the Synoptists, the successive parables, with different symbols, convey different aspects of the great truth of *the Spirituality of the New Kingdom.* The typical parable of the Sower is followed in each Gospel by our Lord's words 'unto you it is given to know the mysteries (St Mark 'the mystery') of the divine, the heavenly kingdom' (Matt. xiii. 11; Mk. iv. 11; Luke viii. 10).

(*b*) In the Revelation the symbol of 'seven stars' (i. 20) shews the present and continuing government of His Church by Christ; the symbol of 'seven trumpet-angels' (x. 7) points to the successive triumphs of the Church over sin; the symbol of 'Babylon, the woman, the beast' (xvii.

5, 7) points to the obstinate development of evil against the Church. In each case the word used of these symbols is 'mystery.'

(c) In St Paul's earliest writings we find the symbol of 'the lawless man' akin to the last passage quoted described as 'the mystery' (2 Thess. ii. 7). In the second group of writings we trace still the idea of the 'symbol' 'proclaiming to you the mystery of God—Jesus Christ the *crucifixus*' (1 Cor. ii. 1, 2), and again 'God's wisdom in a mystery—had they known it, they would not have crucified the Lord of glory' (ver. 7, 8). That is, Christ upon the Cross is the symbol of symbols, proclaiming the truth of truths, the Atonement.

Henceforth the word seems—for St Paul—to have passed over from the sign to the thing signified, from the symbol to the doctrine symbolised. But our ecclesiastical use of 'mystery' for 'sacrament' appears to be a survival of this narrower use where 'symbol' is still part of the notion of the word.

(2) We seem to trace in St Paul's very writing of his first letter to Corinth his passage from the narrower to the wider conception, from the half-concealing symbol and parable to *the wholly revealed truth and doctrine*. When we reach 1 Cor. iv. 1, we find him speaking of the doctrines of Christ generally as 'the mysteries of God' which he and other 'ministers of Christ' are 'dispensing' freely and fully, and so again of the N.T. prophets in xiii. 2 and xiv. 2 as 'speaking' 'all mysteries and all knowledge.' And lastly in xv. 51 he calls the particular doctrine of the 'new spiritual bodies' of which he is 'telling' them plainly 'a mystery.' So in the Epistle to the Romans, written almost immediately after, he calls the particular doctrine of the temporary fall of Israel a 'mystery' (Rom. xi. 25); while at the close of the same epistle (Rom. xvi. 25) he has the same name for the particular doctrine of the universality of the Gospel, or Christ's oneness with both Jews and Gentiles in His 'one body' the Church, which is now 'revealed' and 'manifested' far and wide. This use of 'mystery' bridges over the five years' interval before the writing of the Epistles to the Ephesians and Colossians which are filled entirely with this doctrine thus described (see Eph. vi. *passim*, Col. iv. *passim*). And the one possible exception to this meaning of the word throughout these letters Eph. v. 32 is more apparent than real. For the exact point of the 'mystery' there is the *completeness* of the union of Christ with His whole Church, no part being separated; after which analogy the marriage state is completely to unite husband and wife.

Five years more pass; and all these different doctrines and proclaimed mysteries are gathered up in the expressions now used in the Letter to Timothy where the singular word in 'the mystery of the faith' (1 Tim. iii. 9) and 'the mystery of godliness' (1 Tim. iii. 16) embraces 'the whole doctrine of Christ,' 'the historic Faith,' the creed of 'Christ the Life,' the life of 'Christ the Creed.'

The medieval use of 'mystery' in *mystery plays* appears to be a survival of St Paul's later use of the word in the wider conception. For they were representations, acted revelations (so to speak) of the Scripture story in its different parts and bearings.

H. PUDENS AND CLAUDIA.

THE late Dean Merivale, the author of the *History of the Romans*, gives the following reasonable estimate of the recent efforts made to throw light on these members of the Christian Church at Rome.

"The attempt has been made to identify the Pudens and Claudia, whose greetings are mentioned, 2 Tim. iv. 21, with persons of distinction in the city. Pudens, it is surmised, is the son of the Pudentinus, whose name is read together with his own in a well known British inscription at Chichester. This was the seat of a king Cogidubnus, who had attached himself to the gens of the Emperor Claudius and assumed his gentile designation. It is conjectured that this Claudius Cogidubnus may have had a daughter called after himself Claudia; that she may have married Pudens, and have eventually settled at Rome with him. These two suppositions granted, she may, very possibly, it is said, be the same Claudia who is complimented more than once by Martial as a British lady of great accomplishments, and the wife of a certain Pudens, a friend of his own. The dates of Martial's compositions are too uncertain to allow us to argue upon them one way or the other; but, at least, it must be remarked that the Pudens of the poet was a man of licentious morality, such as might pass indeed with little comment among men of the world at the time, but from which the Apostle would surely have turned with indignation. Another guess that the Claudia of the epistle was the daughter of the British hero Caractacus, brought up as a client of the emperor's during her father's captivity at Rome, is hardly less attractive, but this can only be regarded as at best an idle fancy, besides that it is liable to the same fatal objection as the former."

St Paul at Rome, p. 149.

I. THE CRETE OF ST PAUL.

THE story of the Crete of St Paul is the story of those 'white-marked' eventful years A.D. 33—70, when between Pentecost and the Fall of Jerusalem Crete gained the blessings of the Gospel and the Church. '*Cressa ne careat pulcra dies nota.*' The notices in the Acts and the Epistle to Titus gain in clearness and brightness, if we pass in review what is known otherwise of the natural features and products of the island, the history and character of its inhabitants, and their religious life.

(1) *Natural Features and Products.*

Physically Crete is the southernmost of the "Isles of Greece," being 'a prolongation of that mountain chain which breasts the waters at Cape Malea, with the island of Cythera interposed.' The inhabitants still use the name of St Paul's days and of previous historic and mythical times, *Kriti*; the name *Candia*, now in general use by foreigners, being the Italian form of *Khandax*, the Saracenic name of *Megalo-Kastron*, formerly Heracleum, the chief northern port. The island is 160 miles in length, a continuous mass of highland from 2000 to 5000 feet high running through its whole length, from the centre of which rise the three lofty peaks of Mt Ida (8,059 ft.), now called *Psilor-iti*, or 'the smoother wooded Ida,' and further west the White Mountains (8,081 ft.), still bearing the old name, *Leuca-Ori*, but called also now *Asprabuna*, 'the rougher heights.' The snow-clad summits of both these mountain heights have looked down for centuries before and since St Paul on very varied scenes of hill and valley, rock and plain, wood and water. As one consequence of this variety of climate, the natural fertility of Crete in old days was remarkable; according to Pliny (XXV. 8) everything grew better in Crete than elsewhere. Particular mention is made of the Cretan wines, and especially of the *passum* or raisin wine called 'sack' in Bekker's *Gallus*, p. 493, Eng. Trans. So Pliny (XIV. 9), 'Passum a Cretico Cilicium probatur et Africum,' and Juvenal (XIV. 270) 'pingue antiquae de litore Cretae Passum.' Martial (XIII. 106) calls this wine 'the poor man's *mulsum*' or 'honey-wine cup,' used by *bon vivants* at the beginning of banquets. All these Roman writers were living when St Paul was working in and writing to Crete. The repute of wine from Crete was not confined to the ancient world, but has apparently descended through the middle ages to our own day. We remember how the Duke of Clarence in A.D. 1478, being allowed to choose the mode of his death, chose that of being drowned in a butt of Malmsey wine; and Stanford's recent work, *Geography and Travel in Europe*, p. 321, informs us that 'the best wine is still made from grapes, in the district of *Malevesi*, near Candia, a district which gave its name to the famous *Malvoisie* or Malmsey.' Cf. Tit. i. 7, 8, 12; ii. 2, 3.

(2) *History and Character.*

The character of the Cretans as 'always liars' (Tit. i. 12) may have been originally won by the supreme magnificence of the claims made in their early myths. Minos, King of Gnossus, the early capital of Crete, the son and friend of Zeus, was their ideal ruler and lawgiver, lord of a navy that mastered the whole Ægean, who forced, they said, the proud Athenians to send him an annual tribute of seven youths and seven maidens, to be devoured in the legendary 'labyrinth' at Gnossus by the fabled man-bull, the Minotaur. In a cave on the western slope of Mt Ida they dared to shew the birthplace of Zeus himself; and they claimed too to possess the tomb of Kronos his sire, 'the father of gods and men'; while 'the Dorian invaders made Crete the headquarters of the worship of Apollo.' But this character must also have been sustained by the degeneracy from the Homeric traits of hardy, daring corsairs—the vikings of Greece, and from the Spartan principles of their early communities, into the isolated quarrelsomeness and turbulent license of the historic days of Epimenides (B.C. 600). The bickerings and fightings among themselves of the 'hundred cities' of Virgil and other writers, and their making common cause only when attacked from outside, from which the term *syncretism* was coined, were brought to an end some hundred and thirty years before St Paul's visits by Q. Metellus Creticus taking the island and attaching it to the Roman province of Cyrene, on the opposite coast. It remained in this connexion with Africa till the days of Trajan (A.D. 100), when it was more naturally united with Achaia and Macedonia.

A glimpse of the government of the island by Roman Cretarchs is given us 250 years after by an inscription on the walls of the theatre at Aphrodisias in Lycia, of date A.D. 357, which is given by Fellowes (*Lycia*, p. 304) and seems to breathe the spirit of the classical revival under Julian, against the recently-established State Christianity of Constantine, 'May fortune be favourable! For the good health and the safety and the honours and the victory and perpetual welfare of our lords Fl. Jul. Constantius, the pious the never-vanquished Augustus, and [Fl. Cl. Julianus], the most excellent and noble Caesar, Fl. Qu. Eros Monaxius, the most distinguished governor and one of the Cretarchae, has erected it on his own expense...for the splendid metropolis of the Tauropolitans, the relations of the Cretans.' If Fellowes' conjecture is correct, the name of Julian was erased, as that of an apostate, after his death by the Christians. Subsequently the island, after being held successively by the Arabs, the Greeks, and the Venetians, passed under the sway of the Turks, a sway against which the old turbulent independent spirit is frequently still asserting itself.

With all this change, the fashions and manners of the people have changed but little. 'Mr Pashley (*Trav.* vol. I. p. 245) has detected in the games and dances of modern Crete the tumblers and the old cyclic chorus of 3000 years ago. The dress of the peasant continues to resemble that of his ancestors; he still wears the boots described by Galen, and the short cloak, *Creticum*, mentioned by Eupolis and Aristophanes' (*Dict. Geog.*, s. voc.). We can realise from these particulars something more vividly of the life amid which St Paul and his lieutenant moved, and can appreciate the force of the Apostle's plea for plain practical exhortation. 'Naturally turbulent, the Cretans are to be constantly reminded of the duty of submission in all things right and good. Naturally ferocious, they are to be exhorted to meekness of word and deed towards all men. For even so God showed gentleness to us when we were living in foolish and disobedient error, the slaves of various passions, in a bitter atmosphere of reciprocal hatred' (Farrar, *Life of St Paul*, p. 828).

(3) *Religious Life.*

Looking back to the native religion of Crete, we trace a natural connexion with the Ophite form of the incipient Gnostic heresy sketched in the Introduction. 'There is an evident analogy between the religion of Crete and Phrygia; and the legendary Curetes and Idæan Dactyls are connected on the one hand with the orgiastic worship and on the other with the arts of Phrygia.' And again we see the naturalness of the Judaic character of the budding Gnosticism from the very early connexion formed between the Cretans and the Jews. Tacitus, himself a boy at Rome probably at the date of St Paul's martyrdom, bears witness to this in giving the following as one of the reputed traditions in the Roman world respecting the origin of the Jews:—'Some say that the Jews were fugitives from the island of Crete who settled on the nearest coast of Africa about the time when Saturn was driven from his throne by the power of Jupiter. They look for evidence in the name. There is a famous mountain in Crete called Ida; the neighbouring tribe, the

Idæi, came to be called Judæi by a barbarous lengthening of the national name' (*Hist.* v. 2, Church's Trans.). Among the historic notices we find mention made of Gortyna as the chief place of Jewish residence in Crete about B.C. 143; when 'the prudence and wisdom of Simon, the last of the Maccabæan brothers, gained for the Jews the active support of Rome' (Westcott, *Dict. Bib.* II. p. 166), and notices of this were sent to all the Jewish populations, among others '*to Gortyna and Cnidus and Cyprus and Cyrene*' (1 Macc. xv. 23). And again Philo reports the embassy of Jews to Caligula, A.D. 40, as speaking of the many Jews in Crete and all the larger islands of the Mediterranean (*Leg. ad Cai.* § 36). Cretan Jews were among the multitudes gathered in Jerusalem at Pentecost, A.D. 30; and they probably carried back to the island the first scanty message of the Gospel. We hear of no visit to Crete of apostle or evangelist till St Paul in A.D. 61 involuntarily reached the southern shores in the 'ship of Alexandria,' which, prevented by the Etesian winds from taking the direct course to the north of the island, steered past Cape Salmonè, the eastern promontory, and coasted half way along Crete as far as Fair Havens, which still is called by the same name. There the ship stayed some weeks apparently, till towards the beginning of October, waiting for a change of wind. It is possible, as Captain Pratt supposes, that St Paul may have used this breathing-time to preach to the natives, as the ruins of a church dedicated to St Paul are found on the ridge above the bay (Lewin, *Life of St Paul*, II. p. 192). And the mention of Lasæa, whose ruins were discovered in 1856, a few miles east of Fair Havens, perhaps suggests some action or intercourse beyond what the narrator has room to relate. An attempt was made at length, on the wind becoming favourable, to reach Phœnix, a safe harbour in all weathers, some 40 miles to the west, for the purpose of wintering there; but a sudden gale from the N.-E. coming down from the high ground of Crete between the lofty peaks of Mt Ida, swept the ship along some 25 miles to the little island of Clauda, and thence to St Paul's Bay, as it has been known ever since, at Malta. Such a visit, made under such critical circumstances as the narrative in Acts xxvii. indicates, may well have made St Paul determine, if he were spared and set at liberty, to bring his gospel to shores of which he had only so tantalising a glimpse.

That Christianity had been spreading in Crete for some time before St Paul's visit with Titus (see Int. p. 74), A.D. 64, and his subsequent letter (A.D. 66) seems probable from the fact that St Paul charges Titus 'to appoint elders *in every city*,' or 'city by city' (Tit. i. 5), implying that there were a considerable number already possessed of a Christian congregation and in need of supervision; and further from the stipulation, implying a Christianity of some standing, that the 'elder' or 'bishop' is to be the father of a family with children who are believers and orderly persons (Tit. i. 6); and again from the notice of heresies already existing among the Cretan Christians. There is teaching of a seriously erroneous kind, not merely the errors of ignorance or the misbelief of the newly-converted (Tit. i. 11—16 &c.). See Plummer, *Pastoral Epistles*, p. 212.

The Christian Church long continued to remember with veneration the ministry and work of Titus, as appears from Howson's note, *Life and Epistles of St Paul*, II. 475. 'The cathedral of Megalo-Castron, on the north of the island, was dedicated to him. His name was the watchword of the Cretans when they fought against the Venetians, who came under the standard of St Mark. The Venetians themselves when in the island seem to have transferred to him part of that respect, which, elsewhere, would probably have been manifested for Mark alone. During the celebration of several great festivals of the Church, the response of the Latin clergy of Crete, after the prayer for the Doge of Venice, was *Sancte Marce, tu nos adiuva*; but after that for the Duke of Candia, *Sancte Tite, tu nos adiuva*.'

The same Christian Church in Crete at the present day claims a share in the prayers and sympathies of Christendom, contending as it does feebly and imperfectly for 'the faith once delivered' by a Paul and a Titus against the dominant persecuting rule of the Moslem creed. The cave of Melidóni, on the western slope of Mt Ida, which is noticed above p. 177, and which is remarkable for the beauty of the stalactites which bedeck its walls, was the scene in A.D. 1822 of such 'an evil-entreating and wandering in mountains, caves and the holes of the earth' (Heb. xi. 38), when about 300 Christians—mostly women, children and aged men—who had taken shelter in the cavern were suffocated by the Turks, who burnt a quantity of straw, sulphur and other combustible matter at its entrance. See Stanford, *Geography and Travel*, p. 322.

'*And these all having had witness borne to them through their faith received not the promise, God having provided some better thing concerning us, that apart from us they should not be made perfect*' (Heb. xi. 39, 40).

J. ST PAUL AND SLAVERY.

THE striking character of St Paul's teaching as to the duty of slaves in 1 Tim. vi. 1, 2; Tit. ii. 9, 10, is well illustrated by the following remarks on slavery in the Roman Provinces under the Empire by Dr E. C. Clark, Regius Professor of Laws in the University of Cambridge. They are quoted from Dr Moule's 'Colossians and Philemon' in this Series, p. 191, as shewing the intolerable condition of things from the legal point of view. "Little is known of the administration of ordinary justice in the Provinces. But almost all except serious cases seem to have been left to the native local authorities. I should think that *no treatment* of a slave by his master could come under the cognizance of a Roman governor; and I see no reason to suppose that the local authorities would be more likely to interfere than the Roman magistrates in similar cases at Rome. Power of life and death would be, I imagine, the rule. The introduction of a theory of the Law of Nature may have led to a few ameliorations in the slave's condition mediately, i.e. through the individual action of humane emperors. But these modifications of the old barbarity have been overrated. I doubt whether any prohibition of the arbitrary killing of a slave was *regularly* made before the time of Hadrian. Philemon would have power to treat Onesimus *exactly as he pleased.*"

Socially and morally the condition of slaves was no less deplorable. Dr Plummer hardly overstates the case when he writes of it as 'inhuman,' or Wallon (quoted by Lightfoot, 'Colossians and Philemon,' p. 389 note) who says, "L'esclave appartenait au maître: par lui-même, il n'était rien, il n'avait rien."

And yet St Paul advocates no political revolution. "The institution of slavery in the Roman Empire in the first age of Christianity was not only unchristian but inhuman; and it was so widespread that the slaves outnumbered the freemen. Nevertheless the Apostles and their successors taught neither to the slaves that they ought to resist a dominion which was immoral both in effect and in origin, nor to the masters that as Christians they were bound to set their servants free. Christianity did indeed labour for the abolition of slavery but by quite other methods. It taught masters and slaves alike that all men have a common Divine parentage, and a common Divine redemption, and consequently are equally bound to show brotherly love and equally endowed with spiritual freedom. It showed that the slave and his master are alike children of God, and as such free; and alike servants of Jesus Christ, and as such bondmen,—bondmen in that service which is the only true freedom. And thus very slowly, but surely, Christianity disintegrated and dispersed those unwholesome conditions and false ideas, which made slavery to be everywhere possible, and to seem to most men to be necessary. And wherever these conditions and ideas were swept away, slavery gradually died out or was formally abolished. ......St Paul knew what he was about when he urged Titus to commit the 'adorning of the doctrine of God' in a special manner to slaves...... by cultivating precisely those virtues which contribute most to their masters' comfort and interest—submissiveness, gentleness, meekness, honesty, truthfulness, and a faithful discharge of all duties." (Dr Plummer, *Pastoral Epistles*, pp. 248—258.)

The past and present results of Christian life and progress in this respect are summed up by Bp Lightfoot, 'Philemon,' p. 394. "It is a broad and patent fact that throughout the early and middle ages the influence of the Church was exerted strongly on the side of humanity in this matter. The emancipation of slaves was regarded as a principal aim of the higher Christian life; the amelioration of serfdom was a matter of constant solicitude with the rulers of the Church. And at length we seem to see the beginning of the end. The abolition of slavery throughout the British Empire at an enormous material sacrifice is one of the greatest moral conquests which England has ever achieved. The liberation of 20 millions of serfs throughout the Russian dominions has thrown a halo of glory round the name of Alexander II. which no time can dim. The emancipation of the negro in the vast republic of the New World was a victory not less important than either to the well-being of the human race. It is a fit sequel to these achievements that at length a well-directed attack should have been made on the central fortress of slavery and the slave trade, the interior of Africa. May we not venture to predict that...this epoch will stand out in the history of mankind as the era of liberation? If so, the Epistle to Philemon, as the earliest prelude to these magnificent social victories, must be invested with more than common interest for our generation."

May we not add that the Epistles to Timothy and Titus gain new lustre, as their seed principles are seen to bear this noble fruit after so many ages? '*We have our hope set on the living God, who is the Saviour of all men.*' '*Godliness is profitable for all things, having promise of the life which now is.*' '*Our great God and Saviour Jesus Christ; who gave himself for us, that he might redeem us from all iniquity, and purify unto himself a people for his own possession.*' (1 Tim. iv. 10, 8; Tit. ii. 14.)

K. ST PAUL'S METAPHORS.

THE following list of the metaphors occurring in the Pastoral Epistles will shew to the student of St Paul's letters generally that in this characteristic of authorship it is the same St Paul, free to use, either largely or sparingly, the old familiar metaphors, and yet not barren in brain or limited to the old well-worn stock. For the special force of the words used in the metaphors see the notes upon them in the commentary.

a. Imperial Warfare.

1 Tim. i. 18, 'thou mayest war the good warfare.'
1 Tim. v. 14, 'give none occasion to the adversary.'

The word for 'occasion' is peculiar to St Paul in N.T.; is frequent in Classical Greek, e.g. Thuc. I. 90, 'a base of operations' in war.

2 Tim. ii. 3, 'as a good soldier of Jesus Christ.'
2 Tim. iii. 6, 'take captive silly women.'

b. Classical Architecture.

1 Tim. iii. 13, 'a good standing.'
1 Tim. iii. 15, 'the house of God which is...the pillar and ground of the truth.'
1 Tim. vi. 19, 'a good foundation.'
2 Tim. ii. 19, 'the firm foundation of God standeth.'

c. Ancient Agriculture.

1 Tim. iv. 10, 'we labour and strive.'
1 Tim. v. 17, 'those who labour in the word.'
1 Tim. v. 18, 'the labourer is worthy of his hire.'
1 Tim. vi. 10, 'a root of all kinds of evil.'
Tit. i. 13, 'reprove them sharply' (lit. 'cutting away as with a sharp pruning knife').
Tit. iii. 14, 'that they be not unfruitful.'
2 Tim. ii. 6, 'the husbandman that laboureth.'

d. Greek Games.

1 Tim. iv. 7, 'exercise thyself unto godliness.'
1 Tim. vi. 12, 'play thou the man in the good contest of the Faith.'
2 Tim. ii. 5, 'if a man contend in the games.'
2 Tim. iv. 7, 'I have finished the course.'

e. Roman Law.

Tit. iii. 7, 'that we might be made heirs.'

f. Medical Science.

1 Tim. vi. 3, 'consenteth not to sound words.'
Tit. i. 9, 'to exhort in the sound doctrine.'
Tit. i. 13, 'that they may be sound in the faith.'
Tit. ii. 1, 'things which befit the sound doctrine.'
2 Tim. ii. 17, 'eat as doth a gangrene.'
2 Tim. iii. 17, 'complete, furnished completely.'
2 Tim. iv. 3, 'not endure the sound doctrine.'

g. Seafaring Life.

1 Tim. i. 19, 'made shipwreck concerning the faith.'
1 Tim. vi. 9, 'such as drown men in perdition.'

h. Mercantile Life.

1 Tim. vi. 5, 'godliness is a way of gain.'
2 Tim. i. 12, 'my deposit.'
2 Tim. i. 14, 'the good deposit.'

i. The Fowler's Craft.

1 Tim. iii. 7, 'the snare of the devil.'
1 Tim. vi. 9, 'fall into a temptation and a snare.'
2 Tim. ii. 26, 'out of the snare of the devil.'

Of these nine classes of metaphor, the first five recur very frequently in the other Epistles of St Paul. Compare, for example, the metaphors from Roman law;—*adoption*, Rom. viii. 14, 21; Gal. iv. 3; Eph. i. 5; *subjection of the son to the father*, Rom. iii. 25; Gal. i. 4, iv. 1; Phil. ii. 8; Col. i. 19; *testation and inheritance*, Gal. iii. 15, iv. 1, &c. The word for 'heirs' and its kindred phrases occur 18 times in St Paul.

The words and phrases in the last four classes of metaphors are almost entirely peculiar to the Pastoral Epistles.

INDEX.

Words specially defined or explained are printed in *italics*. Such references are omitted as are sufficiently indicated by chapter and verse of the three Epistles.

Cambridge:
PRINTED BY J. & C. F. CLAY,
AT THE UNIVERSITY PRESS.

THE PITT PRESS SERIES.

COMPLETE LIST.

1. GREEK.

Author	*Work*	*Editor*	*Price*
Aeschylus	Prometheus Vinctus	Rackham	*In the Press*
Aristophanes	Aves—Plutus—Ranae	Green	3/6 *each*
,,	Vespae	Graves	3/6
,,	Nubes	,,	*In the Press*
Demosthenes	Olynthiacs	Glover	2/6
Euripides	Heracleidae	Beck & Headlam	3/6
,,	Hercules Furens	Gray & Hutchinson	2/-
,,	Hippolytus	Hadley	2/-
,,	Iphigeneia in Aulis	Headlam	2/6
,,	Medea	,,	2/6
,,	Hecuba	Hadley	2/6
,,	Alcestis	,,	2/6
,,	Orestes	Wedd	4/6
Herodotus	Book V	Shuckburgh	3/-
,,	,, VI, VIII, IX	,,	4/- *each*
,,	,, VIII 1—90, IX 1—89	,,	2/6 *each*
Homer	Odyssey IX, X	Edwards	2/6 *each*
,,	,, XXI	,,	2/-
,,	Iliad VI, XXII, XXIII, XXIV	,,	2/- *each*
Lucian	Somnium, Charon, etc.	Heitland	3/6
,,	Menippus and Timon	Mackie	3/6
Plato	Apologia Socratis	Adam	3/6
,,	Crito	,,	2/6
,,	Euthyphro	,,	2/6
,,	Protagoras	J. & A. M. Adam	4/6
Plutarch	Demosthenes	Holden	4/6
,,	Gracchi	,,	6/-
,,	Nicias	,,	5/-
,,	Sulla	,,	6/-
,,	Timoleon	,,	6/-
Sophocles	Oedipus Tyrannus	Jebb	4/-
Thucydides	Book III	Spratt	5/-
,,	Book VII	Holden	5/-
Xenophon	Agesilaus	Hailstone	2/6
,,	Anabasis Vol. I. Text.	Pretor	3/-
,,	,, Vol. II. Notes.	,,	4/6
,,	,, I, II	,,	4/-
,,	,, I, III, IV, V	,,	2/- *each*
,,	,, II, VI, VII	,,	2/6 *each*
,,	,, II	Edwards	1/6
,,	,, III	,,	1/6
,,	Cyropaedeia I, II (2 vols.)	Holden	6/-
,,	,, III, IV, V	,,	5/-
,,	,, VI, VII, VIII	,,	5/-

2. LATIN.

Author	*Work*	*Editor*	*Price*
Caesar	De Bello Gallico		
	Com. I, III, VI, VIII	Peskett	1/6 *each*
,,	,, II–III, and VII	,,	2/- *each*
,,	,, I–III	,,	3/-
,,	,, IV–V	,,	1/6
,,	De Bello Gallico I ch. 1–29	Shuckburgh	1/6
,,	,, ,, II Belgic War	,,	1/6
,,	De Bello Civili. Com. I	Peskett	3/-
,,	,, ,, Com. III	,,	*In the Press*
Cicero	Actio Prima in C. Verrem	Cowie	1/6
,,	De Amicitia	Reid	3/6
,,	De Senectute	,,	3/6
,,	Div. in Q. Caec. et Actio Prima in C. Verrem	Heitland & Cowie	3/-
,,	Philippica Secunda	Peskett	3/6
,,	Pro Archia Poeta	Reid	2/-
,,	,, Balbo	,,	1/6
,,	,, Milone	,,	2/6
,,	,, Murena	Heitland	3/-
,,	,, Plancio	Holden	4/6
,,	,, Sulla	Reid	3/6
,,	Somnium Scipionis	Pearman	2/-
Cornelius Nepos	Miltiades, Themistocles, &c.	Shuckburgh	1/6
,,	Hannibal, Cato, Atticus	,,	1/6
,,	Lysander, Alcibiades, &c.	,,	1/6
,,	Timotheus, Phocion, &c.	,,	1/6
Horace	Epistles. Bk I	,,	2/6
,,	Odes and Epodes	Gow	5/-
,,	Odes. Books I, III	,,	2/- *each*
,,	,, Book II, IV	,,	1/6 *each*
,,	Epodes	,,	1/6
Juvenal	Satires	Duff	*In the Press*
Livy	Books IV, VI, IX, XXVII	Stephenson	2/6 *each*
,,	,, V	Whibley	2/6
,,	,, XXI, XXII	Dimsdale	2/6 *each*
Lucan	Pharsalia. Bk I	Heitland & Haskins	1/6
,,	De Bello Civili. Bk VII	Postgate	2/-
Lucretius	Book V	Duff	2/-
Ovid	Fasti. Book VI	Sidgwick	1/6
,,	Metamorphoses, Bk I	Dowdall	1/6
Plautus	Epidicus	Gray	3/-
,,	Stichus	Fennell	2/6
,,	Trinummus	Gray	3/6
Quintus Curtius	Alexander in India	Heitland & Raven	3/6
Tacitus	Agricola and Germania	Stephenson	3/-
,,	Hist. Bk I	Davies	2/6
Terence	Hautontimorumenos	Gray	3/-
Vergil	Aeneid I to XII	Sidgwick	1/6 *each*
,,	Bucolics	,,	1/6
,,	Georgics I, II, and III, IV	,,	2/- *each*
,,	Complete Works, Vol. I, Text	,,	3/6
,,	,, ,, Vol. II, Notes	,,	4/6

3. FRENCH.

Author	*Work*	*Editor*	*Price*
About	Le Roi des Montagnes	Ropes	2/-
Biart	Quand j'étais petit, Pts I, II	Boïelle	2/- *each*
Corneille	La Suite du Menteur	Masson	2/-
,,	Polyeucte	Braunholtz	2/-
De Bonnechose	Lazare Hoche	Colbeck	2/-
,,	Bertrand du Guesclin	Leathes	2/-
,,	,, Part II (*With Vocabulary*)	,,	1/6
Delavigne	Louis XI	Eve	2/-
,,	Les Enfants d'Edouard	,,	2/-
D'Harleville	Le Vieux Célibataire	Masson	2/-
De Lamartine	Jeanne d'Arc	Clapin & Ropes	1/6
De Vigny	La Canne de Jonc	Eve	1/6
Dumas	La Fortune de D'Artagnan	Ropes	2/-
Erckmann-Chatrian	La Guerre	Clapin	3/-
Guizot	Discours sur l'Histoire de la Révolution d'Angleterre	Eve	2/6
Lemercier	Frédégonde et Brunehaut	Masson	2/-
Mme de Staël	Le Directoire	Masson & Prothero	2/-
,,	Dix Années d'Exil	,,	2/-
Malot	Remi et ses Amis	Verrall	2/-
Merimée	Colomba	Ropes	2/-
Michelet	Louis XI & Charles the Bold	,,	2/6
Molière	Le Bourgeois Gentilhomme	Clapin	1/6
,,	L'École des Femmes	Saintsbury	2/6
,,	Les Précieuses ridicules	Braunholtz	2/-
,,	,, (*Abridged Edition*)	,,	1/-
,,	Le Misanthrope	,,	2/6
,,	L'Avare	,,	2/6
Perrault	Fairy Tales	Rippmann	1/6
Piron	La Métromanie	Masson	2/-
Ponsard	Charlotte Corday	Ropes	2/-
Racine	Les Plaideurs	Braunholtz	2/-
,,	,, (*Abridged Edition*)	,,	1/-
Sainte-Beuve	M. Daru.	Masson	2/-
Saintine	Picciola	Clapin	2/-
Scribe & Legouvé	Bataille de Dames	Bull	2/-
Scribe	Le Verre d'Eau	Colbeck	2/-
Sédaine	Le Philosophe sans le savoir	Bull	2/-
Souvestre	Un Philosophe sous les Toits	Eve	2/-
,,	Le Serf & Le Chevrier de Lorraine	Ropes	2/-
,,	Le Serf (*With Vocabulary*)	,,	1/6
Thierry	Lettres sur l'histoire de France (XIII—XXIV)	Masson & Prothero	2/6
,,	Récits des Temps Mérovingiens, I—III	Masson & Ropes	3/-
Villemain	Lascaris ou les Grecs du XVe Siècle	Masson	2/-
Voltaire	Histoire du Siècle de Louis XIV, in three parts	Masson & Prothero	2/6 *each*
Xavier de Maistre	La Jeune Sibérienne. Le Lépreux de la Cité d'Aoste	Masson	1/6

4. GERMAN.

Author	*Work*	*Editor*	*Price*
Andersen	Six Fairy Tales	Rippmann	2/6
	Ballads on German History	Wagner	2/-
Benedix	Dr Wespe	Breul	3/-
Freytag	Der Staat Friedrichs des Grossen	Wagner	2/-
	German Dactylic Poetry	,,	3/-
Goethe	Knabenjahre (1749—1761)	Wagner & Cartmell	2/-
	Hermann und Dorothea	,, ,,	3/6
,,	Iphigenie	Breul	*In the Press*
Grimm	Selected Tales	Rippmann	3/-
Gutzkow	Zopf und Schwert	Wolstenholme	3/6
Hackländer	Der geheime Agent	E. L. Milner Barry	3/-
Hauff	Das Bild des Kaisers	Breul	3/-
,,	Das Wirthshaus im Spessart	Schlottmann & Cartmell	3/-
,,	Die Karavane	Schlottmann	3/-
Immermann	Der Oberhof	Wagner	3/-
Klee	Die deutschen Heldensagen	Wolstenholme	3/-
Kohlrausch	Das Jahr 1813	,,	2/-
Lessing	Minna von Barnhelm	Wolstenholme	3/-
Lessing & Gellert	Selected Fables	Breul	3/-
Mendelssohn	Selected Letters	Sime	3/-
Raumer	Der erste Kreuzzug	Wagner	2/-
Riehl	Culturgeschichtliche Novellen	Wolstenholme	3/-
,,	Die Ganerben & Die Gerechtigkeit Gottes	,,	3/-
Schiller	Wilhelm Tell	Breul	2/6
,,	,, (*Abridged Edition*)	,,	1/6
,,	Geschichte des dreissigjährigen Kriegs Book III.	,,	3/-
,,	Maria Stuart	,,	3/6
,,	Wallenstein I. (Lager and Piccolomini)	,,	3/6
,,	Wallenstein II. (Tod)	,,	3/6
Uhland	Ernst, Herzog von Schwaben	Wolstenholme	3/6

5. ENGLISH.

Author	Work	Editor	Price
Bacon	History of the Reign of King Henry VII	Lumby	3/-
,,	Essays	West	3/6 & 5/-
Cowley	Essays	Lumby	4/-
Earle	Microcosmography	West	3/-
Gray	Poems	Tovey	*In the Press*
Lamb	Tales from Shakespeare	Flather	1/6
Macaulay	Lord Clive	Innes	1/6
,,	Warren Hastings	,,	1/6
,,	William Pitt and Earl of Chatham	,,	2/6
Mayor	A Sketch of Ancient Philosophy from Thales to Cicero		3/6
More	History of King Richard III	Lumby	3/6
,,	Utopia	,,	3/6
Milton	Arcades and Comus	Verity	3/-
,,	Ode on the Nativity, L'Allegro, Il Penseroso & Lycidas	,,	2/6
,,	Samson Agonistes	,,	2/6
,,	Paradise Lost, Bks I, II	,,	2/-
,,	,, Bks III, IV	,,	2/-
,,	,, Bks V, VI	,,	2/-
,,	,, Bks VII, VIII	,,	2/-
,,	,, Bks IX, X	,,	2/-
,,	,, Bks XI, XII	,,	2/-
Pope	Essay on Criticism	West	2/-
Scott	Marmion	Masterman	2/6
,,	Lady of the Lake	,,	2/6
,,	Lay of the last Minstrel	Flather	2/-
,,	Legend of Montrose	Simpson	2/6
Shakespeare	A Midsummer-Night's Dream	Verity	1/6
,,	Twelfth Night	,,	1/6
,,	Julius Caesar	,,	1/6
,,	The Tempest	,,	1/6
,,	King Lear	,,	1/6
,,	Merchant of Venice	,,	1/6
Shakespeare & Fletcher	Two Noble Kinsmen	Skeat	3/6
Sidney	An Apologie for Poetrie	Shuckburgh	3/-
Wallace	Outlines of the Philosophy of Aristotle		4/6

West	Elements of English Grammar	2/6
,,	English Grammar for Beginners	1/-
Carlos	Short History of British India	1/-
Mill	Elementary Commercial Geography	1/6
Bartholomew	Atlas of Commercial Geography	3/-
Robinson	Church Catechism Explained	2/-

6. EDUCATIONAL SCIENCE.

Author	*Work*	*Editor*	*Price*
Colbeck	Lectures on the Teaching of Modern Languages		2/-
Comenius	Life and Educational Works	Laurie	3/6
	Three Lectures on the Practice of Education		
Eve	I. On Marking	1 Vol.	2/-
Sidgwick	II. On Stimulus		
Abbott	III. On the teaching of Latin Verse Composition		
Farrar	General Aims of the Teacher	1 Vol.	1/6
Poole	Form Management		
Locke	Thoughts on Education	Quick	3/6
Milton	Tractate on Education	Browning	2/-
Sidgwick	On Stimulus		1/-
Thring	Theory and Practice of Teaching		4/6

7. MATHEMATICS.

Ball	Elementary Algebra		4/6
Euclid	Books I—VI, XI, XII	Taylor	5/-
,,	Books I—VI	,,	4/-
,,	Books I—IV	,,	3/-
	Also separately		
,,	Books I, & II; III, & IV; V, & VI; XI, & XII		1/6 *each*
,,	Solutions to Exercises in Taylor's Euclid	W. W. Taylor	10/6
	And separately		
,,	Solutions to Bks I—IV	,,	6/-
,,	Solutions to Books VI. XI	,,	6/-
Hobson & Jessop	Elementary Plane Trigonometry		4/6
Loney	Elements of Statics and Dynamics		7/6
	Part I. Elements of Statics		4/6
	,, II. Elements of Dynamics		3/6
,,	Solutions of Examples, Statics and Dynamics		7/6
,,	Mechanics and Hydrostatics		4/6
Smith, C.	Arithmetic for Schools, with or without answers		3/5
,,	Part I. Chapters I—VIII. Elementary, with or without answers		2/-
,,	Part II. Chapters IX—XX, with or without answers		2/-
Hale, G.	Key to Smith's Arithmetic		7/6

LONDON: C. J. CLAY AND SONS,
CAMBRIDGE UNIVERSITY PRESS WAREHOUSE,
AVE MARIA LANE.
GLASGOW: 263, ARGYLE STREET.

CAMBRIDGE: PRINTED BY J. & C. F. CLAY, AT THE UNIVERSITY PRESS

THE CAMBRIDGE BIBLE FOR SCHOOLS AND COLLEGES.

General Editors:

J. J. S. PEROWNE, D.D., *Bishop of Worcester.*

A. F. KIRKPATRICK, D.D., *Regius Professor of Hebrew.*

Opinions of the Press.

Guardian.—"*It is difficult to commend too highly this excellent series.*"

Academy.—"*The modesty of the general title of this series has, we believe, led many to misunderstand its character and underrate its value. The books are well suited for study in the upper forms of our best schools, but not the less are they adapted to the wants of all Bible students who are not specialists. We doubt, indeed, whether any of the numerous popular commentaries recently issued in this country will be found more serviceable for general use.*"

Baptist Magazine.—"*One of the most popular and useful literary enterprises of the nineteenth century.*"

Sword and Trowel.—"*Of great value. The whole series of comments for schools is highly esteemed by students capable of forming a judgment. The books are scholarly without being pretentious: and information is so given as to be easily understood.*"

Sunday School Chronicle.—"*There are no better books in exposition of the different parts of Scripture than those contained in the Cambridge Bible for Schools and Colleges. The series has long since established its claim to an honourable place in the front rank of first-rate commentaries; and the teacher or preacher who masters its volumes will be, like Apollos, 'mighty in the Scriptures.' All conscientious and earnest students of the Scriptures owe an immense debt to the Cambridge University Press for its Bible for Schools and Colleges. Take it for all in all, it is probably the most useful commentary alike on the Old Testament and on the New that has been given us in recent years.*"

II. Samuel. *Academy.*—"Small as this work is in mere dimensions, it is every way the best on its subject and for its purpose that we know of. The opening sections at once prove the thorough competence of the writer for dealing with questions of criticism in an earnest, faithful and devout spirit; and the appendices discuss a few special difficulties with a full knowledge of the data, and a judicial reserve, which contrast most favourably with the superficial dogmatism which has too often made the exegesis of the Old Testament a field for the play of unlimited paradox and the ostentation of personal infallibility. The notes are always clear and suggestive; never trifling or irrelevant; and they everywhere demonstrate the great difference in value between the work of a commentator who is also a Hebraist, and that of one who has to depend for his Hebrew upon secondhand sources."

I. Kings and Ephesians. *Sword and Trowel.*—"With great heartiness we commend these most valuable little commentaries. We had

10.1.98
10000

rather purchase these than nine out of ten of the big blown up expositions. Quality is far better than quantity, and we have it here."

Ezra and Nehemiah. *Guardian.*—"Professor Ryle's Commentary is quite the best work on these books accessible to the English reader."

Christian World.—"This book should be in the library of every Bible Student."

The Book of Job. *Spectator.*—"Able and scholarly as the Introduction is, it is far surpassed by the detailed exegesis of the book. In this Dr DAVIDSON'S strength is at its greatest. His linguistic knowledge, his artistic habit, his scientific insight, and his literary power have full scope when he comes to exegesis."

Methodist Recorder.—"Already we have frequently called attention to this exceedingly valuable work as its volumes have successively appeared. But we have never done so with greater pleasure, very seldom with so great pleasure, as we now refer to the last published volume, that on the **Book of Job**, by Dr DAVIDSON, of Edinburgh.... We cordially commend the volume to all our readers. The least instructed will understand and enjoy it; and mature scholars will learn from it."

Psalms. Book I. *Church Times.*—"It seems in every way a most valuable little book, containing a mass of information, well-assorted, and well-digested, and will be useful not only to students preparing for examinations, but to many who want a handy volume of explanation to much that is difficult in the Psalter.......We owe a great debt of gratitude to Professor Kirkpatrick for his scholarly and interesting volume."

Literary Churchman.—"In this volume thoughtful exegesis founded on nice critical scholarship and due regard for the opinions of various writers, combine, under the influence of a devout spirit, to render this commentary a source of much valuable assistance. The notes are 'though deep yet clear,' for they seem to put in a concentrated form the very pith and marrow of all the best that has been hitherto said on the subject, with striking freedom from anything like pressure of personal views. Throughout the work care and pains are as conspicuous as scholarship."

Psalms. Books II. and III. *Critical Review.*—"The second volume of Professor KIRKPATRICK'S Commentary on the Book of Psalms has all the excellent qualities which characterised the first....It gives what is best in the philology of the subject. Its notes furnish what is most needed and most useful. Its literary style is attractive. It furnishes all that is of real value in the form of introduction, and it has a studious regard for the devout as well as intelligent understanding of the Psalms."

Baptist.—"This volume of the Cambridge Bible for schools and colleges is a very valuable contribution to the expository literature of the Old Testament. The introduction, which occupies some 70 pages, is a compact compendium of explanatory and critical information upon the whole Psalter. The notes are brief, but full, and very suggestive."

Job—Hosea. *Guardian.*—"It is difficult to commend too highly this excellent series, the volumes of which are now becoming numerous. The two books before us, small as they are in size, comprise almost everything that the young student can reasonably expect to find in the way of helps towards such general knowledge of their subjects as may be gained without an attempt to grapple with the Hebrew; and even the learned scholar can hardly read without interest and benefit the very able introductory matter which both these commentators have prefixed to their volumes."

Isaiah. Chapters I—XXXIX. Professor W. H. Bennett in the *British Weekly.*—"Dr Skinner's name on the title-page of this book is a guarantee for extensive and exact scholarship and for careful and accurate treatment of the subject. This little volume will more than sustain the high reputation of the series in which it appears...readers will look forward with much interest to Dr Skinner's second volume on chapters xl—lxvi."

School Guardian.—"This last addition to 'The Cambridge Bible for Schools and Colleges,' is a most valuable one, and will go far to increase the usefulness of what we have no hesitation in calling the most useful commentary for school purposes. There ought to be two copies, at least, of this in every parish—one in the clergyman's and the other in the teacher's library."

Jeremiah. *Church Quarterly Review.*—"The arrangement of the book is well treated on pp. xxx., 396, and the question of Baruch's relations with its composition on pp. xxvii., xxxiv., 317. The illustrations from English literature, history, monuments, works on botany, topography, etc., are good and plentiful, as indeed they are in other volumes of this series."

Ezekiel. *Guardian.*—"No book of the Old Testament stands more in need of a commentator than this, and no scholar in England or Scotland is better qualified to comment upon it than Dr A. B. Davidson. With sound scholarship and excellent judgement he combines an insight into Oriental modes of thought which renders him a specially trustworthy guide to a book such as this....His commentary may be safely recommended as the best that has yet appeared. Nor is it unlikely that it will remain the best for some time to come."

Nahum, Habakkuk and Zephaniah. *Literary World.*—"An admirable little book, worthy of Dr A. B. Davidson's high scholarship and of the excellent series to which it belongs. The introductions are so comprehensive and thorough, and the notes so entirely useful, that one feels the book is all that can be required for the study of these prophecies by most biblical students, and by many Christian ministers."

Guardian.—"Prof. Davidson has laid all students of the Old Testament under a fresh debt of gratitude by the publication of this scholarly little volume. It is quite the best commentary on these books that has yet appeared....Small as it is, the volume is well worthy to take its place by the side of the same author's invaluable commentaries on Job and Ezekiel."

Spectator.—"We may say without hesitation that Professor Davidson's guidance is amply satisfactory. The theological student or the preacher who may have to deal with the subject cannot do better than consult him."

Malachi. *Academy.*—"Archdeacon Perowne has already edited

Jonah and Zechariah for this series. Malachi presents comparatively few difficulties and the Editor's treatment leaves nothing to be desired. His introduction is clear and scholarly and his commentary sufficient. We may instance the notes on ii. 15 and iv. 2 as examples of careful arrangement, clear exposition and graceful expression."

The Gospel according to St Matthew. *English Churchman.*—"The introduction is able, scholarly, and eminently practical, as it bears on the authorship and contents of the Gospel, and the original form in which it is supposed to have been written. It is well illustrated by two excellent maps of the Holy Land and of the Sea of Galilee."

St Mark. *Expositor.*—"Into this small volume Dr Maclear, besides a clear and able Introduction to the Gospel, and the text of St Mark, has compressed many hundreds of valuable and helpful notes. In short, he has given us a capital manual of the kind required—containing all that is needed to illustrate the text, i.e. all that can be drawn from the history, geography, customs, and manners of the time. But as a handbook, giving in a clear and succinct form the information which a lad requires in order to stand an examination in the Gospel, it is admirable......I can very heartily commend it, not only to the senior boys and girls in our High Schools, but also to Sunday-school teachers, who may get from it the very kind of knowledge they often find it hardest to get."

St Luke. *Spectator.*—"Canon FARRAR has supplied students of the Gospel with an admirable manual in this volume. It has all that copious variety of illustration, ingenuity of suggestion, and general soundness of interpretation which readers are accustomed to expect from the learned and eloquent editor. Anyone who has been accustomed to associate the idea of 'dryness' with a commentary, should go to Canon Farrar's **St Luke** for a more correct impression. He will find that a commentary may be made interesting in the highest degree, and that without losing anything of its solid value....But, so to speak, it is *too good* for some of the readers for whom it is intended."

The Gospel according to St John. *English Churchman.*—"The notes are extremely scholarly and valuable, and in most cases exhaustive, bringing to the elucidation of the text all that is best in commentaries, ancient and modern."

Acts. *School Guardian.*—"We do not know of any other volume where so much help is given to the complete understanding of one of the most important and, in many respects, difficult books of the New Testament."

Epistle to the Romans. *Expositor.*—"The 'Notes' are very good, and lean, as the notes of a School Bible should, to the most commonly accepted and orthodox view of the inspired author's meaning; while the Introduction, and especially the Sketch of the Life of St Paul, is a model of condensation. It is as lively and pleasant to read as if two or three facts had not been crowded into well-nigh every sentence."

Galatians. *Modern Church.*—"Dr PEROWNE deals throughout in a very thorough manner with every real difficulty in the text, and in this respect he has faithfully followed the noble example set him in the exegetical masterpiece, his indebtedness to which he frankly acknowledges."

English Churchman.—"This little work, like all of the series, is a scholarly production; but we can also unreservedly recommend it from a doctrinal standpoint; Dr E. H. PEROWNE is one who has grasped the distinctive teaching of the Epistle, and expounds it with clearness and definiteness. In an appendix, he ably maintains the correctness of the A. V. as against the R. V. in the translation of II. 16, a point of no small importance."

Ephesians. *Baptist Magazine.*—"It seems to us the model of a School and College Commentary—comprehensive, but not cumbersome; scholarly, but not pedantic."

Guardian.—"It supplies matter which is evidently the outcome of deep study pursued with a devotional mind."

Philippians. *Record.*—"There are few series more valued by theological students than 'The Cambridge Bible for Schools and Colleges,' and there will be no number of it more esteemed than that by Mr H. C. G. MOULE on the *Epistle to the Philippians.*"

Colossians. *Record.*—"Those who have already used with pleasure and profit Mr Moule's volumes of the same series on Ephesians and Philippians will open this little book with the highest expectations. They will not be disappointed.......No more complete or trustworthy volume has been contributed to this series."

Expository Times.—"This is now the Commentary on Colossians and Philemon to have at your hand, whether you are schoolboy or scholar, layman or clergyman."

Thessalonians. *Academy.*—"Mr FINDLAY maintains the high level of the series to which he has become contributor. Some parts of his introduction to the Epistles to the Thessalonians could scarcely be bettered. The account of Thessalonica, the description of the style and character of the Epistles, and the analysis of them are excellent in style and scholarly care. The notes are possibly too voluminous; but there is so much matter in them, and the matter is arranged and handled so ably, that we are ready to forgive their fulness....Mr FINDLAY'S commentary is a valuable addition to what has been written on the letters to the Thessalonian Church."

Baptist Magazine.—"Mr FINDLAY has fulfilled in this volume a task which Dr Moulton was compelled to decline, though he has rendered valuable aid in its preparation. The commentary is in its own way a model—clear, forceful, scholarly—such as young students will welcome as a really useful guide, and old ones will acknowledge as giving in brief space the substance of all that they knew."

Timothy and Titus. *The Christian.*—"The series includes many volumes of sterling worth, and this last may rank among the most valuable. The pages evince careful scholarship and a thorough acquaintance with expository literature; and the work should promote a more general and practical study of the Pastoral Epistles."

Hebrews. *Baptist Magazine.*—"Like his (Canon Farrar's) commentary on Luke it possesses all the best characteristics of his writing. It is a work not only of an accomplished scholar, but of a skilled teacher."

James. *Expositor.*—"It is, so far as I know, by far the best exposition of the Epistle of St James in the English language. Not schoolboys or students going in for an examination alone, but ministers and preachers of the Word, may get more real help from it than from the most costly and elaborate commentaries."

The Epistles of St John. *Churchman.*—"This forms an admirable companion to the 'Commentary on the Gospel according to St John,' which was reviewed in *The Churchman* as soon as it appeared. Dr Plummer has some of the highest qualifications for such a task; and these two volumes, their size being considered, will bear comparison with the best Commentaries of the time."

Revelation. *Guardian.*—"This volume contains evidence of much careful labour. It is a scholarly production, as might be expected from the pen of the late Mr W. H. SIMCOX....The notes throw light upon many passages of this difficult book, and are extremely suggestive. It is an advantage that they sometimes set before the student various interpretations without exactly guiding him to a choice."

Wesleyan Methodist Sunday-School Record.—"We cannot speak too highly of this excellent little volume. The introduction is of the greatest possible value to the student, and accurate scholarship is combined with true loyalty to the inspired Word. There is much more matter of practical utility compressed into this volume of pp. 174 than is contained in many a portentous tome."

The Smaller Cambridge Bible for Schools.

Sunday-School Chronicle.—"*We can only repeat what we have already said of this admirable series, containing, as it does, the scholarship of the larger work. For scholars in our elder classes, and for those preparing for Scripture examinations, no better commentaries can be put into their hands.*"

Record.—"*Despite their small size, these volumes give the substance of the admirable pieces of work on which they are founded. We can only hope that in many schools the class-teaching will proceed on the lines these commentators suggest.*"

Educational Review.—"*The Smaller Cambridge Bible for Schools is unique in its combination of small compass with great scholarship.... For use in lower forms, in Sunday-schools and in the family, we cannot suggest better little manuals than these.*"

Literary World.—"*All that is necessary to be known and learned by pupils in junior and elementary schools is to be found in this series. Indeed, much more is provided than should be required by the examiners. We do not know what more could be done to provide sensible, interesting, and solid Scriptural instruction for boys and girls. The Syndics of the*

Cambridge University Press are rendering great services both to teachers and to scholars by the publication of such a valuable series of books, in which slipshod work could not have a place."

Christian Leader.—"*For the student of the sacred oracles who utilizes hours of travel or moments of waiting in the perusal of the Bible there is nothing so handy, and, at the same time, so satisfying as these little books..... Nor let anyone suppose that, because these are school-books, therefore they are beneath the adult reader. They contain the very ripest results of the best Biblical scholarship, and that in the very simplest form.*"

Joshua. *School Guardian.*—"This little book is a model of what editorial work, intended for the use of young students, should be; and we could scarcely praise it more highly than by saying that it is in every way worthy of the volumes that have gone before it."

Schoolmistress.—"A most useful little manual for students or teachers."

Judges. *Educational News* (Edinburgh).—"The book makes available for teaching purposes the results of ripe scholarship, varied knowledge, and religious insight."

Schoolmaster.—"The work shows first-rate workmanship, and may be adopted without hesitation."

Samuel I. and II. *Saturday Review.*—"Professor KIRKPATRICK'S two tiny volumes on the First and Second Books of Samuel are quite model school-books; the notes elucidate every possible difficulty with scholarly brevity and clearness and a perfect knowledge of the subject."

Kings I. *Wesleyan Methodist Sunday-School Record.*—"Equally useful for teachers of young men's Bible classes and for earnest Bible students themselves. This series supplies a great need. It contains much valuable instruction in small compass."

St Mark. St Luke. *Guardian.*—"We have received the volumes of St Mark and St Luke in this series....The two volumes seem, on the whole, well adapted for school use, are well and carefully printed, and have maps and good, though necessarily brief, introductions. There is little doubt that this series will be found as popular and useful as the well-known larger series, of which they are abbreviated editions."

St Luke. *Wesleyan Methodist Sunday-School Record.*—"We cannot too highly commend this handy little book to all teachers."

St John. *Methodist Times.*—"A model of condensation, losing nothing of its clearness and force from its condensation into a small compass. Many who have long since completed their college curriculum will find it an invaluable handbook."

Acts. *Literary World.*—"The notes are very brief, but exceedingly comprehensive, comprising as much detail in the way of explanation as would be needed by young students of the Scriptures preparing for examination. We again give the opinion that this series furnishes as much real help as would usually satisfy students for the Christian ministry, or even ministers themselves."

CAMBRIDGE: PRINTED BY J. AND C. F. CLAY, AT THE UNIVERSITY PRESS.